MW00453956

From Selma to Moscow

HOW HUMAN RIGHTS ACTIVISTS TRANSFORMED
U.S. FOREIGN POLICY

Sarah B. Snyder

Columbia University Press
New York

Columbia University Press
Publishers Since 1893
New York   Chichester, West Sussex
cup.columbia.edu
Copyright © 2018 Columbia University Press
All rights reserved

Library of Congress Cataloging-in-Publication Data
Names: Snyder, Sarah B., 1977– author.
Title: From Selma to Moscow : how human rights activists transformed
U.S. foreign policy / Sarah B. Snyder.
Description: New York : Columbia University Press, 2018. | Includes
bibliographical references and index.
Identifiers: LCCN 2017032475 | ISBN 9780231169462 (cloth : alk. paper) |
ISBN 9780231169479 (pbk : alk. paper) | ISBN 9780231547215 (e-book)
Subjects: LCSH: United States—Foreign relations—1945–1989—Case studies. |
Human rights advocacy—Case studies.
Classification: LCC E840 .S595 2018 | DDC 327.73009/04—dc23
LC record available at https://lccn.loc.gov/2017032475

Columbia University Press books are printed on permanent and durable acid-free paper.
Printed in the United States of America

Jacket image: © Bettmann/Getty Images

Jacket design: Chang Jae Lee

In memory of
Abbott Gleason and Nancy Bernkopf Tucker

CONTENTS

CONTENTS

ACKNOWLEDGMENTS

This project began in response to a question posed to me in 2008 by Mark Lawrence, who asked if I had done any research on human rights during the Johnson years. I hadn't. His question and his subsequent invitation to participate in a conference he organized with Francis Gavin, entitled "Lyndon Johnson and the Beginnings of the Post–Cold War Era," sparked this project.

As the bibliography attests, the research for this book took me to several continents and to congressional collections and presidential libraries scattered across the United States. Numerous organizations offered essential financial support for the research that forms the basis for my analysis, including American University, University College London, Yale University, the Rockefeller Archive Center, the Gerald R. Ford Foundation, the Lyndon Baines Johnson Foundation, Friends of the Princeton University Library, the Kennedy Library Foundation, and the Eisenhower Foundation. My research travels were far more enjoyable when I had the opportunity to stay with friends and family, such as Allison Higgins; Kristin Hay and Paul Rubinson; J. P., Amy, William, and Evelyn Fine; Allison and Nader Akhnoukh; and Lindsey Leininger.

Over the years during which I have been working on this project, a number of colleagues and organizations have offered me opportunities to present my research and receive useful feedback. For these invitations I thank

Jennifer Miller, Mitchell Lerner, Eirini Karamouzi, Simon Rofe, the Washington History Seminar, Ronald Granieri, Jussi Hahnimäki, Georgetown University's International History Seminar, Steven Hewitt, Bevan Sewell, Mark Bradley, Kaeten Mistry, Kelly Shannon, Andrew Preston, Geoffrey Connor, Mark Lawrence, James Loeffler, Pierre-Olivier de Broux, Historians of the Twentieth Century United States, the Organization of American Historians, the American Historical Association, and (last, but certainly not least) the Society for Historians of American Foreign Relations. In addition, Effie Pedaliu, Mark Lawrence, Mark Bradley, Thomas Schwartz, Peter Kuznick, Barbara Keys, Jeremi Suri, David Luban, and Petra Goedde have all commented on sections of this book that were presented as conference papers. James Loeffler, Carl Watts, Brad Simpson, Daniel Sargent, Casey Bohlen, Tanya Harmer, Matthew Jones, and Scott Kaufman all shared with me or steered me toward useful sources.

I deeply appreciate the time that Craig Daigle, Meredith Oyen, Robert Rakove, Steven Jensen, Ryan Irwin, James Loeffler, Patrick Kelly, Paul Rubinson, Eirini Karamouzi, and Danny Fine spent reading chapters of the manuscript. The resulting book was also improved by the anonymous readers of Columbia University Press and by my editor there, Philip Leventhal, who pushed me to reframe my argument in bolder ways. In addition, Miriam Grossman helped facilitate the book's production, and Abby Graves offered excellent copyediting. Most significant was a meeting in Washington in 2015 in which Elizabeth Borgwardt, Thomas Borstelmann, Mark Bradley, Mark Lawrence, Eric Lohr, Andrew Preston, and Alice Friend helped me work through a draft of this manuscript. Their suggestions sent me running in many directions, and the book benefited considerably from their careful readings.

Since I have arrived at American University, the School of International Service has supported my research in numerous ways, including by hosting a book incubator. Perhaps even more invaluable has been the funding the school provided for research assistance. Without the help of Alice Friend, Jaclyn Fox, and Luke Theuma, this book would have taken years longer to finish. Alice, in particular, devoted two years to sorting through arcane questions, demystifying the foreign military sales process, and making the charts for the manuscript that illustrate the *New York Times'* growing attention to human rights.

Choosing a title is always a challenge, and I want to thank in particular Allison Higgins, Aaron O'Connell, Andrew Fine, David Andersson, Brin Frazier, Julie Taylor, and Leila Adler for helping me think through different ideas.

The preceding are my professional debts, but my personal ones are similarly significant to me. In addition to my family, old and new friends made and maintained through two transatlantic moves have supported me through this book-writing process. I want to particularly thank Allison Higgins, Amy Sheridan, Larissa Moniz, Craig Daigle, Lien-Hang Nguyen, Becky Farbstein, Leonie Hannan, Adam Smith, Andrew Preston, Simon Rofe, Angela Romano, Emmanuel Mourlon-Droul, Vanessa Berberian (who shared my early interest in the 1960s), and most of all, my husband, Danny Fine—my toughest critic and greatest supporter.

This book is dedicated to the memory of two people who had profound impacts on my life and career—my undergraduate adviser, Abbott Gleason, and my PhD supervisor, Nancy Bernkopf Tucker.

FROM SELMA TO MOSCOW

At a time of burgeoning interest in the history of global human rights politics, recent works have argued variously that Americans turned their attention to human rights as a result of Jimmy Carter's 1976 election, guilt over the war in Vietnam, or failed political utopias.[1] In contrast, *From Selma to Moscow: How Human Rights Activists Transformed U.S. Foreign Policy* identifies transnational connections and social movements during the "long 1960s" as the foundation for human rights activism. It offers in-depth analyses of the most significant debates about the role of human rights in U.S. foreign policy during these years, examining how Americans responded to human rights violations in the Soviet Union, in Southern Rhodesia after the 1965 unilateral declaration of independence, in Greece after the 1967 coup, in authoritarian South Korea, and in Chile after the 1973 coup. The focus on these sites of human rights abuse is based on an extensive examination of records from the relevant presidential administrations, the State Department, Congress, the United Nations (UN), and nongovernmental organizations (NGOs). The five countries chosen for this study had human rights records of significant interest to all these constituencies; they also represent geographic diversity, ideological diversity, and diversity in terms of human rights violations.[2] Taken together, this book shows that Americans were engaged with a wide range of human rights issues across the long 1960s. People who had transnational connections—ties to foreign people and places forged through travel or other border-crossing interactions—united with other Americans who were motivated by broader international and domestic movements; the activism they produced ushered in the institutionalization of human rights in U.S. foreign policy and the expansion of human rights activism in the United States during the late 1970s, the 1980s, and beyond.

I define the "long 1960s" as the years between John F. Kennedy's inauguration in 1961 and Jimmy Carter's in 1977.[3] Like a number of other scholars, I have found the term "long 1960s" useful in explaining the years between the early and late periods of the Cold War.[4] Domestically, the long 1960s was a distinctive period characterized by the height of the civil rights movement, other rights-based movements, and the movement to end U.S. involvement in Vietnam, all of which collectively reshaped American politics and society. In terms of foreign policy, the long 1960s were marked not only by the war in Vietnam but also by increasing challenges to U.S. power in the Third World and by efforts to reduce tension with the Soviet Union amid unrelenting Cold War competition.

This book will employ the term "human rights" as activists at the time most often did—to signal support for the rights to due process, to the practice of one's religion, to freedom of movement, and to participation in one's own government, as well as freedom from racial discrimination and torture. To use shorthand, activists were attentive largely to civil and political rights, not to the fuller list of human rights outlined in the UN Universal Declaration of Human Rights (UDHR).[5] Although many activists and policymakers were concerned about what might be labeled "social and economic rights," they rarely used the language of human rights in that respect during those years. Exceptions include Martin Luther King Jr. and some activists who focused on human rights violations in Chile, who were attentive to the intersection among political, civil, social, and economic rights.[6]

In the years after the adoption of the UDHR, a small number of American NGOs focused on domestic and international human rights. During the Eisenhower years, however, human rights was characterized by critics as a project of the UN that threatened American sovereignty; this sentiment hung over all activism by groups such as Freedom House, the International League for the Rights of Man (ILRM), and the National Association for the Advancement of Colored People (NAACP). These organizations were largely headquartered in New York City, where beginning in the late

1940s they could direct attention toward UN bodies and diplomats. There was considerable overlap in the personnel of these organizations, and many even set up their offices in the same building—the Wendell Willkie Building in midtown Manhattan.[7] Rather than being based on mass membership or engaged in political mobilization, as would be experienced in later years, human rights work in these decades was largely a privileged affair.[8] Observers have described the ILRM as an example of an "elite organization" with a membership made up of an "'old boy' network."[9] Similarly, Freedom House's board meetings were often held at the 21 Club in Manhattan, a restaurant known for its extensive Prohibition-era secret wine cellar.[10]

WHAT WAS NEW IN THE LONG 1960S?

The long 1960s marked both a transformation and an expansion of American human rights activism, shaped by transnational connections and reflected by a focus on Washington rather than New York, which led to new approaches to U.S. foreign policy. One signal of this shift is the increased use of the term "human rights." Using the *New York Times* as an example, the term "human rights" was used on average 2.4 times more per year during the long 1960s than during the eight years of the Eisenhower administration. Furthermore, incidence of "human rights" more than doubled between 1961 and 1976, albeit with fluctuations along the way (figure 0.1).

Occurrence of the term "human rights" is only one measure of the growing salience of human rights terminology in the 1960s. As this book shows, the usage of related terminology, including "torture," "dissidents," "political prisoners," and "racial discrimination" also increased meaningfully during these years—which is evidence of, and potentially a cause of, increasing attention to human rights.[11]

What led Americans to care about international violations of human rights during the long 1960s? The reasons for increased and innovative activism were diverse. Many were primed to care about human rights violations due to broader changes taking place both internationally and within the United States during the long 1960s, such as decolonization, the establishment of NGOs devoted to human rights, the achievements of the civil rights movement, attempts to address poverty in the United States, distress about the direction of U.S. foreign policy, and greater congressional activism in foreign affairs. In this context, activists' transnational connections,

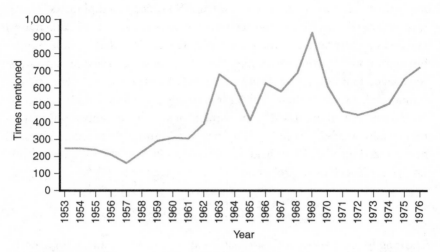

FIGURE 0.1. Usage of the term "human rights" in the *New York Times*, 1953–1976

which were facilitated by decreasing costs for international travel and increasing advances in television and satellite communication during these years, activated or spurred their efforts on behalf of human rights.[12]

The 1960s offered new opportunities for Americans to travel and work abroad, and returning Peace Corps volunteers, missionaries, and academics were often attracted to human rights activism by their international experiences.[13] In his work, historian Patrick Kelly cites Herbert Clemens, a former Peace Corps volunteer who participated in protests for civil rights and against Vietnam and later turned to human rights work, as characteristic of the personal paths of those who became active on human rights during the mid-1970s.[14] In another case, Peace Corps volunteers taught English to Kim Dae Jung, a prominent opposition politician in South Korea. According to Russell Sveda, a Peace Corps volunteer in South Korea in the late 1960s, Kim's Peace Corps connections "gave a certain amount of U.S. government attention to Kim Dae Jung's plight because [Peace Corps] volunteers were visiting him on a daily basis."[15] Sveda's account of how he and his fellow volunteers kept Kim visible to U.S. policymakers demonstrates that Americans overseas can also meaningfully influence U.S. foreign policy.

Travel shaped the activism of a wide range of Americans, not only Peace Corps volunteers.[16] For example, James Becket, one of the two authors of

Amnesty International's first report on torture in Greece, had traveled there with his family and met his future wife during their trip.[17] When University of California–Berkeley law professor Frank Newman began writing about human rights in 1967, he saw the subject as connected with his professional interest in civil rights and civil liberties. But Newman also knew Andreas Papandreou, who was imprisoned in Greece, so he undertook a trip to Athens. This visit further enmeshed him in human rights advocacy, leading to later work with Amnesty International and the International Commission of Jurists.[18] Americans such as David Wiley, Marylee Crofts, and Linda Jones, who were missionaries in Southern Rhodesia and South Korea, became active on human rights based on their intimate connections with violations in the communities they served.[19]

Additional Americans came to feel deep transnational connections to political prisoners and others suffering human rights abuses without ever leaving the United States; they were drawn to human rights based on identity or personal experience.[20] Rita Hauser, who served as the United States' representative to the UN Human Rights Commission, argued that connections forged through immigration fueled American attention to human rights, noting that it was "understandable that many Americans remained concerned over the fate of minorities close to them whose rights were threatened elsewhere in the world."[21] Roberta Cohen, who was the executive director of the ILRM from 1971 to 1977, had a personal family connection to the issue of Soviet discrimination against Jews, as some of her family members had emigrated from Russia due to anti-Semitism.[22] Ginetta Sagan, who was active in Amnesty International USA, had suffered torture in fascist Italy.[23]

Motivations for other individuals' attention to human rights were moral, political, and religious.[24] Andrew Marwick points to a "revived emphasis on the liberal principles of democratic rights and due process" in the 1960s.[25] Furthermore, historian Petra Goedde sees 1970s-era youth as motivated to find "local and personal solutions to global problems."[26] Liisa Malkki depicts Finnish Red Cross workers as being motivated both by their own neediness and by a desire to be connected to something larger than themselves. At a time of domestic and international foment, Americans active on human rights may have similarly been seeking connections to something "greater than themselves."[27] Interestingly, Secretary of State Henry Kissinger, speaking in July 1975 on "The Moral Foundations of

Foreign Policy," made a similar diagnosis, declaring that Americans wanted to think of U.S. policy as representing "something beyond ourselves."[28] Finally, the Catholic Church's commitment to "human dignity" and "religious freedom" in the documents from the Second Vatican Council also likely influenced Americans' thinking about human rights. Specifically, in Vatican II, Pope Paul VI wrote, "With respect to the fundamental rights of the person, every type of discrimination, whether social or cultural, whether based on sex, race, color, social condition, language or religion, is to be overcome and eradicated as contrary to God's intent."[29]

A CHANGING WORLD

Broad developments at the international and domestic levels precipitated and reinforced Americans' individual motivations. Internationally, decolonization increased demands on the United States to take greater account of racial discrimination in its own practices and in its foreign policy. Both abroad and at home, the increasing influence of NGOs, some of which focused on human rights, shaped growing American activism. Domestically, the movements for African American freedom and against the war in Vietnam shaped Americans' thinking about their government's policies and led many to push for new approaches to human rights in U.S. policy. The Cold War consensus that had privileged containment and anticommunism over other priorities was corroded by displeasure with the conduct of the United States, including not only the war in Vietnam but also the 1965 intervention in the Dominican Republic as well as support for military dictatorships and covert intelligence operations abroad. As this consensus weakened, members of Congress asserted themselves more forcefully in the policymaking process and at times used their control of the appropriations process to wield influence.[30]

An analysis of the reasons that prompted greater attention to human rights during the long 1960s must include the role of the UN, which was dramatically transformed in the wake of decolonization.[31] In the words of historian Roland Burke, "Decolonization initiated a global human rights debate."[32] In 1960 alone, seventeen new countries joined the UN. New member states brought with them specific concerns that were often tied to their colonial experiences. Many of these newly independent states bonded together in order to exert greater influence within an organization that was formally managed by the permanent members of the UN Security Council. The "Afro-Asian Group," as these states were often called collectively, focused on racial discrimination, which led the situations in South Africa and eventually Southern Rhodesia to consume a considerable amount of attention and debate at the UN. In addition, these new states targeted European powers, Portugal in particular, that would not relinquish their colonies. UN dynamics fundamentally shaped U.S. policy toward Southern Rhodesia, and in the Chilean case, UN condemnation and pressure heightened American interest in violations there. But for a range of reasons, human rights violations in South Korea, Greece, and the Soviet Union inspired less debate at the UN.

At the same time that some human rights violations garnered greater attention at the UN, American activists increasingly focused on U.S. policymakers in Washington as the most effective avenue for effecting change. In the early 1960s, New York–based Freedom House, the NAACP, and the ILRM remained the most prominent NGOs focused on human rights. Yet they were increasingly frustrated by the UN. Roger Baldwin, the former executive director of the ILRM, repeatedly expressed disillusionment with the UN, writing, "We work against a difficult background—a dis-United Nations too preoccupied with nationalism and colonialism to consider international enforcement of human rights."[33] Arguing that the ILRM needed to intervene in instances of human rights violations abroad, its staff wrote, "As long as international machinery remains rather impotent in confronting human rights violations, the [ILRM] and other such groups must accept a major responsibility for doing so."[34]

The rise of new NGOs as well as the shifting attention of established groups offered outlets for people who were increasingly attuned to human rights and the innovations they brought to human rights activism.[35] The most significant NGO to form during these years was Amnesty International; it would ultimately transform human rights activism into a mass movement. Established in London in 1961, it initially faced challenges as it sought to expand to the United States.[36] In 1965, however, some 750 people responded to a *Reader's Digest* article about its work, which prompted efforts to establish a section of Amnesty International in the United States.[37] Eventually Amnesty International USA (AIUSA) offered a meaningful outlet for the rising number of Americans who wanted to get involved in human rights advocacy.[38]

Other groups that were organized around religion, nationality, or profession also played key parts. For example, the American Association for the International Commission of Jurists saw its mission to be the "protection and independence of foreign lawyers who have been either arrested, incarcerated or intimidated by their governments solely because they are rendering professional services to dissident or unpopular defendants."[39] Similarly, lawyers in the international law section of the American Bar Association expressed concern about human rights violations, particularly of lawyers' rights, in South Korea and Greece.[40]

Support for human rights internationally was closely linked with domestic concerns about civil, political, economic, and social rights as Americans became progressively worried about consistency in the domestic and foreign policies of the United States and the degree to which U.S. leaders championed human rights internationally. During the Eisenhower years, Americans were aware that the country's record on race relations left it open to considerable criticism. As Morris Abram, who was active in the civil rights movement and who served as the U.S. representative to the UN Human Rights Commission, said, "Unless we succeed in solving our own racial and other human rights problems, we may find we are forfeiting our position of leadership and the respect of those many new States to whom questions of racism and exploitation are paramount."[41] As the United States made strides through court decisions such as *Brown v. Board of Education*, protests to end segregation, legislation such as the 1964 Civil Rights Act and the 1965 Voting Rights Act, and greater visibility of African Americans in public life, criticism of the American race record at the UN declined, and U.S. policymakers gained greater confidence in talking about human rights violations abroad.[42]

In many ways, human rights activists were building on the successes of the civil rights movement in that white and black liberals sought to export the movement's victories abroad. This book's title, *From Selma to Moscow*, evokes that impulse.[43] Writing in 1965, the National Citizens' Commission on International Cooperation's Committee on Human Rights argued that as the United States made more progress on the fulfillment of civil rights domestically, it was better situated to contribute internationally regarding human rights. The committee wrote, "We have removed finally most of the domestic obstacles which have in the past prevented our active participation in international efforts to project 'human rights and fundamental freedoms for all without distinction as to race, sex, language, or religion.'"[44] Fundamentally, the civil rights movement wanted the federal government to protect Americans from violations of their rights; that thinking led, by extension, to a belief that the United States could play a role in protecting people from violations abroad in Southern Rhodesia, South Africa, Greece, and elsewhere.[45]

The movement for greater protection of African Americans' rights generally heightened Americans' attention to human rights language, to the plight of those oppressed by illiberal leaders, and specifically to the oppression of black Africans who suffered under colonialism or white minority regimes.[46] Freedom House worked for racial equality in the United States in part because, as Freedom House official Leo Cherne said, "We could not inconveniently, no matter what our inclination, ignore the fact that for a portion of this society, this society was not that much more free than others we were opposing."[47] After Johnson signed the 1964 Civil Rights Act, Secretary of State Dean Rusk wrote to a member of Congress that he was "deeply impressed by the connection between this problem here at home and the great struggle for freedom which is being waged throughout the world. . . . This country is looked upon as a leader of those who wish to be free, and what we do here has an importance far beyond our borders."[48] Other U.S. officials echoed Rusk's perspective, including Harris L. Wofford Jr., a special assistant to the president, when he spoke to the Annual Conference of the National Civil Liberties Clearing House: "If American rights are all that we see at stake, we will lose the perspective that shows this as a world-wide human problem." Wofford also outlined the need to "move this country ahead on the new frontiers at home and abroad, in civil rights here and in human rights everywhere."[49] *From Selma to Moscow* recalls the slogan on a banner at a March 1965 rally for Soviet Jewry—"Selma or Moscow: Human Liberty is Indivisible. End Soviet Anti-Semitism"— which highlighted the historic links between liberal American Jews and the civil rights movement as well as the connections between those engaged in activism on behalf of civil rights and on behalf of human rights (figure 0.2).[50]

Although rights have been significant to the United States since the country's founding, it was the 1960s that produced "an explosion of demands for new rights."[51] According to Risa Goluboff, in the 1960s "reform movements were claiming, and courts were increasingly offering, constitutional protection for new people and new rights."[52] Historian Brian

FIGURE 0.2. Americans protesting the treatment of Soviet Jews in front of Independence Hall in Philadelphia drew an explicit link to the march for voting rights earlier that month. Courtesy of the *Jewish Exponent*.

Balogh suggests, "The civil rights movement provided the 'how-to' guide to would-be organizers, as activists from civil rights moved on to the New Left, feminist, and even the environmental movements."[53] Human rights activists were also inspired by, were students of, and in some cases were participants in the civil rights movements. One notable example of the shift from civil rights work to human rights activism is the Lawyers' Committee for Civil Rights Under Law, which began in response to Kennedy's call to bring a legal approach to the civil rights movement and later defended South Africans who were charged under apartheid legislation.[54] Similarly, James Green, who has written about human rights activism that targeted the Brazilian military government in the 1960s, sees veterans of the civil rights and antiwar movements as drawn to activism regarding Brazil and Chile in particular.[55]

Human rights and intellectual historian Samuel Moyn does not see a strong connection between American attention to human rights internationally and the domestic civil rights movement, writing, "It is tempting to believe that the civil rights movement that had transformed American race relations prompted the new invocations of human rights, but the evidence is thin. Though some participants in the civil rights movement later joined the American human rights movement, the timing of the latter is too late for any truly powerful connection to be made."[56] Moyn's argument is based, to some degree, on the existence of a gap between the dissipation of the freedom movement, to use a broader term, and the development of a mass human rights movement in the late 1970s. Looking at elite-level attention to human rights in the long 1960s, however, suggests a closer relationship between the movements.[57] The two most persuasive links are the overlap of personnel—for example the involvement in human rights debates of prominent freedom leaders such as NAACP executive director Roy Wilkins and executive director of the National Urban League Whitney Young—as well as the claims of many involved—such as Rusk, Abram, and United States ambassador to the UN Arthur J. Goldberg—about the links between U.S. foreign and domestic policies regarding racial discrimination.

The long 1960s were also a period during which American policymakers increasingly tackled Americans' social and economic rights through programs like the Great Society and the War on Poverty.[58] Sending a report to the White House, law professor Louis Sohn echoed the language of many in urging that the Johnson administration pay greater attention to human rights: "As a supporter of the President in his many efforts to create the Great Society at home and to bring peace, justice and economic development to the strife-torn world, I am certain that the new initiatives in the field of human rights suggested in our report are close to the president's heart and are worthy of his attention."[59] Abram declared:

My country recognizes, certainly today, that while man does not live by bread alone, he does not live without bread, and that economic, social and cultural rights are part and parcel of the fabric of American civilization. We are also perfectly aware of the fact that it is not enough simply to open the doors of opportunity, that when the doors are open it frequently is a fact that men do not have the resources, and the society may not have the resources, to permit men to walk through the gates of opportunity to achievement.[60]

Abram sought deliberately to echo Johnson's address at Howard University, where the president had declared: "It is not enough to open the gates of opportunity. All our citizens must have the ability to walk through those gates. This is the next and most profound stage of the battle for civil rights."[61] Historian Ryan Irwin argues that we must see Johnson's policy toward South Africa in the context of his War on Poverty, which was, after all, a war on social injustice and racial discrimination or, as Johnson put it, an effort to "end poverty and racial injustice" in that generation.[62] We can apply this insight to understanding the Johnson administration's approach to Southern Rhodesia as well.

Americans and, importantly, members of Congress viewed U.S. policies as increasingly at odds with American values.[63] Representative Donald Fraser (D-MN), who led a series of highly influential hearings on human rights during these years, later said, "I think American foreign policy has to reflect basic American values. The United States has historically stood as a beacon of hope for oppressed persons around the world, as an example of a free people running their government in a reasonably sensible and civilized way. If our foreign policy fails to reflect our domestic values it loses much of its force."[64] Put another way, they feared that U.S. foreign policy was immoral. Vietnam loomed as the most significant overseas intervention, but United States actions in the Dominican Republic, Chile, and elsewhere also played a role.[65] Criticism of the war in Vietnam by Senator Frank Church (D-ID) during February 1966 hearings set a precedent for condemnation of U.S. foreign policy. As David Schmitz and Natalie Fousekis have noted, in the hearings' aftermath, "the postwar consensus on containment and presidential domination of foreign policy now began to crack."[66] Similarly, Tom Harkin, as a congressional aide in 1970, discovered and publicized the existence of "tiger cages" in an inhumane detention facility on Con Son Island in South Vietnam, raising questions about the record of the South Vietnamese government and American conduct there.[67] Later, as a member of Congress, Representative Harkin (D-IA) was an active proponent of limiting U.S. support to governments that violated human rights.

Congressional skepticism was echoed by NGOs. The ILRM repeatedly expressed its concern over human rights violations in Vietnam.[68] In one statement, it asserted, "Prisoners and civilians have been inhumanely treated, tortured and killed. Wounded have gone uncared for. Dead have been mutilated. Hostages have been taken and in some cases used as human shields. Systematic terror and assassination have been employed as weapons."[69] Later it protested South Vietnam's detention and poor treatment of a hundred thousand political prisoners.[70] Similarly, the U.S. Study Team on Religious and Political Freedom in Vietnam, largely made up of religious leaders, shared with Nixon and members of Congress its concerns about the "suppression of political opposition, using tactics of arrest, harassment, and imprisonment."[71]

As the decade progressed, U.S. support for military dictatorships in Brazil, Greece, and Chile prompted further questions about the wisdom of U.S. policy.[72] Historian Thomas Field has argued that militarization was a "hallmark" of the global 1960s; with military regimes often came repression, which helps explain why there was increasing attention to human rights during that decade.[73] At issue for many was the extent to which Cold War priorities, which were manifested in support for repressive leaders, were diminishing America's image abroad and undermining the morality of U.S. foreign policy. Or, as Daniel Sargent has characterized it, when human rights emerged as an issue in U.S. policy, it "was not just a breakthrough; it was also a backlash."[74]

Connected with growing unease over U.S. foreign policy was "the breakdown of Congressional respect for Executive Branch leadership," as one former diplomat described it.[75] Critics charged that the presidency had become "isolated, autocratic, and imperial," and by 1974 Americans' confidence in their government had fallen to 41 percent, down from 77 percent in 1964.[76]

As their faith in the executive branch eroded due to what were seen as ill-advised foreign policy decisions and abuses of presidential power, members of Congress increasingly asserted themselves in policymaking.[77] Donald Fraser was among the most assertive, and he explained his focus by recalling, "Some years ago, I was in Athens and I was shown a picture of some tanks which were rumbling down the streets. They were tanks made in the United States, and they were being used to suppress students who were protesting against the military junta's destruction of democracy in Greece."[78] As Harry Frankfurt has written, "There are occasions when a person realises that what he cares about matters to him not merely so much, but in such a way, that it is impossible for him to forbear from a certain course of action."[79] Americans such as Fraser came to care about human rights abuses so strongly that they were compelled to reshape U.S. foreign policy.

Frustration with the executive branch and the rise of congressional activism, of course, was heightened by domestic developments, the most prominent of which was Watergate—first, because it accelerated the erosion of trust of the White House, and second, because in the scandal's wake, more liberal elected officials arrived in Washington, leading some to call them "Watergate babies."[80] Kissinger expressed frustration with the impact of Watergate on U.S. foreign policy, saying, "Watergate was circumscribing our freedom of action. We were losing the ability to make credible commitments."[81] Furthermore, members of Congress were drawn into greater activism by the lack of respect shown to them by the White House; as one member of Congress later said, congressional human rights activism developed because "we in Congress were very, very annoyed at the administration."[82] In particular, the congressional hearings held by Frank Church and his United States Senate Select Committee to Study Governmental Operations with Respect to Intelligence Activities further undermined Americans' faith in the executive branch.[83]

The collapse of the Cold War consensus, prodded in part by greater congressional activism in foreign affairs, also produced a degree of democratization in foreign-policy making.[84] Nonstate actors have always played influential roles in shaping U.S. foreign relations, but changes during the 1960s opened up space for them to have an enhanced role in policymaking, which for some time had been dominated by a closed, elite group who subscribed to a consensus view of U.S. policy.[85] The chapters that follow will show how activists, lawyers, and religious leaders who were involved in human rights work seized new opportunities to shape U.S. foreign policy. As Michael Nelson points out, narratives about the 1960s have often emphasized turbulence, division, and potential crisis.[86] These ruptures offered opportunities.

Many accounts chronicling the 1960s focus on protests on college campuses, the radical politics of the left, and the youth counterculture; however, Americans active on human rights were beyond university age, liberal rather than radical, and elite actors rather than participants in a mass movement.[87] Debates at universities were essential to the political climate in which human rights activism transformed, but the figures at the center of *From Selma to Moscow* were motivated by experiences in their professional lives, or at least after their university years. Additionally, while many on the radical left may have sympathized with human rights activism—particularly with respect to Chile—they were more focused on domestic politics and opposing the war in Vietnam, and it was elite liberals like Fraser who spearheaded the international human rights agenda.

The Americans motivated by transnational connections or other personal, political, moral, and religious motivations were political entrepreneurs in the growing movement for human rights during these years. According to sociologist Charles Tilly, "Social movements depend heavily on political entrepreneurs for their scale, durability, and effectiveness."[88] Political entrepreneurs in 1960s-era human rights activism such as James Becket, Joseph Eldridge, and Donald Fraser galvanized other Americans to work alongside them in pressing for greater attention to human rights in U.S. foreign policy. These activists engaged in "contentious politics," which Charles Tilly and Sidney Tarrow define as "interactions in which actors make claims bearing on someone else's interests, leading to coordinated efforts on behalf of shared interests or programs, in which governments are involved as targets, initiators of claims, or third parties."[89]

American human rights activists determined their tactics—namely an unrelenting focus on Washington—based on their diagnosis that U.S. foreign policy was complicit in human rights abuses. The human rights violations at the center of this account—torture, racial discrimination, and religious persecution—drove American citizens and nongovernmental organizations to exert pressure through letter writing, testifying before Congress, and participating in demonstrations among other activities.[90] Members of Congress held hearings to investigate human rights violations, published reports highlighting abuses, and when their concerns were largely dismissed by the executive branch, utilized the "power of the purse"—congressional control over the appropriations process.[91] Their activism led to legislation that limited military and economic assistance to abusive governments, created institutions to monitor human rights internationally, and reshaped U.S. foreign policymaking going forward. Specifically, these activists and their accomplishments imbued the issue of human rights with such salience that it could not be ignored in the subsequent years.

THE WHITE HOUSE RESPONSE

The presidential administrations during the long 1960s responded in a range of ways to external pressure and internal concerns about human rights violations. There were regular in-house debates about the proper course for U.S. policy, with lower-level State Department officials often arguing for more action in the face of resistance at the highest levels. When there was action, frequently it was American diplomats or midlevel officials expressing unease about human rights violations to foreign governments. Despite the reputation of human rights work as a dead end for ambitious foreign service officers, my research shows that many were engaged with dissidents and human rights violations while serving abroad. Occasionally, such as with Rhodesia and Greece, the United States pursued sanctions or implemented an arms embargo. At times, U.S. policymakers— even Henry Kissinger during the 1976 campaign—denounced human rights abuses publicly in what we might think of as "symbolic form[s] of action," but overall, U.S. leaders exercised considerable restraint during these years.[92] Nevertheless, each administration was careful to assert publicly that its commitment to human rights shaped U.S. policy, often to a greater degree than was suggested by its actions.

Kissinger was the driving force of U.S. foreign policy during the Nixon and Ford years, and his long-held perspective, which was shared by many policymakers during the long 1960s, was that protecting human rights was not central to U.S. foreign policy priorities. This dynamic meant that supporters of human rights had a challenging task when it came to shaping U.S. policy—yet they succeeded during the long 1960s in many ways. Importantly, they heightened awareness of human rights violations such that decisions to support repressive regimes led to congressional hearings, front-page news, and some successes in reducing the flow of U.S. dollars to the abusers' coffers. In addition, the country overall became increasingly attuned to the consequences of U.S. foreign policy for human rights abroad.

In the chapters that follow, I demonstrate the range and impact of American human rights activism during the long 1960s. Chapter one highlights growing American attention to and activism on behalf of repressed Soviet citizens during these years. The second chapter demonstrates how Southern Rhodesia's unilateral declaration of independence in 1965 spurred civil rights leaders in the United States and others concerned with racial discrimination to urge Lyndon Johnson's administration to undermine the white regime there. The next three chapters show that Americans became less willing to indulge repressive allies as the Cold War consensus eroded. In the case of Greece, in the wake of the 1967 coup, the junta's harsh treatment of its perceived enemies—arresting them, subjecting them to torture, and imprisoning them in island concentration camps—galvanized many in the United States. Chapter three reveals the varied efforts of academics, members of Congress, and prominent liberals to encourage the United States to moderate its support for the military regime in Greece.

Next, in chapter four, I explore activists' frustrations with U.S. policy toward South Korea and analyze the tool increasingly utilized to signal dissatisfaction with that policy—legislation curbing military and economic assistance to human rights violators. Chapter five examines how the military coup in Chile and the subsequent human rights violations there motivated nongovernmental activists and members of Congress to press for greater distance from the repressive government. In addition to analyzing the influence of nonstate actors, this chapter will demonstrate how Kissinger's intransigence as secretary of state inspired greater congressional activism on human rights.

Across the period of the long 1960s, and reflected in each chapter, activists and members of Congress attempted to utilize available tools but were often stymied by the White House. Their growing frustration produced a congressional revolution led by Donald Fraser. Chapter six explores how, partially motivated by limited executive branch attention, Fraser and his House Subcommittee on International Organizations and Movements held hearings on human rights in 1973 that fundamentally recalibrated U.S. foreign policy formulation. The subcommittee's hearings precipitated a wave of legislation that reshaped the State Department's bureaucracy and formalized human rights as a factor in U.S. policy. These efforts laid the foundation for the institutionalization of human rights as a priority in U.S. foreign policy and assured its continuing significance in the years that followed.

Chapter One

HUMAN RIGHTS ACTIVISM DIRECTED
ACROSS THE IRON CURTAIN

During the long 1960s Americans increasingly became aware of and responded to human rights violations overseas. Not surprisingly, the ideological, military, and economic Cold War with the Soviet Union heightened Americans' focus on human rights abuses in that country. For many observers, the communist system inherently repressed a number of human rights, including the freedoms of religion, movement, and property ownership.[1] Many so-called cold warriors believed that such repression needed to be highlighted for propaganda value with both domestic and international audiences.[2] With the pursuit of détente, the focus on nuclear war lessened, and activists saw an opening to focus more U.S. attention on Soviet human rights violations. Détente, however, also made administrations less likely to press human rights concerns than might have been expected. The White House often felt that more could be gained in its relationship with the Soviet Union by overlooking human rights violations than by championing them, a dynamic that will reappear in later chapters. Such an approach was not uniformly supported in Congress or in nongovernmental circles, which led to ongoing negotiations about the proper place of human rights concerns in Soviet-American relations throughout this period. American activism was also shaped by shifting understandings of the stakes of the Cold War and by increasing questions about whether waging that battle should overwhelm all other foreign policy priorities. Despite uneven attention by successive administrations, the growing prominence of human rights issues helped to ensure their enduring salience in the years that followed.

HUMAN RIGHTS IN THE SOVIET UNION

In the Soviet Union in the 1960s the three greatest violations of human rights were those related to expression, due process, and movement. Soviet leader Nikita Khrushchev's 1956 "secret speech" denouncing Joseph Stalin's excesses offered an opening for some Soviet citizens to express their frustrations with the regime, which had not been permissible under Stalin. But the easing of repression in the wake of Stalin's death extended only so far. It remained illegal to criticize the Soviet government, and those who did so could be charged with Article 70, which targeted speech or propaganda that defamed the Soviet state, or Article 190-1, which banned the circulation of materials that disparaged the state.[3] These prohibitions were largely enforced with censorship and self-censorship. When they were violated, offenders faced harassment and arrest as well as the loss of their employment, apartment, or residence permit. For example, due to what was subsequently characterized as an "antiparty" speech, Soviet authorities deprived scientist Yuri Orlov of his job and exiled him to Armenia.[4] Trials for political offenses in the Soviet Union were demonstrative rather than investigative, with the result and sentence determined either in advance or by the accused's behavior in the courtroom. After conviction, Soviet political prisoners (of which there were thousands) suffered from a caloric intake set at barely subsistence level, beatings, solitary confinement, torture, the interception of packages, poor conditions in punishment cells, and forced commitment to mental institutions.[5] Describing the internal policies of the Union of Soviet Socialist Republics (USSR), Soviet ambassador to the United States Anatoly Dobrynin later wrote, "Dissidents were considered enemies of the regime, and authors who published their works abroad were subjected to reprisals. Nonconformity was still frowned upon. In short, our dogmatic domestic ideology remained unchanged."[6] Most egregious of all, when faced with a government that offered no legal protections and inhibited all types of free expression, there was no escape; the right to emigrate was severely curtailed, often for spurious reasons.

The Soviets, like their Eastern European neighbors, largely declined to grant exit visas, because to do so would represent an admission that not all Soviet citizens were satisfied and that they preferred a life free from the communist system. Those denied the right to emigrate were known as refuseniks, and many would become leading activists against the government. Allowing freer emigration could produce ideological propaganda victories or, as in East Berlin before the construction of the Berlin Wall, a flood of refugees to the West that would threaten to destabilize the regime.[7] In retrospect, however, the international consequences of Soviet policy were far more significant. As Dobrynin writes,

The prohibitive policy of the Soviet authorities over Jewish emigration resulted in growing friction with Israel and contributed to a vigorous anti-Soviet campaign in the United States. . . . Our biggest mistake was to stand on pride and not let as many Jews go as wanted to leave. It would have cost us little and gained us much. Instead, our leadership turned it into a test of wills that we eventually lost.[8]

In response, Soviet citizens protested for their human rights, often in small ways. In the words of activist Lyudmila Alexeyeva, "The human rights movement was born out of the experience of people who lived their lives under conditions of lawlessness, cruelty, and assault on the personality."[9] Expressions of dissent were generally individual initiatives during the late 1950s and early 1960s, focused on freedom of expression, the preservation of national culture, and fairness in the legal system.

In 1965 a network of human rights activists emerged publicly with a demonstration to commemorate the anniversary of the Universal Declaration of Human Rights. Approximately two hundred people assembled in Pushkin Square in December to press for fair trials for imprisoned writers; they focused particularly on Yuli Daniel and Andrei Siniavsky, who had been arrested for violating Article 70 when they published writings abroad that were critical of the Soviet state.[10] The year 1965 also marked the first publication of the *Chronicle of Current Events*, the *samizdat* (self-published) compilation of human rights abuses.[11] Those involved in the Pushkin Square demonstration periodically protested in following years, such as after the Warsaw Pact's 1968 invasion of Czechoslovakia, an action that disillusioned many about the possibilities for progress and reform in the Soviet bloc.[12]

A smaller subset of Soviet activists focused on religious freedom and emigration to Israel. For many Soviet Jews, including prominent refusenik Anatoly Shcharansky, the 1967 Six-Day War in the Middle East awakened their Jewish identity, spurred greater participation in Jewish life, and fostered a desire to live in Israel.[13] Yet the Soviet government refused nearly all applications for emigration. Because of demonstrations for exit visas, Soviet Jews faced police interruption of their holiday celebrations and internal exile. They also suffered discrimination in admission to higher education and in certain professions. More generally, they had little opportunity for a distinct cultural life, including the use of the Yiddish language or access to Jewish schools. Once officially classified as refuseniks, many lost their jobs and faced harassment for wishing to emigrate.[14] The plight of Jewish refuseniks inspired considerable international sympathy, including growing American attention to Soviet Jewry in these years.

Beyond public protests, dissidents began to form organizations to advance their agendas. The two most important groups to develop during the 1960s and early 1970s were the Moscow Human Rights Committee (MHRC) and the Initiative Group for the Defense of Human Rights in the USSR.[15] In describing the MHRC, U.S. representative to the UN Human Rights Commission Rita Hauser commented that such a group was "revolutionary for the Soviet Union, for non-governmental organizations are so rare as to be non-existent."[16] The Soviet government perceived such organizations as threatening and prevented them from operating freely. Members of the MHRC such as nuclear physicist Andrei Sakharov faced a prohibition against living in Moscow as well as the confiscation of written materials, the refusal of exit visas, and the interception of mail.[17] In a notable act of protest, members of the Initiative Group for the Defense of Human Rights in the USSR signed a May 1969 letter that alleged human rights violations in the Soviet Union and addressed it to the UN, making the group the first Soviet NGO to send a letter to that organization.[18] Later, in October 1973, several prominent Soviet dissidents, including Orlov, Valentin Turchin, and Sergei Kovalev, formed a national section of Amnesty International.[19]

Individual acts of protest also persisted. These often took the form of letters, but there were also efforts to escape. For example, after his return from Armenia, an increasingly activist Orlov drafted a September 1973 letter, "Thirteen Questions to Brezhnev," and an appeal to mark Human

Rights Day in December 1974.[20] In one of the more extreme steps taken, a group of Soviet Jews plotted to hijack a plane as a means to escape. The KGB (the Soviet security agency) preemptively foiled the plan, and those behind the plot were sentenced to death. With the exception of the hijacking plot, many refuseniks were hesitant to dissent openly, as it could threaten their ultimate objective—an exit visa.

At times, activism produced positive results from the Soviet government, although on a relatively small scale. In late 1968 Soviet authorities broke their long-standing policy and allowed the emigration of a significant portion of Jewish activists, such that by January 1969, as observer Gal Beckerman writes, "almost the entire old guard" of Jews active in the Baltic republics had left.[21] It seems likely that the Soviets were responding tactically to the growing Jewish emigration movement, hoping that allowing most of the leadership to leave would quell further agitation from the larger Jewish population. Instead, it inspired more Jews to apply for emigration.[22]

The audience for Soviet dissidence was not only internal. Over time, activists sought to reach the international community, particularly the UN, Western governments, and Western citizens, by utilizing the boomerang model described by political scientist Daniel Thomas—that is, through nongovernmental actors making appeals transnationally "in order to circumvent blocked domestic opportunities for protest."[23] In scholar Richard N. Dean's view, Soviet dissidents were initially hesitant to seek support from the West, favoring quiet, private protests. When they shifted tactics, they relied heavily on Western journalists to cover press conferences, solicit interviews, and disseminate *samizdat* materials.[24] A risky but effective way to publicize Soviet human rights abuses was through publication abroad, as Alexander Solzhenitsyn did with *The Gulag Archipelago*, which was released in translation in three volumes in the mid-1970s.[25]

By the 1970s many varied groups were reaching out to the West, including the Initiative Group for the Defense of Human Rights, the MHRC, the Council of Relatives of Imprisoned Baptists, the Working Commission for the Investigation of the Use of Psychiatry for Political Purposes, the Prisoners' Relief Fund, the All-Union Council for Prisoners' Relatives, and the Moscow chapter of Amnesty International. For example, Jewish activist Vladimir Slepak devised a method of smuggling out the names of refuseniks in *matryushka* dolls, one of many creative approaches to ensure that dissidents' reports reached an international audience.[26] Dissidents sought to make stronger, more durable relationships because they believed contacts with the West would facilitate a wider dispersal of their concerns and offer a degree of protection at home.[27] According to dissident Valery Chalidze, being an affiliate of the ILRM and of the Strasbourg Institute for Human Rights protected the MHRC from harsh repercussions, including immediate closure.[28] In a sign that Soviet leaders recognized the effectiveness of those transnational connections, in 1973 and 1974, under Yuri Andropov's leadership, the KGB severed telephone links between Jewish activists and the West, limiting their ability to communicate.

AMERICAN RESPONSE

Of the abuses considered in this book, human rights violations in the Soviet Union produced the most diverse and likely the largest group of Americans driven to action. Whether concerned with dissident scientists, Ukrainian nationalists, or most often Jews who wished to emigrate, members of Congress and interested Americans pressed to make human rights concerns more central to United States foreign policy. One measurement of rising attention to Soviet human rights violations is that the term "dissident" appeared more than twice as frequently in the *New York Times* during the long 1960s than during the Eisenhower administration, with a clear upward trend within the 1961–76 period (figure 1.1).

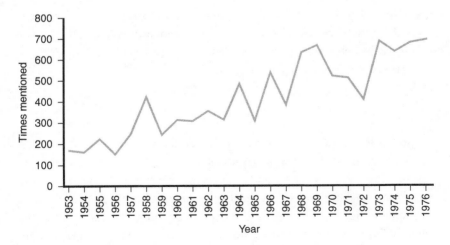

FIGURE 1.1. Usage of the term "dissident" in the *New York Times*, 1953–1976

American citizens, through individual acts such as letter writing, organizational efforts, or participation in mass protests, sought to improve Soviet lives by directly or, more often, indirectly influencing Soviet practices. Direct pressure, whether by Soviet citizens or Americans, had almost no impact on the Soviet leadership. Therefore, activists sought to recruit influential figures who could raise these issues at a higher level, including potentially in bilateral Soviet-American talks. Members of Congress were frequent targets of individual lobbying, and many became advocates for protections of human rights in the Soviet Union, some based on entreaties and others due to personal reasons. Congressional concern about human rights abuses, which often related specifically to Soviet Jewish emigration, was pursued through various channels, the most prominent of which was further lobbying of the executive branch to pressure the Soviet government.

Successive presidential administrations, however, were hesitant to act. Each weighed three principal policy options: first, inaction on human rights, whether out of respect for state sovereignty or to protect other, more important policy priorities; second, quiet diplomacy in which U.S. leaders would raise their concerns privately through diplomatic channels; or third, a louder approach in which Soviet leaders could face public shaming and policy linkage in an aggressive effort to shift their practices. The Kennedy, Johnson, Nixon, and Ford administrations pursued a combination of the first two options. Frustrated by the executive branch's inaction and the limited gains of quiet diplomacy, Congress, with the support of nongovernmental activists, passed the Jackson-Vanik Amendment, weakening the executive branch's monopoly on foreign policy and evaluating the issue of human rights in Soviet-American relations.

Individual Activism

As Soviet leaders were unmoved by dissidents' appeals, external actors, particularly in Europe and the United States, sought to influence the government. Activists in the United States wrote directly to Soviet officials to plead for a prisoner's release, for medical treatment, or for an exit visa. For example, writers, publishers, and members of Congress championed the cause of Soviet dissident writer Andrei Amal'rik, who faced imprisonment for writings that presented the Soviet Union in an unflattering light.[29] In addition, Jerome Shestack, chair of the ILRM, wrote to the chair of the Soviet presidium, Nikolai Podgorny, to object to "what appears to be an official and concerted campaign to restrict the freedom of opinion and expression of its affiliate in the Soviet Union, the Moscow Human Rights Committee."[30]

Members of Congress as well as private citizens such as Townsend Hoopes, the president of the Association of American Publishers, lobbied U.S. officials on these issues in the hope that policymakers would raise the cases in high-level negotiations.[31] In advance of the November 1974 Vladivostok Summit, the White House received many letters asking Ford to bring up the case of Ukrainian political prisoner Valentyn Moroz when he met with Soviet leaders.[32] Even relatives of Soviet prisoners wrote to Ford, asking that he press the Soviet government to release their family members as a humanitarian act.[33]

A considerable amount of activism focused specifically on the problems facing Soviet Jews. This advocacy fits into a much longer history of American concern for religious freedom abroad and of ethnic groups seeking to shape U.S. foreign policy.[34] Jewish Americans as well as missionaries had advocated for human rights dating back at least to the repression of Jews in Romania and Russia during the late nineteenth century. The plight of Soviet Jews resonated for Americans because of the compounding abuse of their human rights—first, that they faced restrictions in practicing their religion, and then second, that they could not emigrate and escape those persecutions.[35] Gal Beckerman describes two reasons that Americans were concerned for Soviet Jewry; the first was based on coreligionists in the United States wanting to aid their Soviet peers, while the other appealed to "universal principles" and framed the struggle as a moral one.[36] Some scholars have pointed to the Holocaust's delayed resonance with Americans as shaping thinking about human rights in the United States.[37] Drawing on such sentiments, the prominent rabbi Abraham Heschel sought to stimulate American Jews into action. In a September 1963 sermon he warned, "The six million are no more. Now three million face spiritual extinction."[38]

One specific source of frustration that prompted considerable rage was the Soviet exit tax, implemented in August 1972, which ostensibly required emigrants to repay the government for their free education. Jews seeking to emigrate had to pay as much as twenty-five thousand dollars to secure their departure.[39] Those concerned with the exit tax sent the White House fifteen hundred telegrams and letters. Such interest prompted the White House to assure letter writers that U.S. officials were raising the issue with their Soviet counterparts.[40]

NGO Efforts

Americans had not been particularly active regarding Soviet Jews during the 1950s and early 1960s; in Beckerman's view, American Jews paid far more attention to the domestic civil rights movement during those years than to Jewish-specific rights violations.[41] Indeed, it was not until October 1963 that the first NGO devoted to Soviet Jewry was established—the Cleveland Committee on Soviet Anti-Semitism.[42] During the next year, twenty-four groups came together to form the American Jewish Conference on Soviet Jewry (AJCSJ), although historian Nathaniel Kurz argues that the AJCSJ did not frame emigration as a human right until after 1967.[43] Subsequently, its successor, the National Conference on Soviet Jewry (NCSJ), undertook what a former staff member called "a campaign to personalize Soviet Jewry."[44]

Other NGOs did emerge. One of the most notable and notorious U.S.-based NGOs focused on Soviet Jewry was the Jewish Defense League (JDL). Beginning in late 1969 the JDL undertook extreme and even violent protests. The group attacked a Soviet airliner on the tarmac at John F. Kennedy International Airport and vandalized the offices of TASS, the Soviet news agency. In 1970 the JDL left Molotov cocktails at the offices of Soviet airline Aeroflot and Soviet tourist agency Intourist.[45]

Beyond highlighting religious or ethnic backgrounds, other NGO efforts sought to galvanize U.S. audiences with initiatives centering on a common profession. For example, the West Coast branch of AIUSA formed an Amnesty International Medical and Scientific Committee for Human Rights. Many members of the committee were scientists, and they spoke out about Soviet pressure on Sakharov and encouraged fellow scientists to join their efforts.[46] Later, in 1973 and 1974, the Federation for American Scientists and the American Psychiatric Association as well as other organizations became engaged in the plight of Soviet dissidents.[47]

Mass Demonstrations

By the mid-1960s there were growing efforts to focus more Jews in the United States on their coreligionists in the USSR.[48] In 1964 Yaakov Birnbaum founded the College Students' Struggle for Soviet Jewry, which was intended to be a "mass grass-roots movement—spearheaded by the student youth." The group organized a demonstration outside the Soviet mission to the UN that drew a thousand students, garnering coverage from the three television networks and major news outlets.[49] Jewish activists often directed their protests at the Soviet mission, as it presented an opportunity to influence Soviet officials directly and resonated with the significant Jewish population in New York City.

The plight of the failed Leningrad hijackers became a cause célèbre among Jewish activists, particularly when the principal conspirators were sentenced to death in December 1970. Later that month twenty-five hundred people demonstrated against the sentences at the Soviet mission in New York, part of a wave of strikes and protests in places as diverse as Israel, Italy, Switzerland, and Sweden.[50] The death sentences of the chief hijackers were quickly overturned and commuted to fifteen-year prison terms. The *New York Times* commented, "It is encouraging that the Kremlin has acknowledged the need for paying attention, in some cases at least, to the sensibilities of the civilized world."[51]

The number of participants in mass rallies devoted to Jewish emigration is one indication of the issue's growing salience among Americans. Activists had a rally of about twenty thousand people in Madison Square Garden in June 1965, and a September vigil outside the White House drew ten thousand people.[52] Thousands rallied in Washington in March and October 1971. More than seven thousand people participated, despite terrible weather, in the October rally in front of the Washington Monument, where Morris Abram referenced the "thousands" who "remained locked in a country neither willing to let them practice their beliefs nor to leave their bondage behind."[53] In 1973 an estimated one hundred thousand people gathered in New York City on behalf of Soviet Jewish emigration; many protesters dressed in striped outfits in an effort to connect Soviet Jews with those imprisoned in concentration camps and Soviet prisons.[54]

Support for Soviet Jews was not confined to Jewish activists. In observer Paula Stern's view, "A human rights objective—that everyone should have the right to emigrate—became both a rallying point and a convenient cause for a wide range of interest groups: ethnic, economic, and ideological."[55] Beyond a commitment to religious freedom, one reason for the issue's high profile was the close link between civil rights activists and those concerned for Soviet Jewry that emerged due to liberal Jews' participation in the campaign for racial equality in the United States. As evidence of this interconnection, a sign during a March 1965 rally in Philadelphia read, "Selma or Moscow: Human Liberty is Indivisible. End Soviet Anti-Semitism."[56] In addition, Reverend Martin Luther King Jr. participated in a phone conference with thirty-two groups supporting Soviet Jews in December 1966, saying, "No person of good will can stand by as a silent auditor while there is a possibility of the complete spiritual and cultural destruction of a once flourishing Jewish community. The denial of human rights anywhere is a threat to the affirmation of human rights everywhere."[57] Making explicit the links between the two movements at a Madison Square Garden rally for Soviet Jews, Abram, a Southern Jew who had served both communities with distinction, said, "We shall protest; we shall march; we shall overcome."[58]

Congressional Activism

An important audience for rallies and allies in the cause were sympathetic members of Congress, some of whom devoted considerable attention to the issue. Within Congress there were no clear predictors of interest in human rights in the USSR. Certainly, members who were Jewish or who represented large numbers of Jewish constituents, such as Senator Jacob Javits (R-NY) or Senator Abraham Ribicoff (D-CT) were particularly active. Liberal Democrats such as Donald Fraser included Soviet abuses as one of the many human rights issues that they followed. Others such as Representative Robert Drinan (D-MA), a Catholic priest, were committed to religious freedom more broadly.[59] A commitment to anticommunism shaped the attitudes of conservatives such as Senators Jesse Helms (R-NC) and Henry M. Jackson (D-WA).[60] Jackson's efforts, which also should be seen in the context of growing congressional activism, culminated with his sponsorship of legislation to restrict Soviet-American trade in an attempt to pressure the Soviet Union to issue more exit visas to Jews. The Jackson-Vanik Amendment will be discussed in greater detail later.[61]

Interested members of Congress and private citizens sought to influence successive administrations to prioritize human rights violations in Soviet-American relations. House members actively sponsored resolutions opposing the Soviet government's treatment of Jews and lent their support to public demonstrations.[62] For example, Representative Gerald Ford (R-MI) spoke at one of the Madison Square Garden rallies for Soviet Jewry, saying, "I feel that it is now very appropriate to remind the Russians of the United Nations Declaration on Human Rights. And I speak specifically about the right of the Jews of the Soviet Union to live as normal human beings with all the rights and freedoms enjoyed by others—and especially the freedom to leave the USSR if they want to."[63] An October 1973 resolution condemned Soviet suppression of dissent: "The intensive and thorough campaign of the Soviet Government to intimidate and deter those who have spoken out against repression of political and intellectual dissent profoundly offends the conscience of a free people." The resolution also highlighted congressional concern for several prominent dissidents, including Sakharov and Solzhenitsyn; criticized anti-Semitism as violating human rights; and called on the Soviets to adhere to the UN UDHR.[64] In a number of instances, Congress held hearings to publicize the scope of abuses in the USSR.[65]

Members of Congress also raised individual cases with the State Department and the White House. For example, Jackson wrote to Ford, encouraging him to pressure the administration to raise Valentyn Moroz's case at the UN.[66] In another instance Fraser wrote to Henry Kissinger about prominent Soviet dissidents such as Andrei Tverdokhlebov of the Moscow chapter of Amnesty International.[67] Despite these examples of activism, the resolutions, statements, and hearings had a limited impact on the White House.

Given the ineffectiveness of some of their other tactics, members of Congress used visits to the Soviet Union to raise the issue of Jewish emigration and other human rights violations with Soviet officials directly.[68] In the USSR members of Congress also met with Jews to offer moral support and to coordinate tactics. When he visited the Soviet Union, Drinan was galvanized by refuseniks such as Shcharansky, and these connections motivated him to address their plight. To that end, Drinan sent a list of refusenik names to the NCSJ and talked to Soviet officials about the obstacles to Jewish emigration.[69]

Administration Response

The United States had noted Soviet human rights violations, to some degree, going back to the Eisenhower administration as part of its propaganda efforts. In 1959 then Vice President Nixon first delivered to Soviet officials lists of individuals whom the United States hoped would be able to emigrate.[70] Since then, the United States had repeatedly declared Captive Nations Week to draw attention to the Soviet domination of Eastern Europe. The initiative was routinely passed by Congress and proclaimed by the president during the early Cold War years. The White House did not raise the topic of human rights with the Soviets during the Kennedy years, and under Johnson indirect criticism was more prevalent, particularly at the UN. There, U.S. ambassador to the UN Arthur J. Goldberg explicitly criticized the Soviet practice of forced detention in psychiatric hospitals, the harsh conditions to which political prisoners were subject in the USSR, and the Soviet conduct of the trials of Vladimir Bukovsky and other dissidents as a "clear violation of Article 11 of the Universal Declaration of Human Rights."[71] Goldberg decried assertions by Soviet diplomats at the Human Rights Commission that foreign diplomats should not address another country's internal affairs, saying, "If violations of human rights do not occur within the confines of sovereign states, where do they occur, on celestial bodies? . . . Human rights are either a concern of the United Nations under the Charter, or they are not. And if they are a concern, as plainly they are, then they must be discussed in reference to the conduct of some states."[72] Soviet officials were sensitive to these criticisms. For example, in June 1969 a Soviet diplomat warned that "any reference would be very badly viewed in Moscow in terms of president's stated express hope for better U.S.-USSR relations."[73]

The Nixon administration was even more conservative in its attitude about raising human rights violations with Soviet officials than the Johnson administration had been. According to Nixon's speechwriter William Safire, Nixon's aides were under strict instructions from Kissinger not to discuss Soviet Jews during the 1972 Moscow Summit. Kissinger warned them, "How would it be if Brezhnev comes to the U.S. with a petition about the Negroes in Mississippi?"[74] Administration officials suggested that there were limits to U.S. influence on Soviet human rights abuses; as Kissinger wrote, "I have no doubt that Soviet Jews as a group are severely disadvantaged, but there is virtually no way in which as a government we can exert pressure on the Soviet Union to ease their plight."[75] The stated U.S. view, which seems disingenuous, was that private citizens could have more impact on Soviet policies than the American government could.[76] Although Soviet authorities had demonstrated some responsiveness to widespread political pressure, such as when they adjusted the Leningrad hijackers' sentence, the administration remained reluctant to make Soviet human rights violations an issue, given its desire to improve relations with the Soviets amid broader Cold War considerations. For much of its first term, the Nixon administration did not do much more than present lists of cases in which the United States was interested.[77]

Growing protests and congressional activism made U.S. officials eventually realize that they should engage with the issue for domestic political reasons. On December 30, 1970, Nixon met with American Jewish leaders in the Oval Office to discuss the plight of Soviet Jewry, the first time a president had ever done so (figure 1.2).[78] At the meeting, which was unlikely to imperil détente, Nixon made no promises. He would later tell Kissinger, "My attitude is I would like to help these people but we cannot jeopardize our

FIGURE 1.2. Richard Nixon and Henry Kissinger meet in the Oval Office with American Jewish leaders on June 5, 1974. Courtesy of the Richard Nixon Presidential Library and Museum, National Archives and Records Administration.

relationship for it." Kissinger responded, "It's not an issue in American foreign policy."[79]

Nixon was motivated to take the issue of Soviet Jewry more seriously only in the lead-up to the 1972 election. The Democratic nominee Senator George McGovern of South Dakota declared in August 1972 that Nixon had "never spoken out" on Soviet Jewry, and Nixon did not want his administration's lack of action to become an issue in the campaign.[80] To that end, in October 1972 Nixon met Soviet foreign minister Andrei Gromyko and outlined public opposition to the exit tax imposed by the Soviet government; later that month, after the two sides had signed a trade agreement, the Soviets started granting exceptions to the tax.[81] In a further effort to demonstrate that the United States was taking action regarding Soviet Jewry, State Department officials wrote, "We have made numerous private, high-level diplomatic approaches to Soviet authorities under-scoring our support for the principle of free emigration and the reuniting of families, and have made repeated representations in cases of Soviet citizens seeking to join relatives in the United States."[82] Evidence suggests that the administration made only an election-year tactical shift; Kissinger would say to Nixon in the subsequent year, "The emigration of Jews from the Soviet Union is not an objective of American foreign policy. Why, if they put Jews into gas chambers in the Soviet Union it is not an American concern."[83]

Soviet officials bristled at the discussions of human rights, which they resented as intervention in their internal affairs, but evidence exists that American entreaties could influence Soviet policy. As Gromyko writes, "Since we genuinely wanted to improve our relations with Washington, we made occasional concessions on individual cases of emigration."[84] This dynamic facilitated the emigration of Lithuanian sailor Simas Kurdika, who had previously attempted to defect. In this circumstance, Ford appealed to Dobrynin for Kurdika's release in a White House meeting less than a week after the new president had assumed office. The Soviets acted on his plea three months later.[85]

Ford was the last in a line of presidents who were disinclined to be aggressive with Soviet leaders regarding human rights.[86] In his memoir, Ford recounts that he favored quiet diplomacy:

I fully agreed that the Soviet anti-emigration policy was deplorable and contrary to my long-held belief that people should be free from oppression. Yet by pursuing quiet but firm diplomacy, Nixon and Kissinger had persuaded the Soviets to ease their restrictions. Jewish emigration from the USSR jumped from four hundred a year in 1968 to about 35,000 in 1973. When I became President, I sought to assure the Soviets that I was going to pursue the same kind of quiet diplomacy.[87]

A preference for quiet diplomacy over other forms of pressure can make sense if it is effective in securing U.S. objectives, and Kissinger's memoirs recount a story of rising emigration numbers through quiet diplomacy.[88] Activists and critics of the administration, however, were focused on the significant numbers of those still waiting for permission to leave and argued that a firmer approach could facilitate even more emigration.

Kissinger, like Ford, argued against direct confrontation with the Soviets over the issue. Speaking at the 1973 Pacem in Terris Conference, Kissinger intoned, "But in the nuclear age we are obliged to recognize that the issue of war and peace also involves human lives and that the attainment of peace is a profound moral concern." Suggesting that the United States should be cautious about pushing the Soviets too far on human rights, Kissinger asked:

How hard can we press without provoking the Soviet leadership into returning to practices in its foreign policy that increase international tensions? Are we ready to face the crises and increased defense budgets that a return to cold war conditions would spawn? And will this encourage full emigration or enhance the well-being or nourish the hope for liberty of the peoples of Eastern Europe and the Soviet Union?[89]

Kissinger sought to defend U.S. policy through, among other tactics, "administrative rhetoric," which is a way of answering protesters but also of "short-circuiting protesters' ideas and influence," by changing the "terms of the argument."[90] For Kissinger, in this context, human rights meant the rights of all people to live free from war and nuclear destruction, which was a reframing that essentially argued that the struggle against communism was a fight to protect human rights.[91]

U.S. diplomats serving in the embassy in Moscow were far more engaged with the issue of Soviet dissent than officials in Washington were by virtue of their responsibilities and location, which enabled them to make transnational connections. Peter Bridges, a political officer in Moscow during the early 1960s, remembers that when Solzhenitsyn published *One Day in the Life of Ivan Denisovich*, it was "a bomb going off in the Soviet intellectual world," a community to which embassy officials were closely attuned.[92] Thompson Buchanan, who served in Moscow during the early 1970s, reported that U.S. officials there had "access, of course, to many dissidents" and devoted considerable time to the problems of Soviet Jewry.[93] During the early years of the Nixon administration, the U.S. embassy had an officer visit a synagogue in Moscow every Friday evening when there were religious services in order to make connections with Soviet Jews.[94] In the mid-1970s the embassy had a staffer who was known, at least informally, as the "dissident officer."[95]

In a limited number of incidents, other executive branch officials intervened on human rights. For example, Treasury Secretary George P. Shultz traveled to Moscow in March 1973, and his agenda for the bilateral talks included Jewish emigration.[96] After meeting with him, Soviet officials lifted the onerous exit visa fee in the hope that it would facilitate congressional agreement to most-favored-nation trading status.[97] In addition, in April 1975 Treasury Secretary William Simon raised individual cases of concern at the Joint U.S.-USSR Commercial Commission and in a meeting with Brezhnev.[98]

THE JACKSON-VANIK AMENDMENT

The most significant American measure to address Soviet human rights violations was the Jackson-Vanik Amendment, which was an amendment to the 1974 trade bill that linked the United States' extension of most-favored-nation trading status to Soviet emigration practices.[99] When Jackson first introduced the amendment in 1972, the legislative session was so near its end that the amendment could not be passed. But the large number of Senate cosponsors he had—seventy-two—signaled the strength of congressional commitment.[100] Congressional support was widespread, because opposing the measure could have led to charges of appeasing the Soviets and would have angered American Jews.[101] As one senator said, "There is no political advantage in not signing. If you do sign, you don't offend anyone. If you don't sign, you might offend some Jews in your state."[102]

Critics of Henry Jackson and his tactics warned that his aggressive stance could worsen the situation for Soviet Jews. Nixon feared that in response to Jackson-Vanik, the Soviets would "slam the door down" on emigration.[103] Yet Soviet Jewish activists were aware of Jackson's efforts and largely supported them. For example, Vitaly Rubin and Anatoly Shcharansky wrote to Jackson: "We categorically deny any allegation which purports to say that your firmness concerning the Amendment affair could do us harm."[104] Similarly, although he did not seek to emigrate, Sakharov wrote an open letter to Congress protesting Soviet interference with the right to choose one's country of residence. His letter argued that there were tens of thousands of Soviet citizens who sought to emigrate, offered support for the Jackson-Vanik Amendment, and disputed those who claimed that passage of the amendment could worsen the situation of Soviet Jews:

Here you have total confusion, either deliberate or based on ignorance about the USSR. . . . As if the techniques of 'quiet diplomacy' could help anyone, beyond a few individuals in Moscow and some other cities.

The abandonment of a policy of principle would be a betrayal of the thousands of Jews and non-Jews who want to emigrate, of the hundreds in camps and mental hospitals, of the victims of the Berlin Wall.[105]

The Jackson-Vanik Amendment was opposed in the Kremlin and in the White House because it presented a considerable threat to détente and to executive branch control of foreign policy.[106] Jackson, his crusade, and his public comments all complicated relations with the Soviets, according to Kissinger.[107] Gromyko later characterized the Jackson-Vanik Amendment as "pathetic," arguing that it "slowed" rather than "smoothed" Soviet-American relations.[108] In an effort to curb some of its potential damage, Kissinger negotiated that if the Soviets met certain conditions that were agreed on in advance with Kissinger and Jackson, Ford would be able to waive the amendment. Thus Kissinger conferred simultaneously with Jackson and Dobrynin regarding broad principles that would govern emigration, such as promising not to harass those seeking to emigrate and establishing the minimum number that would be allowed to emigrate each year, with Jackson asking for one hundred thousand and the Soviets more comfortable with forty-five thousand.[109] Kissinger sought to resolve the impasse with an exchange of letters, but in his view, Jackson's language "not only went far beyond what I could in conscience assert the Soviets had promised, but what any sovereign state would tolerate another government say about its internal order."[110] By October it seemed that Kissinger had been able to broker a deal with Jackson, which included broad principles for Soviet action toward potential emigrants and a target number for visas set at sixty thousand.[111]After meeting with Ford and Kissinger, Jackson publicized the results of their negotiations in a White House press conference. According to Paula Stern, "Jackson, the presidential candidate, was more interested in declaring victory for the benefit of his domestic audience and less concerned about the negative consequences that such publicity might have on the arrangement with the Soviet Union."[112] Jackson's grandstanding angered the Soviets, who had not expected that the terms of their letters with the secretary of state would be trumpeted as a triumph for Jackson and his supporters.

Only a week later Gromyko wrote to Kissinger, arguing that the publicizing of correspondence between Jackson and the secretary of state had offered "a distorted presentation of our position and of what was said by us to the American side of this question."[113] Gromyko was frustrated that Kissinger's exchange with Jackson did not sufficiently highlight the fact that the Soviet Union would follow its own laws in determining emigration cases, and he disavowed any agreements that had been made relating to the Jackson-Vanik Amendment. According to Kissinger, "The Jackson-Vanik Amendment had performed a useful purpose when first put forward, eliciting from Moscow a more precise definition of emigration procedures than had existed previously. But once Congress went beyond those useful achievements to translating informal Soviet assurances into permanent legislation and an annual review, a blowup was foreordained."[114]

In the aftermath of the breakdown in Soviet-American negotiations and the passage of the Jackson-Vanik Amendment, the Soviets canceled their 1972 trade agreement with the United States and ceased making Lend-Lease payments. Emigration also dropped significantly in the years that followed. Whereas twenty-one thousand Soviet Jews had emigrated in 1974, in 1975 the number decreased to thirteen thousand and rose only to fourteen thousand in 1976.[115] The cause of the drop in exit visas is disputed by scholars, with some noting that emigration numbers fluctuated throughout those years and others attributing the declining numbers to the broader decline of détente. In the face of falling emigration numbers, Jackson faced pressure regarding the efficacy of his amendment, with some journalists suggesting that the legislation could be seen as a failure.[116]

Jackson's commitment to human rights has at times been disparaged as politically motivated, with critics arguing that it was formulated with an eye on the 1976 election.[117] Such rhetoric was common among Kissinger and his aides, who saw activism by members of Congress such as Jackson and Fraser as intended to score political points.[118] In Stern's view, however, Jackson was motivated by concerns about Soviet Jewry and by his opposition to détente and increased Soviet-American trade.[119] Yet others see his involvement as rooted in a deeper commitment; political scientist Robert G. Kaufman argues that his dedication to Jewish emigration was driven by "bedrock conviction" and that his efforts did not ebb and flow with the presidential election cycles (figure 1.3).[120]

Jackson's emphasis on human rights can be attributed to many factors beyond simply politics. First, Jackson highlighted his mother's defense of Jews who faced prejudice in their Washington community, saying, "She taught me to respect the Jews, help the Jews! It was a lesson I never forgot."[121] Second, Jackson, like other Americans who became active on human rights, was influenced by his experiences traveling abroad, including a visit to the Buchenwald concentration camp soon after it was liberated and a 1956 visit to the Soviet Union, which historian Jeff Bloodworth argues "reinforced what he had already come to believe—the USSR was a totalitarian society that routinely trampled on human rights to achieve its revolutionary goals."[122] In addition, his former aide Charles Horner argues that Jackson's human rights activism was tied to his brief early career as a prosecutor as well as to his reading of Robert Conquest's account of Stalin's purges in *The Great Terror*, which shaped his view of Soviet human rights abuses.[123] According to Kaufman, Jackson also believed that improving respect for human rights abuses would reduce the risk of international conflict.[124] Finally, Jackson told Israeli ambassador to the United States Yitzhak Rabin that his Norwegian roots made him sensitive to Israeli security concerns and that his own father's emigration from Norway had influenced his commitment to unfettered emigration.[125] Whether all these varied reasons meaningfully shaped Jackson's thinking, the result is that Jackson saw the repression of Soviet Jewry as not just a Jewish issue "but an American issue and a great humanitarian issue."[126] In addition, Jackson disagreed in principle with the administration's emphasis on trade in favor of human rights; he said, "Today, while we're bargaining with the Russians

FIGURE 1.3. Senator Henry F. Jackson championed the cause of emigration for Soviet Jews. Courtesy of the University of Washington Libraries, Special Collections, HMJ0823.

over dollars and rubles, let's do some bargaining on behalf of helpless human beings. When we talk about free trade let's talk about free people, too."[127]

THE 1976 PRESIDENTIAL ELECTION

In connection with Soviet and other human rights abuses, the 1976 presidential campaign led the Ford administration to alter its approach, which demonstrates that concern for human rights could be politically beneficial.

As Hugh Arnold has shown, 1976 was a turning point in Kissinger's discussion of human rights; twice as many mentions of human rights appeared in his speeches that year than in all earlier years combined.[128] In addition to increasing usage of the term, Kissinger sought to highlight the administration's actions in support of human rights. For example, speaking to an audience in Oregon, Kissinger claimed, "We have repeatedly and successfully submitted lists of people in prison to the Soviet Union, and we have achieved the release of a large percentage of those lists that we have submitted."[129]

Strikingly, at an April 1976 meeting between Ford and ethnic leaders in Milwaukee, the president told those gathered that he would raise the names of prisoners of concern with Soviet authorities. Ford's statement spurred considerable discussion within the administration; Myron Kuropas, Ford's special assistant for ethnic affairs, urged more presidential involvement, whereas National Security Council (NSC) staff members such as A. Denis Clift and Brent Scowcroft raised concerns about the negative impact that such intervention might have on Soviet-American relations.[130] In the end, a U.S. diplomat in Moscow brought Americans' concern regarding five Soviet political prisoners to the attention of a Soviet official at the Ministry of Foreign Affairs.[131] The impetus for Ford's action likely derived from two factors. First, Ford was in a tight race for the Republican nomination with former California governor Ronald Reagan, and Ford's toughness with the Soviets and his support for human rights were both at issue in the campaign.[132] Second, the value of détente was declining in the White House's view as relations were becoming more complicated and given the policy's political liability.

Although the administration's fierce resistance to discussions of Soviet human rights violations dissipated, there was not a wholesale transformation of U.S. policy. In the White House, Kuropas sought more NSC activity on Moroz's case in late June 1976, in part due to congressional activism that included efforts to grant Moroz honorary citizenship and the introduction of a "Free Moroz Resolution."[133] Kuropas and Scowcroft, however, fundamentally disagreed about the efficacy of U.S. intervention on Moroz's case, with Scowcroft arguing that "high level interventions on behalf of Moroz likely would not be fruitful and, in fact, could be counterproductive and harmful to his interests."[134] The divide between Scowcroft and Kuropas reflected the growing divergence between official policy and popular sentiment regarding human rights, which contributed to declining support for détente and to Gerald Ford's defeat in the 1976 election.[135]

Yet incremental support for human rights did not seem to be imperiling détente any more than other issues were. As a November 1976 memo for Vice President Nelson Rockefeller suggested,

The Soviets are still deeply committed to détente for considerations which have not significantly changed—the need for foreign credits, technology and food imports; the threat from China; the desire to loosen Western alliance ties and promote leftist gains in Europe; the wish to avoid Soviet-Western confrontations; and their firm belief that détente serves their own foreign policy and ideological ends.[136]

Such analysis suggests that there likely was more room for pressure on human rights and humanitarian issues had it been desired by the Ford administration or its predecessors.

With only episodic attention from the administration to human rights in the Soviet bloc, congressional pressure remained. Notably, it led to the establishment of the Commission on Security and Cooperation in Europe to monitor compliance with the 1975 Helsinki Final Act, which was a broad East-West agreement containing commitments to respect human rights and to facilitate human contacts. Although the United States did little to ensure the agreement's implementation at first, the commission, transnational activism, and the Carter administration would ultimately transform U.S. attention to and engagement with human rights violations in the Soviet bloc.[137] These efforts built on increasing American activism on behalf of Soviet human rights throughout the previous decade.

During the long 1960s, Americans became increasingly opposed to Soviet human rights abuses and sought multiple allies to address their concerns. Their activism, which was motivated largely by transnational connections and religious identity, took a range of forms but achieved only limited successes in the short term. In the years that followed, however, transnational activism spurred by the Helsinki Final Act would have far more significant successes.

In Gal Beckerman's view, the campaign for Soviet Jewry is what made human rights a part of U.S. foreign policy: "Human rights have since become a pivotal guide of our relations with other countries, from China to Zimbabwe. But this was not the case before the movement to save

Soviet Jewry."[138] Indeed, the plight of Soviet Jews, like that of Soviet dissidents, focused Americans' attention on the Soviet record and complicated presidential efforts to improve relations with Moscow despite Soviet abuses. Yet, as the subsequent chapters will show, human rights violations in many other countries during the long 1960s galvanized Americans and influenced U.S. foreign policy.

Chapter Two

A DOUBLE STANDARD ABROAD
AND AT HOME?

Rhodesia's Unilateral Declaration of Independence

Southern Rhodesia's unilateral declaration of independence from Great Britain in 1965, which was intended to ensure the continuation of white minority rule, elicited a global response that fit into a broader pattern of concern about racial discrimination both at home and abroad during Lyndon Johnson's presidency and in the years that followed.[1] Racial discrimination in Southern Rhodesia was a violation of the human rights of black Africans living in that territory; specifically, Article 2 of the Universal Declaration of Human Rights states, "Everyone is entitled to all the rights and freedoms set forth in this Declaration, without distinction of any kind, such as race, colour, sex, language, religion, political or other opinion, national or social origin, property, birth or other status."[2]

American activists at the time framed their domestic struggle against racial discrimination in human rights terms. For example, Martin Luther King Jr. characterized Johnson's March 15, 1965, call for voting rights legislation as "one of the most passionate pleas for human rights ever made by a President," and he increasingly used the term "human rights" in 1965 and 1966.[3] Similarly, King's aide Harry G. Boyte said, "The Civil Rights movement is becoming a Human Rights movement in this country."[4] They likewise saw the unilateral declaration of independence by the white Southern Rhodesian leader Ian Smith through the lenses of the American civil rights or black freedom movement and of legislative efforts such as the 1965

Voting Rights Act to address African Americans' status as second-class citizens.[5]

These activists—veterans of the black freedom movement as well as others concerned about the United States' racial record—were committed to the universality of human rights: U.S. citizens, as much as people living elsewhere, had the right to be free of discrimination based on race. In contrast to the administrative inaction regarding Soviet human rights violations, the Johnson administration implemented a range of measures intended to signal its opposition to Smith's white, discriminatory regime and its support for majority rule. When sanctions were not immediately effective, activists within the United States and Africa sought more-assertive measures. Furthermore, they opposed efforts such as the Byrd Amendment, which enabled American purchase of Rhodesian chrome and weakened U.S. compliance with UN sanctions. The increasing distance between activists and the White House, particularly during the Nixon and Ford administrations, precipitated a struggle about how aggressive the United States should be in the face of Smith's intransigence.

HUMAN RIGHTS VIOLATED

At stake in Rhodesia were the deprivation of black Rhodesians' rights, the imposition of a racially discriminatory government, and the use of a harsh justice system for dissenters or opponents of Smith's leadership. Robert Lagamma, who served in the U.S. consulate in Salisbury in 1963, reported that for black Africans, white rule "was a daily humiliation."[6] In the State Department's estimate, the Smith regime "systematically denied effective political rights to the nearly 5.3 million Africans who comprise 95 percent of Southern Rhodesia's population."[7] In the wake of Smith's unilateral declaration of independence, observers were concerned about censorship, restrictions on individual liberties, detention camps, beatings, and employment regulations.[8] As of the fall of 1966, Amnesty International reported, "The problem with Rhodesia is that people are being 'restricted' (sent to concentration camps) in such volume, and in such an arbitrary and capricious manner, that the Smith de facto regime probably could not provide meaningful background information on the POC's [prisoners of conscience] in Rhodesia if it wanted to."[9] In describing conditions in Rhodesia, American lawyer E. Clinton Bamberger, who had observed a trial for the Lawyers'

Committee for Civil Rights Under Law, wrote, "The Government's attempt to conduct a facade of judicial review must be seen as just that, a facade—a shameful degradation of judicial office and function." Beyond the problems in the judicial hearing that he observed, Bamberger also wrote about Rhodesia's "protected villages," which he, like Amnesty International, likened to concentration camps.[10] As of December 1974 Amnesty International estimated that there were more than three hundred political prisoners in Rhodesia, and by November 1975 it put the number at more than six hundred.[11] Furthermore, in the armed conflict that followed the unilateral declaration of independence, between twenty thousand and thirty thousand people died.[12]

Earlier accounts have largely framed U.S. policy toward Southern Rhodesia in terms of the Cold War, allied unity, and domestic political developments.[13] I argue, however, that the crisis in Rhodesia was conceived of in human rights terms by black Africans, nonstate actors seeking to influence U.S. policy, and American policymakers.[14] Furthermore, even when American leaders viewed Rhodesia though other lenses, they remained careful to couch their policies in human rights language, suggesting that the term "human rights" had achieved salience with this case.

REACTION TO SMITH'S UNILATERAL DECLARATION OF INDEPENDENCE

The United States signaled its nonrecognition of Smith's unilateral declaration of independence in many ways, including at the UN. There, U.S. representatives repeatedly emphasized American support for self-determination in Rhodesia, but in what would become a continuing source of tension, African leaders wanted a stronger British and Western response.[15] For example, the government of Ghana declared that members of the Security Council should use their military force to "destroy" the Rhodesian army and air force.[16]

UN activism on Southern Rhodesia fit into a general increasing of concern about human rights at the UN during the late 1960s.[17] Certainly, the UN General Assembly (UNGA) was transformed by an influx of new members from Africa and Asia in the early 1960s, and this change in demographics inspired increased pressure for self-determination and against racial discrimination. As a demonstration of concern at the UN, in 1965 the

General Assembly adopted the International Convention on the Elimination of All Forms of Racial Discrimination.[18]

The UN Security Council repeatedly acted in response to the situation in Rhodesia. In November 1965 it passed Resolution 217, which repudiated the unilateral declaration of independence and charged Great Britain with resolving the crisis. Five months later the Security Council voted that UN states should "do their utmost to break off economic relations with Southern Rhodesia." Furthermore, the Security Council authorized Great Britain to prevent the delivery of oil to Rhodesia "by the use of force if necessary."[19] On December 16, 1966, it characterized the Rhodesian declaration of independence as a "threat to international peace and security" and passed sanctions preventing member states from importing Rhodesian products.[20]

Besides official condemnation at the UN, many American voices outside policymaking circles spoke out against Smith's action. Initially American newspapers were strongly opposed to Smith's declaration.[21] For example, the *Washington Post* opined that it was "built upon a false basis, upon a denial of human rights that affronts much of the world."[22] A. Philip Randolph and Donald S. Harrington, the cochairs of the American Committee on Africa (ACOA), encouraged Secretary of State Dean Rusk to recall American officials from Southern Rhodesia and to sever trade relations with the regime.[23] A wide range of U.S.-based groups supported sanctions against Rhodesia, including religious, labor, legal, student, advocacy, and regional organizations.[24] These efforts were part of a broader transnational network, including the UK-based Campaign for the Relief of Rhodesian Political Prisoners and the Canadian Committee for Zimbabwe.

African Americans drew connections between freedom movements in the United States and Africa, and civil rights leaders repeatedly weighed in on American policy.[25] For example, in the wake of Smith's declaration, Martin Luther King Jr. spoke from Paris, declaring, "I think that it is very urgent for the world, for all of the nations of the world to take a stand against this attempt on the part of the Government of Rhodesia to turn the clock of history back. Rhodesia, Southern Rhodesia will become another South Africa and the world cannot stand another South Africa."[26] Similarly, Representative Adam Clayton Powell (D-NY), one of the most prominent African American elected officials at the time, wrote to Johnson and called for a "world economic boycott of Rhodesia and severance of all diplomatic relations." Urging the United States to take a position of leadership on the issue, Powell asserted, "Colored peoples of the world look to our great democracy to bring about the moral imperatives of freedom and equality throughout Africa."[27] Roy Wilkins wrote to the White House several months later, drawing links between the administration's domestic and foreign policies: "We in the NAACP believe it is essential that the United States ally itself with the cause of racial equality in Africa, as it is doing at home, rather than with an isolated and embattled minority."[28]

This activism fits with historian James Meriwether's analysis of the transnational connections that African American leaders felt to black Africans struggling for greater rights:

African Americans had turned to contemporary Africa and included it in their lives for a number of positive reasons: for the inspiration it provided for the struggle in America; for a sense of solidarity, be it from a common sense of oppression or from a shared heritage; for the price and confidence that came from seeing black men and women win their freedom and run their own countries.[29]

Johnson administration officials were cognizant of African American interest in Rhodesia, and one warned that "a 'Zionist' type of emotional concern, affecting local voting, could emerge."[30]

In terms of NGOs' reactions, ACOA was the leading American voice on African affairs. Utilizing Cold War rhetoric, it framed Rhodesia and South Africa as "Captive Nations."[31] The Washington office of ACOA focused on interacting with Congress by serving as a floating aide to a number of members, providing briefings in advance of travel to Africa, and supplying materials for insertion into the *Congressional Record*. In addition, its staff disseminated *Washington Notes on Africa* to nearly a thousand addressees.[32]

Beyond ACOA, Amnesty International USA was active on Southern Rhodesia; by the mid-1970s it had adopted several hundred Rhodesians as prisoners of conscience.[33] ACOA also facilitated the establishment of the American Negro Leadership Conference on Africa (ANLCA) to bring together civil rights leaders on behalf of African causes, including Southern Rhodesia.[34] ANLCA passed resolutions in 1964 calling on the U.S. government to undertake steps to signal its resistance to a possible declaration of independence, but ANLCA ultimately had little influence on U.S.

policy.[35] Echoing dynamics that were at play as U.S.-based human rights activism in general transformed, Anthony Lake explained that ANLCA's narrow influence was due to its focus, "at least until the late 1960s, on New York and the United Nations rather than on Washington and the American government."[36] ANLCA was also limited by its lack of allies within the U.S. government due to what historian Carl Watts terms "institutional racism within the power structure."[37]

Finally, ACOA worked to ensure U.S. compliance with UN sanctions against Rhodesia.[38] When ACOA had advance notice that ships carrying Rhodesian cargo were arriving, the group notified the UN, encouraged protests, and reached out to longshoremen's unions to prevent offloading.[39] In a connected effort, the New York Coalition to Stop Rhodesian Imports held a protest in New York City in June 1974 with the aim of inspiring longshoremen to refuse to offload nickel from a Rhodesian cargo ship.[40] In Baltimore, Militant Action Dockers engaged in protests, and longshoremen boycotted ships carrying Rhodesian nickel cathodes.[41] News that an Argentine ship might arrive with Rhodesian chrome set off protests in Louisiana as well.[42] The Coalition to Stop Rhodesian Imports even organized a rally at the U.S. Capitol in July 1974 to pressure Congress to overturn the Byrd Amendment, which allowed the use of Rhodesian chrome.[43]

Despite the range of external pressures on the U.S. government, there were divisions within it about the importance of opposing Smith.[44] Some, such as Under Secretary of State George Ball, argued that the United States had little interest in Rhodesia and should leave the problem to Great Britain.[45] The main potential cost of sanctions would be lost access to Rhodesian chrome, of which the United States bought three hundred thousand tons in 1965, comprising about 20 percent of the country's total chrome imports.[46] Others in the administration argued that U.S. interests did not necessitate opposing Smith and that such a move would risk increasing the spread of communism in Africa.

U.S. diplomats on the ground at the U.S. consulate in Salisbury had a different perspective. According to labor attaché Herman Cohen, when Smith declared independence, "the State Department went ape over that." The problem, in Cohen's view, was that "this was moving backwards, a blow to democracy and all that. We refused to recognize them, and to show our displeasure, we were going to reduce the size of the mission of the consulate general."[47]

Similarly, the State Department's African bureau supported an aggressive response to Smith's declaration. Assistant Secretary of State for African Affairs G. Mennen Williams' connection with the civil rights movement likely shaped his position; according to historian Ryan Irwin, Williams "conflated the line between the national and the global, and argued that reform at home mandated change abroad, most obviously in the form of UN sanctions against white regimes in South Africa."[48]

After Smith declared independence, the United States withheld recognition of his government, recalled the American consul, shelved its United States Information Agency activity, froze loans and credits, opposed American travel to Rhodesia, and demanded that those who did travel there have British visas.[49] In addition, the United States put in place an embargo against shipments of military equipment and arms, encouraged American businesses to cease dealings with Rhodesia, and suspended sugar imports from the territory. Furthermore, the United States and Great Britain supported ending the shipment of oil and petroleum products to Rhodesia.[50] The administration's response provoked opposition from both the right and the left, including proponents of human rights who wanted the White House to act more forcefully against the white minority regime.[51] Activists particularly concerned with racial discrimination urged a hard-line approach to Smith and other white minority governments in Southern Africa.

After the initial few months, the Johnson administration became increasingly focused elsewhere and paid little attention to Rhodesia until the execution of five political prisoners in March 1968 led the UN Security Council to target Smith's government with comprehensive sanctions.[52] Clearly under pressure to defend U.S. actions, U.S. ambassador to the UN Arthur J. Goldberg declared that the United States had "joined in every resolution the Security Council has adopted on Rhodesia."[53] In a sign of the Cold War's implications for U.S. policy, the United States and the Soviet Union sparred over the United States' relationship with Southern Rhodesia in dueling speeches at the UNGA in October 1968, with the Soviets charging that the United States was violating UN sanctions and profiting from doing so. Not surprisingly, the American representative refuted the Soviet charges.[54]

African nations demanded a stricter approach to Smith's regime, urging the use of force and cutting off all communications, but they could not gain sufficient support for their agenda.[55] In an interesting contradiction with its avowed anticolonialist stance, the UNGA found itself calling for the United Kingdom, the incumbent colonial power, "to suppress the racist and illegal minority regime in Southern Rhodesia."[56] The Johnson administration was not responsive to calls for more-aggressive action and, in a message to Congress, outlined the United States' efforts to be "moderate but responsible" and to pursue the problem of apartheid in a "rational and effective way." The president emphasized, "In the modern world peace is threatened not only by the illegal use of force but also by violations of human rights which offend the conscience of man."[57] The United States regarded the comprehensive sanctions as "livable from our point of view," and as successfully avoiding "more drastic action previously demanded by the Africans."[58]

Arguments against the American position from the right linked Smith's declaration of independence to the United States' own in 1776 and claimed that due to the Cold War, the United States should support Smith and his government because they were Christian, white, and anticommunist.[59] Critics of Johnson's stance reasoned further that American support for the British position was unnecessary, given what they perceived to be that government's lackluster assistance to the United States in Vietnam.[60] Opponents also argued that the United States was not bound to act just because it disagreed with the racism of Smith's government. Former secretary of state Dean Acheson and his former aide Charles Burton Marshall were among the administration's principal opponents on the Rhodesian issue, with Acheson arguing against UN sanctions on legal grounds.[61]

American interest in disavowing Smith's regime, despite opposition, was driven by several factors. First, U.S. leaders felt a connection to the Rhodesian situation, given the country's own struggle to improve the conditions of African Americans, and American leaders hoped they could build upon the goodwill that Johnson's civil rights policy had engendered in African leaders. Second, the United States was committed to self-determination and anticolonialism. According to several observers, in the face of external pressure, the Johnson administration made a political calculation that it could curry favor by opposing Smith without being forced to follow suit against South Africa, which would have had far greater costs.[62] U.S. efforts to win adherents in Africa created a record of opposition to racial discrimination and enabled it to claim support for self-determination and human rights in Africa.[63] Third, the United States was genuinely concerned about respect for human rights. Fourth, given the significance attributed to black African leaders' views of the United States, some saw a cost in black African and African American support of the Johnson administration if it did not act against Smith.[64] Fifth, Cold War considerations could be ignored in formulating U.S. policy toward Southern Rhodesia because "there was no significant communist activity" there.[65] Sixth, Johnson's fight against social justice and racial equality through the War on Poverty shaped his approach to Southern Rhodesia.[66] And finally, the United States had limited material interests in the territory.[67]

Given these considerations, members of Johnson's National Security Council urged him to support the British response to Smith in order to "stay on the right side of all the Afro-Asians."[68] Deputy national security adviser Robert Komer further emphasized this point in a memorandum, writing, "Rhodesia itself isn't very important to us. But the point is that it's critical to all the other Africans. They see it as a straight anti-colonial issue, and all their anti-white instincts are aroused. So our stance on this issue will greatly affect our influence throughout Africa—it will be a test of whether we mean what we say about self-determination and racialism."[69] Komer argued to Johnson, "Vietnam, South Asia, or Berlin are far away, but these African issues are seen by Africans as an intimate part of their own struggle for independence of colonialism."[70] American officials were highly cognizant of the potential positive public relations aspects of their policy: "The U.S. public position on [Rhodesia] is one about which we can crow as we are standing on such honored principles as racial equality, human rights and government by the consent of the governed."[71] In a National Security Council meeting, Arthur Goldberg explained the American position on a recent UN vote that would limit the importation of minerals and goods and curtail most sales of arms, munitions, and materials to be used by the military in Southern Rhodesia: "We were obliged to vote in the UN as we did because to do otherwise would have caused us domestic racial difficulties and hurt our business interests in every African country."[72] Yet American opposition to Smith did not precipitate stronger pressure against his regime, as the interest in what Komer termed the "Rhodesian mess" was limited.[73]

FIGURE 2.1. Ambassador Arthur J. Goldberg confers with Lyndon B. Johnson aboard Air Force One. Courtesy of the Lyndon Baines Johnson Presidential Library, photo by Yoichi Okamoto.

Goldberg would have liked an even firmer approach, not only against Rhodesia, but also with respect to South Africa.[74] He spoke out repeatedly against the system of racial discrimination in Rhodesia, and his speeches demonstrate a full commitment to racial equality among other human rights issues.[75] Interestingly, according to former U.S. diplomat Seymour Maxwell Finger, Goldberg believed in sanctions as an effective means to shift the Rhodesian government based on the successful use of boycotts in the South by the civil rights movement.[76] His strong opposition to Smith's regime was consistent with his commitment to civil rights and his position at the UN, and he advocated a harder stance by the United States.[77] Speaking about Rhodesia, Goldberg said, "Experience demonstrates that in Africa today peace and stability are inseparable from orderly progress toward self-determination and equality for all the people of that continent."[78] He explained that U.S. policy was intended "to open the full power and responsibility of nationhood to all the people of Rhodesia—not just six percent of them."[79] He also linked the U.S. position on Rhodesia to historic anticolonialism, to the UN Charter's language in support of "human rights and fundamental freedoms without distinction as to race," and to the civil rights movement in the United States.[80]

Like Goldberg, Donald Fraser wanted the United States to implement more aggressive sanctions against Rhodesia: "We should not wait until we are pushed by the African and Asian nations and then try to achieve the weakest possible compromise."[81] Fraser declared, "We shun minority rule at home, and we cannot stand for this position abroad."[82] The evidence demonstrates that Goldberg and others concerned with Rhodesia conceived of the crisis in human rights terms; Fraser and Goldberg were among the many Americans arguing that connections between the movements for black freedom in the United States and elsewhere necessitated a firmer anti-Smith stance.

Those committed to opposing racial discrimination in Rhodesia, from the Oval Office down, often framed U.S. actions in the context of U.S. support for domestic civil rights. On May 26, 1966, Johnson said, "We will not support policies abroad which are based on the rule of minorities or the discredited notion that men are unequal before the law. . . . We will not live by a double standard, professing abroad what we do not practice at home or venerating at home what we ignore abroad."[83] In 1965 Rusk, too, declared that "how we handled civil rights in the United States" was highly relevant to the United States' relationships with foreign countries.[84] Given the White House's support for domestic civil rights, officials such as Goldberg argued that the United States needed to oppose racial discrimination abroad as well. Goldberg made the link between the domestic civil rights movement and opposition to Smith's regime explicit in a letter to Benjamin Bradlee of the *Washington Post*: "Frankly I don't see how we can have a double standard with respect to civil rights—one at home and another abroad."[85] Goldberg argued that the "movement toward self-determination and equality" taking place in southern Africa was "every bit as important to the cause of human rights as the making of international agreements and conventions."[86] In Goldberg's view, American opposition to Smith's regime was necessary in order for U.S. policy to remain consistent with the country's values:

First, the basic issue in Rhodesia is self-government for all the people, regardless of race. Our country, founded on the proposition that all men are created equal—and currently engaged in a vigorous nationwide program to make that equality real for our own Negro citizens—cannot honorably turn its back on what is happening in Rhodesia.[87]

Goldberg was not the only official to emphasize this theme; NSC staffers Charles E. Johnson and Ulric Haynes wrote to the president, "Your accomplishments in race relations and civil rights here at home make it essential that our position on similar issues abroad be consistent with domestic policy. Failure to do so if this issue becomes widely publicized would alienate some members of Congress, American Negroes, civil rights groups, labor, church groups and liberals in general."[88] Those pressing for greater consistency were cognizant of the potential domestic benefits but seemed genuinely committed to racial equality in principle, suggesting that U.S. policy was not motivated by political gain alone. Examining U.S. policy toward Southern Rhodesia during the Johnson years demonstrates that the human rights at stake were a factor in shaping that policy.

THE UNITED STATES' POSITION WEAKENS

After a year in office, the Nixon administration undertook a significant shift in policy toward southern Africa to emphasize more "communication" with the white regimes of Southern Rhodesia and South Africa.[89] Echoing divisions within the administration that had existed during the Johnson years, Africanists in the State Department, not surprisingly, opposed such a change. Members of the NSC staff and the Department of Defense, however, favored a new approach, believing that the United States could exert more influence through closer relations and that American businesses should not suffer for an ineffective policy.[90] The Nixon administration decided to change course, easing restrictions on Rhodesia, reducing its profile at the UN, improving relations with South Africa, and limiting criticism of Portugal. This led, in effect, to "balancing our relations in the area by compensating for—rather than abandoning—our tangible interests in the white states."[91] Both Gerald Horne and Thomas Borstelmann make a link between Nixon's Southern Strategy—his effort to appeal to southern white Democrats in the United States—and his move toward to white Rhodesians. As Horne writes, "In both cases, deflecting the aspirations of blacks was the priority."[92] In order to avoid a backlash against such a shift, Henry Kissinger proposed increasing aid to black African states by about $5 million and undertaking "other gestures to the black states."[93] In addition, although it was formulated through extensive NSC work, the new policy was not announced and was successfully kept quiet.[94]

The White House sought to limit any outcry over its change in position by downplaying or, arguably, mischaracterizing it. For example, in a letter to Representative Charles Diggs (D-MI), chair of the House Foreign Affairs Subcommittee on Africa and one of the critics of potential concern to the administration, Kissinger wrote, "There has not been, or is any consideration being given, to a relaxation of U.S. support for UN resolutions prohibiting Rhodesian imports. Neither has there been, nor is any consideration being given, to following a policy of expediency toward the arms embargo on South Africa."[95] Kissinger's letter to Diggs was at best disingenuous given the White House's maneuvers behind the scenes. Congressional pressure on Southern Rhodesia was minimal, which likely reflects support for Johnson's sanctions and deft maneuvering as the Nixon administration shifted its policy.

As the United States' position evolved, American officials repeatedly framed it in human rights terms. In a March 1970 policy statement on southern Africa, Secretary of State William Rogers used the phrase "fundamental human rights," signaling an awareness of the issues at stake.[96] Similarly, when discussing U.S. policy toward Africa that same year, Assistant Secretary of State for African Affairs David Newsom repeatedly spoke about U.S. objectives for the continent, and particularly southern Africa, in human rights terms: "Our actions and policies toward Rhodesia receive wide publicity and are looked upon as a concrete measure of America's commitment to self-determination, majority rule and human rights."[97]

At the same time that it was formulating a new approach to southern Africa, the United States came under increasing pressure to close the American consulate in Salisbury. The secretary of state, the UN secretary general U Thant, and the British government urged the White House to shutter the consulate in 1970.[98] In addition, thirty-two members of Congress wrote to Nixon, calling for its closure.[99] The Nixon administration had kept it open as long as politically possible, but three days later Nixon's closure of the consulate was formalized with National Security Decision Memorandum 47.[100]

In advance of the Nixon administration's shift on southern Africa, a key NSC official, Winston Lord, questioned such an approach. Writing to

FIGURE 2.2. Winston Lord confers with Henry Kissinger. Courtesy of the Gerald R. Ford Presidential Library.

Kissinger about a possible move away from white regimes in southern Africa, Lord asserted, "The Administration already is in trouble on its civil rights policy at home. To move closer, or to appear to move closer, to the racist regimes of southern Africa will reverberate domestically and reinforce doubts about the commitment to racial justice in our own society."[101] Furthermore, he argued that the United States faced "a younger generation which insists on matching rhetoric with action."[102] Lord emphasized that South Africa "represented a direct affront" to 10 percent of the U.S. population.[103] In his memorandum to Kissinger, under the subtitle "The Moral Imperatives," Lord urged that the United States disengage from minority governments in Africa and argued that the reasons to do so were "domestic and moral, not foreign."[104] Over the course of the Nixon and Ford administrations, other State Department officials would join Lord in an effort to push Kissinger, and therefore the United States, toward a more "moral" approach to U.S. foreign policy. Demonstrating again that his approach to Africa differed from that of the administration and Kissinger, Lord suggested "giving strong Administration support for repeal of the Byrd provision."[105]

THE BYRD AMENDMENT

The Byrd Amendment, Section 503 of the 1971 Defense Procurement Bill, which came into effect January 1, 1972, and prevented the United States from banning Rhodesian chrome, was particularly troubling for opponents of Smith's regime, as it meant that the United States would be out of compliance with UN sanctions.[106] The *New York Times* condemned the White House's silence regarding this amendment, which it charged was due to "a well-financed Rhodesian lobby which has exploited shrewdly the racism of Southern Senators and Congressmen" as well as congressional anticommunism and opposition to the UN.[107] The Byrd Amendment demonstrates the continuing adherence to a zero-sum-game view of the Cold War, even as tensions were ostensibly reducing due to détente. Interestingly, the Byrd Amendment is the only instance under review here in which Congress pressed for and passed legislation that undermined rather than enhanced U.S. policy regarding human rights.

In the years that followed, the administration walked a fine line between seeking to keep the principal Byrd Amendment supporters—U.S. businesspeople and conservative members of Congress—satisfied and minimizing the consequences of not complying with UN sanctions. In order to lessen domestic and UN criticism of the measure, U.S. ambassador to the UN George Bush urged the Nixon administration to state publicly that it supported overturning the Byrd Amendment. Given that the repeal was not expected to pass the House, NSC staffer Mel Levine argued that what Bush "really wants [is] the Administration's moral skirts kept clean, rather than the repeal itself."[108] Levine's language demonstrates that even in a White House that was proud of its realpolitik approach to international relations, policymakers recognized that the controversy was viewed externally in moral terms. In September 1973, as part of his confirmation hearings to become secretary of state, Kissinger said that the administration favored repealing the amendment.[109] Yet the White House did not lobby to make it happen, which suggests that there was not much depth to the administration's support.

The White House sought to minimize any blame for the Byrd Amendment by issuing statements asserting that "U.S. legislation should be in line with our international treaty obligations." In the view of Kissinger's aides, such a statement would "relieve us of responsibility for the Byrd

Amendment and its treaty violations, put the monkey squarely on the Senate's back where it belongs, and help defuse criticism in Africa and the UN."[110] Jerry Warren, a spokesperson for the White House, did deliver such a message, saying on May 19, 1972, "The White House feels it is appropriate for the Senate to seek conformity between our domestic laws and our international treaty obligations." But in an awkward exchange with reporters, Warren would not confirm that his statement meant that the White House wanted a repeal of the amendment.[111]

Administration records demonstrate how contentious the issue of Rhodesian chrome became, with NSC staffers J. F. Lehman and Harold Horan writing to Kissinger, saying, "On the Hill, the conservatives led by Harry Byrd consider this a very emotional issue. The liberals equally so." In their view, most galling of all to liberal members of Congress was that "we have had our cake and eaten it successfully." In this context, pressure increased for the White House to support more fully the repeal of the Byrd Amendment.[112]

For those who were committed to sanctions against Smith's regime, the Byrd Amendment remained an affront as long as it was U.S. law. There were multiple efforts to overturn it, all of which failed in the years before Carter's election. Members of Congress such as Senator Gale William McGee (D-WY), who sought to repeal the amendment in 1971 and 1972, viewed the White House as continuously refusing to support their efforts: "After all the high sounding rhetoric, the White House alone must bear the burden and the responsibility for the failure of legislative efforts to turn this country around on the issue of sanctions against Rhodesia."[113]

Liberals such as Fraser were upset that the Byrd Amendment put the United States in the company of Portugal and South Africa, other states that were violating UN sanctions against Rhodesia.[114] He was one of thirty-eight members of the House who sought to repeal the Byrd Amendment in 1973.[115] In Fraser's view, the American companies pushing for chrome importation believed that "their corporate interests in making a profit are more important than international law, self-determination, and U.S. relations with almost all the nations in Africa."[116] When ACOA lobbied members of Congress to repeal the Byrd Amendment, the group utilized the administration's ostensible support for such an endeavor, asserting that a repeal would be "in accord with Henry Kissinger."[117] Speaking in favor of overturning the Byrd Amendment, Ted Kennedy argued that the United

States must "use all available legal avenues to serve this country's own concept of human and social justice."[118] The Washington Office on Africa also mobilized in an effort to revoke the Byrd Amendment; urging U.S. compliance with sanctions, it framed the case in terms of the United States' security, economic, and diplomatic interests.[119]

Efforts continued through the final months of Nixon's presidency and gained new adherents. Members of the administration began pressing more forcefully for the repeal of the amendment, with Assistant Secretary of State for African Affairs David Newsom asserting, "In my four years as Assistant Secretary, the exemption of Rhodesian sanctions has been the most serious blow to the credibility of our African policy."[120] Speaking in support of the amendment's repeal, Representative John Buchanan (R-AL) said, "We are the only nation [that], while trying to fulfill the role of an advocate for human rights, was first a party to the sanctions, then made their violation a matter of public law and official policy." Buchanan's statement demonstrates the extent to which those who were active on Rhodesia saw the United States' policy as contradicting its ostensible commitment to human rights. In his view, "Our national interest does not lie in the encouragement of repressive regimes of the left or the right but in the achievement of freedom and justice in the world."[121]

Gerald Ford's assumption of the presidency did not initially shift U.S. policy. Although House support for repealing the Byrd Amendment was growing on a relative scale, the votes were not yet sufficient to overturn the amendment. On September 25, 1975, the House refused to repeal the Byrd Amendment by a vote of 209–187, and Congress was not able to revoke the Byrd Amendment before the end of Ford's presidency, despite the support of the American Federation of Labor and Congress of Industrial Organizations (AFL-CIO), the United Steelworkers of America, the Washington Office on Africa, and other progressive and religious organizations.[122] Despite this failure, during the 1976 campaign Ford said, "We have to be on the right side morally, and the right side morally is to be for majority rule."[123]

Beginning in spring 1976, in a surprising turn of events given the administration's toleration of white minority regimes, Kissinger engaged in shuttle diplomacy with British, South African, Tanzanian, Zambian, and liberation movement leaders as well as, eventually, Ian Smith in an attempt to negotiate an end to the crisis in Rhodesia. Kissinger sought a political solution that would lead to majority rule as well as economic assistance to the country.[124] Kissinger framed his activism in human rights terms, saying in his April 27, 1976, Lusaka Declaration, "We support self-determination, majority rule, equal rights and human dignity for all the peoples of southern Africa—in the name of moral principle, international law and world peace."[125] He also called for "racial justice" for Zimbabwe, using the name preferred by the black majority rather than the one preferred by Smith's regime.[126] In September, after extensive negotiations with Kissinger, Smith finally agreed with the principle of majority rule, but negotiations broke down as Ford's presidency was coming to an end, with acrimony between American and British officials and between Kissinger and Zambian president Kenneth Kaunda.[127] The crisis was not effectively addressed in the short term; a power-sharing agreement between whites and blacks was not meaningfully implemented until 1980, but in getting Smith to agree to majority rule, Kissinger ensured that "there was no going back," as Andrew DeRoche has characterized it.[128]

In the wake of Smith's unilateral declaration of independence, each administration engaged with the issue to the degree that doing so aligned with its interests. For Johnson, supporting Britain's stance against Smith and participating in UN sanctions that targeted his government were low-cost ways to demonstrate his bona fides as an opponent of racial discrimination to black Africans and to civil rights supporters in the United States. The Nixon administration—which was less attentive to civil rights concerns, more focused on superpower détente, and more sympathetic to business interests—weakened the U.S. stance. Not until Kissinger feared that the growing instability in southern Africa could enable the expansion of communist influence in the region did Kissinger begin efforts to seek a diplomatic solution.

Throughout the crisis, many members of Congress, nongovernmental actors, and lower-level officials pressured the White House to take a strong stand against Smith's discriminatory and repressive regime. Through activism that was motivated by shared racial identity and a universal commitment to racial equality, activists firmly signaled that the rights of black Africans were a human rights concern. Their activism shaped U.S. policy and set the stage for movements against apartheid and racial discrimination elsewhere in the years that followed.

Chapter Three

CAUSING US "REAL TROUBLE"

The 1967 Coup in Greece

In the wake of the 1967 coup in Greece, prominent American academics were concerned about the fate of Greek political leader Andreas Papandreou, whom many knew personally. Their efforts to prevent Andreas's execution and to secure his release from prison evolved into broader advocacy aimed at the repressive regime. Despite nongovernmental activism, the Johnson administration and those that followed did not actively oppose the new military leaders, precipitating years of struggle among the White House, the State Department, congressional critics, and concerned citizens. At the center of the debate, which lasted until Greece returned to democracy in July 1974, were the United States' short- and long-term strategic interests as well as the potential costs of close association with the Greek regime. Responses to the coup in Greece—and to human rights violations in South Korea and Chile as discussed in the next two chapters—show that in the 1960s and early 1970s Americans became less willing to countenance U.S. government support for repressive regimes.

THE "RAPE OF GREEK DEMOCRACY"

The Greek coup d'etat prompted international outcry and engendered deep concern for the abrogation of human rights. On April 21, 1967, a group of colonels seized power amid fears that George Papandreou's Center Union

Party might come to power in the upcoming elections.[1] The party's opponents had effectively tarred it with the taint of communism and suggested that it could threaten Greece's role in the Atlantic alliance.[2] Among the first to be arrested were George Papandreou and his son, Andreas, who was a rising political leader. In the wake of the coup, the Greek junta dealt severely with its perceived opponents, arresting them, subjecting them to torture, and imprisoning them in island concentration camps.

Yet Greece's membership in the North Atlantic Treaty Organization (NATO) and Cold War security concerns meant that many governments were hesitant to criticize the leadership too harshly.[3] Greece's strategic location along the eastern flank of NATO territory—Greece shared its borders with two Warsaw Pact countries—precipitated American caution.[4] Although the Johnson administration condemned the nature of the Greek regime, repeatedly inquired with the junta about the fate of political prisoners, and implemented an embargo against heavy military exports to Greece, the United States did not actively undermine the new leaders. The Johnson administration became increasingly focused on access to Greek bases after the outbreak of war in the Middle East in 1967, which heightened the strategic significance of the Mediterranean. As a result, in the aftermath of the Six-Day War, the United States lessened its criticism of the military junta, and the Johnson administration opposed and defeated Senate efforts to end military assistance to Greece.[5] Moreover, the selective embargo implemented in May 1967 was later lifted during the Nixon administration due to concerns that stemming the flow of military aid to Greece could weaken the NATO alliance.

As with Southern Rhodesia and the Soviet Union, debates concerning the United States' policy toward Greece drew new adherents to the cause of human rights and galvanized many others.[6] Discussions about the situation in Greece previewed many of the trends that made human rights rise in prominence over the subsequent decade. First, the plight of an identifiable political prisoner with many transnational connections such as Andreas Papandreou served as a rallying point for disparate actors in the United States. Second, a loosely linked collection of academics, members of Congress, concerned citizens, international human rights groups, and ad hoc NGOs such as the U.S. Committee for Democracy in Greece succeeded in keeping policymakers' attention on human rights violations and limiting the Johnson administration's policy options. Third, although policymakers ultimately privileged their military alliance with Greece over concerns about the country's internal politics, if they signaled such a choice too openly, they risked angering influential members of Congress, which suggests that the issue was becoming increasingly salient in domestic politics. Finally, Greece's location in Europe and its history as the birthplace of democracy meant that human rights abuses there were harder to overlook than those in places that were more culturally or geographically distant. The United States ultimately prioritized its military alliance with Greece at a time of regional and global insecurity. Discussions regarding Greece's human rights record and U.S. policy formulation indicate that many actors were rethinking the advisability of supporting anticommunism without regard to the costs, both to foreigners and to the United States' international reputation.

Concerns about the administration's tepid position toward Greece were raised in the context of a transnational campaign against the politically repressive junta, and nonstate actors played a significant role in forcing the president and his aides to grapple with human rights concerns. Amnesty International, in particular, actively responded to reports of human rights violations in Greece, and its reporting maintained international attention on the junta's authoritarianism. The group sent a delegation to Greece in December 1967, which interviewed prisoners and took testimony from their family members.

James Becket, one of the two authors of Amnesty's first report, was drawn to the Greek case through a transnational connection. Traveling in Europe in 1958, he had met Maria Zafiro Hary, and the two later married. They settled in Geneva, where news of the 1967 Greek coup and subsequent repression spurred them into action.[7] Becket emphasizes that his personal background had primed him to become active on Greece. He highlights the McCarthy hearings as initially heightening his "sense of justice," as did extensive time spent in Chile during the 1950s and early 1960s.[8] In addition, he had attended Harvard Law School "at the time of the civil rights movement," which also shaped his "left-wing" political views.[9]

Together James and Maria reached out to Amnesty International and to "everyone who might be interested" in the wake of the coup. They met with Amnesty head Sean MacBride, and he proposed a mission to Greece. The Beckets' goal was to get greater attention for the repression in Greece; as James put it later, they were engaged in a "battle for public opinion in Europe and in America." Torture "became the key issue" because it "drew

FIGURE 3.1. James and Maria Becket arrive at the European Commission of Human Rights, 1968. Courtesy of James Becket.

attention."[10] Becket describes himself as having been motivated to defend human rights because he was "ashamed about American policy."[11]

In its January 1968 report, "Situation in Greece," Amnesty International outlined its argument, stating that "torture as a deliberate practice is carried out by the Security Police . . . and the Military Police," and the report detailed twelve different physical methods being used to torture political prisoners. Investigators found that the psychological torture employed by the regime was equally devastating to political prisoners and stated that the security police and military police operated without any restrictions on their behavior.[12] Embassy officials in Athens characterized the first report as "probably substantially true," but sought to emphasize that "such methods have long been used by Greek police against political and other prisoners."[13]

Amnesty's reporting inspired a range of governmental and nongovernmental actors to oppose ongoing U.S. support for the Greek regime. Many American critics viewed the U.S. government's attitude toward the Greek colonels in the context of their own opposition to the war in Vietnam and to intervention in the Dominican Republic.[14] Donald Fraser expressed concern about support for the regime, especially in terms of military assistance, information policy, and public and private investment in the country. He pushed the State Department to do more than have a "hands off, no comment, position regarding the denial of human rights in Greece today" and indicated that he was particularly troubled at reports that the Greek regime was torturing its political prisoners.[15] He also wrote to the secretary of state and the White House to express concern specifically for Andreas Papandreou, who had formerly been a professor at the University of Minnesota.[16] He later said that his position on U.S. policy toward Greece was shaped by the knowledge that U.S. tanks had been used "to suppress students who were protesting against the military junta's destruction of democracy in Greece."[17]

Fraser traveled to Greece in May 1968, and his visit solidified his disagreement with U.S. policy toward the junta.[18] While there, he sought to learn about political prisoners, the junta's administration of the country, and the relationship between the Greek and American militaries.[19] After his return Fraser gave a speech in the House of Representatives on the repressive nature of the regime: "Torture of political prisoners has occurred in some Greek prisons. . . . Arrests and imprisonment of persons who speak critically in public continue. Thousands of Greeks have been imprisoned." Fraser recommended taking steps to pressure the Greek junta, which included American condemnation of the regime and a significant reduction in military assistance to the government.[20]

Fraser had like-minded colleagues in Congress, such as Representative Benjamin Rosenthal (D-NY) and Representative Don Edwards (D-CA), who kept attention on the situation in Greece. Rosenthal chaired the House Foreign Affairs Subcommittee on Europe and held a series of hearings on the United States' policy toward Greece. Edwards was also a leader of anti-junta activism, working among members of Congress to pressure the State

Department and corresponding with interested observers outside the government. For example, when the House of Representatives voted overwhelmingly, 321–42, to extend the lease of two destroyers and a submarine to Greece, Edwards released a statement characterizing it as a "bad mistake" that "constitutes approval of military dictatorship in Greece."[21] In evocative language, members of Congress collectively wrote to the secretary of state to express concern about the "deprivation of liberty in Greece" and to ask that the United States "not close its eyes to the human indignities" occurring there; they sought to capitalize on the United States' "moral power," arguing, "The world has looked to America for sensitivity to the human condition and for moral leadership."[22]

Fraser and Edwards both took steps on their own and acted in concert with an NGO devoted to the issue, the U.S. Committee for Democracy in Greece, which was part of a broader network of groups and individuals in Australia, Canada, Denmark, Great Britain, France, the Federal Republic of Germany, Italy, Norway, Sweden, and Switzerland who were opposed to the Greek regime.[23] The committee, which was organized by many well-known Washington-based liberals, including Edwards, former attorney general Francis Biddle, labor organizer Victor Reuther, and Senator Claiborne Pell (D-RI), warned that the United States risked tarnishing its international image if it failed to separate itself from the leadership in Athens.[24] The U.S. Committee for Democracy in Greece published a bimonthly newsletter with a circulation of thirty-five thousand, one of several ways it sought to disseminate information on the regime's activities.[25] In one issue of the newsletter the Committee cautioned, "The presence of the Greek dictatorship is a constant threat to the unity of the Western world. . . . By continuing assistance to the present regime, the United States would risk seriously undermining the entire Western alliance."[26]

Other organizations expressed their concerns by disseminating advertisements, corresponding with members of Congress, donating to aid Greek prisoners, pressing for the release of political prisoners, and fundraising to support public awareness activities. The group Minnesotans for Democracy and Freedom in Greece was primarily focused on achieving its aims by pressuring the U.S. government.[27] To that end, it organized several hundred people to write to Fraser, conveying their concern about the situation in Greece.[28] The involvement by Minnesotans was likely spurred by Andreas Papandreou's deep connections to the state; he had taught at the University of Minnesota for nine years. But Americans organized against the junta in many other corners of the country as well. Some, such as the California Committee for Democracy in Greece, raised funds to aid Greek political prisoners and their families as well as to "fight for Freedom in Greece."[29] The American Committee for Democracy and Freedom in Greece wrote to Johnson, asking him to intercede on behalf of composer Mikis Theodorakis, and organized a silent "March in Mourning" to mark the "death of human rights and freedoms in Greece."[30] The Boston Ad Hoc Committee for Freedom in Greece, the International Longshoremen's and Warehousemen's Union, and Amnesty International USA undertook similar efforts to influence U.S. policy.[31] Evidence of the development of a broader network of activists can be seen in the Inter-American Federation for Democracy in Greece, which was an umbrella organization overseeing nineteen regional committees.[32]

THE IDENTIFIABLE POLITICAL PRISONER

Concerns about human rights violations in Greece drew wide attention as former colleagues, friends, and supporters of Andreas Papandreou mobilized on his behalf in the United States. After an academic career during which he taught at Harvard, the University of Minnesota, Northwestern University, and the University of California–Berkeley, Papandreou returned to Greece, where he became increasingly involved in politics.[33]

In the years leading up to the coup, Andreas's critics increasingly had painted him as a communist, which was a dangerous label in postwar Greece. Andreas was one of many Greek politicians arrested when the coup was launched, and the threat that the colonels perceived in him was clear in their trumped-up charges that he had participated in a military conspiracy.[34] His wife, Margaret, was instrumental in keeping international attention focused on her husband's plight, and she repeatedly appealed to the United States embassy in Athens for assistance. She wrote to economist and former U.S. ambassador to India John Kenneth Galbraith, Stephen Rousseas of New York University, and George Linias at Purdue University to enlist their support for her husband. Academics from Minnesota Leo Hurwicz and John Buttrick as well as many others campaigned on his behalf.[35] Overall, 250 economists were said to have written to the White House.[36] Indeed, Andreas's former colleagues were among those most

FIGURE 3.2. Andreas Papandreou at the University of Minnesota.
Courtesy of the University of Minnesota Archives, University of
Minnesota-Twin Cities.

attentive to Greek repression soon after the coup, and White House aides
were cognizant of the extent to which Andreas's incarceration focused
attention on the United States' policy toward Greece: "Our major problem
here in the White House is domestic concern for the safety of Andreas
Papandreou. . . . Andreas' friends—Walter Heller, Carl Kaysen and others—
have mounted a major telephone campaign, which some of us fear could
cause real trouble."[37]

Margaret's efforts bore fruit when Galbraith called Johnson aide Joseph
Califano at the White House to express the widespread concern for Papandreou in academic circles. Johnson reportedly said of the campaign, "This
is the first issue in history on which all the American economists seem to
have agreed."[38] According to Galbraith, Under Secretary of State Nicholas
Katzenbach later telephoned him to report a message from Johnson: "Call

up Ken Galbraith and tell him I've told those Greek bastards to lay off that son-of-a-bitch—whoever he is."[39] Economist Walter Heller, who was particularly active, wrote to Johnson: "The academic grapevine was crackling from coast to coast last night with the good news that you were taking a direct hand in the Papandreou case. . . . The word of your quick and direct interest is spreading fast and favorably."[40]

The State Department's assistant secretary for congressional relations offered assurances to Fraser and other members of Congress regarding the United States' efforts on Andreas's behalf: "Ambassador Talbot has made a series of strong representations in Athens on behalf of all the political detainees, including both Andreas and his father."[41] Andreas later wrote in his memoirs, "There was some fear in the United States, I learned, that I was to be taken before a kangaroo court and summarily executed, and my friends in that country had been pressuring President Lyndon Johnson to intervene on my behalf. It was to the concern of those friends, I concluded, that I owed the fact that I was still alive."[42] Margaret also believed that this pressure had been essential, and she wrote to Johnson, expressing her appreciation for his "swift humanitarian action" on behalf of her husband."[43] The actual influence of the United States, however, is less clear. Andreas, who was released after eight months, reports that Ambassador Philips Talbot told him after his release that the junta had never planned to kill him, but its true intentions are difficult to assess.[44] Andreas later served as prime minister of Greece from 1981 to 1989 and again from 1993 to 1996.

The campaign by Andreas's supporters to pressure the Johnson administration had begun immediately.[45] His father-in-law, Douglas Chant, visited the United States embassy the day of the coup, seeking American intervention to protect Andreas. Talbot reportedly told Chant that the United States "has and would by every means discourage Greek military leaders from any resort to violence or bloodshed."[46] Talbot asserted that any harm suffered by political prisoners would "greatly increase complications of already complicated situation."[47] The next day, the State Department asked Talbot how feasible it would be for him to speak to the newly installed prime minister about the "possibility of obtaining release of younger Papandreou on condition that he be immediately ousted from country and forbidden to return." The State Department was concerned that Andreas's execution would "provoke a strong reaction outside Greece" and that poor treatment of political prisoners more generally "would seriously damage the image" of the junta abroad, including in the United States: "execution of Andreas would give coup regime such a black eye that it might never gain favor of American public opinion."[48]

State Department officials in Washington repeatedly pressed Talbot to convey American concerns about the poor treatment of prisoners and how that would resonate internationally. These instructions acknowledged the growing salience of human rights concerns at this time and demonstrated U.S. fears that Greek actions could weaken NATO unity and undermine domestic support for close Greek-American relations.[49] The ambassador arranged a meeting with the Greek minister of the interior, who told Talbot that the regime "intends to kill no one."[50] Furthermore, internal State Department documents reveal, "Ambassador Talbot has expressed U.S. concern to the new Prime Minister about the fate of the prisoners, and he was assured none would be harmed. . . . There is some uneasiness about the fate of the younger Papandreou should he remain incarcerated."[51]

U.S. officials also pursued these concerns outside State Department channels. Deputy national security adviser Francis Bator reached out to the director of the Central Intelligence Agency (CIA), Richard Helms, to highlight the fact that Andreas had a range of supporters in intellectual and academic circles in the United States. Bator also noted a "consular rationale"—the fact that Margaret and the Papandreou children were American citizens—for "special attention" to Andreas's case.[52] American analysts did not believe that Papandreou was in immediate danger, but they noted, "The junta desires to eliminate Andreas from the Greek political scene." They hoped to avoid "summary action" against him.[53]

The support for Andreas was varied and went well beyond economists. For example, former California governor Pat Brown and California lawyer James Schwartz visited Margaret and met with Greek officials to advocate on Andreas's behalf at the end of May 1967. The two hoped to convince the Greek government to deport Andreas.[54] Berkeley law professor Frank Newman also undertook a trip to Greece, which led to his active opposition to the junta for several years. Newman coordinated with Galbraith, Senator Claiborne Pell (D-RI), Stephen Rousseas, and Senator Joe Clark (D-PA) to develop a strategy to secure Andreas's release.[55] In addition, Paul Lyons, executive director of AIUSA, wrote to the Greek interior minister to request that a representative of AIUSA or another Amnesty group be allowed to visit Andreas in prison.[56]

Even after Andreas's release in December 1967, many in and out of Congress, remained disturbed by the Greek junta's character and urged the United States to exert more influence on the regime's practices.[57] Elise Becket, the mother of Amnesty investigator James Becket, sent countless letters to members of Congress about human rights violations in Greece, including a long letter to Senator Claiborne Pell, making the case that torture was occurring in Greece. As James describes it, "She got involved because the family was involved." It was with Greece that she "found herself as an activist." According to her son, Elise even took her lobbying directly to the halls of Congress, roller-skating to enhance her effectiveness.[58]

Attention to Andreas's plight fit into a broader pattern of growing concern for political prisoners during these years. To use one illustrative metric, the term "political prisoners" appeared in the *New York Times* on average 2.2 times more frequently across the long 1960s than during Eisenhower's presidency (figure 3.3). Furthermore, usage of the term increased markedly within the long 1960s, with the first three years of the junta's reign in Greece showing a notable upswing.

Interestingly, few Greek-Americans were prominent voices among the nongovernmental and congressional efforts to influence U.S. policy toward Greece.[59] Scholars have suggested that the junta's anticommunism and support for Greek-American Vice President Spiro Agnew led many to remain

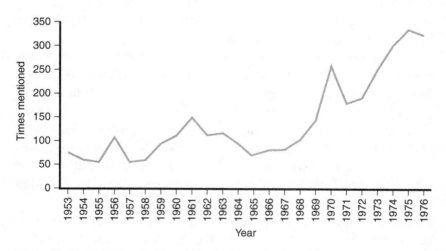

FIGURE 3.3. Usage of the term "political prisoners" in the *New York Times*, 1953–1976

silent about the junta.[60] Despite later interpretations of Greek-Americans as "notably cohesive and politically active," none of the traditional Greek-American religious and social organizations protested against the junta.[61] Historian Effie Pedaliu has argued that transnational connections forged through widespread tourist visits to Greece and "philhellenism" played a role in drawing foreign attention to events there.[62] Yet the transnational connections experienced by Frank Newman, James Becket, and others were more significant than ties based on national heritage.

ADMINISTRATION RESPONSE

U.S. embassy officials in Athens sought to balance their efforts to ensure that Andreas's rights were respected, especially given American attention to his case, with their desire to avoid angering the junta by championing one of its strongest opponents.[63] According to CIA analysis, Greek officials had "not taken kindly to what they regard as unwarranted American interest in the welfare of their 'enfant terrible,' Andreas Papandreou."[64] Such resistance to American entreaties would continue in the years that followed.

Beyond its immediate focus on Andreas and a number of other political prisoners, the United States government struggled with how to respond to the coup other than to make it clear that it was not involved.[65] According to Pedaliu, the Johnson administration was surprised and did not formulate a strong response. [66] The U.S. ambassador's initial reaction to the coup represents a dynamic that is apparent in many cases examined here—U.S. diplomats serving abroad appraised the human rights violations more seriously than officials in Washington did. Whereas Talbot referred to the coup as the "rape of Greek democracy," national security adviser Walt Rostow suggested that Talbot's characterization might have been overly dramatic; however, he noted in a memo to Johnson, "We do regret the coup."[67] Rostow wrote to Johnson on April 21, 1967:

At some point soon, I feel we should express regret—even if softly—that democratic processes have been suspended. I fear that our posture before the Greek Americans and the Greek people will look weak-kneed if we completely avoid judgment. Greek democracy is something all the world cherishes, and we have made a strong effort through Ambassador Talbot to stave this off. However, State logically argues that we should hold off on any substantive comment this morning lest we encourage violence against the coup government.[68]

In an April 24, 1967, teleconference between the State Department and the U.S. embassy in Athens, policymakers searched for the right American response. The secretary of state asserted that the United States had "important leverage" over the coup leaders that could be exercised by delaying the delivery of military equipment, and officials in Washington outlined their approach toward the coup leaders as "stand-offish and neutral." Embassy officials regarded cutting off military assistance shipments to Greece to be a "very serious step" that should only be undertaken in the course of a new U.S. policy toward Greece.[69]

Several days later Rostow reported to Johnson that the United States was "doing business with the new government, but Phil Talbot has made clear that our cooperation will depend on quick restoration of civil liberties and return to constitutional government as soon as possible."[70] State Department officials characterized the United States' stance toward Greece in the wake of the coup as "cool but correct," likely intended to indicate some displeasure without damaging the historically close relationship.[71] According to Barrington King, who served in the U.S. embassy in Athens at the time of the coup, "Phil Talbot was basically quite unhappy with the situation that he had to deal with. But I think that he felt that he had to work with what was there, as best he could, and try to move the situation back to a more democratic regime."[72] Presumably, Talbot's proximity to the violence magnified the crisis for him, whereas the State Department viewed the coup and its aftermath in the broader context of the Cold War and the upheaval of the 1960s.[73]

Although the administration unilaterally halted major arms shipments to Greece after the coup in order to signal its displeasure to domestic and foreign audiences, by late July the State Department believed the arms suspension had ceased to be effective.[74] In a memorandum to Johnson, Dean Rusk argued that existing U.S. policy was "no longer useful," particularly given U.S. interests in the Mediterranean and the Middle East.[75] Interestingly, several memoranda demonstrate American fears that Greece could follow Charles de Gaulle's lead and leave NATO's integrated military command if the United States did not end its suspension.[76] Rostow argued that the United States could "make a convincing case that the foreign policy considerations should override our understandable distaste for doing business with a military regime in a country like Greece."[77] Rostow was hesitant to face the inevitable congressional displeasure; he wrote that, given congressional debates on military aid, "this obviously isn't the best time."[78]

When the administration signaled that it might shift its policy on aid to Greece, a range of actors and groups cabled the White House, asking that it not begin shipping arms again. In response, administration officials, including Rusk, Assistant Secretary of State for Congressional Relations William Macomber, and Paul Warnke of the Defense Department, tried to put a positive spin on the progress that the Greek government was making toward returning to democracy, citing the release of nearly thirty-five hundred political prisoners and "concrete steps" that it had taken toward a constitutional government.[79]

Beyond highlighting this purported progress, State Department officials shared their efforts to encourage Greek leaders to liberalize. Under Secretary of State Nicholas Katzenbach wrote to assure Frank Newman that the United States was pressuring the Greek government, telling him, "If you could read the cables, I'm sure your judgment about our policy in Greece would not be so harsh as that expressed in your letter."[80] In later correspondence between Newman and Rostow, the under secretary for political affairs reiterated that the United States government was circumscribed in what it could say publicly.[81] The available cable traffic, however, does not provide much evidence that the United States leaned on the Greek government. Despite the absence of evidence of such appeals in the documentary record, anecdotal evidence suggests that Greek leaders were hearing expressions of concern from the United States. According to Walter Heller, who traveled to Athens in July 1967, "The Greek junta leaders continually complain that the American government seems preoccupied with protesting about Andreas and their political prisoners, that it tends to impede their efforts to restore clean, constitutional, and democratic government to Greece."[82]

REPORTS OF TORTURE IN GREECE

Beyond Andreas's imprisonment, Americans were galvanized by reports of torture in Greece. Their concerns reflected a growing American awareness of and opposition to torture internationally. One means of measuring that

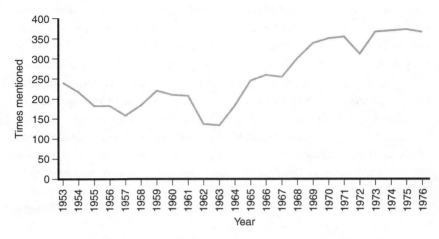

FIGURE 3.4. Usage of the term "torture" in the *New York Times*, 1953–1976

dynamic was that on average the *New York Times* used the term "torture" 1.4 times more during the long 1960s than the average across the eight years of Eisenhower's two terms (figure 3.4). In addition, mentions of "torture" nearly doubled in the *New York Times* between 1961 and 1976 and increased noticeably between 1967 and 1971.

More specifically, Amnesty's report on Greece highlighted the thousands of Greeks who were detained without trial, the persecution of those prisoners' relatives, and the "widespread" use of torture in interrogations.[83] The report detailed physical and psychological torture inflicted on detained Greeks, including the sustained beating of a prisoner's feet (called *falanga*), the insertion of fingers or other objects into prisoners' vaginas and anuses, near suffocation, electric shock, burning, and other methods designed to inflict considerable pain. Amnesty reported that the police subjected prisoners to mock executions; threats of torture, harm, or rape; the sound of others' physical torture; and other tactics used to break their will.[84] A memo reporting the Amnesty findings asserted, "The Delegation can objectively state that torture is deliberately and officially used and was convinced that the use of torture is a widespread practice against Greek citizens suspected of active opposition to the Government."[85] When Greek officials and others sought to dismiss Amnesty's report, prisoners from the

Laki camp on the island of Leros clandestinely issued a statement offering evidence of torture.[86]

The U.S. government was slow to accept these reports, arguing in April 1968 that "there have been unfortunately instances of mistreatment of prisoners in individual cases" instead of acknowledging more widespread problems.[87] Nevertheless, officials in Athens noted a significant decline in torture in the wake of the Amnesty International report, which indicates that intervention, even by an NGO, could have an impact on abuses.[88] Reports by Amnesty and others documenting the use of torture have held up over time, including *Look* magazine's May 1969 report that graphically recounted torture methods such as *falanga*, which produces very painful swelling. The piece included horrifying accounts of torture and prolonged abuse of Greeks, and it drew considerable attention within the United States and from the junta.[89]

U.S. officials such as Rostow were skeptical that American influence could induce Greek reform, yet as it was formulating a new approach, the administration was cognizant that it needed to be seen as considering human rights violations. The White House weighed resuming aid to Greece against a possible backlash by "a group of liberal Democrats" who might abandon the president's foreign aid bill.[90] Indeed, members of Congress such as Don Edwards registered their opposition to increasing military aid to Greece.[91] In congressional debate regarding American policy, Fraser said that the United States "ought to come down firmly on the side of free and open societies and firmly against those repressive and oppressive governments which are characterized by the present regime that rules Greece."[92] Earlier he had recommended that military aid to the junta be "ended or sharply reduced" to signal that the United States did not support the "full-blown police state" that Greece had become.[93]

As months passed, the United States' relationship with the Greek leadership remained complicated, which suited neither side. By January 1968 the United States wanted a "normalization" of relations.[94] At the same juncture, the Greek prime minister George Papadopoulos wrote directly to Johnson, rationalizing the coup. According to Rostow's analysis of the letter, "It shows some discomfort over our keeping our distance and the value he apparently still places in a relationship with us."[95] The Johnson administration's Greek policy had failed in its objective of encouraging democratic reforms and a return to constitutionalism. Instead, it inspired opposition from some members of NATO, liberals in the United States, and the opposition in Greece.[96]

In October 1968, with the arms embargo still under discussion, Rostow continued to urge the president to focus on Greece's strategic value rather than on its repression: "The time has come to separate our NATO relationship from our disapproval of domestic Greek politics. . . . It doesn't make sense to let our security relationships with Greece—NATO role, commo [sic] facilities, Sixth Fleet support—deteriorate further."[97] According to Rostow, resuming aid to Greece would garner domestic opposition: "A vocal group on the Hill will object to any resumption. You have already had letters from Congressmen Edwards and Fraser, who are active with Melina Mercouri and other friends of Greek democracy." Yet Rostow recommended releasing 40 percent of the suspended military equipment.[98] The Warsaw Pact invasion of Czechoslovakia in August 1968, which unsettled the United States' European allies in NATO, influenced the White House's determination to resume shipments of military aid to Greece.[99] The decision that was made in October focused on materials such as minesweepers and fighter jets that were tied to Greece's role in NATO.[100]

In a rather disturbing example of conflicting thinking among U.S. policymakers, at the same time that the United States considered renewing military shipments, Talbot weighed how far the United States could or should push the regime to reform:

Although I recognize the risks in terms of our long-term relations with Greece inherent in undly [sic] protracted effort to convert present Greek regime into democratic and representative government, particularly in absence of concrete evidence from Papadopoulos and co. of some genuine intention to move in this direction, I believe we can still allow them a little more rope before we are faced with critical decision of whether only acceptable alternative is to support concerted attempt to depose them.[101]

Talbot's telegram suggests that despite the American decision to resume aid, the United States was nonetheless open to a coup against the junta. U.S. policy toward Greece remained muddled throughout Johnson's time in office, and the United States' relationship with Greece became increasingly controversial during the Nixon administration, heightening concerns about the character of American foreign policy and spurring activism against the junta in Washington and beyond.

RICHARD NIXON AND THE JUNTA

When Nixon assumed the presidency on January 20, 1969, Greece had not returned to constitutional democracy nor had the United States fully normalized its relations with Greece as a NATO ally.[102] The new administration had to weigh its short- and long-term interests in the region against the costs of American involvement with the junta.[103] Overall, the Nixon administration prioritized stability and security in the eastern Mediterranean.[104] Nixon's ambassador to Athens, Henry Tasca, feared that a "Greek Nasser" could follow the collapse of the junta, referring to the Egyptian leader who was viewed as too independent by American policymakers.[105] Therefore, U.S. policy sought to maintain NATO military strength and slowly prod the Greek leaders to return to democracy. In embassy staffer Charles Stuart Kennedy's view, Tasca's role was to "represent a new positive policy from President Nixon toward the colonels." As Kennedy remembered it, Tasca "was sent there to try to bring the colonels around to a more democratic form of government."[106]

Although the administration claimed to be interested in reform, it exerted little pressure to move the junta in that direction.[107] In one instance, Nixon wrote to the Greek prime minister in June 1970 to convey that "developments in Greece have become a matter of intimate concern to Greece's friends and allies," yet Nixon's language suggested only a mild degree of concern.[108] Kennedy candidly characterized the United States' relationship with the Greek regime as being "under the sheets in bed with them."[109] As the United States moved closer to the ruling regime, the embassy stayed at a greater distance from other Greek voices; according to embassy staffer Barrington King, "Relations with the opposition were a good bit inhibited under Tasca."[110]

Indeed, the Nixon administration continued to soften its position. Whereas the Johnson administration had allowed around 40 percent of the suspended military equipment to be shipped to Greece, Nixon decided to go further and resume full military aid. Nixon and Kissinger had discussed selling $20 million more in equipment, but fundamentally they determined that military aid should not be dependent on a return to constitutional government and ended the arms embargo.[111] One dissenting voice within the administration's inner circle was NSC staffer Winston Lord, who in a memorandum to Kissinger, under the subtitle "The Moral Imperatives," urged the United States to take a different approach to Greece, making an argument similar to the one he had made regarding Rhodesia.[112]

Throughout the Nixon years, members of Congress and others attentive to Greek prisoners wrote to the administration in the hope that it would intervene in individual cases. In spring 1969 and onward, a number of people sent letters specifically about imprisoned Greek composer Mikis Theodorakis.[113] In another example, Senator Birch Bayh (D-IN) wrote to the U.S. ambassador to Greece about a young prisoner who may have been tortured and was in poor health: "I'm sure, Mr. Ambassador, that you share my belief that an integral part of our responsibility as citizens of this country is to our fellow man in other parts of the world. Thus, when one man suffers injustice and degradation, it is our burden, as well as that of his countryman, as long as his call for humanity goes unheard."[114] And, just as when Andreas was arrested, Henry Kissinger received letters from former colleagues regarding the plight of John Pesmazoglou, a former vice-governor of the Bank of Greece who was being held for his antigovernment activism. Consistent with the trend of the Nixon administration demonstrating less concern about the violations than Johnson's had, Kissinger chose not to get involved in Pesmazoglou's case.[115]

Members of Congress also wrote to the State Department, pushing for clearer signs that the United States disapproved of the junta, including the appointment of a career diplomat as ambassador to Greece.[116] Assistant Secretary of State William Macomber, in reply, falsely claimed that American-Greek relations were under "intensive review" given the conflict between Greece's role as a key NATO ally and its "autocratic government denying basic civil liberties."[117] In the context of the ongoing debate, Fraser used the *Congressional Record* to highlight reporting that was critical of U.S. policy in Greece, including an author's charge that the United States had "almost stealthily renewed full military aid, on the pretext that the adoption of a new constitution represented progress toward the restoration of democracy."[118] One congressional concern was that U.S. contact with the Greek military, under the guise of NATO, increased popular anti-Americanism in Greece.[119]

Given significant congressional interest, the White House sought to resume military aid to Greece in a way that would "minimize

Congressional and international objections."[120] According to NSC talking points, one of the principles guiding U.S. policy toward Greece was "a general presidential insistence on not involving ourselves in the internal political disputes of other countries."[121] Of course, throughout the Cold War the United States selectively, and at times with great consequence, involved itself in the internal affairs of other countries.

NGOs remained engaged with U.S. policy toward Greece, although with less influence than during the Johnson years. In a June 1969 meeting between members of the U.S. Committee for Democracy in Greece and State Department officials, for example, Fraser urged the Nixon administration to develop an approach to the Greek regime that was more in line with the moral tenets of the United States.[122] Similarly, Niall MacDermott, secretary general of the International Commission of Jurists (ICJ), sought more U.S. involvement in the cases of political prisoners in Greece, which as of March 1970 exceeded three thousand, according to Amnesty, who had "adopted" three hundred of them.[123]

Building on long-standing connections, different NGOs began to cooperate with one another regarding Greece. For example, the International League for the Rights of Man offered its mailing list of sixty-five hundred names to the U.S. Committee for Democracy in Greece, and AIUSA facilitated the mailing of its newsletter.[124] In addition, the American Civil Liberties Union (ACLU) and the ILRM divided their targets regarding Greek repression, with the ACLU focusing on Washington and the ILRM directing its pressure at Athens.[125] In addition, the ICJ and Amnesty published a joint appeal by Greek political prisoners, alleging torture by Greek military police.[126] And after six Greek lawyers were detained in March 1973, American lawyer William Butler, Morris Abram, Canadian lawyer and former head of the UN Division of Human Rights John Humphrey, and British politician Sir Elwyn Jones traveled to Greece on behalf of the ILRM and the ICJ to investigate their condition.

Although, on the surface, Nixon's policies were more accommodating than Johnson's, Nixon administration officials characterized the pressure exerted on the Greek junta under Johnson to be "more symbolic than real," which suggests continuity between the two administrations, even if the policies appeared different at the time. As the Nixon administration assessed U.S. interests in Greece, the "strategic benefits," rather than political or economic ones, were considered "significant" given the role Greece could play in holding off an advance of Warsaw Pact forces as well as the communications and basing capabilities the country offered.[127] Furthermore, an NSC memo noted, "Over the years the relationship we enjoyed with Greece permitted to us almost unrestricted use of Greek air space, naval bases, staging areas, communications and transshipment points to and from areas in the Middle East."[128] Administration documents acknowledged that military shipments might not have been essential to short-term U.S. interests in Greece, but that continued suspension could damage Greece's role in NATO in the long run.[129]

When sending Ambassador Henry Tasca to Athens, the administration instructed him to tell the Greek prime minister that the United States intended to resume military aid shipments but also to highlight the American wish for greater progress toward a constitutional government. Notably, however, the shift in U.S. military shipments was regarded by the White House as "unconditional."[130] In historian James Miller's view, Tasca's selection as ambassador "reflected the Nixon administration's desire to have a tough, politically reliable, and experienced diplomat in a country where it could expect conflict over policy with U.S. liberals."[131] During his time in Athens, Tasca had a challenging job. Political counselor Elizabeth Brown remembers, "We bent over backwards to get along with the 'colonels.'"[132] At the same time, Dan Zachary, who was in the embassy in Athens from 1969 to 1973, recalls that Tasca "put pressure on the colonels to avoid any actions that would bring retaliatory measures by the U.S."[133] Zachary's recollection fits with those of foreign service officers working with other repressive regimes, most notably in Chile and South Korea.

The new U.S. ambassador sent Nixon a report in 1970 that diminished the current repression by describing military intervention as a "recurrent phenomenon" in Greek political life. Tasca's report offered a rationalization for the repression of the regime given its "ambitious and radical program." In contrast to Talbot's telegram immediately after the coup, Tasca cited a remarkably crass article that claimed, "Democracy in Greece is no virgin."[134]He also enumerated positive steps that Greece was taking, particularly with its diplomatic relations in the eastern Mediterranean. In Tasca's view, "It makes no sense whatever . . . for the U.S. to refuse to *sell* NATO-related equipment to another NATO member country."[135] In Tasca's analysis, United States policy was not facilitating a return to constitutional government; instead, the American stance was slowly damaging U.S.

interests by bolstering the opposition, undermining NATO unity, hampering Greek-American military cooperation, and giving military sales to other governments. Tasca argued, therefore, that the United States should abandon an ineffective policy that offered the Soviets the opportunity to capitalize on intra-alliance differences.[136]

On the other side of the debate, members of Congress who wanted a firmer stance against the junta argued that such a shift would benefit American standing in Western Europe.[137] Fraser and Edwards maintained pressure on the White House, writing to Nixon in April 1970, asking him to indicate American disapproval of Greek judicial proceedings, allegations of torture, and potential use of capital punishment.[138] Critics of U.S. policy such as Senator Ted Kennedy (D-MA) accused the government of "coddling" the Greeks and of "cold and calculated indifference."[139] Edwards argued that the United States should instead be "joining the international outcry against the excesses of the Greek dictatorship."[140] In May 1970 Representative Paul Findley (R-IL), who had visited Greece nine months previously, wrote to Nixon, urging the maintenance of the American arms embargo. Similar to many others, Findley expressed concern for how resuming aid would be perceived by the Greek populace. In addition, he minimized worries that Greece would withdraw from NATO, arguing, "It has no other place to go."[141] More concretely, in June 1970 liberal Senator Vance Hartke (D-IN) introduced an amendment that would prohibit American military aid to the Greek junta, although it had little chance of success. Joseph Sisco, chair of the NSC's Interdepartmental Group for Near East and South Asia, predicted that in order to squash congressional efforts to cut off security assistance to Greece, the administration "will probably require increasing effort."[142]

The Nixon White House wished that developments in Greece in late summer and early autumn 1970 would provide enough political cover for it to announce the resumption of military aid. Specifically, the administration hoped that, in addition to the recent release of five hundred political prisoners, martial law would be lifted or municipal elections called.[143] When justifying its September 22, 1970, decision to resume sending aid to Greece, the United States did point to steps that the Greek government was taking toward resuming democracy as well as Greece's status as a loyal NATO ally.[144] The administration's rationalizations did not persuade the regime's critics such as Findley. In a letter to Nixon, he expressed concern that the resumption of aid could be "misinterpreted by the Greek public and politicians as an overt embrace of the military dictatorship." Findley warned, "The U.S. must avoid paying the politically embarrassing price, both at home and among our European NATO allies, of appearing to be installing and supporting dictatorships."[145] Similarly, when the United States announced plans to resume the shipping of military aid, Fraser and Edwards denounced the decision as "the final bankruptcy of American policy in Greece."[146]

By early 1971 Greek leaders had made little of the hoped-for progress on returning to democracy, which prompted NSC staffer Harold Saunders to recommend a review of U.S. policy.[147] Sisco outlined possible shifts for U.S. policy, which boiled down to "do somewhat more or do somewhat less." Sisco warned that to "do somewhat less . . . would significantly elevate the risk of serious division in NATO and arouse strong reactions among some elements of the Congress."[148] The review provoked no new stance toward the Greek leaders, although State Department officials in Washington later sent Tasca instructions to encourage Papadopoulos to end martial law.[149]

Meanwhile, human rights abuses continued, but the junta was generally effective in limiting attention to them. Evidence of continued torture reached an international audience through a letter smuggled out of a Greek prison in November 1970 in which Alexandros Panagoulis, who had tried to assassinate Papadopoulos, detailed tortures he had suffered, including whippings, *falanga*, beatings with an iron bar, cigarette burns, sexual abuse, kicking, hair pulling, suffocation, sleep deprivation, and other inhumane acts.[150]

It is difficult to determine how influential external pressure was on the Greek government, although in Amnesty International's view, it had facilitated the closing of island concentration camps and the amnesty of political prisoners.[151] In a letter to Fraser, the Greek ambassador to the United States described "the closing down of all prisoner's camps and the release of all persons detained in Greece." In addition, he asserted that Greece was working to move away from martial law, showing that the government cared about conveying at least an impression of progress to members of Congress.[152] Despite these steps, critics such as Edwards were not mollified. He remained concerned that America was supplying the means of repression—namely guns—to the Greeks, charging the American government with being "guilty of complacency if not complicity."[153]

Two months later eighty-one members of Congress joined Edwards in asking Nixon to make a "serious review" of U.S. Greek policy given the "strategic, moral, and political interests" affected.[154] Fraser also remained highly critical of U.S. policy; in testimony before the House Foreign Affairs Subcommittee on Europe, he argued that U.S. policy "towards Greece since 1967 has shown an extraordinary indifference to the fate of the Greek people." He said, "The continued support by the United States of the Greek regime can only underline its contempt for the basic values which NATO was set up to preserve, and the hypocrisy of U.S. assertions in support of the value of freedom under law."[155] In July Fraser urged that the United States call for Greece's suspension from NATO.[156]

Recognizing that they did not share an agenda with the Nixon White House, members of Congress who were opposed to the junta escalated their tactics further.[157] In the same month that Fraser testified, the House Foreign Affairs Committee voted to cut off U.S. aid to Greece, which was $117 million at that point.[158] Representative Wayne L. Hays (D-OH), who had introduced the amendment cutting off aid, opposed the junta's antidemocratic nature, saying, "I am not going to stand here and let anybody say that the nation that invented democracy, the nation from which the word 'democracy' derives, from the Greek word 'demos,' cannot run a democracy in 1971."[159] The New York Times editorial board supported the House vote, declaring, "The Foreign Affairs Committee has projected the national interest on a broader canvas than that employed by the State and Defense Departments. It would be foolhardy for the Administration to ignore the meaning of its actions."[160] In addition, members of Congress affiliated with the U.S. Committee for Democracy in Greece wrote to their supporters, imploring them to pressure the Senate to follow Hays's lead.[161] The vote complicated U.S.-Greek relations but also gave U.S. officials in Athens demonstrable proof of American frustration at the slow pace of Greek reform.[162] Although the amendment passed, it did not end aid, because Nixon signed a waiver characterizing continued funds as being in the national security interests of the United States.[163]

Debates about military assistance persisted and were heightened in early 1972 when the U.S. Navy decided to homeport a carrier task force in Greece, which represented to congressional critics such as Representative Donald W. Riegle Jr. (D-MI) an increasingly close Greek-American military relationship.[164] In addition, Nixon again waived a ban on security assistance or sales to Greece based on national security.[165] Military assistance to Greece even became an issue in the 1972 presidential campaign, with candidate Senator George McGovern (D-SD) asserting that he would cut off all aid to Greece within ten days of taking office.[166] Greece, however, independently removed a thorn in the side of congressional-executive relations by turning down American military assistance for 1973, which White House analysis attributed to Greek leaders' desire to appear independent and the relatively small amount being offered.[167]

In 1973 tensions rose within Greece, pitting the regime in open confrontation against its opponents. In March student protests escalated, and a crackdown ensued, which included the arrest of six lawyers who had defended students participating in the demonstrations.[168] These new human rights violations incited congressional critics of Greece. For example, in May 1973 Edwards called for a review of U.S. policy, given what he identified as problems with the Greek navy and air force as well as the increasing unpopularity of the junta.[169]

Given ongoing pressure, American officials often were attentive to domestic perceptions of their foreign policy. In the face of upcoming Greek elections, which U.S. officials worried might not be free and fair, a debate ensued about whether the United States should warn the Greek prime minister that flawed elections could worsen bilateral relations. The primary motivation for a U.S. demarche seemed to be making the White House "somewhat less vulnerable to charges in Greece, the U.S. Congress, and elsewhere that we have been supporting Papadopoulos' recent actions."[170]

Although the Greek prime minister declared a wide amnesty for political prisoners on August 19, 1973, martial law was reintroduced in November.[171] Several days later there was a military coup in Greece in which Papadopoulos was overthrown and new leaders emerged. Tasca was increasingly weary of military dictators, but Kissinger did not want the United States to get involved, saying, "We work with whoever is in power as long as they are not anti-American."[172] Within four months the country finally returned to democracy in the wake of the Greek-Turkish crisis over Cyprus, with former prime minister Konstantine Karamanlis returning from exile to lead Greece on July 24, 1974.[173]

As the United States had reviewed its policy toward Greece in the months between the 1973 coup and the return to democracy in July 1974, Winston Lord noted that the United States' decision between a "hands-off approach" or a "moralist/interventionist approach" was relevant to countries beyond Greece, specifically the Soviet Union, South Africa, and Rhodesia. Disavowing the two "pure" strategies that were initially outlined in their memorandum, State Department officials argued that the United States should formulate its policy based on an assessment of whether "a given policy offer[s] a promise of maximizing our interests over the full range of foreseeable circumstances."[174] Lord was cautious about the risks of intervening in Greece, noting, "We could at most bring down a government, but not dictate a successor. The result might be chaos or a government more harmful to our interests than the Ioannides regime."[175] In a subsequent meeting to assess U.S. policy, Sisco said, "I'm not entirely satisfied with our present policy, and I have never been entirely satisfied with the totally hands-off policy we have pursued. I feel that our present policy does not sufficiently and clearly enough disassociate ourselves from Greece in this respect."[176] Not surprisingly, suggestions that the United States should distance itself from the Greek leadership prompted a tirade from Kissinger:

Why is it in the American interest to do in Greece what we apparently don't do anywhere else—of requiring them to give a commitment to the President to move to representative government? . . . Well, I'm just being the devil's advocate. You can say the Department of State doesn't have a Political Science Division. It conducts the foreign policy of the United States. It deals with any government—communist or non-communist—within the context of the foreign-policy objectives of the United States.[177]

Kissinger's meeting with his aides did not resolve what course the United States should take.[178] Their discussion, however, demonstrates how the White House and State Department debated their formulation of U.S. foreign policy as pressure to respond to evidence of human rights abuses increased.

In September 1975 Greece put accused torturers on trial, with convictions resulting in imprisonment of five months to twenty-three years.[179] The trials demonstrated that reports by Amnesty and others about the widespread use of torture by the Greek junta had merit, countering official American doubts throughout the years.[180] In a notable column, William F. Buckley Jr. issued an apology for discounting earlier reports and wrote, "Certainly the evidence exists that the Colonels were engaging in torture."[181] The United States had long diminished such accounts as isolated excesses in order to overlook the most serious Greek human rights violations in its policymaking process.

Speaking in May 1974, Fraser was dismissive of U.S. attention to human rights violations in Greece, saying, "Our country's performance in Greece in this area is unfortunately typical not only of our feeble efforts elsewhere but also of the prevailing standards operating among all countries today."[182] Fraser's frustration with American inaction was shared by many liberals, and it laid the groundwork for more-focused attention on international human rights and greater congressional activism in foreign relations.[183] American activism against the junta marks the first of three instances, followed by efforts targeting South Korea and Chile, in which human rights violations prompted Congress to pass legislation cutting off aid to a repressive government.

Americans concerned with human rights violations in Greece in the wake of the 1967 coup mobilized to protect Andreas Papandreou from execution, participated in fact-finding missions to reveal patterns of torture of Greek prisoners, and worked to end U.S. military assistance to the junta. These Americans were drawn to such efforts through their transnational connections to Greeks such as Andreas and Maria Papandreou as well as a belief that the United States should not support governments that torture their citizens. Their activism called into question one of the tenets of U.S. foreign policy since the 1920s—that the United States preferred reliable, stable allies. These activists' challenge to what David Schmitz has characterized as a "lesser-of-two-evils approach to foreign policy" continued in the years that followed.[184]

Chapter Four

DOES THE UNITED STATES STAND FOR SOMETHING?

Human Rights in South Korea

During the years between Park Chung Hee's seizure of power in 1961 and Carter's inauguration in 1977, American attention to human rights violations in South Korea, or the Republic of Korea (ROK), fluctuated considerably.[1] Not unusual for the era and the region, the United States relied on an authoritarian leader to preserve stability in the country. Throughout the period, the United States remained largely reticent about human rights abuses in South Korea, content with a politically stable, anticommunist ally and distracted by more-pressing problems such as the war in Vietnam. Top U.S. leaders directed their attention to Park's repression only when the instability it produced seemed to threaten U.S. interests in the region directly, such as in March 1963, when Park announced a four-year extension of military rule, and in August 1973, when they believed that Kim Dae Jung, a dissident South Korean politician who had been kidnapped in Tokyo, would be murdered. Debates over U.S.–South Korean relations highlight the extent to which the Korean peninsula remained a potential Cold War flashpoint throughout the long 1960s, even as the United States sought détente with the Soviet Union and rapprochement with the Chinese.

Those concerned with human rights violations in South Korea sought firmer pressure on Park and a reduction in U.S. support for his repressive government. Unlike the situation with Greece, pressure to shift U.S. policy came largely from members of Congress and lower-level diplomats, as there was limited nongovernmental attention paid to South Korean human rights abuses. American activists in South Korea and the United States sought to use military and economic assistance as levers to reduce Park's human rights violations. American missionaries, like diplomats serving in Seoul, were often drawn into activism based on personal connections to those facing repression. The actions of those motivated by specific acts of South Korean authoritarianism complemented broader congressional concerns about U.S. support for dictators. Together, they succeeded in raising awareness about Park's human rights violations and limiting U.S. assistance to him for several years.

PARK CHUNG HEE COMES TO POWER

The United States did not pursue a clear policy toward South Korea in the wake of the 1961 military coup that brought Park to power, and a lack of clarity would complicate U.S. policy in the years that followed. U.S. officials hoped for a speedy return to civilian rule, but did not take steps to advance such a goal.[2] Given the lack of meaningful pressure or action, the United States' stance was essentially acceptance of the junta.[3] When Park announced in August 1961 that South Korea would return to civil rule in two years, U.S. officials reported, "Although this timetable is somewhat slower than we would have preferred, General [Park]'s announcement does represent a step in the right direction in that it provides a public commitment to return to representative constitutional government by a specific time."[4] Park also released more than five thousand political prisoners and announced amnesty for other prisoners, which were encouraging signals to U.S. observers.[5] When Park and John F. Kennedy met in 1961, they issued a communiqué in which Park reasserted his "solemn pledge of the revolutionary government to return the government to civilian control" within two years.[6]

On March 16, 1963, however, Park declared it necessary to push off plans for a transition to civilian government for four more years.[7] He now believed that "two years were too short."[8] Park's plan to continue military rule for four more years risked sparking deeper unrest; the threat to South Korean stability prompted the United States to press him to hold democratic elections. In a March 21 meeting with Park, U.S. ambassador to

Seoul Samuel Berger advised that the United States "cannot possibly approve, and might be compelled openly to oppose, continuation of military government for four more years."[9]

Although U.S. officials had viewed Park's rule as acceptable, if not ideal, for some time, the administration now sought an end to military control. Kennedy wrote to Park, communicating that the United States did not seek to impose its will on him, but rather expected that he should come to his own decision to pursue the preferred American outcome.[10] U.S. officials in Seoul stated that they would not publicize Kennedy's letter if progress were made, implicitly threatening to release it if Park did not reform.[11] In addition, during the Kennedy years, the South Korean government was highly dependent on American aid, which was approximately $270 million annually.[12] In an effort to signal its seriousness, the United States withheld $25 million that was promised to and needed by South Korea.[13] Shortly thereafter, Park announced that elections would go forward. As embassy official Philip Habib put it, "We laid down the law to them, and we made it stick."[14] Habib had traveled to South Korea in 1962 to serve as political counselor. During his three years there, Habib remembers, "I used to play poker with

FIGURE 4. 1. Philip Habib in the White House Cabinet Room. Courtesy of the Gerald R. Ford Presidential Library.

the Prime Minister every Sunday afternoon. I knew everybody in the country."[15] Habib would build on and extend those connections when he returned to Seoul as ambassador in 1971.

Despite South Korea's return to civilian rule, an open, democratic system did not develop, and Park's increasing authoritarianism complicated American–South Korean relations for years to come. The United States had hoped to encourage greater respect for political and civil rights, but the White House ultimately overlooked the limits on democracy in South Korea, given the close security relationship between the two countries. High-level U.S. officials prioritized South Korea as a strategic and stable pillar in Asia, even while recognizing that South Korean leaders were "far from benevolent despots" who "carried out inexcusable transgressions against the basic human rights of their citizens."[16] As some members of Congress, diplomats, and nongovernmental activists became uncomfortable with formal U.S. support for "despots," South Korean abuses were increasingly a source of unease.

"A BIT MORE STABILITY": PARK, LBJ, AND VIETNAM

U.S. policymakers were aware of deficits in South Korean domestic politics. When widespread student demonstrations broke out in opposition to the government in March 1964, NSC staffer Robert Komer displayed a callous attitude toward the security of South Korean students who were protesting the government:

Korean student riots, ostensibly against [the South Korean–Japanese] settlement but actually against [the government] are getting worrisome. No one expected they'd reach such intensity (students are normally feisty this time each year). . . . All in all, instead of urging Park and his Rasputin, Kim Chong-pil, to be more democratic, maybe we ought to tolerate a little more dictatorship in this messy fief.

Conveying his perception of the U.S. government's priorities in stark language, Komer wrote, "Korea is still a mess. . . . So I'd settle for a bit more stability."[17] Komer's preference for stability, which American policymakers often believed was more favorable to safeguarding U.S. national security interests, characterized U.S. policy toward South Korea throughout these years.[18]

Park imposed martial law when the protests shifted to violent riots in early June. The government closed schools and implemented censorship in an effort to suppress the demonstrations, arresting more than thirteen thousand people in its crackdown.[19] The United States expressed concern about the actions of South Korean forces—there were reports that they had threatened the *Donga Ilbo* newspaper—which led the American ambassador to stress that the United States did not want its military assistance to support "undisciplined troops which threaten orderly processes."[20] Komer was concerned that the United States could "be over-identified with yet another repressive campaign by one of our Asian clients."[21] However, unlike the Kennedy administration, the Johnson White House exerted no meaningful pressure for change.[22] The White House's repeated decisions to prioritize stability and Cold War loyalty slowly galvanized critics. To those concerned about the morality of United States foreign policy, American policy toward South Korea and other authoritarian allies during the Cold War suggested that fears of communism had disturbed the relationship between American ideals and the framework of U.S. foreign relations. In the case of South Korea, these critics included foreign correspondents; religious figures, including missionaries in South Korea and U.S.-based leaders; academics; members of Congress; and a number of diplomats who sought to use American economic and military power as leverage to moderate Park's increasing repression.

Although Johnson's attention was elsewhere, U.S. officials remained focused on the stability of Park's regime. Recently declassified National Security Council files indicate the NSC's assessment that the government "faced recurrent political conflict" and "internal disputes."[23] After another cycle of student protests and police repression, there was hope in late November 1967 among American officials in Seoul that the internal political situation would "soon be restored to something approaching normalcy."[24]

In January 1968, however, North Korean agents attacked Seoul's presidential palace, the Blue House. They killed several South Koreans, but did not reach the president or his close aides. Park often pointed to the threat that South Koreans faced from the North when rationalizing his repressive measures, and the Blue House raid and the subsequent capture of the USS *Pueblo*, a naval intelligence ship, bolstered his point.[25] The attacks also crystallized the broader Cold War context in which Park was a key

American ally. The raid on the Blue House and concerns that domestic instability presented opportunities for North Korean attacks might have heightened the Johnson administration's attentiveness to Park's repression; however, Johnson was consumed with Vietnam and his failed reelection campaign, and he ultimately left office twelve months later.

During the Kennedy and Johnson years, there were few examples of external observers focused on human rights violations in South Korea.[26] One noteworthy exception was Yong-jeung Kim, president of the Korean Affairs Institute, a nonprofit, nonpartisan organization based in Washington, DC, that advocated for Korean reunification.[27] Yong-jeung Kim wrote to Dean Rusk, "Instead of South Korea being a showcase of freedom it is an ugly billboard for all Asia to see."[28] In addition, the International League for the Rights of Man, which had an affiliate in South Korea, expressed its concern.[29] During the late 1960s, American foundations and the United States Operations Mission, which administered U.S. assistance in South Korea, worked to encourage democracy and the rule of law there.[30] Such activism was limited in scope and did not meaningfully influence U.S. policy.

Richard Nixon's victory in the 1968 election ushered in an administration that was even more concerned with the Cold War balance of power. Such a worldview meant that Henry Kissinger (who at the time was national security adviser and Nixon's chief foreign policy aide) was not particularly interested in South Korea outside the levels of U.S. troops there and Korean forces serving in Vietnam.[31] Not surprisingly, their realist approach meant that Nixon and Kissinger were far less troubled by the character of Park's government than, for example, Kennedy had been.[32] The new administration remained publicly silent about South Korean repression and privately conveyed the message that American officials would not intervene in South Korean politics.[33] United States military assistance from 1968 to 1972 was greater than any previous or future five-year span during the Cold War, which indicates that the Nixon administration viewed Park as an important ally.[34] Nevertheless, the administration did face congressional pressure regarding military assistance for authoritarian regimes in general, and in Vice President Spiro Agnew's view, Park did not understand the relationship between the legislative and executive branches sufficiently, which meant that he could not grasp why his repression might limit the level of assistance that Nixon could send to South Korea.[35]

Domestically, Park became increasingly focused on potential electoral opponents and used undemocratic means to limit their influence, particularly with opposition politician Kim Dae Jung. The United States embassy in Seoul recognized the threat that Kim posed to Park as the two campaigned for the presidency in November 1970.[36] When NSC staffer John Holdridge traveled to South Korea in March 1971, he reported on Kim's dynamism in the presidential election and noted that Kim and his family were subject to "skullduggery" such as police harassment; as it turned out, this would be the beginning of an escalating campaign by the state against Kim.[37] The situation was likely exacerbated by Kim's visit to the United States in early 1971, when he met with Secretary of State William P. Rogers and Senators William Fulbright, Ted Kennedy, and Hubert Humphrey as well as Representative Gerald Ford.[38] As further evidence of his growing stature, Kim was also present at the National Prayer Breakfast, although he did not speak with Nixon or Agnew.

In December 1971, several months after his reelection, Park instituted greater controls on the freedom of expression and the free flow of information.[39] According to the argument for such measures that Park made to Ambassador Philip Habib, as the two superpowers moved toward détente, North Korea might take advantage of shifting international priorities.[40] When faced with Park's institution of emergency powers, the U.S. embassy urged the State Department to exert "pressure [on the South Korean government] to prevent abuse."[41] Although there is no evidence that it did so, this advice is consistent with the pattern seen in other instances where in-country diplomats were more concerned about human rights violations than officials in Washington were.

MARTIAL LAW AND THE *YUSHIN* CONSTITUTION

Park's steps to limit political debate and any challenges to his rule culminated in his declaration of martial law on October 17, 1972. He dismissed the National Assembly; initiated a process to ratify a new constitution, which would enhance presidential powers and curb opportunities for political dissent; imposed a ban on political activity; closed the universities; and continued existing censorship policies.[42] As Park moved toward authoritarianism, Habib urged Washington to disassociate itself from Park. Holdridge, however, disagreed with Habib's preference, writing to

Kissinger, "While we regret the character of Park's reorganization and believe it unnecessary, his new system is not inevitably de-stabilizing," which demonstrates the degree to which Washington's overriding priority was stability.[43]

Under martial law, Park imprisoned opposition leaders, and courts sentenced critics of his government to three years in prison. According to Habib, the United States maintained a public position of noninterference and nonassociation. Privately, the embassy "clarified that the changes are not being well received in the U.S. and that this could have an adverse effect on U.S. public and Congressional attitudes toward Korea."[44] Notably, the embassy did not convey executive branch or White House displeasure with Park's leadership.

In the shadow of Park's crackdown, a national referendum was held in November, and a new national constitution was "approved" with 92 percent of the vote, although, as the U.S. embassy reported, it was "more an exercise in conformity than a reflection of national sentiment for or against the constitutional change. The pressures for conformity on the voters were both official and social. No dissenting voices were permitted."[45] Park justified the new *Yushin* Constitution, meaning "rejuvenation" or "revitalization," by pointing to a broad array of changing international and domestic factors, including superpower détente, the Unites States' opening to China, the normalization of Sino–Japanese relations, the break in diplomatic relations between Japan and Taiwan, U.S. efforts to end the war in Vietnam, menacing behavior by North Korea, the facilitation of industrialization, and the need to create a "Korean-style democracy."[46] In addition, he argued that South Korea sought greater unity to negotiate more effectively with North Korea, where there was no dissension.[47] The United States did not see *Yushin* as necessary, given South Korea's economic strengths and the domestic political situation, but recognized that Park was worried about détente and other changes.[48] More skeptical, Kim Dae Jung argued that Park had heightened fears of North Korean aggression to ensure his permanent political position.[49] Antagonism toward the *Yushin* Constitution began among students and religious figures and then spread to opposition politicians as well. Not surprisingly, Park's reaction was to repress the dissent. His first emergency measure made it illegal "for any person to deny, oppose, misrepresent or defame the Constitution" or "to assert, introduce, propose, or petition for revision or repeal of the Constitution."[50]

Park's imposition of martial law and his general repression against perceived opponents spurred increasing attention and concern from diplomats working in Seoul. Stanley Zuckerman, who was the information officer and press attaché in the U.S. embassy between 1971 and 1973, remembers how his friends who were journalists were arrested by the Korean Central Intelligence Agency after "printing unacceptable stories" and suffered *falanga*.[51] As Zuckerman recalls it, Habib, who knew many of those journalists through regular poker games among other connections, "communicated firmly that press repression was a strong irritant in our relationship."[52] David Blakemore, who was an economic officer in Seoul, remembers that in 1971 Park "was getting a little more heavy handed. He had always been heavy handed but it was getting to be a little unpleasant, a little nasty. It was harder and more awkward for us to maintain a close relationship and be quiet about the repression that was going on."[53] Park's imposition of martial law and the new constitution, Blakemore says, "made me uncomfortable and it made most of the people in the embassy uncomfortable to have such an intimate and close relationship with that kind of government."[54]

Although the new constitution was seen as disruptive and largely unjustified by State Department officials in Seoul and Washington, when Nixon met with Korean prime minister Kim Chong-pil in January 1973 in the wake of Park's reelection, he did not suggest that the South Korean leadership change course.[55] When Kim Chong-pil brought up his government's plans for reopening the National Assembly and a timetable for elections, Nixon said, "I won't lecture you like some do on your internal affairs," sending a strong signal about the administration's lack of interest in South Korean abuses of power.[56] Yet Park was aware of growing concern about his record within government circles in Washington; therefore, in 1973 Korean officials launched a campaign to build more American support for Park and his *Yushin* Constitution, which targeted members of Congress, journalists, academics, and business people.[57]

Despite Nixon's declaration of nonintervention, a brazen attack by Park's regime forced U.S. involvement several months later when on August 8, 1973, South Korean agents kidnapped Kim Dae Jung from his room at Tokyo's Grand Palace Hotel.[58] He was driven to Osaka and put on a high-speed boat. Restrained with weights, Kim expected to be tossed into the sea. Instead, Philip Habib and Donald Ranard, the country director for

South Korea, quickly mobilized an effective campaign that was outside the normal chain of command at the State Department.[59] They and Japanese diplomats "made forceful appeals" to the South Korean government to save Kim's life, and officials in Washington issued a statement calling for his release, which occurred in Seoul five days later. Donald P. Gregg, who was the CIA station chief in Seoul when Kim was kidnapped, reported, "Habib made a representation to the Korean government saying it is your own agency that has done this, and you damn well better keep him alive or it is going to be a tremendous spot on your escutcheon and it will do huge damage to our relations."[60] State Department official Daniel A. O'Donohue remembers that Habib's message was, "The U.S. wants this man alive."[61]

At the same time, U.S.-based Korean organizations called on the United States to expel the Korean ambassador, Kim Dong-Jo, and to exert pressure on the Korean government to free Kim Dae Jung.[62] According to William H. Gleysteen, who returned to Washington shortly thereafter to serve as deputy assistant secretary of state for East Asian affairs under Habib, "The kidnapping of Kim Dae Jung caught peoples' attention in a spectacular fashion." In Washington, church groups, labor unions, and the press all responded.[63]

Talking to Kissinger and other State Department officials some months later, Habib argued, "I think Kim [Dae] Jung was not killed partly because of the reaction of the United States and the reaction of Japan."[64] Habib's reflections demonstrate again that U.S. officials were aware of the impact that their pressure could have on South Korean repression; left unsaid was that they rarely chose to utilize such leverage. Kim may not have been well known to a significant number of American elites—such as the economists who mobilized on Andreas Papandreou's behalf in the case of Greece—but key diplomats in Seoul and Washington were aware of his plight and acted quickly and forcefully to save his life. Ambassador Habib described the kidnapping as "stupid governmental thuggery." Moreover, the operation may have been counterproductive because, in Habib's view, the incident enhanced Kim's reputation among South Koreans.[65] After years in prison, in exile, and under house arrest, Kim became president of the Republic of South Korea in 1998, and he later recounted the story of his kidnapping when accepting the Nobel Peace Prize in 2000.[66]

One of the reasons that Kim's kidnapping drew such swift attention was that U.S. embassy officials in Seoul had maintained contact with him and other members of the opposition. Paul Cleveland, who was a politico-military officer in Seoul between 1973 and 1977, said later, "I did insist that it was proper and indeed our job to talk to the opposition. Accordingly, I saw Kim Dae Jung regularly during this period."[67] According to Cleveland, "We had a major interest in [Kim's] welfare."[68] Political Counselor Edward Hurwitz remembers that when Kim was under house arrest, Hurwitz hosted Kim at his house three or four times, primarily to speak privately with visiting members of Congress; embassy officials also visited Kim "on occasion," and Kim once had lunch at the deputy chief of mission's house. [69]

Similarly, George Lichtblau, the labor attaché in the U.S. embassy in Seoul from 1972 to 1975, was deeply involved with South Korean labor unions and with Catholic and Protestant churches that were targeted for government repression. He recalls that one of his roles was to be a "pipeline of information into the Embassy on civil rights abuses and torture." Lichtblau reports that he was "constantly under surveillance" but that Habib "fully supported my activities and wanted me to do this kind of work." Furthermore, in Lichtblau's memory, Habib and the deputy chief of mission at the time backed his efforts to intervene on behalf of a labor leader who had been arrested and, it was feared, might be killed.[70]

Such incidents invariably affected diplomats' views of their host governments. J. D. Bindenagel, an economics officer at the embassy during the mid-1970s, describes Park as "ruthless."[71] Richard A. Ericson, who became deputy chief of mission in Seoul at the end of 1973, recalls that Park's violations of human rights "went against all of our values, all of our instincts, etc. And that it could not help but fail to influence attitudes in significant sectors of the American public, including the Congress, and the media, to develop anti-ROK government attitudes and that this in turn would impinge heavily on our material and psychological support for the Korean government in all of its doings."[72]

Habib, who spent six years in South Korea between 1961 and 1974, was deeply connected with South Koreans through professional and personal ties. Along with these connections, his longstanding concerns about political and religious repression based on his family's and his own personal history led Habib to press for the rights of individual South Koreans facing abuses under Park as well as to urge official pressure on Park to alleviate human rights conditions more broadly.[73] Habib stretched the parameters of his official role to address human rights concerns when possible.

According to Lichtblau, there was a shift in embassy support when Habib moved to Washington in September 1974 to serve as assistant secretary for East Asian affairs and Richard Sneider arrived as the ambassador in Seoul.[74] As Hurwitz put it, Sneider "had no time" for dissidents.[75] There were also differences of opinion regarding Kim in the U.S. embassy. In Cleveland's view, Sneider regarded Kim as a "political hack"; Cleveland disagreed with that assessment and argued that Kim's remarks had to be reported to Washington because he was "the recognized leader of the Korean opposition."[76]

Kim's kidnapping did not stifle opposition to Park's government, and in October 1973, tens of thousands of students protested. In January, Park issued emergency decrees that made criticizing the constitution or pressing for its reform punishable by up to fifteen years in prison. William Butler, an American lawyer who traveled to South Korea on behalf of Amnesty International as he had to Greece earlier, characterized Emergency Decree Four, one of Park's repressive measures, as "one of the most extreme suppressive laws against students and universities anywhere."[77] Students who skipped their classes or who participated in demonstrations or even discussions of politics faced possible death sentences. Butler recounted reports by students' lawyers and relatives that they were subject to torture, including the use of electric prods.[78]

Students were not alone in expressing opposition or being persecuted. Sixty-one cultural figures, including the national poet Kim Chi Ha and other literary notables, demanded that "the basic rights of the people, including the freedom of conscience and freedom of expression . . . be guaranteed constitutionally." The government quickly responded by detaining the signatories of the petition.[79] According to Ericson, Kim Chi Ha became a cause célèbre in the United States, and members of Congress brought up his case whenever they visited South Korea.[80] Protestant ministers were also targeted by the regime, with ten arrested on January 21, 1974. During that year, Butler estimated, there were eleven hundred people imprisoned for political reasons.[81] In addition, he characterized the torture of political prisoners as a "foregone conclusion" and cited reports from detainees' lawyers, describing methods such as "forcing cold water through nostrils of individuals, causing extreme fatigue, the use of screams and yelps in adjoining rooms as a warning, and the physical beating of prisoners themselves." Butler offered evidence from arrested intellectuals who reported that they had been hung upside down and had suffered burns at the hands of their interrogators.[82]

Butler was well equipped to undertake a mission on behalf of Amnesty. He was staff counsel at the ACLU, worked closely with Roger Baldwin, and had argued and won two significant civil rights cases in front of the Supreme Court. His career, which also included considerable work with the International Commission of Jurists as well as service to the American Jewish Congress, Amnesty International, the New York City Bar Association, the New York Civil Liberties Union, and the International League for the Rights of Man, demonstrates the overlapping roles and commitments of many human rights activists in this era.

Escalating repression in South Korea drew more Americans to condemn Park's regime and call for Washington to influence his policies. The ILRM, in association with its affiliate, the International Human Rights League of Korea, called for the release of all political prisoners.[83] Christians for Democracy in Korea put together an extensive analysis of the political landscape there, which made its way to policymakers such as Senator James Abourezk (D-SD). The Committee for Human Rights in Korea, formed in 1974 by Fletcher School professor and former foreign service officer Gregory Henderson and Presbyterian leader Newton Thurber, was made up of academics and religious figures and worked to mobilize support for Abourezk's amendment to cut off military and economic assistance to repressive governments.[84] The World Student Christian Federation, the Board of Global Ministries of the United Methodist Church, and the National Council of the Churches of Christ in the USA also reported on repression in South Korea and expressed their concerns to members of Congress.[85]

Other voices outside of government circles condemning the Park regime included noted East Asian scholar and former ambassador to Japan Edwin O. Reischauer, who wrote in the *New York Times* that Park's regime "continues to trample on civil liberties and imprison its citizens for political reasons."[86] Therefore, he noted, "We face a conflict between our commitment to democracy and human rights and the strategic considerations that lie behind our military involvement in Korea."[87] He also wrote to Kissinger to express his concern about Park's declaration of martial law and his revisions to the constitution.[88] The *Los Angeles Times* also weighed in on "The U.S. and Repression in Korea," arguing that "the obligation to avoid intervention is not an obligation to continue supporting and strengthening regimes built on repression, nor is it an obligation to refrain from forthright criticism. South Korea is a case in point. Furthermore destruction of freedom and the mistreatment of those who protest that destruction is never a private affair. . . . The United States should recognize that it does, after all, stand for something."[89] Nevertheless, Nixon and Kissinger did not engage more deeply with reports of South Korean human rights abuses, focusing instead on Sino-American relations, the end of the war in Vietnam, and other international developments.[90]

Among the most significant nonstate voices regarding Korean repression were American missionaries living in South Korea.[91] Historian David A. Hollinger has described missionaries as developing "through their work abroad a concern for human equality," which translated into criticism of racism in the United States and human rights activism. This pattern manifested in Southern Rhodesia, South Korea, and Chile as well.[92] Missionary Randy Rice remembers that fifty people, mostly Americans, organized in South Korea in the late 1960s in opposition to Park's regime, calling themselves the Monday Night Group. Among other activities, they collaborated with Amnesty International to monitor trials and reached out to officials at the U.S. embassy in Seoul, reporting on human rights abuses. Both Ambassador Habib and Donald Fraser met with the Monday Night Group.[93] Missionaries even participated in a demonstration outside the U.S. embassy against what they viewed as "ineffective" diplomacy regarding human rights.[94] Unlike many other organizations focused on human rights during these years, women were involved in significant ways in the Monday Night Group, including, notably, Linda Jones, who worked to distribute clandestine materials.[95]

The missionaries' activism also inspired greater efforts in the United States. For example, after their visit to South Korea, where they interacted with dissidents and human rights activists, missionary Louise Morris reports that her parents became active in writing to members of Congress and to the White House.[96] In addition, Faye Moon spoke about opposition to Park's dictatorship at the July 1976 Women's National Assembly of the Presbyterian Church USA, and in her view, hearing her perspective on the dictatorship in South Korea inspired those women to write letters to U.S. officials and to support human rights activists in South Korea financially.[97]

Philip Habib's activism continued after he returned to Washington, where he sought to draw high-level attention to problems in South Korea by, for example, speaking about the issue at length in a meeting with Kissinger and other senior State Department staff: "The situation is now reaching a stage where I think [the relationship between the government and the opposition] is serious from the standpoint of our own interests." He went on to argue, "[Park] faces a serious problem of maintaining power, and that affects our interests because if you get political instability you can logically presume the possibility of North Korean adventurism and you can largely perceive the possibility of internal disarray in such a manner as it affects the military structure." Habib sought a reevaluation of American objectives in South Korea, arguing, "When faced with the reality of oppression, I think the United States has to make clear that it's not on the side of oppression—that it doesn't condone."[98] Kissinger remembers that his assistant secretaries, including Habib, were "insistent on sharing their own views forcefully if they felt I was the one in need of guidance."[99]

In both Habib's and Kissinger's telling, their first meeting in Vietnam set the tone for their relationship.[100] Habib remembers that Kissinger turned up at his office in Saigon, hoping to learn more about the war, and Habib said shortly, "Professor, you don't know a god-damn thing about this place. . . . You go around the country, spend a couple of weeks looking the situation over, then you come back and I'll have time to talk to you. In the meantime, get the hell out of my office."[101] In Kissinger's memory Habib had said, " 'I bet you are one of those Harvard smart alecs who knows everything.' Then he told me to go to the provinces and 'see what was really going on.' "[102]

Kissinger, however, was not convinced that Park's human rights abuses could produce instability that might threaten U.S. interests. In a classic expression of his position on human rights, Kissinger responded, "First, in general, I've tried to abolish the political science department in the State Department which tries to restructure the domestic situation of other countries—especially allies—because either we're involved because we have American foreign-policy interests or we shouldn't be involved at all. I don't think it is worth our investment to democratize Korea."[103] Kissinger's discussion was held at a time when Korean students faced mass arrests, torture, and potential execution under two emergency decrees that Park had issued to stem protests.

Habib and other officials continued to lobby the South Korean government on human rights, but without the imprimatur of Nixon or Kissinger, their influence was limited.[104] For example, Habib had advised Park not to execute those who violated South Korea's emergency measures because it would be "stupid."[105] Yet Park's ultimate decision to allow the executions to go forward illustrates that he felt empowered by Nixon's hands-off stance. Furthermore, Habib's freelancing did not go unnoticed in Washington. According to Donald Ranard, Kissinger admonished Habib in the spring of 1974 to reduce his entreaties to the South Korean government about its repression.[106] Kissinger's actions fit into a broader and recurring trend of efforts by the White House, and Kissinger specifically, to thwart human rights activism by diplomats and members of Congress. Ranard's reflections highlight the limits of that activism, even by an ambassador, during these years. According to a second, unnamed official who served in the embassy, Washington indicated that there would be "no change in U.S. policy no matter what you might report."[107] In Ranard's view, "The known disinterest of Kissinger for human-rights issues completely undermined any possible effectiveness those concerned in the department might have had."[108] Ranard argues that Kissinger's rebukes of aides who pressed human rights concerns created a "climate of intimidation" that stifled those who wanted to advance human rights in U.S. foreign policy.[109]

Disparate actors were attuned to South Korean abuses. Students from the University of Hawai'i issued a resolution condemning the death sentences of Kim Chi Ha and South Korean students. In addition, missionaries testified against Park's repression, and representatives of Amnesty International traveled to South Korea to monitor human rights violations.[110] However, in contrast to the plight of Soviet Jewry, for example, Park's actions drew less nongovernmental action.

One notable example was support for George Ogle. The case of Reverend George E. Ogle, a Methodist missionary, drew considerable attention within Methodist and other religious communities in South Korea and the United States. Ogle became involved in human rights activism in part due to an encounter with the wives of eight men who had been arrested by Park's government.[111] His public prayers on their behalf and his behind-the-scenes work precipitated seventeen hours of Korean Central Intelligence Agency interrogation at its notorious headquarters, followed by expulsion from the country when he refused to sign an apology for praying for the accused men.[112] Shortly after his expulsion, Ogle testified before Congress. His exodus produced considerable press coverage about his case and about abuses of human rights in South Korea generally, although relatively less coverage than violations in the Soviet Union and Chile did.[113]

Yong-jeung Kim also continued to press the U.S. government to shift its policy toward South Korea: "It appears that the United States has become a senior partner of the police-state establishment, and Seoul, an appendage of Washington."[114] The State Department assured Kim that it "has, through a variety of channels, formal and informal, in Seoul and in Washington, ensured that Korean officials are aware of the seriousness with which the United States views deprivation of human rights."[115] In much the same way that Johnson administration officials had oversold the degree of their pressure on the Greek junta, the response to Yong-jeung Kim was disingenuous at best. But, overall, the flow of correspondence to the White House was minimal, wide-scale protests did not develop, and anti-Park activism remained confined to a small, albeit passionate group.

In the absence of activist groups, journalists played a key role in raising American awareness of South Korean human rights violations, as Patrick Chung has demonstrated. Before 1972 American journalists had depicted South Korea as a loyal, anticommunist ally of the United States, but with the *Yushin* Constitution, observers revised their views. Chung shows that after 1972, the incidence of terms such as "dictator" and "authoritarian" to describe Park and his government increased meaningfully in U.S. newspapers.[116] According to Chung, "American journalists felt compelled to inform the American public of the South Korean people's plight."[117] *Washington Post* reporter Don Oberdorfer, who had served in Korea and was the paper's Northeast Asia correspondent between 1972 and 1975, wrote, "With the death sentence for a poet, the trial of an ex-president, the arrest of a bishop, the world has awakened with something of a start to the political condition of South Korea."[118] Jim Stentzel, a missionary-journalist based in Japan, remembers that Kim Dae Jung's kidnapping marked a real shift for him, as the two had talked in Tokyo only weeks earlier.[119] Examining the relationship between American journalists and South Korean dissidents shows evidence of a "boomerang effect," whereby South Koreans utilized foreign journalists to get around domestic obstacles in order to protest.[120] In Chung's view, the news coverage of Park's regime "made it impossible for U.S. policy makers to ignore the Park government's actions."[121]

Records demonstrate that despite Kissinger's hard line, members of the State Department's policy planning staff, led by Winston Lord, had a more nuanced approach to South Korea's poor human rights record; reflecting on problems of authoritarianism in East Asia, they noted in a memo that Korea had experienced "a major regression from the quasi-democratic system which had begun to take root by the late 1960s."[122] These diplomats expressed concern about cases "where it can be argued that U.S. assistance programs—by providing resources which help to keep incumbent regimes in power—in themselves constitute 'interference' in the internal affairs of those countries and, in effect, made us accomplices of authoritarianism."[123] Such a relationship was disconcerting for the policy planners: "Thus, for reasons of national interest, as well as to develop a policy more clearly in accordance with American political values, it is arguable that a more active and less ambivalent U.S. posture toward authoritarianism is necessary."[124] With this approach, there were multiple ways for the United States to signal its concerns about authoritarianism, including the suspension of high-level visits, an increase in communication with opposition elements, and a curtailment of bilateral exchanges. Yet the authors of this memo recognized the risks of publicly condemning and withholding substantive support from such governments; instead, they urged "reticence" as the administration's policy when dealing with authoritarian regimes in East Asia:

There is probably no government in East Asia against which we would wish to apply punitive measures, such as reductions in our assistance programs and other forms of cooperation, in response to that government's non-democratic actions. The complex of U.S. interests at stake in these various countries, and our fundamental objective of developing a stable equilibrium in the region militate against such measures and their unpredictable consequences.[125]

The United States, these State Department officials concluded, could take small steps, such as indicating disapproval through "gestures" and occasional comments on internal matters as well as engaging in more-active bilateral diplomacy to encourage liberalizing the political process. Such steps would "help to blur our identification with the non-democratic aspects of their regimes and reaffirm our conviction that human freedoms, where abridged should be restored as soon as possible."[126] Although certain State Department officials in Washington and Seoul were clearly uncomfortable with the Nixon administration's fervent support for Park, they, like activists outside the government, made little progress in shifting U.S. policy.

CONGRESSIONAL HEARINGS

With louder bully pulpits and the power of appropriation at their disposal, select members of Congress attempted to shape U.S. policy toward South Korea because of their concerns about the character of Park's leadership, the support of the U.S. military for a repressive government, and the negative way such an affiliation could reflect on U.S. foreign policy. In three sessions during 1974, the House Foreign Affairs Subcommittees on Asian and Pacific Affairs and on International Organizations and Movements held joint hearings examining the human rights situation in South Korea and discussing how the United States should respond to reports of violations there. In explaining the rationale for holding the hearings, Fraser argued, "The increasingly oppressive nature of the South Korean Government demands a thorough reevaluation of U.S. policy."[127] He specifically raised concerns about political prisoners, harsh sentences, due process, and torture. In his view,

U.S. military assistance to countries with oppressive regimes is not only morally wrong, but practically unsound. In deciding upon the level of military assistance to South Korea, we should have not only taken into account the threat of aggression by the North Koreans, but the fact that our assistance strengthens the South Korean Government's ability to oppress its own people.[128]

Fraser also sought to broach broader questions about whether the United States should send military assistance to repressive governments. The administration, not surprisingly, was more concerned with military stability than with human rights. During the hearings, acting Assistant Secretary for East Asian and Pacific Affairs Robert S. Ingersoll disagreed in principle with ending assistance to human rights violators, and he explained the department's position by suggesting that the suspension of aid removed a potential restraint on future repressive actions and deprived the United States of any leverage with the government.[129]

The 1974 hearings on South Korea brought together a range of experts from inside and outside the government. Gregory Henderson, a former foreign service officer, Korea expert, and founder of the Committee for Human Rights in Korea, testified that "Political repression, political imprisonment, political detention and incarceration, political torture and gross miscarriages of justice for the political preservation of the present regime are rampant in today's South Korea."[130] Documentation submitted to the subcommittees detailed 174 politically motivated arrests.[131] Representative Leo Ryan (D-CA) raised the concern that American support for the Park regime could produce anti-American sentiment in South Korea, and he directly linked the South Korean case to the relative inaction by the United States against Greek repression, which, he argued, had soured the Greek people on the United States. Ryan, thinking of his constituents, said, "They say, come on, you supported the government of Pakistan against India and lost, you supported the government of Greece and you went wrong there, you supported the government of South Vietnam and are knocking the hell out of people all over the place there."[132] At the conclusion of the second hearing, Fraser declared, "I should tell you that I am not prepared to vote to send American troops back in Korea in the defense of an essentially totalitarian regime. The issue is probably important to an increasing number of others because of our experience in Vietnam."[133] Whereas Johnson, Nixon, and Kissinger ignored South Korean abuses because of Vietnam, Fraser's declaration shows how Vietnam also served as a cautionary example of the risks of supporting authoritarian regimes and served to erode the Cold War consensus on U.S. foreign policy.

Park's regime also had supporters who testified at the hearings and sent supportive statements, suggesting, perhaps, that South Korean efforts to cultivate support in Congress had worked. For example, Representative H. R. Gross (R-IA) commented that the United States "dealt with a lot of dictatorships around the world" and should not single out South Korea.[134] In addition, Representative G. V. Montgomery (D-MS) pointed out that no U.S. service personnel or military equipment was involved in South Korean human rights violations, which he cited as evidence that U.S. military assistance should not be linked to the South Korean record, implicitly arguing that there was no need for congressional oversight.[135]

The hearings were one indication of congressional activism on South Korea. Other signals included an October 1974 letter to Ford in which members of Congress expressed concerns about the human rights situation in South Korea; they urged that "unless human rights are restored to the Korean people, the United States will begin to disengage from South Korea."[136] In addition, the House Foreign Affairs and Senate Foreign Relations Committees, led by Fraser and Frank Church, took initial steps to restrict military assistance to South Korea.[137]

In between the second and third sessions of hearings, Nixon resigned, and Ford took over the presidency. The administration's stance toward Park and human rights in South Korea, however, was unchanged. In the words of William Gleysteen, "As much as possible the [Ford] administration avoided confrontation over political and human rights issues, desisting from public criticism and generally relying on diplomatic and other traditional means to convey its views to the Park government."[138] In fact, Ford's first foreign trip was to South Korea.

In advance of Ford's planned visit to Seoul, interested citizens wrote to him, urging him to cancel. For example, Asian Studies professor Harold Sunoo suggested to Ford that his visit would "be interpreted by the Korean people that you are supporting President Park Chung Hee's suppression of their human rights."[139] Similarly, Yong-jeung Kim warned Ford that South Koreans would see the planned visit as "honoring the Park regime which is depriving them of their freedom and inalienable rights."[140] The United Presbyterian Church in the United States of America and the Association of Korean Christian Scholars in North America both wrote to the president in advance of his trip to signal their concerns about human rights violations in South Korea.[141]

In Seoul, Ford emphasized to Park that he sought to build a "personal relationship" and to ensure "continuity" in U.S.–South Korean relations. Ford also underscored his long commitment to South Korean security, dating back to his support for Truman's intervention in 1950. Based on available records, it seems that Ford, continuing the pattern of presidents since Johnson, did not discuss internal South Korean politics with Park.[142] In his memoirs, however, Ford writes that he spoke alone with Park about "the sensitive issue of human rights." Ford remembers telling Park that "a more reasonable approach" was necessary to mollify congressional critics.[143]

The 1974 hearings offered a sustained examination of South Korean human rights violations, which led members of Congress, including Fraser, to support limiting military aid. In Fraser's view, Park led "the most repressive and thoroughly anti-Democratic of all the governments with whom the United States has close relations."[144] An amendment to the Foreign Assistance Act of 1974 that was introduced by Fraser ultimately passed in both houses, limiting South Korea to $145 million in assistance rather than the $252.8 million that Ford had sought.[145] Fraser's amendment allowed for an increase in funding of $20 million if the Ford administration certified that South Korea was making "substantial progress in the observance of international recognized standards of human rights."[146]

In the aftermath of the hearings and related legislation, officials in the State Department reflected on U.S. policy. Habib and Kissinger remained divided regarding the potential for the United States to pressure the Park government effectively. In a discussion of Fraser's hearings, Kissinger complained, "[Fraser] is out of his mind. We don't have that kind of bargaining position." However, Habib argued that the United States should "approach Park" because Fraser "might try to end MAP [Military Assistance Program] or cut U.S. forces." Habib criticized Park's record and argued, "It is in our interests to get Park to moderate his actions."[147] Winston Lord warned, "The human rights problem might erode the ROK domestic cohesion." In the end, Kissinger said he was "not opposed to a telegram."[148] State Department officials in Washington subsequently cabled the embassy in Seoul, saying that officials there should "raise directly with Park our concerns." Kissinger directed the ambassador to meet with Park and emphasize that if he

persists in any long-term effort to implement emergency measure no. 9, it will inevitably affect support of important elements of our society for our Korean policies and programs. . . . Further, drastic actions against prominent domestic opponents of the government can only seriously complicate our efforts. (For example, a death sentence against poet Kim Chi Ha or prison terms for church leaders would seriously affect the ROKG image in the U.S.)[149]

Two days later Sneider cabled back to Washington to report that he had met with Park, as instructed, "to express concerns about impact on U.S. of ROKG Emergency Measure (EM) No. 9."[150] In response, Park "express[ed] understanding of Secretary's motives in raising this issue and recogniz[ed] pressures in U.S. on administration."[151] Nevertheless, repression continued, including the execution in April of eight prisoners for political crimes as well as stringent limits on political activity and limited freedom of expression.[152]

State Department telegrams from Seoul also indicate that U.S. officials did raise the issue of human rights violations with their South Korean counterparts as complications to bilateral relations. Ambassador Sneider reported that the embassy in Seoul had "pointed out the impact of domestic political actions on congressional and public support of U.S. commitments to Korea and urged the [government] to view treaty relationship as two-way street imposing obligations on its part and to recognize the continued potential for influencing U.S. opinion positively." In his appraisal, South Korean officials were concerned that, as with Vietnam, Congress might cut off its funding or even withdraw U.S. forces from the peninsula.[153] Yet, given that Sneider only highlighted disquiet within Congress and in some public opinion, but did not express high-level executive branch dissatisfaction, Park may have felt free to utilize repressive tactics.

Congressional attention to Park's abuses meant that embassy officials such as Richard Ericson had to devote considerable time to hosting "the United States Congress' more liberal members, who came in a seemingly endless stream to investigate political oppression and human rights violations and to determine whether the United States should support a government that resorted to such measures."[154] For example, Fraser and several aides traveled to South Korea in April 1975 to assess human rights conditions there through meetings with Park and opposition figures such as Kim and the poet Kim Chi Ha. According to Ericson, Fraser and his aides were not able to talk to dissidents because most of them had been removed from the capital in advance of the representative's visit.[155]

Congressional hearings on human rights in South Korea continued; in 1975 Fraser asked whether the United States' "special relationships" with some countries were "contributing to ends consistent with our democratic traditions."[156] A range of witnesses, including a South Korean defector and Donald Ranard, argued that the U.S. government and the American people were morally compromised by their ongoing support for Park. Ranard testified, "I find it unbecoming to our heritage and to our role in world affairs, that the United States should be tonguetied in expressing its revulsion and disdain for the violations of basic human rights that are taking place currently in Korea."[157] Harvard Law School professor Jerome Alan Cohen and Columbia University professor Gari Ledyard suggested that Park's conduct was weakening South Korea's security and urged greater U.S. condemnation of Park's record.

Habib's testimony before Congress in June 1975, underscoring the competing priorities that the United States faced in South Korea—"the maintenance of peace and security on the peninsula" while ensuring the observance of human rights—is particularly significant because of his activism on human rights issues. In his testimony Habib described human rights as being "valid foreign policy objectives in their own right," acknowledged congressional concern about ongoing human rights violations, highlighted State Department efforts to institutionalize attention to the issue, provided updates on Park's emergency decrees, and noted that the United States had "publicly expressed our regret" at the eight executions.[158] He sought to assure members of Congress that "the U.S. Government is genuinely and deeply concerned about human rights matters. This concern reflects both our own traditions as well as a realization that human rights and respect for them are valid foreign policy objectives in their own right."[159] His testimony revealed rising attention to human rights in U.S. foreign policy formulation and implementation, ongoing interbranch discussions on the issue, and continuing limitations on greater prioritization—in this case, that local, regional, and international considerations restricted the steps that the U.S. government would take in response to Park's abuses.

Repeated open discussions about Park's human rights record may have eroded broader public support in the United States for his government. For example, polling in July 1975 showed that declining numbers of Americans were committed to defending South Korea in the face of an attack. Whereas in May 1975 a plurality of Americans polled (43 percent) had favored sending U.S. troops, by July a plurality (46 percent) was opposed.[160] After the conclusion of the House hearings, Kissinger, likely concerned with growing congressional activism, met with Fraser and afterward asked his aides to pull together a memorandum that outlined possible implications of domestic unrest in South Korea.[161]

There is evidence that principals in other executive branch agencies differed on U.S. tactics regarding Park's repression. A memorandum concerning Secretary of Defense James Schlesinger's conversation with Park in Seoul noted that the second item the two discussed—after Japan—was human rights and the potential problems that the administration faced with Congress.[162] Schlesinger's approach was notable both in his decision to discuss human rights with the South Korean leader and in how high the issue ranked on their agenda. It is probable that Schlesinger's entreaty reflected that Pentagon officials were more concerned than Kissinger was that Park's repression could jeopardize congressional support for military programs in South Korea; alternatively, it might represent a broader evolution of the administration's position, as indicated by Kissinger's willingness to "send a telegram," although other documentation suggests that the former interpretation is more likely. For example, a Pentagon memorandum, presumably from January 1976, focused on the danger to the U.S. military presence in South Korea: "We have witnessed Congressional efforts to remove our troops by denying aid and threatening U.S. withdrawal."[163] Interestingly, when Ford asked Schlesinger, regarding his meeting in Seoul, "Did civil rights come up?" Schlesinger said he raised the issue only "indirectly."[164] Schlesinger's characterization likely reflects his efforts to bring up the issue in a "diplomatic" fashion. Separately, Ford's language shows how policymakers continued to blur civil rights and human rights as late as the mid-1970s.

By this point, South Korea was paying for almost all of its military expenditures, in a marked shift from the past, but the changing burden did not lessen apprehensions at the Pentagon. A March 1976 memorandum to Schlesinger's successor, Donald Rumsfeld, was explicit: "We are deeply concerned by the increasing repression in Korea and its impact on Congressional support of Korea."[165] U.S. officials were uncertain how to respond to such considerations. Harry Bergold, the acting assistant secretary of defense for international security affairs, told Rumsfeld, "It may become necessary for us to lean heavily on the Park regime in order to mollify U.S. Congressional and public criticism and retain support for our Korean posture." Bergold noted, "Dr. Kissinger is strongly opposed to any 'leaning' on Park."[166] Kissinger's position, however, had not prevented Schlesinger from raising the issue of South Korea's human rights record in his meetings in Seoul.

Congressional concern persisted, and in March 1976, Ted Kennedy and Alan Cranston (D-CA) called on the State Department to review South

Korean human rights practices as a step to reassessing U.S. assistance to South Korea.[167] The next month, 120 members of Congress communicated to the White House their unease with the United States' relationship with Korea: "The policies of President Park toward political dissidents not only violate internationally recognized standards of human rights but also raise serious questions about the supportive role of the United States in its relations with the Republic of Korea." They warned further, "Many Americans and Koreans suspect that United States military support somehow condones or even contributes to the long wave of repression, in the absence of strong public signals to the contrary from our government."[168] Later that year, in September 1976, eighteen senators wrote directly to Park to share their "profound distress" about actions taken against those calling for a return to democracy in South Korea.[169] Although there was momentum in Congress, other members did not waver in their support for Park, due to financial payments, anticommunism, and other factors.[170]

Congress escalated its intervention into U.S. foreign-policy making and ultimately passed legislation limiting military assistance to Korea for the 1976 fiscal year to $55 million and dramatically decreasing appropriated funds for fiscal year 1977 to $8.3 million. Congress expressed "distress" at "the erosion of civil liberties in the Republic of Korea" and asked Ford to share congressional concerns with South Korean leaders.[171] Fraser had sought to limit U.S. economic aid to South Korea for 1976 and 1977 as well, but the State Department and agricultural interests ultimately thwarted his efforts.[172] Ranard, however, argues that the House International Relations Committee's approval of Fraser's amendment, before its defeat in the full House, demonstrated heightened concern about American support for South Korea.[173]

In one of the final legislative-executive battles over South Korea during the Ford years, members of Congress requested to see the State Department human rights reports on South Korea, which were intended to facilitate decisions on foreign assistance. The State Department under Kissinger, however, made limited attempts to fulfill the June 1976 legislation mandating the reports.[174] Given Kissinger's intransigence, Congress responded by requiring the secretary of state to "transmit to Congress . . . a full and complete report . . . with respect to practices regarding the observance of and respect for internationally recognized human rights in each country proposed as a recipient of security assistance."[175] Unyielding congressional pressure ensured the eventual comprehensiveness of the reports. As will be discussed in greater length in the final chapter, the reports facilitated the institutionalization of human rights in U.S. foreign policy and remain a significant feature of the State Department's work.

During Ford's presidency, nongovernmental attention to human rights violations in South Korea persisted. Most notably, after a 1975 mission to South Korea, Amnesty International declared, "Torture is frequently used by law enforcement agencies both in an attempt to extract false confessions and as a tactic of intimidation." Amnesty investigators outlined thirteen methods of torture, including electric shock, beating, and burning. The report also recounted a lack of due process faced by detainees, harassment by the police, and poor prison conditions. In many of the cases profiled in the report, detainees were beaten with "the side pole of an army cot," a consistent detail that lends considerable credence to their claims.[176] In addition, individuals such as Harvard biologist George Wald traveled to Seoul in August 1974 to transmit a petition signed by seventeen thousand people asking for the release of political prisoners. While in Seoul, Wald met with several prisoners, including Kim Dae Jung, who reported that he was physically suffering.[177]

In the subsequent months, which coincided with the final stage of Ford's race against Reagan for the Republican nomination, Kissinger increased his public engagement with human rights as an issue, declaring, "America cannot be true to its heritage unless it stands with those who strive for freedom and human dignity." Yet, in evidence of his varied position on human rights, he also asserted, "We should not bemuse ourselves with false choices between defense or domestic needs, between security or social justice."[178] Speaking in Seattle in July 1976, Kissinger similarly signaled at least rhetorical concern about Park's record, saying, "We will continue to remind the South Korean Government that responsiveness to the popular will and social justice are essential if subversion and external challenge are to be resisted."[179] But, in a further indication that little had changed in Kissinger's commitment to nonintervention, he argued that the United States was not overly concerned with South Korea's human rights record: "We are not in Korea because of the practice of the Korean Government, but because of the importance that Korea has for the stability of Northeast Asia. Therefore we have to balance our security necessities against some of the feelings with respect to certain governmental practices."[180] Amid this legislative activity, on August 30, 1976, Kissinger wrote to the Korean ambassador in Washington to express the concern of members of Congress about restrictions on the rights of Korean citizens.[181]

South Korea was in the spotlight during the 1976 campaign due to the sharper focus on the Ford administration's record on human rights. In his second debate with Carter, Ford said, "I have personally told President Park that the United States does not condone the kind of repressive measures that he has taken in that country. But I think in all fairness and equity we have to recognize the [security] problems South Korea has."[182] In contrast, Carter effectively framed Ford's foreign policy—as formulated by Kissinger—as immoral because it neglected human rights. Although Carter sought to shift U.S. policy once in office, the American military presence in South Korea, and by extension U.S. support for Park, remained largely unchanged.

Transnational connections shaped activism against Park's regime by missionaries, foreign service officers, and members of Congress. Yet very few organizations focused on human rights abuses in South Korea, particularly in comparison to those that arose in connection with Greece, the Soviet Union, and Chile. What explains this disparity in nongovernmental activism? First, Kim was not a prominent figure with the American public, but rather was known mainly in American diplomatic circles. The lack of popular pressure was also due to the strategic significance of South Korea, its geographic and cultural distance from the United States, and minimal Korean diaspora in the United States.[183] Furthermore, the experience of the Korean War meant that many Americans who were deeply connected to South Korea might have been inclined to excuse the excesses of an anticommunist ally.

These factors made it easier for the White House to ignore Park's human rights violations. Johnson was overly focused on Vietnam and thus was most concerned with maintaining South Korean forces there.[184] His administration therefore devoted little attention to Park's human rights abuses, and Nixon and Kissinger were fundamentally opposed to intervening in the domestic political affairs of other countries. Only in the mid-1970s, when enough members of Congress threatened to reduce military assistance to South Korea, which could endanger U.S. national security interests in Northeast Asia, did the State and Defense Departments become more attentive to Park's record in order to ensure that it did not threaten administration priorities.

During these years, members of Congress were exercised with U.S. support for military dictatorships more broadly, and South Korea eventually became one of the most prominent targets. Fraser's extensive hearings in 1974 and 1975 enabled concerned Americans to detail Park's repression and signal their dissatisfaction with U.S. policy. In repeated sessions, disparate actors outlined the ways in which U.S. support for Park might be at odds with the country's stated commitment to upholding human rights, and Congress succeeded in limiting support to South Korea in 1975, 1976, and 1977. Although such actions had little effect on the South Korean political system, the United States had minimized its support of Park's repression, signaling greater significance for human rights in U.S. foreign policy.[185]

Chapter Five

TRANSLATING HUMAN RIGHTS INTO THE LANGUAGE OF WASHINGTON

American Activism in the Wake of the Coup in Chile

The overthrow of democratically elected Chilean president Salvador Allende in a violent coup on September 11, 1973, was the start of a repressive regime under General Augusto Pinochet, which lasted until 1990. As journalist John Dinges has characterized it, "The first September 11 was a day after which everything changed in Latin America."[1] The junta killed more than three thousand Chileans while in power, and approximately eleven hundred people were "disappeared" by the National Intelligence Directorate (DINA) and other arms of the military. In addition to the killings and arrests that are often noted in catalogues of Chilean repression, Pinochet's Chile sent two hundred thousand people into exile, which represented about 2 percent of the country's population.[2]

U.S. policy toward Chile was largely shaped by Secretary of State Henry Kissinger's skepticism about prioritizing human rights. Consistent with his worldview that influenced U.S. policy toward the Soviet Union, Southern Rhodesia, Greece, and South Korea, Kissinger maintained that human rights violations were internal matters in which the United States should not intervene; he even admonished one ambassador to Chile, whom he viewed as pressing the issue too forcefully, to "cut out the political science lectures."[3]

Despite ongoing White House support for Pinochet, many Americans viewed the Chilean government differently. American activism, which was spurred in part by the murder of two U.S. citizens in the early days of the coup, fit within a broader pattern of opposing U.S. support for right wing, anticommunist regimes. Those concerned with the United States' close ties to Pinochet's junta built on tactics that had previously proved effective, including conducting fact-finding missions by internationally respected NGOs, holding congressional hearings, making direct appeals to the White House, identifying high-level allies, targeting U.S. assistances, and increasing participation in efforts to signal displeasure with U.S. policy. Dismay at events in Chile led both liberal Democrats and more-radical leftists to undertake anti-Pinochet activities. Their participation in antijunta activism connected them with a broader and growing transnational community that was concerned about violations of human rights and laid the groundwork for new forms of activism in later years.

AFTER THE COUP

The threat to human rights presented by the military coup was immediately clear to observers inside and outside of Chile.[4] Soon after securing power, the junta announced an extensive list of Chileans who needed to turn themselves in to the Ministry of Defense.[5] The next day, Freedom House declared that Chile was no longer on its list of "free nations."[6] Furthermore, U.S. officials in Washington reported within days that there were "a few summary executions, . . . at least several thousand" prisoners, efforts to deport at least twelve thousand non-Chileans living in the country, and "heavy bombardments" on the capital.[7] The first protests against the coup in the United States were led by academics calling themselves the Chile Emergency Committee, who placed a full-page ad in the New York Times on September 23.[8]

Officials in Washington were hesitant to be seen as too welcoming of the coup. Although the Nixon administration had worked actively to prevent Allende's election and had undertaken efforts to destabilize his government, it still exhibited caution in its public response to the coup.[9] The junta immediately requested flares and helmets from the Americans, and U.S. officials expected that requests for ammunition and riot control equipment would be next.[10] Outlining possible responses, U.S. officials seemed most concerned with the public relations implications of their assistance to the junta, particularly relating to the issue of human rights.[11] U.S. ambassador to Chile Nathaniel Davis suggested that the United States "accommodate this request—discreetly if possible."[12] A memorandum for a meeting of the Washington Special Action Group, which managed crises during the Nixon administration, asserted that the Chilean government needed to foster "a reasonably good international image with respect to human rights." To use more-contemporary terms, the optics, not the actual human rights violations, were most significant in shaping U.S. policy.[13] In a memo to Kissinger, NSC staffers Richard Kennedy and William Jorden described Chilean actions a week after the coup as "mopping up," and as further evidence of the callous treatment of White House aides toward human rights violations in Chile, the two characterized the junta's policy thus far as "effective actions against terrorists and extremists."[14] Using language most associated with Kissinger's policy toward Vietnam, Kennedy and Jorden claimed that the United States' hesitation to recognize the new regime was a decision to wait a "decent interval" in order to allow other states the opportunity to formalize relations with the junta first. But by September 19, when they wrote to Kissinger, there were concerns that the United States could not wait much longer and that it needed to "reassure" Chile. [15]

The focus on the perception of U.S. policy was due to pressure Nixon felt from members of Congress, the public, and the press who wanted him to address human rights violations in Chile. U.S. officials struggled to balance the insistence that they make U.S. concerns known in Santiago with the realization that junta leaders would be "extremely sensitive" to such demarches and with the belief among U.S. leaders that the new Chilean leaders faced "serious problems of security."[16] High-level officials responsible for policy on Chile were thus caught between competing pressures, highlighting the extent to which the issue of human rights was becoming a factor in U.S. foreign-policy making.

ANTIJUNTA ACTIVISM

In the wake of the coup, Chileans opposed to the junta mobilized in many ways; in one formulation, lawyers joined with the Catholic Church.[17] Eventually some Chileans formed international connections, which linked them with groups such as Amnesty International. In addition, a North-South alliance developed among the Ford Foundation, former Allende officials, and Democrats in the United States.[18] According to historian

Tanya Harmer, "Exiles skillfully appealed to different audiences when mobilizing solidarity," and many antijunta forces connected through Mexico City [19] In addition, former foreign minister Orlando Letelier rallied antijunta activism from and in Washington.[20] Yet none of these efforts, which were often quite fractured, were particularly effective in stemming the junta's repression.

With limited ability for Chileans to influence the junta, international governments and NGOs were left to take a stand. The cause had some high-profile supporters helping it gain momentum; for example, folk singer Joan Baez sent a letter to Kissinger asking for an investigation into the use of torture and executions in Chile.[21] The involvement of prominent individuals, such as writer Rose Styron, who was a board member of Amnesty International USA, drew attention to allegations of Chile's abuses, and she wrote an account of human rights violations for the *New York Review of Books* that was particularly notable.[22] Styron's gripping essay, relying on Amnesty's reporting as well as other eyewitness testimony, described physical and psychological torture. One victim whom she highlighted recounted being tied to a table while wet and then repeatedly electrocuted before receiving "blows" to his "abdomen, ribs, chest, testicles, etc." Yet, he said, there were other "things that cannot be told" that were even more disturbing. Styron also recounted the abuse of teenagers, the lack of due process, and the targeting of professional groups such as doctors. Her account finished with a call to protest the junta in Santiago and its representatives in Washington as well as to support the efforts of AIUSA and the National Council of Churches.[23] *New York Times* columnist Anthony Lewis wrote about Styron's column, giving a wider audience to her discussion of young female prisoners "with their hair pulled out and their nipples and genitals badly burned."[24]

A wide range of organizations in the United States—some already established and many created in response to the coup—protested Chilean repression.[25] Existing groups, such as the Authors League of America and the Committee on Latin-American Studies at Harvard University, appealed to U.S. government officials to exert pressure on the Chilean junta to respect human rights.[26] Non-Intervention in Chile became a network of more than a thousand people who worked to free Chilean political prisoners through letter-writing campaigns and other efforts to influence American and Chilean leaders.[27] In addition, a number of new groups specifically focused on Chile, such as the Chicago Committee to Save Lives in Chile, the National Coordinating Center in Solidarity with Chile, the Chile Solidarity Committee, and the Chile Committee for Human Rights, sought to raise awareness through conferences, publications, rallies, and events, including one featuring Allende's widow, Hortensia, which was attended by approximately thirty-five hundred people.[28]

Similar to the movement opposing the Greek junta, Americans also mobilized against Pinochet's regime based on professional connections. For example, the Federation of American Scientists sponsored a mission to Chile in June 1974 to investigate the conditions of doctors there; groups such as the the Emergency Committee to Save Chilean Health Workers and the New York–based Lawyers Committee on Chile formed as well. The Ford Foundation funded a range of efforts to aid Chilean academics and students who had become refugees in the wake of the coup, making grants to organizations based in Argentina, the United States, Canada, and the United Kingdom; one organization working to place Chilean academics in the United States was the Latin American Studies Association.[29] The professional and geographic range of these efforts shows the diversity of Americans engaged with the Chilean case.[30]

The genesis behind many of the newly formed organizations was often idiosyncratic. For example, the wives of imprisoned former officials in the Allende government reached out to U.S. embassy officials in Santiago for help in facilitating their attendance at their husbands' trials and for improvements in the prison conditions and increased family visits.[31] The embassy used its standard excuse in these cases—that it could not make representations on behalf of non–U.S. citizens.[32] In its place, American citizens got involved. Former representative Charles Porter (D-OR) formed the Fair Trial Committee for Chilean Political Prisoners, and members of the group traveled to Santiago in April 1974 to monitor the trials of political prisoners.[33]

Several church organizations founded the Washington Office on Latin America (WOLA) to focus attention on human rights violations across Latin America in the wake of the 1973 coups in Chile and Uruguay.[34] Joseph Eldridge, one of WOLA's longtime leaders, had served as a Methodist missionary in Chile until the coup. His path to human rights activism had begun in segregated Tennessee, built upon a growing consciousness about race that he developed during his university years, manifested itself in protests against segregation and the war in Vietnam, and was influenced by liberation theology and his missionary training experiences.[35] As a missionary, Eldridge worked with others who were concerned about U.S. corporate and government influences in Chile. After the coup and the arrest of two Maryknoll seminarians with whom he worked, Eldridge left the country. Back in the United States, Eldridge was drawn into WOLA by his personal connection to the situation. His objective was to influence U.S. policy at a time when few members of Congress cared about Latin America—"the backwater of U.S. foreign policy."[36] To this end, Eldridge monitored hearings, collected information, and met regularly with members of Congress and their staff. In Eldridge's view, what WOLA did was "take a prophetic view of Latin America and translate it into the clinical language of Washington, the language of legislation and lobbying."[37] WOLA asked its network to write to members of Congress to pressure them to stop military aid to repressive governments as well as to disseminate information about abuses in Chile.[38] The organization also supported congressional hearings by suggesting witnesses and offering "its expertise in the region and its credibility."[39]

The other prominent branch of nongovernmental activism focused on Chile was pursued by solidarity groups—namely those who conceived of their efforts as being aligned with leftists facing repression in Chile. The National Coordinating Center in Solidarity with Chile (NCCSC), which was affiliated with the Communist Party of the United States, organized petition drives, facilitated speaking tours for Chileans, lent films and relevant literature, and organized a letter-writing campaign to Pinochet to "end torture in Chile."[40] The NCCSC was explicit that its campaign was following a "well-established and accepted vehicle of protest coming out of the Vietnam war."[41] The NCCSC also organized a national legislative conference and a People's Lobby in which more than two hundred people lobbied members of Congress to end assistance to Pinochet's government.[42]

THE CONGRESSIONAL RESPONSE

Members of Congress acted within a week of the coup by introducing concurrent resolutions to express their concerns.[43] In addition, Representative Dante Fascell (D-FL), through the Subcommittee on Inter-American Affairs that he headed, exerted pressure on the Nixon administration to share American distress at human rights abuses with the government of Chile.[44] During the five weeks following the coup in Chile, his subcommittee received 2,693 pieces of correspondence condemning the military and only two that were supportive, illustrating the sentiment of the American public.[45]

Senator Edward Kennedy's aide Mark Schneider notes, "There were maybe five Senators who were concerned at all about Latin America."[46] Their activism, however, would prove to be significant. In Schneider's view, Kennedy's interest in Chile stemmed from broader attentiveness to Latin America as an outgrowth of his older brother's Alliance for Progress initiative. Kennedy had also traveled to Chile twice before embarking on his congressional career; the first trip had been his honeymoon.[47] Kennedy began using his Senate subcommittee to focus attention on Chile almost immediately after the coup. The first hearing on "refugee and humanitarian problems in Chile" was on September 28, 1973.[48] In October, Kennedy proposed a sense of Congress resolution to urge the president to "deny Chile any economic or military assistance" until he certified the fulfillment of human rights obligations by that government; Kennedy declared, "This amendment expresses my own deep sense of shock at the continued violations of human rights occurring in Chile."[49] As it was nonbinding, the amendment had little effect. Later, his efforts would prove more successful. In a subsequent hearing, Kennedy connected his concern about U.S. policy toward Chile with his opposition to four other instances in which he viewed U.S. actions as inadequate—the aftermath of the coup in Greece, repression in South Korea, widespread violence in Bangladesh, and human rights violations in the Philippines.[50]

REACTION IN THE WHITE HOUSE

The administration responded to external calls for action by downplaying the Chilean repression but still claiming to convey stern messages, although, in fact, the content of American communications to Chile can be more accurately described as moderate. In one instance, in late September, U.S. ambassador Davis sought out Chilean foreign minister Ismael Huerta Díaz to discuss American concerns about detainees and due process for their cases. Davis reported the foreign minister's assertion that his government "shares fully our concern for human rights."[51] Yet Huerta was hesitant to allow State Department officials to disclose such assurances publicly. Davis secured some concessions on this point as a means to assuage congressional anger; the ambassador suggested that a statement outlining "the measures the Chilean government is taking to ensure protection of human rights" would "not cause serious trouble" for the junta. More broadly, in the wake of the meeting, Davis made a strong argument in favor of quiet diplomacy when he wrote to officials in Washington: "We will be more effective in protecting human rights of Chileans and foreigners if we can convince the Chilean government of our ability to talk about these matters in private and not to make the [government] the object of public humiliation and embarrassment."[52] When Ambassador Davis raised American concerns directly with Pinochet in early October, he responded with the same rhetoric as his foreign minister: "The Chilean government shares fully [your] concern for human rights, and is doing its best to prevent violations and loss of life."[53] Furthermore, Pinochet explained the junta's actions in the context of threats from leftist extremists who were attacking the military, which was an overstatement of their threat.[54]

The previous day, Huerta had met with Kissinger at the State Department. Kissinger had assured Huerta that the United States would not tell Chilean officials "how to run their business," but that American leaders would be uneasy with any practices that made U.S. foreign policy "more difficult." Also "difficult" for the United States would be supplying Chile with equipment that could be used in domestic repression.[55]

Chilean-American relations were complicated by a lack of cooperation regarding U.S. citizens in Chile. The U.S. embassy in Santiago reported that working through normal consular channels was ineffective and that it was forced to make informal contact with members of the military to locate and secure the release of American citizens.[56] Most were eventually freed and returned to the United States with firsthand accounts of violent repression. For example, Patricia and Adam Garrett-Schesh, who had been detained in Chile's national stadium, spoke with the American press about "mass executions" in Chile, and the negative publicity caused considerable concern in the State Department.[57] Several days later they testified about their experience before Kennedy's subcommittee.[58] Of greater concern, the murder of two American citizens, Charles Horman and Frank Teruggi, precluded many Americans from supporting positive relations with Pinochet.

The Horman and Teruggi cases would negatively color congressional and public opinion of the junta in the years to come and would complicate, to some degree, Chilean-American relations. After Edmund Horman returned from a trip to Chile, during which he learned that his son, Charles, had been killed, he wrote to Senator William Fulbright (D-AR) to express his frustration that the United States had not adequately supported the search for his son. Horman charged that the State Department's agenda was "to clear the Chilean government of responsibility and, at the same time, clear themselves of their obligation to hold a foreign government accountable for killing an American citizen." Horman accused the U.S. embassy of "negligence, inaction and failure" in connection with his son's disappearance and death.[59] As the issue festered, the U.S. embassy formally notified the Chilean Ministry of Foreign Affairs of the "strong Congressional and public interest" in the deaths of Horman and Teruggi. The embassy's memo, although dressed in diplomatic pleasantries, asked direct and tough questions about the Chilean narratives regarding Horman's and Teruggi's deaths, for which the government denied all responsibility, arguing that it had released both before they were killed.[60] The Chilean government stuck to its story, including at a November 26 meeting between the Chilean ambassador and Assistant Secretary of State for Latin American Affairs Jack Kubisch.[61] Several months later the U.S. embassy wrote to inquire whether any American citizens were being detained by the junta, which suggests that a degree of distrust had developed between U.S. officials in Santiago and the government on this issue.[62]

NONGOVERNMENTAL EFFORTS

As human rights abuses such as arbitrary arrest, violation of due process, torture, forced expulsion, and indefinite detention persisted, Amnesty International was quick to organize against the junta. Amnesty sent a three-person fact-finding mission to Chile in November 1973, made up of Frank Newman, California judge Bruce Sumner, and Amnesty researcher Roger Plant.[63] The resulting report argued that Chileans were being imprisoned for their political beliefs and that some prisoners had been subjected to torture and other inhumane treatment. According to the report's authors, "Among many immediate problems that distressed us— holding prisoners anonymously and incommunicado, torture, restrictions on the right to counsel, etc.—we single out preventative detention as perhaps the worst."[64] In releasing the report, Amnesty headquarters characterized the torture of political prisoners as taking place "on a large scale." Amnesty's secretary general Martin Ennals declared, "There is substantial evidence of a persistent and gross violation of the most fundamental human rights."[65] Amnesty International subsequently called on Chile to cease arrests and executions and worked to assist individuals in danger by issuing Urgent Action press releases, which were intended to provoke a rapid response when the subjects of the appeals were in imminent danger.[66] Due to its continued concern, Amnesty International again reported on ongoing torture in Chile in 1974.[67] By allowing Amnesty International to visit, the Chilean government sought to correct its negative image internationally, but the visit increased rather than decreased critical press attention.[68]

Amnesty's mission was the first of many after the coup. For example, the Women's International League for Peace and Freedom visited Chile early in 1974. The group toured some detention centers, spoke with victims of torture, and charged the junta with violating seventeen articles of the UN Universal Declaration of Human Rights.[69] The Chicago Commission of Inquiry into the Status of Human Rights in Chile also traveled to Santiago. Upon its return, commission members reported that a "campaign of terror developed by the junta seems to have assumed a systematic and organized character." In addition, it expressed concern about "politically motivated detentions" and torture as well as limits on the press and universities.[70]

The International Commission of Jurists also sent its secretary general, Niall MacDermot, as well as Max Planck Institute for Comparative Public Law and International Law professor Kurt Madlener and University of Pennsylvania law professor Covey Oliver to Chile in April 1974. Their resulting report enumerated a range of human rights that were being violated, including free assembly, participation in political parties, freedom of expression, freedom of movement, protection against undue search and seizure, and freedom from arbitrary arrest and detention. The ICJ delegation reported the decrease in effectiveness of amparo, a legal remedy akin to habeas corpus, and the fact that more than five hundred people were regarded as "disappeared." The ICJ lawyers found reliable evidence of torture, generally immediately following an arrest, which included "electric shock, blows, beatings, burning with acid or cigarettes, prolonged standing, prolonged hooding and isolation in solitary confinement, extraction of nails, crushing of testicles, sexual assaults, immersion in water, hanging simulated executions, insults, threats, and compelling attendance at the torture of others."[71] In the ICJ's view, "torture is likely to occur whenever detainees are held for a considerable time incommunicado and without access to a lawyer."[72] The report urged, therefore, greater attention to due process, including arrests based on written orders, limits on the time prisoners were detained incommunicado, notification of family members and lawyers of the detention, and other steps to regularize the process.[73] After the report's publication, MacDermott testified before Congress and described Chile as having a "highly repressive system of government."[74] Indeed, the ICJ declared that as of late October 1974, repression in Chile was "more ubiquitous and more systematic than at any time since the coup d'état."[75] Finally, the Inter-American Commission on Human Rights visited Chile from July 22 to August 2, 1974, and published a report recounting "extremely serious violations" of human rights, including the use of torture, detention of political prisoners as well as the lack of habeas corpus and due process.[76]

"REPRESENTATIONS AT APPROPRIATE LEVELS"

Despite widespread congressional and nongovernmental antijunta activism, U.S. executive branch officials still recycled the junta's claim "that it does not intend to persecute anyone for their ideas or for their support of the previous government and that it expects to release most of the people who have been detained."[77] Yet State Department records show that officials were aware of the scope of arrests and summary executions, noting that an "internal, confidential report prepared for the Junta" estimated the number of executions between September 11 and 30, 1973, to be 320. Furthermore, U.S. officials estimated that 13,500 people had been arrested and that between fifteen hundred and three thousand had died by mid-November 1973.[78]

Given domestic pressure, the State Department considered intervening with Chilean officials to convey its concern and to explain how Chilean repression was affecting the U.S. government's ability to maneuver. The State Department seems to have been particularly concerned with how Chilean human rights practices might influence congressional action on foreign aid and military assistance, which would be a growing issue in the months and years to come.[79] In response, the new U.S. ambassador to Chile, David Popper, notified State Department officials in Washington in April 1974 that he was "beginning to carry out department's instructions to weigh in very confidentially and carefully with government in effort to induce it to ease up on its current human rights practices."[80] Writing to Washington, Popper warned that controversial Chilean trials could occur as Congress debated foreign aid. Notably, Popper said, "I question whether we can be put in position of advising Chilean re timing of their judicial proceedings." Popper rightly recognized that that would be a considerable intervention into Chilean affairs, but his consideration of such a step indicates U.S. officials' concerns about the impact of these trials on U.S. foreign policy.[81] On that day, April 4, Popper saw Huerta and expressed the State Department's unease "over continuing criticism of junta for alleged human rights violations." The U.S. ambassador highlighted the criticism rather than the violations themselves, which he qualified as "alleged." Popper urged the junta to offer "evidence that the rights of accused persons were being protected" in order to assuage congressional opinion.[82] Reporting back to the State Department, Popper suggested a "very high-level approach" to Huerta on human rights during his upcoming visit to the United States to convey the significance of the issue politically.[83] To a greater degree than with Greece or South Korea, the United States did seem to be making "appropriate representations at appropriate levels to the government of Chile," as a U.S. official put it. Demonstrating the degree of sensitivity around such communications, however, the Chilean foreign minister claimed not to know about such protests.[84]

DISTRESS AT CHILEAN ABUSES

The House Subcommittees on Inter-American Affairs and on International Organizations and Movements regularly held joint hearings on Chile that highlighted Chilean human rights abuses and juxtaposed them to the administration's efforts to downplay concerns and decouple human rights violations from U.S. foreign policy overall. In assessing the Chilean record based on his participation in Amnesty's fact-finding mission, Frank Newman estimated that several thousand political prisoners remained in custody and asserted that Chile had misrepresented its record on human rights.[85] Yet he did say that the situation was improving, arguing that there were "fewer killings" and "less torture" and that thousands had been released from prison. Charles Porter, the former representative from Oregon, who had traveled to Chile with the Fair Trial Committee for Chilean Political Prisoners, like Newman, divided his testimony into "good news" and "bad news." The negatives—including ongoing use of torture, contravention of the Chilean constitution, and problems with due process—still outweighed improvements, leading Porter to advocate that the United States end military aid to Chile.[86] Distress about the repression in Chile built upon earlier outrage at the how little the executive branch was responding to human rights violations in South Korea, Greece, and Brazil. These connections were recognized by State Department officials, who suggested that Chile was "becoming another Greece."[87]

Former attorney general Ramsey Clark traveled to Chile in the spring of 1974 as a trial observer, and he testified before Congress, "There are no human rights in Chile today in the only sense rights have value. The military government of Chile can transgress any human right with impunity; for any reason it chooses, or no reason at all, and [this] goes on regularly in Chile."[88] In dramatic testimony, Clark described the consequences of the coup as "a violent and lawless reign of arbitrary power dealing death to thousands, imprisonment and torture to tens of thousands, and terror to hundreds of thousands."[89] Although State Department officials acknowledged failings in Chile's human rights record, they would not tie this to withdrawing support. Fraser expressed considerable frustration with the testimony of Deputy Assistant Secretary of State for Inter-American Affairs Harry W. Shlaudeman, saying, "I don't find in your statement any indication that human rights considerations had any practical effect on shaping U.S. relations with Chile."[90] Showing his exasperation with U.S. policy, Fraser asked, "Since the military coup in Greece in 1967, we have had essentially the same statements from the Department with respect to the Government of Greece, and there has not been any significant restoration of democratic liberties. Is there any reason to think there will be a different pattern in Chile?"[91]

Although members of Congress were limited in their ability to affect U.S. foreign policy, they could exert influence through the "power of the purse." As was the case with Greece and South Korea, members of Congress used their role in appropriations to shape U.S. policy. Indeed,

Representative Fascell framed the May 23, 1974, hearing as part of an effort to determine how much, if any, economic and military assistance should be granted to Chile. Fascell asked several witnesses for their position on American assistance, suggesting that the Chileans were "desperate" for economic assistance and believing they required further military assistance in the face of a serious threat from Peru.

Members of Congress increasingly viewed withholding economic and military assistance to be a means of accomplishing two goals: protecting human rights and separating the United States from repressive regimes. Using this tactic with Chile, South Korea, and Greece, members of Congress had achieved a degree of success. In a letter to a constituent, Fraser outlined his philosophy on tying military and economic assistance to human rights:

My general impression is that in the absence of an overriding U.S. security interest, military assistance should be withheld from an authoritarian regime—especially one which shows no sign of progressing in the restoration of the rule of law and the protection of basic human rights. . . . Generally, aid which is directly supportive of an authoritarian regime such as budget support should be avoided for the same reasons that military aid should be withheld.[92]

As the subcommittees held their hearings, the State Department sought to prevent any limitations from passing the full Congress by arguing that Chile's human rights record was improving and that the United States should maintain close relations with, rather than face estrangement from, Chile.[93] As it turned out, Kennedy, Fraser, and their allies were able to garner enough votes to cut off all new military assistance to Chile for 1975. Kennedy's 1974 amendment passed the Senate by a vote of forty-seven to forty-one. It did not, however, expressly prohibit military aid that was already in the pipeline or commercial sales, and Kissinger resisted implementing the legislation, often using legal arguments to skirt congressional intent.[94] In Joseph Eldridge's view, Kennedy's amendment was a "huge breakthrough" because it "convinced a dubious Congress that they could take on the administration and win."[95] Kissinger, on the other hand, characterized it as a "disaster."[96] Despite Kennedy's amendment, the White House sought to secure congressional support for a $15 million program of spare parts for Chile in 1976.[97] As with Greece, U.S. officials worried that withholding military assistance to Chile might create a "group of Nasser-like colonels."[98]

Shortly thereafter, Kennedy attached an amendment to the International Security Assistance and Arms Export Control Act that banned any shipment of U.S.-manufactured weapons to Chile, heightening the role of the legislative branch in decisions about foreign military sales. The amendment was intended to cut off cash sales not expressly prohibited by earlier efforts.[99] It banned all military assistance, credits, and cash sales of military equipment to Chile. Only the pipeline of funds that had been appropriated but not yet spent remained, and Chilean officials exerted considerable pressure on Ford administration officials to extract them.[100]

Whereas initially Congress had settled for a declaration that Chile must respect human rights and had reduced military assistance for 1974 to $16 million, its more-extreme actions signified growing discontent with the administration's policy.[101] The International Security Assistance and Arms Export Control Act of 1976 marked the first time that Congress had ended military assistance to another country without any exceptions or loopholes. Yet, after the bill banning additional military assistance to Chile had been agreed on in conference but before it had been signed in the White House, the Ford administration pushed through $9.2 million of military supplies to Chile. The maneuver, which demonstrated the lengths to which the administration would go to continue the flow of military assistance to Chile, angered Hubert Humphrey, who called it a "shoddy deal," and Kennedy, who labeled the effort "outrageous."[102]

REACTION IN NEW YORK: THE UNITED NATIONS AND CHILE

As with Southern Rhodesia, UN diplomats were highly engaged on Chile, which reinforced activism in the United States and constrained Washington to some extent. In 1974 the UN General Assembly expressed concern about Chile's human rights record, particularly relating to torture, political imprisonment, and indefinite detention, and voted ninety to eight, with twenty-six abstentions, including the United States, to appeal to Chile to release its political prisoners.[103] Chile's decision to bar the UN Commission on Human Rights' ad hoc working group, despite assurances from the government that it would be granted entry, angered many diplomats at the UN.[104]

Without visiting Chile, the UN working group nonetheless described the situation there: "The chaotic and inhuman brutality which characterized indiscriminate arrests in the immediate period following the coup of September 1973 has been replaced recently by more systematic methods directed against selected individuals." According to the working group, prisoners in Chile faced poor conditions of imprisonment as well as physical and psychological torture, whereas Chileans more broadly faced a range of violations of their human rights.[105] The UNGA therefore extended the working group's mandate and called on Chile to allow the body to conduct its visit.[106]

Given widespread condemnation at the UN of the junta's record, as well as that of the apartheid government in South Africa, which the United States supported, the United States sought to reframe the debate at the UN to deflect criticism from itself and its allies. To that end, Daniel Patrick Moynihan, the U.S. ambassador to the UN, called for a worldwide amnesty for political prisoners in November 1975, a more aggressive position than the United States had previously taken; then, however, he criticized UN committees for "selective morality" and, noting that they had been focused only on the plight of political prisoners in South Africa and Chile, asked, "Is there, however, any reason to stop there, to limit our concerns to only two members of the United Nations, when there are altogether 142 members?"[107] He pointed out that many of the countries condemning the records of South Africa and Chile had political prisoners of their own.[108] Moynihan's tack echoed Chile's efforts to undermine criticism of its human rights record by suggesting that many of those states that targeted the junta were themselves using the same tactics. Moynihan's speech also served as a defense of Chile in that he noted that the regime had allowed international observers such as Amnesty and the Red Cross to visit.[109]

FRUSTRATION IN WASHINGTON

In a signal of its frustration with the press coverage of Chile in the *New York Times* and a range of other publications, the Chilean embassy in Washington chose to implement an advertising campaign in late 1973 and 1974 to change its image in the United States.[110] Similarly, Chilean ambassador to the United States Walter Heitmann was so frustrated by *Washington Post* coverage of the situation in Chile that he wrote a letter to the editor refuting claims in the newspaper.[111] The embassy's actions suggest that anti-junta activism was striking at the government's sense of impunity; it also prompted increased focus from U.S. officials.

American policymakers were also cognizant of the increasing need to manage the press regarding Chilean-American relations. When the NSC considered a visit by foreign minister Patricio Carvajal, one potential drawback was that news of the meeting would inevitably leak. The NSC was particularly concerned about the potential that the *Washington Post*'s Jack Anderson would write a column.[112] Anderson was one of the most prominent critics of U.S. policy among journalists, repeatedly chronicling Chilean repression and American complicity in the junta's coup.[113] Reporting by Anderson, Seymour Hersh of the *New York Times*, and others enabled the American public to discuss the intersection of human rights and U.S. foreign policy.[114]

Efforts to improve Chilean human rights violations through the executive branch, either directly or indirectly, remained at a stalemate through the transition from Nixon to Ford. A State Department briefing paper for Ford after his inauguration identified Chile as "the focal point of international criticism, seriously affecting its image and our ability to provide assistance."[115] The memo for Ford did not whitewash the situation; it noted that the Chileans had engaged in summary executions, massive detentions, and general human rights violations and that the abuses complicated American-Chilean relations: "The Junta looks to the United States for help and support. But we in turn are seriously hampered by hostile Congressional attitudes. It is virtually certain that the Foreign Assistance Act this year will restrict military assistance to Chile. A ceiling on economic aid is also possible."[116] The memorandum's authors justified a hands-off approach by noting that "undue pressure on human rights" could undermine the junta.[117] According to Thomas D. Boyatt, who served as deputy chief of mission in Santiago from 1975 to 1978, "The Pinochet regime was committing human rights violations, and we were reporting these, and suggesting to some degree we ought to do something about it. And Kissinger didn't want to hear that. So we had sort of a realpolitik from the executive branch, and human rights driven pressures from the legislative branch, and the media, and so on. And we were in the middle."[118] In a pattern that can be seen in previous chapters, officials in Washington favored caution more than U.S. diplomats overseas did.

Many news outlets were broadly critical of U.S. policy toward Chile, and op-eds disavowing the regime persisted. For example, Anthony Lewis of the *New York Times* made a forceful argument for why Americans should care about human rights violations in distant places: "American attitudes do make a difference—an enormous one. We cannot remove totalitarian regimes, but we can shame them. And we can help their victims. All of which makes it depressing that the reaction of the United States Government to official terror, in Chile and elsewhere, so often appears to be a studied indifference."[119] Continued press coverage of the junta's measures in Chile was in part due to NGOs' efforts to keep the topic in the news. Joseph Eldridge, for example, remembers that he talked regularly with journalists he hoped to influence, introduced them to Latin American dissidents, and shared leads with them.[120]

More significantly, as he had in previous instances, Ambassador Popper raised human rights concerns in a meeting with the Chilean minister of defense Oscar Bonilla in September 1974. In response, Kissinger, using a formulation he often deployed to diminish State Department officials concerned with human rights, urged the ambassador to "cut out the political science lectures."[121] Press reports of Kissinger's comments provoked those who were active on human rights, including Fraser, who found his actions, "outrageous—incredible." Fraser declared, "In effect, the Secretary of State has dressed down the Ambassador for raising the human rights issue."[122] Fraser wrote directly to Kissinger to express his displeasure, asking the secretary of state to "clarify" his views.[123] Kissinger's defenders asserted that he was upset only because Popper raised the issue in a meeting focused on military assistance, but the explanation did not convince many critics.[124] According to Hersh's reporting, Kissinger's message had its intended effect—Popper's attention to human rights in discussions with Chilean officials subsequently diminished.[125]

Poor treatment of U.S. citizens continued to cause considerable problems in U.S.–Chilean relations, particularly when American citizens' stories made their way into the press.[126] For example, a notable Jack Anderson column in November 1974 detailed the psychological torture and physical abuse that U.S. citizen Amy Conger suffered in Chilean custody as well as other violence that she witnessed or saw evidence of while imprisoned.[127] Conger's situation was particularly problematic for Chilean-American relations because the U.S. embassy had not been notified of her detention, as it should have been under the Vienna Convention on Consular Relations.[128] After her return to the United States, Conger sought to influence U.S. policy toward Chile by writing to members of Congress with her story.[129] After reading her account, Representative Paul Findley (R-IL) characterized Conger's report as "most astonishing" and "an eye opener." He pledged that he would raise the issue of her "inhuman treatment" in discussions of foreign assistance.[130]

As with other cases of human rights violations during these years, Congress and the State Department diagnosed the situation differently and prescribed incompatible U.S. responses. More meaningfully, there were significant differences among key officials within the State Department. For example, in a December 1974 meeting with his aides, Kissinger questioned how bad the human rights situation in Chile was in comparison to Allende's years in power. Assistant Secretary of State for Inter-American Affairs William D. Rogers noted that in terms of freedom of the press and freedom of association, Pinochet's regime was certainly worse, suggesting that Kissinger faced assistant secretaries in addition to Philip Habib who assessed human rights situations differently than he did.[131] Two days earlier, Kissinger had asked Rogers if Pinochet's record was inferior to its neighbors. Rogers answered in a word: "Yes."[132] Rogers and Kissinger continued to spar over how "bad" the human rights situation in Chile really was. Almost a year later, Rogers argued that Chile's record was "as bad on human rights as you can find."[133]

Kissinger repeatedly expressed exasperation to his aides about activism on human rights. In one instance, Kissinger sarcastically remarked, "We won't rest until we have left wing governments in power everywhere."[134] Later that month, Kissinger was again irate about the infringement on executive branch authority, declaring, "My position is that I don't yield to Congress on matters of principle."[135] In a meeting the following week, Kissinger expressed frustration that public opinion supported ending foreign assistance. He and his staff expressed concern that Korea, the Philippines, and Vietnam would be Congress's next targets, suggesting that the "principle" of concern to Kissinger had higher stakes than just assistance to Chile.[136] The United States' ability to support its Cold War allies and protect its national interests were at risk due to congressional interference, in Kissinger's view. The secretary of state repeatedly warned that if pushed or if denied military assistance, Chile might become the next Portugal, which had experienced a left-wing coup the previous year.[137] When Kissinger had warned that cutting off military sales might imperil sales to South Korea, Habib had argued that the South Korean case was "clearer," likely due to security concerns on the Korean peninsula. Habib's comments suggest, however, that U.S. officials did not see "clear" security considerations at stake in Chile.[138]

Although Kissinger asserted that he would not alter U.S. policy due to congressional sentiment, the reality is that it did influence him, or at least his tactical decision-making. At the end of December 1974, the Chilean government asked that Kissinger stop there during his upcoming trip to the region, likely believing that a visit by the secretary of state would convey some legitimacy for its leadership in the face of international pressure.[139] Kissinger pointed out that such a decision "would be unpopular in the United States and entail a domestic political price" for the United States."[140] Nonetheless, Kissinger reported that he was giving "serious consideration" to a stop in Chile and noted that it would be easier if improvements in human rights could be made, and if Pinochet sent signals that he was willing to take positive steps to facilitate a visit.[141] Assistant Secretary Rogers pointed out to Chilean leaders that the United States would face less criticism for a Kissinger visit if more prisoners were released or if the state of siege was lessened.[142] It was revealed both in cables from Santiago and in NSC discussions about an upcoming foreign policy address by Ford—where an early draft was characterized as "a chastisement of Congress"—that American diplomats prioritized lessening opposition to a Kissinger visit to Chile over improving human rights practices there.[143] In the end, Kissinger did not stop in Santiago. His decision was one signal that there were limits to U.S. support for the junta.[144]

Kissinger nonetheless met with Chilean leaders at the Organization of American States (OAS) General Assembly in Washington that same month. A State Department briefing paper for Kissinger's meeting with Foreign Minister Carvajal offered a highly distorted view of international criticism of Chile's human rights record, characterizing it as "an effective international campaign orchestrated by the Soviets and designed to isolate and topple the [government of Chile]."[145] Kissinger was to assure Carvajal that the United States would make as much funding available to Chile as possible through Public Law 480 grain sales, a $55 million housing guaranty, and the extension of credits from international institutions, which were some of the various ways that Kissinger compensated for legislation that had been passed in Congress.[146]

As Chilean human rights practices remained largely unchanged into 1975, there were policy differences within the embassy in Santiago, with several foreign service officers proposing that the United States "inform [the Chilean government] that we will take no new initiatives to assist Chile politically, economically, or militarily unless and until its human rights practices have reached an acceptable standard," because the existing policy of "friendly persuasion has not worked." Popper, however, argued that it was impossible for "a major change of this character in U.S. policy toward Chile to be justified in present circumstances."[147]

NSC records make it clear that there were also disagreements throughout the government about the best course forward, with the State Department's Bureau of Inter-American Affairs expressing the most concern about supporting the junta militarily or economically.[148] For example, the bureau's Richard J. Bloomfield suggested that the United States needed to signal its displeasure with Pinochet by targeting the Chilean government on sensitive issues: debt rescheduling, loans, condemnations at the UN, or arms sales. He asserted that the United States should reconceive the significance of Chile's human rights abuses: "The human rights problem in Chile may not be 'secondary' but may be a major U.S. interest in the present domestic and international context." Bloomfield argued that the United States should not overlook human rights violations in Chile in order to ensure a warm relationship with the junta in Santiago.[149]

In contrast, other parts of the State Department as well as the Departments of Treasury and Defense favored arms sales to Chile. For example, James Wilson and Ronald Palmer, officials in the State Department's Office on Humanitarian Affairs, argued,

We do not believe that continued withholding of security assistance to Chile will improve [the government's] human rights performance. . . . Providing U.S. military aid does give credibility to the charge that we support a repressive regime. Nevertheless, we believe that the best policy is to restore security assistance while increasing our efforts to persuade the [government] to reduce human rights violations.[150]

Inter-American Affairs continued to oppose listing Chile on the foreign military sales credit list and approved only minimal sales ($10 million) for fiscal year 1976; here, Rogers and his bureau were not in line with Kissinger's policy.[151] Debating U.S. policy with Kissinger, Rogers pointed out that the United States had been "pretty forthcoming" in terms of aid and asserted, "Who governs Chile and what they do about human rights . . . are absolutely separate."[152]

As the U.S. government deliberated, political repression continued, and opposition to Pinochet's regime did not abate among Americans concerned with human rights. One diplomat based in Santiago told a *Time* magazine journalist, "With the single exception of detainees released, I defy you to find any tangible improvement in human rights."[153] Only further inflaming its opponents, the junta made tone-deaf political moves, such as its decision to expel a *Washington Post* journalist and the previously mentioned cancellation of the UN human rights mission in July 1975.[154] As Popper put it, they "must have some kind of death wish."[155] Furthermore, in December 1975 hearings before Congress, Reverend Daniel Panchot, who had been arrested, held incommunicado for twelve days, and then expelled from Chile, gave an account of the Chilean system of detention and torture based on his own experience.[156] Other witnesses testified that Chileans faced infringements on their rights to free expression and academic freedom.[157] Activists remained focused not only on the junta's repression, but also on U.S. complicity; according to Reverend Philip Devlin, continued U.S. support for the Chilean junta was leading to "a tremendous loss in the moral values the United States pretends to promote, especially among those peoples who respect human lives and human dignity."[158]

A flashpoint in congressional and public frustration with U.S. policy toward Chile occurred when, in testimony before the House Armed Services Subcommittee on Intelligence, CIA director William Colby acknowledged that the CIA had devoted more than $8 million from 1970 to 1973 to destabilizing Allende's government. Not only were members of Congress dismayed at the revelation, they were also angered to conclude that the administration had deliberately misled them about American involvement in Chile during the Allende years.[159] Allende's widow charged that such actions made U.S. leaders "morally" responsible for Pinochet's coup.[160] Later that year Representative Michael Harrington (D-MA) sued the CIA in federal district court in an effort to prevent further covert intervention in foreign countries.[161]

Some on Kissinger's staff, including director of the policy planning staff Winston Lord, proposed in September 1975 ways to reduce friction with Congress over human rights, including acknowledging abuses in Chile and reducing foreign assistance. Kissinger, however, refused to agree to public or private criticism of countries for their human rights records or to propose reductions in foreign aid on that basis, which continued his pattern of rebuffing Lord's prodding to modify U.S. policy.[162] The State Department under Kissinger persisted in its confrontational approach to congressional legislation by disagreeing whether the Harkin Amendment, a prohibition on economic aid to governments that engaged in gross violations of human rights, applied to Chile, arguing, "The Department of State believes a serious question exists as to whether Chile is a 'country which engages in a consistent pattern of gross violations of human rights.'"[163] As opposed to some State Department officials who regarded reports of torture in Chile as "circumstantial," however, James Wilson, the new coordinator for human rights in the State Department, characterized Chile as a "classic example" of a state that engages in a "consistent pattern of gross violations of internationally recognized human rights."[164] As will be described in the next chapter, interbranch tensions were further exacerbated when Kissinger withheld from Congress the 1975 human rights country reports that the State Department had drafted, in part due to the wide range of human rights abuses that they catalogued and his characterizations of the judgments as "subjective."[165] In response, members of Congress passed more-stringent legislation intended to clarify abusive countries' human rights records and ensure that they would not receive foreign assistance.[166]

Not only would Kissinger not take steps to mollify congressional critics, he actively undermined diplomatic criticism of Chile's human rights record by repeatedly signaling his lack of concern about human rights abuses to Chilean officials, such as when he told foreign minister Patricio Carvajal, "I hold the strong view that human rights are not appropriate for discussion in a foreign policy context."[167] Similarly, in his meeting with a Chilean official in September 1975, Kissinger said, "I read a Briefing Paper for this meeting and it was nothing but Human Rights. The State Department is made up of people who have a vocation for ministry." Kissinger described criticism of Chile's record as "a total injustice," but he noted, "It would help enormously if something can be done."[168] In these meetings, as political scientist Kathryn Sikkink puts it, Kissinger gave "verbal green lights" to Chilean officials, which were intended to portray American concern about human rights violations as limited to a few members of Congress.[169]

Kissinger's disregard for congressional opposition to Pinochet was epitomized by the U.S. government's welcoming of Manuel Contreras Sepulveda, the head of DINA—the intelligence directorate responsible for many of the human rights violations in the aftermath of the coup—to Washington in October 1975.[170] Contreras's visit was for the ostensible purpose of briefing Congress and other U.S. officials on Chile's "human rights" policy. As Heraldo Muñoz, a Chilean diplomat who was in exile in the United States at the time, said, "It was unbelievable: the executive head of the bloodiest repression machine in South America traveled to Washington to explain Pinochet's human rights policy."[171] Indeed, the CIA regarded Contreras as "the principal obstacle to a reasonable human rights policy with the Junta."[172] Contreras, of course, dismissed reports of Chilean human rights abuses as a Marxist conspiracy: "There is no torture, and there wasn't much before."[173] Contreras's visit was a testament to the undiminished executive branch commitment to the junta and a signal of how little congressional opposition was initially perceived to be a threat to U.S. foreign policy prerogatives.

Nongovernmental activism against Chilean human rights abuses continued. The NCCSC focused on the release of prominent political prisoners such as Luis Corvalán and Laura Allende, an end to torture and political imprisonment, and a return to the rule of law.[174] It also hoped to influence U.S. policy, mobilizing its mailing list to support the McGovern/Abourezk Amendment to suspend economic assistance to governments that abuse human rights.[175] A May 1976 National Legislative Conference on Chile covered topics such as "how to lobby" to enable interested Americans to pressure their representatives.[176] Furthermore, groups in Washington and Baltimore mobilized against the Chilean ship *Esmeralda's* participation in a bicentennial celebration, calling the ship a "floating torture chamber."[177]

Hearings investigating U.S. policy persisted. At one, Rogers notably declared, "The State Department is convinced that the observance of human rights must be an important factor in our relations with other countries."[178] With his statement before the Senate subcommittee, Rogers demonstrated, as he had repeatedly in private discussions with Kissinger, that he recognized both the scope of Chilean human rights abuses and the potential political costs to the State Department if it denied Chilean abuses or suggested that they were beyond the parameters of U.S. concern. Unlike other instances of State Department testimony on human rights, Rogers's record indicates that the sentiment was genuine.

THE TREASURY SECRETARY INTERVENES IN FOREIGN POLICY

The first sign that the Ford administration might moderate its policy toward Chile came with Treasury Secretary William Simon's trip to Santiago in May 1976.[179] Ford sent Simon to convey the message that continued economic assistance to Chile would be conditioned on improved respect for human rights.[180] Simon was in touch with Rose Styron, and she influenced him to press the issue of political prisoners during his visit.[181] Styron also sent Simon a list of prisoners who had been adopted by AIUSA and who were "of deep concern to Amnesty groups and members through the U.S."[182] Similarly, Kennedy aide Mark Schneider supplied the treasury secretary with the names of hundreds political prisoners before his trip.[183] When he landed in Santiago, Simon said, "We must all recognize that there is an inextricable relationship between our economic freedoms and our personal and social freedoms. One without the other is not sustainable for the long term."[184]

Chile released forty-nine political prisoners in advance of Simon's visit, which was the first by a U.S. cabinet member since the coup. In the view of the embassy in Santiago, Simon's trip "resulted in specific human rights achievements and generated leverage which will assist further progress."[185] Simon, in a memorandum to Ford, laid out a similarly positive view of his accomplishments in Santiago, including prisoner releases, further discussions about a visit from the UN Commission on Human Rights, and public acknowledgment of the trial and sentencing of officials committing human rights abuses.[186] Other observers were more cautious. A Chilean dissident noted that these forty-nine people released represented "little more than 1 percent of the political prisoners still in jail."[187] Moreover, the Chilean ambassador subsequently disavowed the suggestion that any Chilean releases were tied to Simon's visit, disagreed with the characterization of detainees in Chile as "political prisoners," and argued that Chile "is taking and will continue to take all the measures necessary to guarantee rights to all citizens, including the right to live in peace, without fear of violence, terrorism, or criminal political actions."[188]

KISSINGER GOES TO SANTIAGO

The next month Kissinger made a trip to Santiago to participate in the OAS General Assembly. While there, Kissinger raised human rights concerns in his public remarks, although his relatively strong language on human rights had not been part of his original plan. Indeed, in a preparatory meeting with his staff, he betrayed considerable skepticism about the role of human rights in U.S. foreign policy, saying, "Human Rights make me love the State Department. Am I supposed to make a revolution in Chile? I can't say what you want me to. I can't launch a broad scale attack on Chile. I am willing to make a general statement on human rights in the Western Hemisphere." But Kissinger's staff was firm in its advice.[189]

Despite Kissinger's skepticism, the issue of human rights was high on the agenda for his conversation with the Chilean foreign minister in Santiago—due to Chilean insistence. The American interpretation was that the Chileans wanted to get the issue "out of the way as early as possible to clear the atmosphere."[190] Members of the embassy in Santiago urged Kissinger to address U.S. human rights concerns directly in his meeting with Pinochet. According to deputy chief of mission Thomas Boyatt, "Pinochet is so narrow-minded and convinced of his righteousness that it takes sledgehammer blows to all [sic] his attention to some unpleasant facts of life." Popper advised, "The traditional norms of diplomatic phraseology can be lost on the president. He needs direct treatment, and clear and specific statements."[191]

Declassified documents show that the Chilean leader was less upset than might have been expected, because before giving his speech, Kissinger told Pinochet "We are sympathetic with what you are trying to do here."[192] Kissinger warned him, "In my statement, I will treat human rights in general terms, and human rights in a world context. I will refer in two paragraphs to the report on Chile of the OAS Human Rights Commission. I will say that the human rights issue has impaired relations between the U.S. and Chile. This is partly the result of Congressional actions. I will add that I hope you will shortly remove those obstacles."[193] In their joint session, Kissinger asked Pinochet to outline the steps the junta was taking to improve human rights and even advised the Chilean leader on tactics, suggesting, "If you could group the releases, instead of 20 a week, have a bigger program of releases, that would be better for the psychological impact of the releases."[194] Although Pinochet may not have been perturbed by Kissinger's speech, the Chilean leader complained directly that the United States should be offering even more support to his government.[195]

According to Kissinger, his speech at the OAS General Assembly was "the most extensive statement we have made on the subject." Kissinger's address did acknowledge human rights violations in Chile and the Americas more broadly, although his remarks lacked much specificity, particularly on the abuses that were occurring. Kissinger said, "Basic human rights must be preserved, cherished, and defended if peace and prosperity are to be more than hollow technical achievements. For technological progress without social justice mocks humanity; national unity without freedom is sterile; nationalism without a consciousness of human community—which means a shared concern for human rights—refines instruments of oppression."[196] The speech was motivated by, among other factors, Ford's upcoming election.[197] In other words, Kissinger was, in his mind, forced to signal to domestic and international audiences a U.S. commitment that did not fit with his broader strategic goals. He later wrote, "Congress was reflecting single-issue ideological and political agendas, pushed to a point that the administration considered inimical to broader United States strategic or geopolitical interests, or oblivious to them."[198] Similarly, at Rogers's suggestion, Kissinger met with Chilean Cardinal Raúl Silva in June 1976 in an effort to demonstrate the secretary's commitment to human rights.[199]

Kissinger's speech was widely covered in the press and was of interest to many who cared about human rights. Thomas C. Jones Jr., who was active in Amnesty International, had high praise for Kissinger's address in Santiago, calling it the "best statement ever made by a U.S. Secretary of State on human rights." He argued to an Amnesty staffer in London, "It must be stressed that never before Kissinger's Santiago Statement has there been any broad open support for human rights concerns by anyone with decision-making authority at State—at least not since the Eisenhower Administration took office in 1952."[200] Similarly, the *Wall Street Journal* asserted that Kissinger's speech demonstrated that "the U.S. government is also seeing, more than it has in the past, benefits in taking a strong stand on human rights."[201]

Kissinger's address, however, did not deter Chile. In a sign of the junta's hubris, on September 21, 1976, Orlando Letelier, a former Chilean ambassador to the United States and a key aide to Allende, was killed by a car bomb in Washington, DC.[202] In a *New York Times* op-ed written a few days before his death, Letelier had detailed the junta's continuing repression of him for his service in Allende's government. First, he was jailed in a concentration camp for a year, and then he was expelled from Chile. Shortly before his death, the junta had stripped Letelier of his Chilean citizenship.[203] In response to his strong condemnations of the junta, Chilean officials executed their critic in a spectacular bombing in the heart of their ally's capital.[204] Early NSC analysis that the Chileans were "too obvious" a culprit proved misguided.[205] The CIA spread information suggesting that Letelier had been targeted by leftists, but all signs ultimately pointed to the Chilean government, and any hopes for progress in Chilean-American relations ceased.[206] Not only was Letelier the victim of international, state-sponsored terrorism, but an American citizen, Roni Moffitt, was also killed in the explosion. The assassination only worsened many Americans' appraisal of the junta. On Capitol Hill, members of Congress such as Abourezk and Kennedy spoke about their "sadness and outrage" at Letelier's death.[207] Abourezk asserted that with Letelier's death, "the tyranny of the dictatorship in Chile has now been extended in part to the United States."[208]

As the assassination illustrated, the junta largely defied international pressure to change. Chilean officials were emboldened in part by Kissinger's signals that they would not face repercussions from the United States. Like South Korea, which eventually grew so economically independent that it could eschew U.S. assistance, Chile also decided that the increasingly meager assistance from the United States was not worth the hassle. In late October 1976 the Chilean government notified Washington that it was not seeking any economic assistance from the United States.[209]

Although the United States no longer supported Chile financially, its alliance with Pinochet remained controversial domestically. As the 1976 presidential election progressed, Carter attacked the Ford administration's record on Chile. The Chilean ambassador to the United States, Manuel Trucco, was so angered by Carter's comments that he sent the candidate a fifteen-page letter rebutting Carter's understanding of the situation in Chile; Trucco said that he wanted to call "attention to the factual vacuum of your information regarding Chile."[210] The news of Trucco's letter leaked, prompting considerable embarrassment among the Chilean leadership and an urgent investigation into the source of the leak within the Chilean embassy.[211]

Pinochet's tactics were a topic of discussion at the second presidential debate, when Ford was asked about potentially changing his policy to address the "bloodshed in Chile, Chilean prisons," and other issues. Ford's answer concentrated on China, South Korea, South Africa, and the Middle East, but neglected Chile, an omission that Carter highlighted: "I notice that Mr. Ford didn't comment on the prisons in Chile. This is a typical example, maybe one of many others, where this administration overthrew an elected government and helped to establish a military dictatorship." Carter further pointed out that 85 percent of U.S. Food for Peace aid to South America was going to Chile, suggesting that the United States was sending a disproportionate and unwarranted amount of support to that country.[212]

Political repression and violence in Chile resonated broadly with protests in Argentina, France, Italy, Mexico, Switzerland, and Venezuela.[213] Historian Tanya Harmer attributes the international reaction to the coup in Chile in part to the "ambitious scope" of Allende's foreign policy, which had "increased Chile's visibility around the globe."[214] In David Popper's view, American and Western European opposition to Pinochet's coup was connected with the reversals of Allende's "revolutionary" reforms as much as it was with the nature of the "repressive, strongly anti-Communist government" that followed.[215] Patrick Kelly argues that there was a "real and perceived . . . emergency" in the wake of the coup, in part due to "what increasingly came to be seen as massive state human rights abuses."[216]

Of all the examples of human rights concerns examined in this book, Chile created the most trouble for administration officials, which is somewhat surprising, given how limited U.S. interests there were. This was the country, after all, that Kissinger had described as a "dagger pointed at the heart of Antarctica."[217] Kissinger's condescension toward Latin America more broadly is noteworthy: "Nothing important can come from the South. History has never been produced in the South. The axis of history starts in Moscow, goes to Bonn, crosses over to Washington, and then goes to Tokyo. What happens in the South is of no importance."[218] Even the foreign service officers stationed in Santiago who had urged a new approach to Chile argued that it was "a country of little strategic importance whose natural resources are not important to the United States."[219]

Why, then, was there such attention on Chile? The timing of the coup was important, as it came after years of increasing attention to human rights in the United States. By late 1973 many of the trends responsible for heightening concern for human rights during the long 1960s had come to a head. In particular, Donald Fraser's human rights hearings were already underway when Pinochet seized power. Furthermore, as with other cases, because of the erosion of trust in the U.S. government due to U.S. actions in Vietnam, the Watergate scandal, and questions about covert actions overseas, many had lost faith in the White House and were more skeptical of the government's embrace of the junta.[220] In many ways, Americans were primed to react to the Chilean coup. Liberals broadly rallied to the anti-Chile cause, gaining support from the young and old as well as from those motivated by religion, opposition to Vietnam, or a commitment to the law.[221] Frank Church explicitly linked his opposition to the war in Vietnam to his position on Chile, writing, "While I was no supporter of President Allende, he was democratically elected and we should have honored the very principle on which our nation exists. For this reason I supported in the recent foreign aid debate both the Abourezk and Kennedy amendments stopping aid to anti-democratic regimes in Saigon and now in Santiago."[222]

More than with South Korea and Southern Rhodesia, the repression in Chile resonated with Americans because there were stronger and more numerous personal connections. Americans who had traveled to Latin America through churches or the Peace Corps returned to the United States and became active in U.S. policy toward the region.[223] Among the prominent actors on Chile, Kennedy's chief foreign policy aide, Mark Schneider, had served in the Peace Corps in El Salvador from 1966 to 1968.[224] Robert Fagen, a political scientist at the University of California–Berkeley, who later testified before Congress on Chile's human rights record, had a personal connection to Teruggi and Horman through his Ford Foundation posting in Chile; he wrote to Kissinger and a range of members of Congress about events in Santiago and about the questionable role of the United States embassy during that time.[225] Eldridge similarly knew victims of Pinochet's repression personally. In addition, Chilean exiles in the United States, although small in number, actively pressured the U.S. government to limit its support for the junta.[226]

Congressional activism was also heightened through personal encounters, including through travel to Chile in which members of Congress experienced the political climate firsthand. For example, Representatives Tom Harkin, George Miller (D-CA), and Toby Moffett (D-CT) traveled with Eldridge to Chile in 1976.[227] Harkin had a particularly eventful visit to Santiago, as he and Eldridge managed to get inside Villa Grimaldi, an infamous torture center, before being quickly removed by Chilean security forces.[228] Upon their return, the three representatives declared, "During our stay, it became increasingly clear that the junta, with all the sincerity and conviction imaginable, rules nonetheless by terror. We found a silent and pervasive fear in all segments of Chilean society, the oldest of Latin American democracies."[229]

FIGURE 5.1. Representative Tom Harkin met with Cardinal Raúl Silva to discuss human rights violations in Chile. Courtesy of the Drake University Archives and Special Collections.

Furthermore, Chile had a long democratic history, which made the military coup there shocking, even more so than in Greece. Barbara Keys has emphasized that feelings of guilt, embarrassment, and shame over the Vietnam War drove liberals in the 1970s to pick up human rights language.[230] Perhaps guilt over American complicity in destabilizing Allende, which facilitated the betrayal of Chilean democracy, played a similar role.

Taken together, the human rights violations in Chile were made immediate to Americans through transnational connections, a shared democratic tradition, geographic and cultural closeness, and the intertwined tragedies of Americans being murdered in Chile and a Chilean assassinated in the United States.[231] Looming ominously over the Chilean case were the dead bodies of Salvador Allende, who many at the time suspected had not taken his own life; Charles Horman; Frank Teruggi; and later, Orlando Letelier. The junta's complicity in their deaths rendered status-quo relations unacceptable to many involved Americans. Yet the Nixon and Ford administrations remained immune to public displeasure with Pinochet's regime, leaving congressional action as the principal way that the United States demonstrated distance from Santiago. Eventually, the rise of liberal members of Congress who asserted their commitment to human rights enabled an end to military and economic assistance for Chile—a visible signal of opposition to the junta's repression.[232]

Chapter Six

"A CALL FOR U.S. LEADERSHIP"

Congressional Activism on Human Rights

The preceding chapters, particularly those on human rights activism relating to Greece, South Korea, and Chile, have shown that the White House largely resisted congressional, nongovernmental, and even State Department pressure to take greater account of human rights violations in foreign-policy making during the long 1960s. Frustrated members of Congress demonstrated their policy differences with Nixon, Ford, and Kissinger through hearings and legislation. They initially targeted country-specific appropriations and eventually pursued a more comprehensive approach to changing U.S. foreign policy. This chapter explores the House Foreign Affairs Subcommittee on International Organizations and Movements' hearings on human rights, the subcommittee's resulting report, and legislation implementing much of its recommendations, which collectively marked a key turning point in the rise of human rights as a priority in U.S. foreign policy.[1]

FRASER'S HEARINGS

Historian Robert David Johnson has characterized members of Congress who wanted to emphasize cultural and economic elements of foreign policy over military ones as "new internationalists."[2] These members of Congress believed that the United States had been too willing to support right-wing dictators and had become overly reliant on military solutions; they pushed instead for a more moral foreign policy. Members of Congress who subscribed to these tenets asserted themselves, beginning in the Johnson administration, criticizing U.S. policy and pressing for changes in the United States' relations with the world, although their impact started being felt more meaningfully during the Nixon years.

As head of the House Foreign Affairs Subcommittee on International Organizations and Movements, Donald Fraser organized a series of hearings in 1973 and ultimately pressed a number of measures that forced the U.S. government to take greater account of human rights when formulating and executing its foreign policy.[3] Fraser, whose activism has been seen in each chapter of this book, began publicly questioning the morality of U.S. foreign policy in the 1960s. He believed that the Cold War framework inhibited consistency between American morality and the government's foreign policy; his calls for greater attention to human rights were part of an effort to develop a new approach to relations with the wider world.[4]

Fraser has said that international events, including the war in Vietnam, coups in Chile and Greece, and the United States' intervention in the Dominican Republic, all influenced his interest in human rights and his attention to it as a member of Congress.[5] Speaking to past and present federal government lawyers on "the importance of a Human Rights policy," Fraser said,

When I began my first term in Congress in 1963 I was assigned to the House Committee on Foreign Affairs—a field in which I had long been interested as a private citizen. I soon became very unhappy with United States policies toward countries like the Dominican Republic, Greece and Chile.

The Dominican Republic was invaded by U.S. marines a little over 2 years after I was first elected to Congress. I was dismayed to see our alleged security interests override the rights of the people of the Dominican Republic.[6]

The subcommittee's hearings should be viewed as part of a larger pattern of congressional activism in foreign policy during these years, spurred to a large degree by the Vietnam War and the Watergate scandal. Increasingly at odds with the White House, Congress sought to reassert itself against the embattled president and his "imperial" style of conducting foreign policy.[7] In a letter to the editor of the *Washington Post*, Representative

Jonathan Bingham wrote, "The rebellious mood prevalent in the Senate reflects the high-handed way Mr. Nixon has treated the Congress in regard to Vietnam."[8] Additional notable instances of congressional activism in foreign policy during the these years include the Jackson-Vanik Amendment, which was examined in chapter one; the Mansfield Amendment, which was intended to reduce U.S. forces stationed overseas; and the passage of the War Powers Resolution.[9]

Fraser chose to focus on the international protection of human rights extensively because, he wrote, "After becoming chair, within reason I had the ability to set the agenda," and "I felt that a more systematic approach to this topic made sense."[10] According to John Salzberg, Fraser's close aide, his boss believed that U.S. support and especially military assistance for dictators was not in the long-term interests of the country.[11]

Fraser suggested that "the continuing erosion of human rights in the world" motivated the hearings.[12] He also believed that they might lead to a more bipartisan approach to human rights:

I had noted that in the preceding years, expressions of concern about countries tended to follow ideological lines in the U.S. Congress. The Republicans would tend to focus on left-leaning countries, and the Democrats on the rightist countries. I believed it would be useful to find a framework for viewing countries' human rights practices that would provide a more objective measure of the abuses that were occurring.[13]

Furthermore, over time Fraser came to see concern for human rights as a new framework for U.S. foreign policy that moved beyond Cold War concerns of ideology and containment. During the subcommittee's human rights hearings, Fraser had said,

Because we have been so preoccupied with the contest of ideologies that formed the framework of the cold war, . . . we have not replaced that way of measuring events, judging nations and looking to international relationships with some new framework. It is my impression that one useful framework would be an increased emphasis on the observance of human rights by various societies around the world, which has the value, in pragmatic terms, of putting to societies, both the left and right, a rather standard set of ideas in terms of how they treat their own people.[14]

At a more basic level, support for human rights was also popular politically.[15]

The subcommittee comprised eleven members of the House Committee on Foreign Affairs, including four who demonstrated a level of commitment to human rights similar to Fraser's.[16] However, according to Salzberg, "there were times when Fraser was the only member of the subcommittee present," which highlights his central role in the process.[17] Dante Fascell, Jonathan Bingham, Benjamin Rosenthal, and Paul Findley also contributed regularly, and throughout, their questioning revealed concerns about violations of human rights.[18] Fascell was a longtime representative from South Florida who regarded his experience in the African and Italian campaigns of World War II as formative to his desire to enter public service, saying, "If Americans are going to be sent to war, I want to know why and be part of the process that decides whether they should go."[19] Fascell served nineteen terms in Congress and had a seat on the Foreign Affairs Committee for thirty-six years.[20] For nine of those years, he served as its chair.

Before Bingham's election to nine terms in Congress, he had served as a diplomat at the UN. He represented New York City and was interested in Soviet Jewish emigration in particular. Rosenthal also hailed from New York City, where he practiced law before serving in Congress for more than twenty years. He was an early opponent of the war in Vietnam, openly dissenting by 1965, and was a vocal critic of the Nixon administration's policy toward the Greek junta.

As the representative from Abraham Lincoln's district in Springfield, Illinois, Findley consciously supported civil rights and sought to "encourage the Republican party to take the leadership" in that area.[21] To that end, Findley introduced legislation intended to achieve desegregation and an end to racial discrimination through federal programs such as food stamps and aid to schools.[22] His congressional correspondence demonstrates sympathy for the victims of the coup in Chile, support for the Universal Declaration of Human Rights, concern for the plight of Jews wishing to emigrate from the Soviet Union, and condemnation of the My Lai massacre in Vietnam.[23]

The subcommittee held its hearings between August 1 and December 7, 1973, investigating the efforts of international organizations, regional organizations, and international NGOs to protect human rights.[24] In addition, it considered U.S. policy toward states that abused human rights. Fraser said, "For its part, the U.S. cannot ask the UN to be forceful in protecting human rights without at the same time giving human rights considerations the highest priority in conducting its own affairs."[25] The subcommittee also focused on the human rights situations in a number of individual countries; specifically, the hearings considered abuses in Bangladesh, Northern Ireland, and Chile, among other countries, as case studies for examining the successes and failures of American and UN attempts to protect human rights. Fraser said, "This is not a theoretical study. . . . We are going to take a close look at actual situations involving gross violations of human rights in many places around the world."[26]

During the hearings, Fraser repeatedly criticized American reluctance to condemn governments that violated their citizens' human rights:

Our Government . . . does not believe that human rights should be a significant factor in determining our bilateral relations with other states. Human rights issues are not raised with other states—except in the most discrete manner—for fear of jeopardizing our friendly relations. To the victims of the human rights violations, we may appear to condone these practices in order to retain the economic, political and other benefits which flow from our maintenance of friendly relations with the repressive government.[27]

While discussing the UN and U.S. reactions to massacres in Burundi, Fraser advocated for more aggressive and comprehensive American responses when clear evidence of human rights abuses was available: "When a government commits gross violations of human rights, such as massacre, torture, and apartheid, it should be our policy to terminate all military assistance and sales to the government and to suspend any economic assistance directly supportive of the government."[28] Ted Kennedy echoed Fraser's sentiment when he testified: "A policy of silence toward human tragedy, wherever it occurs, violates the traditions of our people and does a disservice to the best interests of our country."[29]

Congressional hearings offer a platform for nonstate actors to be heard, and a range of witnesses testified at Fraser's hearings, including many active on human rights outside of Washington. Some, such as Jerome Shestack, emphasized that defending human rights was in the United States' national security interests: "One of the critical concepts that must be accepted if we are to advance human rights is that human rights and peace in the world community are interrelated. . . . If history teaches us anything it is that today's violations are the seeds of tomorrow's armed conflicts."[30] Those concerned about the United States' close identification with authoritarian regimes warned that such relations were not in the United States' long-term interests. They raised the specter that subsequent governments could adopt anti-American policies, given U.S. support for previously repressive governments.

Others who testified, including Rita Hauser, criticized the lack of consistency in the American approach to human rights. Hauser said, "We speak out against violations of countries we are not particularly close to or where we feel we can do so with some measure of safety politically, and we are largely silent, as are other countries, when human rights violations occur on the part of our allies or friendly countries we do not wish to offend."[31] The double standard described by Hauser frustrated many human rights advocates who believed that American policy was undermined by Cold War politics.

HUMAN RIGHTS IN THE WORLD COMMUNITY: THE SUBCOMMITTEE'S REPORT

After fifteen sessions in which more than forty witnesses testified, the subcommittee drafted a report entitled *Human Rights in the World Community: A Call for U.S. Leadership.* The report made a series of suggestions, many of which were eventually implemented. First, the subcommittee formulated ideas about how Congress could enhance U.S. support for human rights internationally. Specifically, the subcommittee advised the Senate to ratify the Convention on the Prevention and Punishment of the Crime of Genocide and other human rights treaties that had not yet been approved by the Senate.

In its report, the subcommittee pressed the State Department to "treat human rights factors as a regular part of U.S. foreign policy decision-making" and advocated greater U.S. attention to human rights in its foreign policy:

The human rights factor is not accorded the high priority it deserves in our country's foreign policy. Too often it becomes invisible on the vast foreign policy horizon of political, economic, and military affairs. Proponents of pure power politics too often dismiss it as a factor in diplomacy. . . . Our relations with the present Governments of South Vietnam, Spain, Portugal, the Soviet Union, Brazil, Indonesia, Greece, the Philippines, and Chile exemplify how we have disregarded human rights for the sake of other assumed interests.

In the subcommittee's view, "The State Department too often has taken the position that human rights is a domestic matter and not a relevant factor in determining bilateral relations."[32] In addition, it outlined a range of tactics that the United States could use to influence governments to end the abuse of human rights, such as discreet bilateral conversations, public efforts in international organizations, and termination of military and economic assistance. The subcommittee advocated repealing the Byrd Amendment and suggested that human rights abuses in the Soviet Union should not be overlooked in deference to Soviet-American détente. Finally, the subcommittee recommended that the State Department study the human rights treaties that the United States had not yet acted on.

The subcommittee's report advocated reorganizing the State Department to better equip it to consider human rights as an element of U.S. foreign relations. First, it suggested the establishment of an Office for Human Rights in the Bureau of International Organization Affairs. Second, it proposed designating a human rights officer in each regional bureau in the department. Third, the subcommittee urged the department to appoint an assistant legal adviser on human rights and form an advisory committee on human rights. The report's authors also suggested expanding the mandate of the United States Civil Rights Commission to include international human rights. Last, it proposed facilitating the development of an association of legislators interested in human rights internationally.[33]

Not surprisingly, the recommendations of the subcommittee were not well received by the Nixon administration. In describing executive-legislative relations during the hearings, Fraser reports that the subcommittee did not have "a cordial relationship" with the Nixon White House and the State Department.[34] Salzberg was more explicit, suggesting that the relationship between Congress and the State Department was actually "confrontational."[35] In Fraser's recounting, the palpable conflict emerged when the hearings were critical of American policy toward certain countries: "It was in the specifics where tension would develop." [36] Nevertheless,

Fraser believed that "congressional prodding [resulted] in limited upgrading of human rights in U.S. foreign policy" and argued that with their efforts, "at least, the seed had been planted."[37]

Kissinger's opposition to congressional legislation and changes in the State Department's bureaucracy were rooted in two factors. First, his adherence to realpolitik meant that he saw concern for human rights as a lower priority than his congressional critics did. Second, he resented the interference of Congress in the formulation and implementation of U.S. foreign policy.[38] Despite its resistance to Fraser's hearings, the department nonetheless tried to anticipate and blunt the subcommittee's suggestions by making administrative changes before the report's release. Specifically, the State Department tasked Charles Runyon III with following human rights issues in the Office of the Legal Adviser and gave Warren E. Hewitt responsibility for human rights issues in the Office of United Nations Political Affairs.[39]

In what was likely a similar, preemptive effort, Kissinger spoke about the administration's stance on human rights in an October 1973 address to the Pacem in Terris Conference. The fact that Kissinger addressed the topic amid the subcommittee's hearings suggests that the committee's activism had put human rights on the foreign policy agenda. He said,

So let us not address this as a debate between those who are morally sensitive and those who are not, between those who care for justice and those who are oblivious to humane values. . . . We shall never condone the suppression of fundamental liberties. We shall urge humane principles and use our influence to promote justice. But the issue comes down to the limits of such efforts.[40]

His speech served to articulate the administration's position on human rights, including the view that the United States could not transform the domestic systems of foreign countries and the idea that in an age of nuclear weapons, human rights concerns were at times less significant than achieving détente and the stability of the international system.

Similarly, Nixon felt the need to address the issue publicly. In a commencement address in June 1974, the president strongly articulated U.S. support for human rights: "We can never, as Americans, acquiesce in the suppression of human liberties." Nonetheless, echoing Kissinger's remarks, Nixon suggested that the United States at times pursued higher priorities, saying, "We cannot gear our foreign policy to transformation of other societies. In the nuclear age, our first responsibility must be the prevention of a war that could destroy all societies."[41]

The State Department also conferred with its congressional critics at many levels. Kissinger's aversion to congressional interference was unshakeable, whereas many others in the State Department were open to cooperation. At a meeting with his top aides in October 1974, Kissinger expressed frustration at an upcoming session with Fraser and wondered how it could end in his favor. Kissinger asked, "What am I supposed to do—show that I am a humanitarian?" He indicated that he expected Fraser to hold a press conference after the meeting that condemned administration policies.[42] His advisers, however, assured him that Fraser would adopt a reasonable approach to the meeting. Lynwood Holton, assistant secretary for congressional relations, urged Kissinger to "get hold of Fraser" and "get him on your side."[43] Kissinger dismissed Fraser's agenda, claiming, "These guys don't want to stand for human rights—they want grandstand plays. They want public humiliation of other countries."[44] In contrast, State Department officials described Fraser's staff as "friendlily disposed to work with the Department" on human rights issues.[45] Later, State Department officials tried to assuage Kissinger's anxieties by declaring, "These are all liberal but rational people."[46]

Kissinger's concerns likely led to his December 17, 1974, meeting with Fraser and other members of Congress being off the record. According to State Department sources, Fraser was conciliatory, noting that those attending "know of the many positive things which have been done recently in the field of human rights." Yet he pointed out that members of Congress were less willing to support foreign assistance to governments with poor human rights records.[47] Alan Cranston reported to Kissinger that a recent study had shown that the United States was sending aid to fifty-eight countries that were regarded as dictatorships, which Representative Robert Roe (D-NJ) said was leading to decreasing support for foreign aid.[48] The secretary responded by outlining steps that the administration had taken to raise the issue of human rights with the Chilean and Soviet governments. Furthermore, Kissinger argued that although Congress should "express its view on human rights," he was "allergic" to "obligatory statutes."[49] In future consultations, Kissinger wanted to emphasize attention to human rights in multilateral forums such as the UN rather than press the issue bilaterally,

FIGURE 6.1. Henry Kissinger in his White House office. Courtesy of the Richard Nixon Presidential Library and Museum, National Archives and Records Administration.

while members of Congress sought Kissinger's support to repeal the Byrd Amendment, which was not forthcoming.[50]

STATE DEPARTMENT STUDIES

Fraser's hearings, and congressional activism more broadly, prompted the State Department in 1974 to undertake two studies; the first examined how the bureaucracy of the State Department could better address human rights concerns, and the second assessed current U.S. human rights policy. At a high-level State Department meeting in June 1974, Deputy Assistant Secretary for Congressional Relations Kempton Jenkins noted that only two people were currently working on human rights issues in the department—Runyon and Hewitt. To highlight deficiencies in the organization, Jenkins reported, "They cannot handle their mail."[51] William Buffum, deputy assistant secretary for international organization affairs, suggested that many observers did not regard the United States as supporting human rights, which created a problem: "We are under increasing criticism on the Hill, I find, for not taking enough of a lead and not taking a forthcoming enough approach."[52] State Department officials discussed Fraser's role in the debate, noting that whereas he had once been "a lone Indian" on the issue, he wasn't anymore. Jenkins reported that Fraser had "worked very hard on the issue," had been "very even-handed," and had "not gone just after right-wing organizations." Jenkins correctly warned at the time that rising attention to the issue in Congress would likely produce legislation that prevented military assistance to Chile and that could potentially affect U.S. forces in Korea.[53]

The State Department evaluated the degree to which it should reorganize in order to address human rights concerns, outlining several broad approaches: "do nothing"; enact a "minor reorganization"; take steps that went beyond a "cosmetic" reorganization; undergo a substantive and institutional reorganization; or accede to the Senate-proposed creation of a Bureau of Humanitarian Affairs. Deputy Under Secretary for Management Dean Brown noted that at issue was "how far we want to go and how fast." He evaluated options in terms of the degree of disruption they would cause for the department, their effect on the burdens of the secretary, and the message that such steps would signal to external observers, among other factors.[54] As members of the State Department worked through how they might reorganize themselves, one official noted that "there is no agreement either in the Department or outside as to just what 'human rights' does or should cover."[55] Yet, he noted, "Human rights need the prestige and clout of Seventh Floor backing" from the secretary of state "if they are to have a meaningful impact on foreign policy decisions."[56]

Several months after the subcommittee's report was released, Fraser wrote to Kissinger to express the subcommittee's pleasure at administrative changes within the State Department, including the designation of someone in the United Nations Political Affairs Office to be in charge of human rights, the appointment of an assistant legal adviser for human rights, and the selection of human rights officers in three regional bureaus.[57] Fraser, however, continued to press for greater bureaucratic change, including the appointment of a special assistant on human rights to the deputy secretary of state.[58]

In April 1975, Deputy Secretary of State Ingersoll named James M. Wilson Jr. the coordinator for humanitarian affairs. Ingersoll described Wilson's appointment as a step "to expand and upgrade the time and attention devoted to human rights considerations in the work of the Department of State" and suggested that he was "instituting centralized direction of the Department's efforts on human rights, refugees, humanitarian assistance, prisoners of war."[59] In a letter to Senator James O. Eastland (D-MS), chair of the judiciary committee, Ingersoll intended Wilson's appointment to bring "a clear focus on human rights issues to activities throughout the Department, and to assure attention at the highest level, as these issues deserve."[60]

Wilson was given three deputies—one to cover human rights, one for soldiers who were prisoners of war or missing in action, and one for refugees and migration. Ronald D. Palmer, a longtime State Department official, remembers that Wilson's office needed to convince the regional bureaus at the State Department that this "was now something to which we were going to pay greater attention," because of greater congressional activism.[61] Palmer said, "I see this initial period of the human rights effort being a kind of expansion of the palette of possible inputs that we were able to use in dealing with the international situation."[62]

The second study was more comprehensive and had potentially considerable consequences for the subsequent direction of U.S. foreign policy. A State Department consultant authored what was a significant evaluation of U.S. policy toward authoritarian regimes. It was intended to stave off more-drastic congressional action, enhance the coherence of American policy, and develop greater domestic consensus. The report attributed increased attention on American human rights policy to the developments in the fall of 1973 in South Korea, Greece, and Chile in particular. It also pointed to the imposition of martial law in the Philippines in 1972, the continuing impediments to Jewish emigration from the Soviet Union, the United States' violation of the UN embargo of Rhodesia due to the Byrd Amendment, and the repression in South

Vietnam by Nguyen Van Thieu's regime. Press accounts of human rights violations, including torture by governments with which the United States was closely identified, were also cited. As the report indicated, "It is becoming increasingly clear that nothing 'turns off' large segments of the natural foreign policy 'constituency' . . . [more] than the appearance of insensitivity on the part of U.S. officialdom toward human rights issues around the world." The study noted, "What official Americans say in public about the U.S. position on human rights and authoritarian regimes, either in general terms or in regard to specific situations is not just a matter of public relations. It is an essential element of our policy in this field."[63]

The report proposed that the United States work to develop a "coherent" but "sufficiently flexible" approach to human rights. As with the study that contemplated reorganization of the State Department, this report outlined four possible approaches, which included maintaining the status quo; enacting a "passive approach"; creating "selective change"; or bringing about a "major initiative," which would "signal a decisive turn in U.S. policy toward a stronger position generally on human rights." In determining what option to pursue, policy planners noted that the government needed to take account of the nature of the bilateral relationship, the extent of U.S. influence, the effect on other American interests, the severity of the human rights violations, the degree of the situation's improvement or worsening, the domestic reaction to the violations, the possible consequences of American action, the regional context, and the extent of American identification with the abuses. The study's authors clearly struggled to balance a potentially more assertive role on human rights with concerns about respecting the principle of noninterference in the internal affairs of foreign governments.[64] The report advised the government to adopt a policy of making a "modest modification in our high-level expressions of concern for protection of human rights generally" and to "indicate a willingness, however, on occasion to give public expression to our disapproval of human rights violations in countries besides those in the Soviet bloc whenever that is deemed the best way to achieve results without seriously compromising other important interests." The study's author called for a special assistant on human rights and for an examination of the United States' export of police equipment, its visa policies toward emigrants from authoritarian countries, and its refugee and asylum policies.[65]

LEGISLATIVE IMPLEMENTATION

Following the subcommittee's report, there were several key consequences for U.S. human rights policy. First, members of Congress interested in human rights increasingly shifted their focus to curbing U.S. military assistance to repressive governments, a trend that is discussed in previous chapters. Congressional concern reached a decisive point in September 1974 when 104 members of Congress wrote to Kissinger, suggesting that support in the House for military assistance to authoritarian regimes was declining. They wrote,

In the absence of extraordinary circumstances, we do not believe that long-term U.S. foreign policy interests are served by maintaining supportive relationships with oppressive governments, especially in the military field, since military power is directly associated with the exercise of governmental control over the civilian population.

Unless U.S. foreign policies—especially military assistance policies—more accurately reflect the traditional commitment of the American people to promote human rights, we will find it increasingly difficult to justify support for foreign aid legislation to our constituents.[66]

Responding to the letter, Lynwood Holton suggested that the department was indeed working to assess international human rights violations. He argued that the United States must pay careful attention to the direction of a government's record and highlighted South Korea in particular as a country that might be making improvements that would alleviate congressional interest in reducing assistance.[67]

In the aftermath of the subcommittee's hearings, Congress took incremental steps to try to curb assistance to repressive governments. In 1973 James Abourezk proposed amendments banning foreign assistance to countries with political prisoners. Urging Alan Cranston to support the amendments, he wrote, "It is a grave mistake to turn our heads on the thousands of innocent citizens in many of the countries which we continue to support who are being imprisoned and tortured as political prisoners."[68] Reflecting on a 1973 meeting in which he discussed human rights abuses with a member of the Brazilian parliament, Abourezk wrote, "I was shocked by what I heard. It was something totally new to me, so I asked what I could do." This encounter led him to propose human rights legislation and ultimately led to the shuttering of the United States Office on Public Safety, which trained foreign police officers and which faced allegations that it condoned torture.[69]

Abourezk's amendments failed, and instead Congress passed Section 32 of the Foreign Assistance Act of 1973, which said, "It is the sense of Congress that the President should deny any economic or military assistance to the government of any foreign country which practices the internment or imprisonment of that country's citizens for political purposes."[70] State Department officials advised against Section 32 because it was a "one-time thing" that did not allow the United States to maintain leverage with repressive leaders.[71] After sharing the language of Section 32 with foreign governments, especially in East Asia, the State Department reported that some officials raised questions about the "difficulty of defining" political prisoners.[72]

Congress therefore included language that was far more specific in the subsequent year's legislation. Section 502B of the 1974 Foreign Assistance Act stipulated:

Except under extraordinary circumstances, the President shall substantially reduce or terminate security assistance to any government which engages in a consistent pattern of gross violations of internationally recognized human rights. Those violations are defined to include torture; cruel, inhuman or degrading treatment or punishment; prolonged detention without charges; or other flagrant denials of the right to life, liberty and security of person.[73]

Yet, section 502B of the 1974 Foreign Assistance Act expressed only the sense of Congress and thus could be ignored by the executive branch, and it was.[74] Observers have argued that the executive branch was able to circumvent 502B by determining that human rights violations did not rise to the level of "gross violations" and that when there were significant human rights abuses, they did not constitute a "consistent pattern."[75] Yet, in correspondence with Representative Ed Koch (D-NY), Assistant Secretary of State Robert J. McCloskey thoughtfully outlined the challenges that the State Department faced in developing a definition of a "consistent pattern of gross violations of internationally recognized human rights" and devising metrics to measure it.[76] Nevertheless, between November 1974 and November 1975 no country had its military aid or sales stopped due to 502B.[77] As one scholar has put it, 502B is a "case study of executive frustration of congressionally mandated foreign policy."[78] As Fraser later wrote, "We might as well have opened the barn door and let the horses out right there! The Nixon-Ford administration walked right through that door."[79]

Barbara Keys argues that Kissinger's intransigence on human rights forced Congress to pass increasingly restrictive legislation to force him to address the issue. Kissinger believed that he had to remain firm in the face of congressional pressure or else close U.S. allies would be targeted for their human rights records.[80] Joseph Eldridge similarly contends that human rights legislation was passed as a rebuke to Kissinger: "Had Kissinger been a little more open [to] listening and recognizing that Congress was an equal branch of government legislation would not have passed!"[81] In addition to reacting to Kissinger, these activist members of Congress, according to a December 1974 nationwide survey, were in line with American public opinion; 68 percent of Americans agreed ("strongly" or "somewhat") with the statement that the "U.S. should put pressure on countries which systematically violate basic human rights."[82]

Nevertheless, in January 1975 the State Department began adopting a more proactive approach, which included requesting reports on human rights violations from embassies abroad.[83] Furthermore, Ingersoll wrote to all diplomatic and consular posts in August of that year, urging them to undertake actions that would signal U.S. concern about human rights, such as observing trials.[84] Feedback from the field, however, was not enthusiastic. According to Wilson, chiefs of mission were uniformly negative about how new human rights reporting requirements might affect them: "Practically all of them came back saying that they thought it would cause major problems. They thought it would mess up considerably many of the programs we were facing in the Cold War." He elaborated,

They felt that if the U.S. government had to broadcast publicly what was going on, it would be considered a slap in the face by the government concerned and, in terms of human rights, it would be self defeating. They very much preferred to do things quietly, without the glare of publicity, and said it should certainly not be done with a lot of public flagellation along the way.[85]

Although the department was now compiling reports on individual countries' records, it was loathe to share them with Congress in response to Section 502B.[86] Under Ford and Kissinger, the State Department did not send Congress individual reports on the human rights records of countries receiving military assistance in 1975 as members of Congress had been expecting.[87] Instead, State Department officials wrote, "Our view is that while both security interests and human rights are important, each country needs to be looked at individually to determine where our predominant interests lie in every case."[88] Using language that particularly angered congressional supporters of human rights legislation, State Department officials declared, "We have found no adequately objective way to make distinctions of degree between nations."[89] Hubert Humphrey condemned the State Department language as being as "bland, may I say, as swallowing a bucket of sawdust."[90] Cranston labeled the State Department position "a cover-up of information that American taxpayers and legislators are entitled to."[91] In response to perceived State Department attempts to evade congressional intent, Fraser and Representative Stephen Solarz (D-NY) proposed an amendment that would force the department to submit a human rights report alongside any request for security assistance.[92] Subsequently, Cranston emphasized the executive branch's noncompliance with earlier congressional efforts to limit assistance to repressive governments, charging the State Department with sending a report that was intended to "ignore and evade the spirit and intent of the laws passed by Congress." Cranston lamented, "If we do not respect our own history and hold up the torch of democratic ideas, who will? And if we do not, who are we?"[93]

In response, Congress passed Section 301 of the International Security Assistance and Arms Export Control Act of 1976, which tightened the language in 502B to make the reporting mandatory. Ford vetoed the law, however, forcing Congress to pass a weakened version in order to secure a presidential signature.[94] The International Security Assistance and Arms Export Control Act of 1976 dictated that the United States not extend security assistance to countries that engaged in a pattern of gross violations of human rights "except under circumstances specified in this section."[95] To make such a determination, the State Department needed to compile "full and complete reports" on each country that received security assistance. For purposes of drafting its reports, the State Department focused on Articles 3, 5, 8, 9, 10, and 11 of the UN Universal Declaration of Human Rights, which largely deal with violations of the person. It also needed to determine the depth and frequency of such violations and whether any extenuating circumstances existed.[96] The legislation also made the coordinator for human rights and humanitarian affairs a position that was confirmable by the Senate. Ford designated Wilson, whose earlier title had been coordinator for humanitarian affairs, to that position in November 1976. Congressional legislation had so enhanced the responsibilities of Wilson's office that he requested additional personnel in November 1976.[97]

Furthermore, the Harkin Amendment—or Section 116 of the International Development and Food Assistance language of the Foreign Assistance Act of 1961—prevented the extension of economic aid to governments that engaged in gross violations of human rights "unless such assistance will directly benefit the needy people of such country."[98] The "vague" language in Section 116, including the "needy people" clause, weakened its implementation. Nonetheless, because Section 116 required executive branch explanation when the "needy people" clause was utilized, it was a marginally more effective tool for Congress in ending economic assistance to countries than Section 502B was at facilitating the cutoff of military assistance.[99]

In the wake of stricter legislative language, the State Department and Congress worked together more successfully on monitoring human rights. Humphrey, in his capacity as chair of the Senate Subcommittee on Foreign Assistance, requested human rights information on seventeen countries, including Chile and South Korea, in September 1976. The NSC worried about the release of such reports and the potential impact of the press saying that "according to the State Department so and so tortures its peoples."[100] In the end, the State Department submitted reports on Bangladesh, Brazil, Chile, Ethiopia, India, Mozambique, Nigeria, Pakistan, Paraguay, South Korea, Spain, Uruguay, and Zaire.[101] Reports on human rights in Argentina, Indonesia, Iran, and the Philippines were sent separately. Fraser also successfully requested country reports for his subcommittee.[102] According to Kenneth Hill, who worked on the State Department's early human rights country reports, they "were breaking entirely new ground to report, and in many cases criticize, the human rights records mainly of our allies."[103] Fraser similarly regards the annual reports as allowing "the U.S. to express our views on a country's human rights practices without requiring overt intervention."[104]

With Carter's election in November 1976 and Kissinger's imminent departure from the State Department, human rights activists were hopeful. Wilson began thinking about what human rights policy might look like under the Carter administration. Among Wilson's suggestions were "a policy of cooperation with Congress" and a policy-planning staff report on ameliorating human rights violations internationally.[105] Similarly, Salzberg wrote to the transition staff, making recommendations for how the administration should address human rights.[106] George Aldrich, deputy legal adviser in the State Department, advised that "our first priority, on which all else depends, must be to reverse the general perception of our present policy—i.e., that we do not really care very much about human rights abroad."[107] Wilson sent similar suggestions to the deputy secretary designate on the day after Carter's inauguration, advocating more-informal sharing of information with members of Congress and their staff as well as raising the possibility of making his office a bureau.[108]

Fraser's human rights hearings, the subcommittee's resulting report, and legislation implementing much of its recommendations represented a significant moment in U.S. foreign-policy formulation. Incremental steps by Congress eventually led to the establishment of the Bureau of Human Rights and Humanitarian Affairs in 1977, annual reports on countries' human rights records, and an increase of limits on assistance to repressive regimes.[109] Former State Department official Sandy Vogelgesang writes that congressional activism was a "catalyst to grudging Executive Branch action" because it "raised consciousness in the ranks, if not at the highest reaches of the Administration."[110] In Fraser's view, the legacy of the hearings was "to change the culture of the State Department which in the past had viewed human rights issues generally as not relevant to their work of building and maintaining relationships with other countries."[111] Richard Schifter, who served as assistant secretary of state for human rights and humanitarian affairs during the Reagan administration—and thus is likely to be relatively objective about the hearings' impact—agrees: "I believe that the basic concept of human rights, as part of U.S. foreign policy, is now embedded in foreign policy and has been as a result, as I say, of the congressional actions in the 1970s."[112] In Salzberg's view, the subcommittee's "legacy" was that "human rights became a commonly [accepted] factor in U.S. foreign policy." Specifically, he argues that the country reports on human rights are "the most durable aspect of the Fraser hearings."[113] From a more geographically distant perspective, David D. Newsom remembers that as ambassador to Indonesia, he was able to use congressional activism on human rights in his relations in Jakarta, suggesting that congressional efforts could curb human rights violations and lead to meaningful change beyond the Beltway. Newsom argues, for instance, that he successfully persuaded the government to release prisoners in an attempt to avoid congressional sanction, contributing to the release of nearly thirty thousand political prisoners in Indonesia.[114]

Before the House Foreign Affairs Subcommittee on International Organizations and Movements held hearings on human rights in 1973, the issue had only sporadically captured high-level governmental interest. Fraser's hearings forced a recalibration of U.S. foreign-policy formulation and assured that human rights would be considered. By the fall of 1976, Fraser's subcommittee had held seventy-six hearings on human rights. Fraser noted, "Subcommittee hearings do not, in and of themselves change U.S. foreign policy or improve the observance of human rights in the world. But they can draw attention to neglected problems."[115] Fraser's hearings and those held by other like-minded colleagues, such as Ted Kennedy, Dante Fascell, Charles Diggs, and Benjamin Rosenthal, not only publicized human rights violations internationally but also facilitated legislation to limit U.S. support for repressive regimes. In explaining the end of the slave trade, Steven Pinker has written, "A gradual shift in sensibilities is often incapable of changing actual practices until the change is implemented by the stroke of a pen."[116] In this vein, congressional legislation that curbed military and economic assistance to governments that abused human rights and also created institutions to monitor human rights around the world formalized the growing attention to human rights in the preceding years. As the executive branch's commitment to the issue fluctuated depending on who occupied the White House, persistent congressional attention to the issue was essential to its continued salience. Such steps slowly transformed attitudes at the State Department, and in the United States more broadly, about prioritizing concern for human rights in U.S. foreign policy. In subsequent years, concern for international human rights deepened, and eventually it grew into an international movement comprising nongovernmental organizations, individuals, and key political actors that had far-reaching implications for international relations.

The motivations, targets, and rhetoric of human rights activism during the long 1960s marked significant breaks with activists from the late 1940s and 1950s. Amid the various 1960s-era domestic social movements, Americans were also making transnational connections that drove their interest in international causes; their travel, marriages, Peace Corps service, academic connections, and missionary work drove them to care about human rights violations in foreign countries and to pressure the U.S. government to address their concerns through its foreign policy. In the case of the Soviet Union, American Jews, allies of Soviet dissidents, and notably, Senator Henry Jackson were propelled by personal ties—including religion and connections forged through travel—as well as a broader commitment to freedom of expression and movement. Americans opposed to Smith's discriminatory regime in Southern Rhodesia were inspired by their participation in the black freedom movement in the United States. The most prominent voices on Rhodesia, including African American leaders and Arthur Goldberg, acted based on shared racial identity and universal notions about race and human rights. Transnational connections, particularly to Andreas Papandreou and Maria Becket, as well as broader concerns about torture motivated Americans to work against the colonels in Greece. Diplomats who had served or were serving in Seoul and missionaries working in South Korea, all with significant transnational connections to those facing human rights abuses, were most active in pressing for a new U.S. approach to Park's government. Ideological allies of Allende, missionaries, and liberal members of Congress, prompted in part by transnational connections, urged the Nixon and Ford administrations to limit their support for Pinochet's government.

This activism was driven by nonstate and lower-level actors who saw the U.S. government as the entity that could have the greatest effect on human rights violations abroad rather than the UN or foreign governments—two targets of activism in the early Cold War years.[1] These activists' vision identified the United States—both its values and its power—as being at the center of the international system, which illuminates how these Americans conceived of their role in U.S. foreign-policy making and the role of the United States in the world during the long 1960s.

This shift in focus, away from the UN in New York toward the federal government in Washington, is the second novel and significant characteristic of human rights activism during the long 1960s. Since the late 1940s, human rights groups had been headquartered in New York City, where with UN observer status they could direct attention at UN bodies and diplomats. The model of the International League of the Rights of Man was a standard one for the time: to bring "violations to the attention of the particular government through its Ambassador in Washington or its Mission to the UN. If no reply is forth-coming or is inadequate, the matter is pressed further by bringing it to the attention of the Secretary General of the UN or to the press and the world community."[2] Thus it was notable that in July 1967 the ILRM outlined a plan for more assertively tackling human rights violations by moving beyond correspondence with foreign diplomats and by shifting its attention away from New York.[3] By 1975 the ILRM proposed creating a lawyers' committee in Washington to enhance its effectiveness in achieving the organization's agenda.[4] In a similar move, Amnesty International USA opened a Washington office in 1976.[5] Moving the geographic focus of American human rights activism from New York to Washington also represented deep frustration with the effectiveness of the UN as a forum for addressing human rights violations, which led advocates in the United States, the Soviet Union, and elsewhere to lose faith in the UN as a body through which human rights could be protected.[6]

The long 1960s was a period during which Americans who fought against racial discrimination, U.S. support for repressive regimes, and the use of torture came to adopt the lexicon of "human rights" to describe their activism. For example, Joseph Eldridge commented, "Before the Fraser report, I didn't think of what I was doing as 'human rights' work." John Salzberg, Eldridge remembers, "helped me to recognize that we were in a human rights struggle."[7] Similarly, Ronald D. Palmer, a longtime State Department official, remembers that in mid-1975 James Wilson asked him to join his team working on "something called human rights," which suggests the term's novelty within State Department officialdom; Wilson recalls that when he asked whether he would be interested in taking on a role that included human rights, he replied, "quite truthfully, that I knew nothing about human rights beyond an acquaintanceship with the UN Universal Declaration of Human Rights during my law school days."[8]

The outcomes of this activism included the institutionalization of attention to human rights in U.S. foreign policy and the elevation of the issue among broader American audiences. This is reflected in polls, which show that by 1974, 66.9 percent of Americans agreed "strongly" or "somewhat" that the United States "should put pressure on countries which systematically violate basic human rights."[9] In addition, 72.9 percent of Americans agreed "strongly" or "somewhat" that it was "morally wrong" for the United States to support military dictators that violate their citizens' rights.[10]

Human rights emerged as a relevant issue for U.S. foreign policy despite the obstructionist efforts of Henry Kissinger. Outlining the frustrations that diplomats faced when reporting human rights violations to the Kissinger State Department, Miles Pendleton Jr. recalls writing about two hundred thousand people who were killed in Burundi, mostly with sledgehammers, in 1972. This reporting was seen as "inconvenient," and the message from the secretary's office was, "Do not waste the secretary's time with such a thing." As Pendleton remembers, "This was the kind of non–human rights guidance which prevailed."[11] Such experiences make it unsurprising that Kissinger was often the focus of activists' ire as much as repressive dictators were. Whether from conservative democrats who disagreed that the pursuit of détente should trump the plight of Soviet Jews or from liberals in Congress who recoiled at U.S. complicity in the coup in Chile, Kissinger resisted pressure from many sides. He even faced tough questioning from aides such as Philip Habib, William Rogers, and Winston Lord, who thought that taking greater consideration of human rights, rather than maintaining an intransigent position that largely ignored them as an element of U.S. foreign relations, might better protect U.S. interests. Particularly significant are Lord's memos spanning five years, which seem to represent a surprising dissent from Kissinger's worldview. Lord and other State Department officials, whether in Washington or serving as diplomats overseas, were far more attentive to and concerned about human rights than previous Kissinger-centered studies have recognized. Kissinger, however, held firm in his views; only when political expediency—namely the 1976 election—made a new approach important did he incorporate human rights into his rhetoric and diplomacy.

These three shifts—in inspiration, focus, and language—marked a meaningful transformation in American human rights activism and led to considerable achievements in terms of U.S. foreign policy. Subsequent years saw even greater institutionalization of attention to human rights in the State Department. For example, the coordinator's position was elevated to assistant secretary of state for human rights and humanitarian affairs in August 1977, and several months later the Department of State established the Bureau of Human Rights and Humanitarian Affairs. These bureaucratic reforms as well as the State Department's annual country reports were the result of congressional initiatives.[12] Furthermore, the Carter administration appointed many individuals who had been pressing the issue of human rights from outside the executive branch, such as Mark Schneider and ILRM executive director Roberta Cohen.

Americans active on human rights during the long 1960s achieved congressional legislation that curbed military and economic assistance to repressive governments, established institutions to monitor human rights around the world, and shifted patterns of U.S. foreign-policy making for years to come. These connections during the long 1960s led to the creation of a broader transnational network in the years that followed. By the mid to late 1970s, human rights organizations worked as part of a broad-based network along with labor unions, religious groups, State Department officials, members of Congress and their aides, and professional associations to advocate for a new approach to U.S. foreign policy.[13] An international human rights movement eventually developed, which included people who compiled information on human rights abuses, legal experts who acted as advocates for those whose rights were being abused, medical experts who treated victims, and supporters who offered financial, emotional, and other support.[14]

Although Jimmy Carter's inauguration in 1977 seemed, at the time, to represent the culmination of human rights activists' efforts, with a longer view, *From Selma to Moscow: How Human Rights Activists Transformed U.S. Foreign Policy* is an instructive rather than triumphal tale. The years since the terrorist attacks on September 11, 2001, have revealed that the place of human rights in U.S. foreign policy remains contested, debated by the president, his lawyers, members of Congress, NGOs such as Human Rights Watch and the ACLU, and the American public. Not only did the United States increasingly collaborate with repressive governments with the objective of fighting international terrorism during the years since 9/11, the country also became an abuser of human rights. It violated human rights in Afghanistan, Iraq, Cuba, and the United States among other known and unknown sites. As in the long 1960s, members of Congress, foreign service officers, lawyers, journalists, human rights professionals, and outraged members of the public worked to reveal and curtail American engagement in and support for human rights abuses. Although considerable progress has been made—the United States no longer tortures or operates covert prisons—many troubling policies remain, such as rendition; indefinite detention of prisoners at Guantanamo Bay, Cuba; and the increasing use of drone warfare. *From Selma to Moscow* shows that the challenges facing 1960s-era activists—in particular, deciding how to balance morality and adherence to American values with the preservation of national security as well as determining how to advance a policy agenda that is resisted by the White House—have continuing relevance to U.S. foreign policy today.

NOTES

ABBREVIATIONS

ACLU Records	American Civil Liberties Union Records
ACOA	American Committee on Africa Records
ACOA Addendum	American Committee of Africa Records Addendum
ADST	Foreign Affairs Oral History Collection of the Association for Diplomatic Studies and Training
AI IS	Amnesty International International Secretariat Archives
AIUSA Records	Amnesty International USA Records
CFPF	Central Foreign Policy Files
CPUSA	Communist Party of the United States of America Papers TAM.132, Tamiment Library
FRUS	Department of State, *Foreign Relations of the United States*, 1961–1976 (Washington, DC: United States Printing Office, 1993–2011)
GRFPL	Gerald R. Ford Presidential Library
ILHRC	International League for Human Rights Collection, New York Public Library
JFKPL	John F. Kennedy Presidential Library
LBJPL	Lyndon Baines Johnson Presidential Library
MREC	Archivo General Histórico, Ministerio de Relaciones Exteriores de Chile
NARA	National Archives and Records Administration
NAUK	National Archives, United Kingdom
NPMP	Richard Nixon Presidential Materials Project
S/P	Policy Planning Staff
WHCF	White House Central Files
WOLA Records	Washington Office on Latin America Records

INTRODUCTION

1. On the influence of Carter and his administration in ushering in greater attention to human rights in U.S. foreign policy, see David F. Schmitz and Vanessa Walker, "Jimmy Carter and the Foreign Policy of Human Rights: The Development of a Post–Cold War Foreign Policy," *Diplomatic History* 28 (January 2004): 113, 117. On the legacy of the Vietnam War, see Barbara J. Keys, *Reclaiming American Virtue: The Human Rights Revolution of the 1970s* (Cambridge, MA: Harvard University Press, 2014). I have not seen evidence of the emotions shame or guilt as factors motivating the activism under analysis here. On utopias, see Samuel Moyn, *The Last Utopia* (Cambridge, MA: Harvard University Press, 2010).

2. Other countries such as Iran and China had widespread human rights violations but sparked little outrage in the United States. South Africa did warrant substantial interest during the long 1960s but has already received considerable scholarly attention. See, for example, Ryan M. Irwin, *Gordian Knot: Apartheid and the Unmaking of the Liberal World Order* (New York: Oxford University Press, 2012); Thomas Borstelmann, *The Cold War and the Color Line: American Race Relations in the Global Arena* (Cambridge, MA: Harvard University Press, 2001); Francis Njubi Nesbitt, *Race for Sanctions: African Americans Against Apartheid, 1946–1994* (Bloomington: Indiana University Press, 2004); David L. Hostetter, *Movement Matters: American Antiapartheid Activism and the Rise of Multicultural Politics* (London: Routledge, 2006).

3. Both Kennedy and Carter used the term "human rights" in their inaugural addresses in ways that suggested to listeners the connections between domestic and international human rights. See "John F. Kennedy Quotations: President Kennedy's Inaugural Address, January 20, 1961," John F. Kennedy Presidential Library and Museum, http://www.jfklibrary.org/Research/Research-Aids/Ready-Reference/JFK-Quotations/Inaugural-Address.aspx, accessed April 27, 2016; "Inaugural Address of President Jimmy Carter, Thursday, January 20, 1977," Jimmy Carter Presidential Library and Museum, https://www.jimmycarterlibrary.gov/assets/documents/speeches/inaugadd.phtml, accessed April 27, 2016. Unfortunately, Kennedy's speechwriter Ted Sorensen does not write in his biography about the inclusion of the term "human rights" in Kennedy's inaugural address. Ted Sorensen, *Kennedy: The Classic Biography*, rev. ed. (New York: Harper Perennial, 2009). Taylor Branch points out that Kennedy did not mention "segregation, civil rights, or race" in his inaugural address. Taylor Branch, *Parting the Waters: America in the King Years, 1954–63* (New York: Simon & Schuster, 1988), 384.

4. In another formulation, historian Tanya Harmer characterizes the "long decade of the 1960s" as stretching from the Cuban revolution in 1959 until the 1973 coup against Chilean president Salvador Allende. Tanya Harmer, *Allende's Chile and the Inter-American Cold War* (Chapel Hill: University of North Carolina Press, 2011), 265. Simon Hall's *Peace and Freedom* examines the intersection of the freedom and peace movements during the "long 1960s," this time from 1960 to 1972. Simon Hall, *Peace and Freedom: The Civil Rights and Antiwar Movements in the 1960s* (Philadelphia: University of Pennsylvania Press, 2005), 1–2. Hall's work clarifies for me the distinction between the "long 1960s" and the "long 1970s" in that the former was a period of liberal mobilization whereas the defining characteristic of the latter is a turn toward conservatism. Thus, this book sits firmly in the 1960s. Simon Hall, "Protest Movements in

the 1970s: The Long 1960s," *Journal of Contemporary History* 43, no. 4 (2008): 655–72. See also Andrew Marwick, "'1968' and the Cultural Revolution of the Long Sixties (c. 1958–c. 1974)," in *Transnational Moments of Change: Europe 1945, 1968, 1989*, ed. Gerd-Rainer Horn and Padraic Kenney (New York: Rowman & Littlefield, 2004), 81; Michael Kazin, *American Dreamers: How the Left Changed a Nation* (New York: Knopf, 2011), 210, 229; Akira Iriye and Rana Mitter, Foreword to *1968 in Europe: A History of Protest and Activism, 1956–1977*, ed. Martin Klimke and Joachim Scharloth (New York: Palgrave Macmillan, 2008), vii; Martin Klimke and Joachim Scharloth, "1968 in Europe: An Introduction," in *1968 in Europe: A History of Protest and Activism, 1956–1977*, ed. Martin Klimke and Joachim Scharloth (New York: Palgrave Macmillan, 2008), 2–3, 5; Martin Klimke, *The Other Alliance: Student Protest in West Germany & the United States in the Global Sixties* (Princeton, NJ: Princeton University Press, 2010), 244; Risa L. Goluboff, *Vagrant Nation: Police Power, Constitutional Change, and the Making of the 1960s* (New York: Oxford University Press, 2016), 10; Jan Eckel, "The International League for the Rights of Man, Amnesty International, and the Changing Fate of Human Rights Activism from the 1940s Through the 1970s," *Humanity* 4, no. 2 (Summer 2013): 200. I am conscious of some of the problems with focusing on a decade, even a "long" one, as the most relevant unit of time. Jason Scott Smith, "The Strange History of the Decade: Modernity, Nostalgia, and the Perils of Periodization," *Journal of Social History* 32, no. 2 (Winter 1998): 263–85.

5. "Universal Declaration of Human Rights," United Nations, http://www.un.org/en/universal-declaration-human-rights/index.html, accessed May 20, 2015.

6. For further discussion, see Thomas F. Jackson, *From Civil Rights to Human Rights: Martin Luther King, Jr., and the Struggle for Economic Justice* (Philadelphia: University of Pennsylvania Press, 2007), 341, 351. Among activists who mobilized against abuses in Chile were ideological allies of the socialist president Salvador Allende who were therefore more likely to identify themselves as champions of social and economic rights.

7. Several like-minded organizations were headquartered at the Willkie Building during its early years, including the NAACP, the United States Committee for Refugees, the Inter-American Association for Democracy and Freedom, the Anti-Defamation League, and the Metropolitan Council of B'Nai B'rith. Because the mortgage had been paid off on the building as of May 1946, the organizations housed there did not pay rent. They only contributed to the maintenance of the building. In a 1963 fundraising appeal, the Willkie Building's president articulated its mission as housing "independent non-profit organizations devoted to the cause of freedom." Gideonse Appeal, Folder 13, Box 80, Freedom House Records, Public Policy Papers, Seely G. Mudd Manuscript Library, Princeton University.

8. For further discussion, see Eckel, "The International League," 184–87.

9. The ILRM was established in the United States in 1942 as an effort to reconstitute the French Ligue Française pour la Défense des Droits de L'Homme et du Citoyen, which had fallen apart with the outbreak of war in Europe. Laurie S. Wiseberg and Harry M. Scoble, "The International League for Human Rights: The Strategy of a Human Rights NGO," *Georgia Journal of International & Comparative Law* 7 (1977): 292–93, 296, 300.

10. The awardees of Freedom House's annual Freedom Award reveal the organization's definition of "freedom." Selecting cold warriors, such as Berlin mayor Willy

Brandt in 1961 or the father of European integration Jean Monnet in 1963, signaled that the organization was most concerned with freedom from communism (and particularly freedom behind the Iron Curtain), with peace and democracy, and increasingly with black freedom.

11. For criticism of narrow constructions of human rights based on phrasing, see Sarita Cargas, "Questioning Samuel Moyn's Revisionist History of Human Rights," *Human Rights Quarterly* 38, no. 2 (May 2016): 412; Kenneth Cmiel, "The Recent History of Human Rights," *American Historical Review* 109, no. 1 (2004): 119.

12. Klimke, *The Other Alliance*, 3. For a broader discussion of postwar transnational connections, see Akira Iriye, Introduction to *Global Interdependence: The World After 1945*, ed. Akira Iriye (Cambridge, MA: Belknap Press of Harvard University Press, 2014), 4. See also Jean H. Quataert, *Advocating Dignity: Human Rights Mobilizations in Global Politics* (Philadelphia: University of Pennsylvania Press, 2009), 7.

13. International migration and tourism increased between 1960 and 1980. According to Iriye, the "transnational encounters" of the 1960s and 1970s "served to alter drastically the traditional perception of the world as consisting of nations." Akira Iriye, "The Transnationalization of Humanity," in *Global Interdependence: The World after 1945*, ed. Akira Iriye (Cambridge, MA: Belknap Press of Harvard University Press, 2014), 738–39. Barbara Keys argues that human rights was the purview of "international lawyers and a few church groups" during the 1960s, but my work demonstrates that a much wider range of actors was involved. Keys, *Reclaiming American Virtue*, 57.

14. Patrick William Kelly, *Sovereign Emergencies: Latin America and the Making of Global Human Rights Politics* (New York: Cambridge University Press, 2018). In its first ten years, more than 38,500 Americans participated in the Peace Corps program. A former Peace Corps volunteer reported that his or her experience enabled a critical appraisal of the United States from a distance and a commitment to improve the country upon the volunteers' return. Brent Ashabranner, *A Moment in History: The First Ten Years of the Peace Corps* (Garden City, NY: Doubleday, 1971), 363, 365. See also James N. Green, *We Cannot Remain Silent: Opposition to the Brazilian Military Dictatorship in the United States* (Durham, NC: Duke University Press, 2010), 70. On the history of the Peace Corps, see Elizabeth Cobbs Hoffman, *All You Need Is Love: The Peace Corps and the Spirit of the 1960s* (Cambridge, MA: Harvard University Press, 1998).

15. Russell Sveda, Oral History Interview, June 28, 2000, ADST.

16. Mark Bradley also sees transnational encounters as significant but regards them as not affecting American human rights activism significantly until the 1970s. Mark Philip Bradley, *The World Reimagined: Americans and Human Rights in the Twentieth Century* (New York: Cambridge University Press, 2016), 135.

17. James Becket, *Barbarism in Greece* (New York: Walker, 1970), ix.

18. Frank C. Newman, Oral History Interview Conducted 1989 and 1991 by Carol Hicke, Regional Oral History Office, University of California–Berkeley, California State Archives State Government Oral History Program.

19. Their activism included starting a magazine, the *Rhodesia News Summary*, to disseminate information on the conditions there. Ada J. Focer, "Frontier Internship in Mission, 1961–1974: Young Christians Abroad in a Post-Colonial and Cold War World" (PhD Diss., Boston University, 2016), 213, 405–13. See also Raymond Joseph Parrott, "Struggle for Solidarity: The New Left, Portuguese African Decolonization, and the

End of the Cold War Consensus" (PhD Diss., University of Texas–Austin, 2016), 264–69.

20. Although I had expected to see a greater role for ethnic interest groups, their influence was limited. For a fuller discussion of the influence of ethnic interest groups on the American political process, see Alexander DeConde, *Ethnicity, Race, and American Foreign Policy: A History* (Boston: Northeastern University Press, 1992), 141; Tony Smith, *Foreign Attachments: The Power of Ethnic Groups in the Making of American Foreign Policy* (Cambridge, MA: Harvard University Press, 2000), 94. For a different interpretation, see Joe Renouard, *Human Rights in American Foreign Policy: From the 1960s to the Soviet Collapse* (Philadelphia: University of Pennsylvania Press, 2016), 10, 101–9.

21. Rita Hauser, November 25, 1969, A/C.3/SR.1714 (New York: United Nations, 1969).

22. Roberta Cohen, Oral History Interview, September 26, 2008, ADST. The International League for the Rights of Man changed its name to the International League for Human Rights in March 1976.

23. Kelly, *Sovereign Emergencies*.

24. For more on religious motives, see Andrew Preston, *Sword of the Spirit, Shield of the Faith: Religion in American War and Diplomacy* (New York: Knopf, 2012), 7; David A. Hollinger, *After Cloven Tongues of Fire: Protestant Liberalism in Modern American History* (Princeton, NJ: Princeton University Press, 2013), 46–47.

25. Marwick, "'1968,'" 89.

26. Petra Goedde, "Challenging Cultural Norms," in *Global Interdependence: The World after 1945*, ed. Akira Iriye (Cambridge, MA: Belknap Press of Harvard University Press, 2014), 606.

27. Liisa H. Malkki, *The Need to Help: The Domestic Arts of International Humanitarianism* (Durham, NC: Duke University Press, 2015), 4, 8, 10.

28. Ibid., 162.

29. Pope Paul VI, "Declaration on Religious Freedom," December 7, 1965, The Holy See, http://www.vatican.va/archive/hist_councils/ii_vatican_council/documents/vat -ii_decl_19651207_dignitatis-humanae_en.html, accessed March 25, 2016; Pope Paul VI, "Gaudium et Spes," December 7, 1965, The Holy See, http://www.vatican.va/archive /hist_councils/ii_vatican_council/documents/vat-ii_cons_19651207_gaudium-et -spes_en.html, accessed March 25, 2016.

30. There may have been other factors at play in congressional efforts to reduce assistance to repressive regimes. Assistant to the president for legislative affairs William E. Timmons noted that congressional support for foreign aid had "been eroding steadily. Opposition stems from competition for funds for domestic programs and a 'hangover' from the Vietnam War." Memorandum, September 10, 1974, Congressional (4), Box 2, Wilson Accession, 9/76–8/77, James M. Wilson Papers, GRFPL.

31. Rosemary Foot, "The Cold War and Human Rights," in *The Cambridge History of the Cold War Volume III: Endings*, ed. Melvyn P. Leffler and Odd Arne Westad (Cambridge: Cambridge University Press, 2010), 454; Michael Cotey Morgan, "The Seventies and the Rebirth of Human Rights," in *The Shock of the Global: The 1970s in Perspective*, ed. Niall Ferguson et al. (Cambridge, MA: Harvard University Press, 2010), 240–41. One notable dissenter is Samuel Moyn, who does not see the movement for decolonization as a human rights movement. Moyn, *The Last Utopia*, 85.

32. Roland Burke, *Decolonization and the Evolution of International Human Rights* (Philadelphia: University of Pennsylvania Press, 2010), 12, 148–49.

33. Baldwin to Papanek, May 26, 1968, Folder 4, Box 8, Roger N. Baldwin Papers, Public Policy Papers, Seeley G. Mudd Manuscript Library, Princeton University.

34. "The League and Interventions," ibid.

35. Sidney Tarrow, *The New Transnational Activism* (Cambridge: Cambridge University Press, 2005), 9, 32, 101–2, 120, 124, 145.

36. British lawyer Peter Benenson established Amnesty International at a unique, liberalizing moment during the Cold War. Sarah B. Snyder, "Exporting Amnesty International to the United States: Transatlantic Human Rights Activism in the 1960s," *Human Rights Quarterly* 34, no. 3 (August 2012): 779–99; Tom Buchanan, "'The Truth Will Set You Free': The Making of Amnesty International," *Journal of Contemporary History* 37, no. 4 (2002): 575–97.

37. "They Fight to Free the World's 'Prisoners of Conscience,'" *Reader's Digest* (February 1965): 131–35; Meeting Minutes, November 10, 1965, Meetings 1965, Box 1, Series 1: 1, Record Group 1, AIUSA Records. Moyn, however, has argued that Amnesty International was "practically unknown" during the 1960s. Moyn, *The Last Utopia*, 3.

38. Interestingly, Baldwin termed AIUSA's work "international civil rights." Minutes, October 26, 1970, 1970, Box 1, Series 1: 1, Record Group 1, AIUSA Records; Umberto Tulli, "'Whose Rights Are Human Rights?': The Ambiguous Emergence of Human Rights and the Demise of Kissingerism," *Cold War History* 12, no. 4 (November 2012): 579; Wiseberg and Scoble, "The International League," 290.

39. Butler to Ford Foundation, September 23, 1976, Grant 07690811, Reel 3652, Ford Foundation Records, Rockefeller Archive Center, Sleepy Hollow, NY.

40. Recommendation, Human Rights: Korea—Correspondence September 1, 1974–3/31/1975, Box 1, Entry UD—13D 15, Record Group 59, NARA.

41. "United States and International Human Rights—Retrospect and Prospects," December 1968, Executive IT 47–9/A, Box 13, WHCF, LBJPL.

42. Tape Transcription, "UN Implementation of Human Rights," March 30, 1966, Human Rights Commission: International Conventions on Human Rights, Box 88, Series 1, Morris B. Abram Papers, Manuscript, Archives, and Rare Book Library, Emory University. After Johnson's June 1965 conference on civil rights, Abram reported that he "returned to the United Nations confident that the American record in civil rights, fortified by recent advances in legislation and court decisions, could, like our American productivity, be valuable foreign policy assets." Morris B. Abram, *The Day Is Short: An Autobiography* (New York: Harcourt Brace Jovanovich, 1982), 158. The chronology of American improvements to its human rights record, as well as the timing of increased disillusionment with U.S. foreign policy, explains why there was relatively less human rights activism during Kennedy's presidency.

43. According to Mary Dudziak, after Johnson's signing of the 1965 Voting Rights Act, "The executive branch had come to be believe it had resolved the Cold War/civil rights dilemma, and that race in America no longer damaged the nation's prestige abroad." Mary Dudziak, *Cold War Civil Rights: Race and the Image of American Democracy* (Princeton, NJ: Princeton University Press, 2000), 241.

44. Report of the Committee on Human Rights of the National Citizens' Commission on International Cooperation, Untitled-1970s Corres, Speeches, Printed Mat'l—Human Rights, Box 82, Series 1, Abram Papers.

45. Risa L. Goluboff, *The Lost Promise of Civil Rights* (Cambridge, MA: Harvard University Press, 2007), 266.

46. For further discussion of transnational connections among African Americans and black Africans fighting for greater rights, see James H. Meriwether, *Proudly We Can Be Africans: Black Americans and Africa, 1935–1961* (Chapel Hill: University of North Carolina Press, 2002), 142. The late 1960s were a time of increasing attention to Black Studies in the academy. Jonathan Fenderson, James Stewart, and Kabria Baumgartner, "Expanding the History of the Black Studies Movement: Some Prefatory Notes," *Journal of African American Studies* 16 (2012): 2.

47. Minutes, Trustees Meeting, May 10, 1966, Box 1, George Field Collection, Public Policy Papers, Seeley G. Mudd Manuscript Library, Princeton University.

48. Dudziak, *Cold War Civil Rights*, 212.

49. Address, March 23, 1961, Wofford Speeches, Box 14, Series 1, Harris Wofford White House Staff Files, JFKPL.

50. Gal Beckerman, *When They Come for Us, We'll Be Gone* (New York: Houghton Mifflin Harcourt, 2010), 138.

51. Maurice Isserman and Michael Kazin, *America Divided: The Civil War of the 1960s* (New York: Oxford University Press, 2000), 117. Thomas Jefferson described the United States as a "monument of human rights" in 1809. "Thomas Jefferson to the Citizens of Washington, DC, 4 March 1809," Founders Online, http://founders.archives .gov/documents/Jefferson/03-01-02-0006, accessed May 19, 2015. In Risa Goluboff's description, the civil rights movement shifted from emphasizing social and economic rights to civil and political rights in the 1950s and 1960s, shortly before Johnson stressed greater attention to the former. Goluboff, *The Lost Promise*, 264–65.

52. Goluboff, *Vagrant Nation*, 6. Growing attention to violations of human rights during the long 1960s may also fit with the rising attention to child abuse, and then incest, marital rape, and other types of family violence, in the 1960s and 1970s, which Linda Gordon describes. Linda Gordon, *Heroes of Their Own Lives: The Politics and History of Family Violence, Boston 1880–1960* (New York: Viking, 1988), 1.

53. Brian Balogh, *The Associational State: American Governance in the Twentieth Century* (Philadelphia: University of Pennsylvania Press, 2015), 183. Martin Klimke and Joachim Scharloth have shown how European protesters, like human rights activists, learned many tactics from the civil rights and free speech movements in the United States. Klimke and Scharloth, "1968 in Europe," 2–3, 5. See also Klimke, *The Other Alliance*, 6, 103.

54. The committee turned its attention to South Africa in 1967. Recommendation for Grant, February 10, 1975, Grant 07300040, Reel 4406, Ford Foundation Records; William Korey, *Taking On the World's Repressive Regimes: The Ford Foundation's International Human Rights Policies and Practices* (New York: Palgrave Macmillan, 2007), 147, 153, 175. The American Civil Liberties Union and the Ford Foundation saw their shifts to international human rights as grounded in their commitment to domestic rights. Francis X. Sutton, "Human Rights Freedom, and the Liberal Tradition," Report 009588, Unpublished Reports, Ford Foundation Records.

55. James N. Green, "Clerics, Exiles, and Academics: Opposition to the Brazilian Military Dictatorship in the United States, 1969–1974," *Latin American Politics and Society* 45, no. 1 (Spring 2003): 109–10.

56. Moyn, *The Last Utopia*, 159. Similarly, Joe Renouard, Stephen Hopgood, and Barbara Keys do not see the social movements of the 1960s as very significant in rising attention to human rights. Renouard, *Human Rights*, 11; Stephen Hopgood, *The Endtimes of Human Rights* (Ithaca, NY: Cornell University Press, 2013), 97; Keys, *Reclaiming American Virtue*, 33.

57. For example, historian Benjamin Nathans argues that American Jews turned to the cause of Soviet Jewry as they were increasingly marginalized in the civil rights movement. Benjamin Nathans, "The Wild Desire to Leave: On Soviet Jewry," *The Nation*, November 10, 2010. See also Nathaniel A. Kurz, "'A Sphere Above the Nations?': The Rise and Fall of International Jewish Human Rights Politics" (PhD Diss., Yale University, 2015), 288.

58. Johnson administration officials such as its delegate to the UN Human Rights Commission Morris Abram suggested that Johnson's War on Poverty was extending social and economic rights. "United States and International Human Rights—Retrospect and Prospects," December 1968, Executive IT 47–9/A, Box 13, WHCF, LBJPL. Important texts that further shaped my thinking about this question were Irwin, *Gordian Knot*; Hanne Hagtvedt Vik, "The United States, the American Legal Community and the Vision of International Human Rights Protection, 1941–1953" (PhD Diss., University of Oslo, 2009), 6. See also Jared Michael Phillips, "Toward a Better World: LBJ, Niebuhr, and American Human Rights, 1964–1966," *Ozark Historical Review* 38 (Spring 2009): 31. For a more negative picture of the War on Poverty, see Elizabeth Hinton, *From the War on Poverty to the War on Crime: The Making of Mass Incarceration in America* (Cambridge, MA: Harvard University Press, 2016), 32.

59. Sohn to McPherson, February 14, 1966, United Nations, Box 17, Office Files of Harry McPherson, LBJPL.

60. Press Release, March 4, 1968, Human Rights Commission: International Conventions on Human Rights, Box 88, Series 1, Abram Papers.

61. Lyndon B. Johnson, "Commencement Address at Howard University: 'To Fulfill These Rights,'" in *Public Papers of the Presidents of the United States: Lyndon B. Johnson, 1965: Volume II* (Washington, DC: Government Printing Office, 1966), 635–40.

62. Irwin, *Gordian Knot*, 91.

63. Those who opposed the war in Vietnam overlapped in many ways with those advocating for greater civil rights for African Americans in the United States. For further discussion, see Thomas Borstelmann, *The 1970s: A New Global History from Civil Rights to Economic Inequality* (Princeton, NJ: Princeton University Press, 2012), 181, 204; Foot, "The Cold War," 446, 450, 457, 464; Clair Apodaca, *Understanding U.S. Human Rights Policy: A Paradoxical Legacy* (New York: Routledge, 2006), xiv; Goedde, "Challenging Cultural Norms," 599.

64. Donald Fraser, Speech, May 30, 1979, Folder 5/30/79, Human Rights Conference for the Fed Bar Association, Box 149.C.13.4 (F), Donald M. Fraser Papers, Minnesota Historical Society, St. Paul.

65. Borstelmann, *The Cold War*, 177; Jeremi Suri, *Power and Protest: Global Revolution and the Rise of Détente* (Cambridge, MA: Harvard University Press, 2003), 3, 163.

66. David F. Schmitz and Natalie Fousekis, "Frank Church, the Senate, and the Emergence of Dissent on the Vietnam War," *Pacific Historical Review* 63, no. 4

(November 1994): 579. See also Renouard, *Human Rights*, 26. According to Van Gosse, due to the Vietnam War, after 1967, "opposition to U.S. foreign policy became pervasive instead of marginal," which enabled many to question the government and push for greater protections of human rights. Van Gosse, "Unpacking the Vietnam Syndrome: The Coup in Chile and the Rise of Popular Anti-Interventionism," in *The World the '60s Made: Politics and Culture in Recent America*, ed. Van Gosse and Richard Moser (Philadelphia: Temple University Press, 2003), 100. See also Yves Dezalay and Bryant Garth, "From the Cold War to Kosovo: The Rise and Renewal of the Field of International Human Rights," *Annual Review of Law and Social Science* (2006): 239.

67. Moral opposition to the policy of containment, which had led to American involvement in Vietnam, fueled critiques of United States policy. See, for example, Hans Göran Franck to Johnson, August 4, 1966, AMMO, Box 142, WHCF—Name File, LBJPL; "Human Rights in the Vietnam War," April 21, 1968, U.S. Vietnam Correspondence, 1964–66, Box 36, ILHRC; Donald M. Fraser, "Human Rights and U.S. Foreign Policy: Some Basic Questions Regarding Principles and Practice," *International Studies Quarterly* 23, no. 2 (June 1979): 176. In Joseph Eldridge's view, activists who had opposed the war in Vietnam shifted their attention to Latin America as the war ended. Joseph Eldridge, Interview with the Author, April 13, 2016. In Keys's argument, human rights was not regarded as "a means of coming to terms with the Vietnam war but as a means of moving past it." Human rights was a way to overcome "guilt" and "revulsion" over Vietnam. Keys, *Reclaiming American Virtue*, 3, 63. Others have suggested that congressional interest in human rights during the early 1970s was spurred by attention to the issue of Jewish emigration from the Soviet Union. Richard Schifter, Interview, "The Life and Legacy of George Lister: Reconsidering Human Rights, Democracy, and U.S. Foreign Policy," Bernard and Audre Rapoport Center for Human Rights and Justice, University of Texas School of Law.

68. See, for example, Resolution on Violations of Human Rights in Vietnam, January 24, 1966, U.S. Vietnam Correspondence, 1964–66, Box 36, ILHRC; League to Rusk, February 21, 1968, ibid.; League to Harriman, ibid.; U.S. Study Team to Nixon, June 5, 1969, ibid.

69. "Human Rights in the Vietnam War," Vietnam—Statement on (1968), Box 48, ILHRC.

70. Annual Review 1974–1975, Folder 2812, Box 461, Record Group 3, Rockefeller Brothers Fund, Rockefeller Archive Center, Sleepy Hollow, NY.

71. Press Release, June 10, 1969, Vietnam, 1969, Box 151.I.11.6 (F), Fraser Papers.

72. Kathryn Sikkink, *Mixed Signals: U.S. Human Rights Policy and Latin America* (Ithaca, NY: Cornell University Press, 2004), 20–21; Gosse, "Unpacking the Vietnam Syndrome," 100–101; Carlos Chipoco and Lars Schoultz, Program Evaluation, 1981 Ford Evaluation, Box 28, WOLA Records.

73. Thomas C. Field, *From Development to Dictatorship: Bolivia and the Alliance for Progress in the Kennedy Era* (Ithaca, NY: Cornell University Press, 2014), 3.

74. Daniel J. Sargent, *A Superpower Transformed: The Remaking of American Foreign Relations in the 1970s* (New York: Oxford University Press, 2015), 99.

75. Daniel A. O'Donohue, Oral History Interview, May 28, 1996, ADST. See also Robert D. Schulzinger, "Richard Nixon, Congress, and the War in Vietnam, 1969–1974," in *Vietnam and the American Political Tradition: The Politics of Dissent*, ed. Randall B. Woods (New York: Cambridge University Press, 2003), 283.

76. Thomas Cronin, "A Resurgent Congress and the Imperial Presidency," *Political Science Quarterly* 95, no. 2 (Summer 1980): 210; "Beyond Distrust: How Americans View Their Government," November 23, 2015, Pew Research Center, http://www.people-press.org/2015/11/23/beyond-distrust-how-americans-view-their-government/, accessed March 30, 2017.

77. See Frank Church, "American Foreign Policy in Transition: Who Will Shape It?," February 3, 1971, Folder 3, Box 11, Series 7.9, Frank Church Papers, Special Collections Department, Albertsons Library, Boise State University.

78. Fraser, "Human Rights," 176.

79. Harry Frankfurt, "The Importance of What We Care About," *Syntheses* 53, no. 2 (November 1982): 263.

80. Benedetta Calandra, "The 'Good Americans': U.S. Solidarity Networks for Chilean and Argentinean Refugees, 1973–1983," *Historia Actual Online* (2010): 26; Julian E. Zelizer, *On Capitol Hill: The Struggle to Reform Congress and Its Consequences, 1948–2000* (New York: Cambridge University Press, 2004), 156.

81. Seymour M. Hersh, *The Price of Power: Kissinger in the Nixon White House* (New York: Summit Books, 1983), 637.

82. Keys, *Reclaiming American Virtue*, 155; Jeremi Suri, *Henry Kissinger and the American Century* (Cambridge, MA: Harvard University Press, 2007), 246.

83. David F. Schmitz, "Senator Frank Church and Opposition to the Vietnam War and the Imperial Presidency," in *Vietnam and the American Political Tradition*, ed. Randall B. Woods (New York: Cambridge University Press, 2003), 147.

84. Edward L. Cleary, *The Struggle for Human Rights in Latin America* (Westport, CT: Praeger, 1997), 144. On the other hand, Balogh argues that it was the Great Society that "democratized politics." Balogh, *The Associational State*, 172, 183, 185.

85. Barbara Keys and Daniel Sargent see détente as opening up space in which attention to human rights could flourish. Keys, *Reclaiming American Virtue*, 10; Sargent, *A Superpower Transformed*, 203; Virginia Bouvier, "The Washington Office on Latin America: Charting a New Path in U.S.–Latin American Relations," Box 28, WOLA Records. On the influence of nonstate actors, see, for example, Preston, *Sword of the Spirit*; Christopher McKnight Nichols, *Promise and Peril: America at the Dawn of a Global Age* (Cambridge, MA: Harvard University Press, 2011); Gregory F. Domber, *Empowering Revolution: America, Poland and the End of the Cold War* (Chapel Hill: University of North Carolina Press, 2014).

86. Michael Nelson, *Resilient America: Electing Nixon in 1968, Channeling Dissent, and Dividing Government* (Lawrence: University Press of Kansas, 2014), xiii.

87. The Democrats were in the majority throughout the long 1960s. It seems unlikely, however, that party affiliation alone fueled the transformation of human rights activism, as the Democratic Party had also dominated Congress for much of the first fifteen years of the Cold War with almost no attention to human rights.

88. Tilly defines a social movement as "a sustained, organized public effort making claims on target authorities," which utilizes methods of political action to demonstrate the movement's "worthiness, unity, numbers, and commitment." Charles Tilly, *Social Movements, 1768–2004* (Boulder, CO: Paradigm, 2004), 3–4, 13.

89. Charles Tilly and Sidney Tarrow, *Contentious Politics* (Boulder, CO: Paradigm, 2007), 4.

90. Roland Burke argues that Amnesty, the ILRM, and later, Helsinki Watch shifted from petitioning the UN to appealing "directly to the heart, reviving human rights with the power of pity." Roland Burke, "Flat Affect? Revisiting Emotion in the Historiography of Human Rights," *Journal of Human Rights* (2015): 123–41.

91. Balogh has written about liberal tactics on public policy: "Congressional hearings became an important venue for articulating still-new demands and exposing executive or local foot-dragging." Balogh, *The Associational State*, 191. The same could be said of members of Congress who wanted human rights to be a greater principle in U.S. foreign policy.

92. Terri Bimes, "Understanding the Rhetorical Presidency," in *The Oxford Handbook of the American Presidency*, ed. George C Edwards III and William G. Howell (New York: Oxford University Press, 2009), 216. As early as May 1975 Kissinger recognized, as he told Ford, "This election is one of the most crucial ever." Thomas Alan Schwartz, "'Henry, . . . Winning an Election Is Terribly Important': Partisan Politics in the History of U.S. Foreign Relations," *Diplomatic History* 33, no. 2 (April 2009): 188.

1. HUMAN RIGHTS ACTIVISM DIRECTED ACROSS THE IRON CURTAIN

1. There has been considerable work on Soviet dissidence. See Benjamin Nathans, "The Dictatorship of Reason: Aleksandr Vol'Pin and the Idea of Rights under 'Developed Socialism,'" *Slavic Review* 66, no. 4 (Winter 2007): 630–63; H. Gordon Skilling, *Samizdat and an Independent Society in Central and Eastern Europe* (London: Macmillan Press, 1989); Lyudmila Alexeyeva, *Soviet Dissent: Contemporary Movements for National, Religious, and Human Rights* (Middletown, CT: Wesleyan University Press, 1985); Emma Gilligan, *Defending Human Rights in Russia: Sergei Kovalyov, Dissident and Human Rights Commissioner, 1969–2003* (New York: Routledge, 2004); Paul Goldberg, *The Final Act: The Dramatic, Revealing Story of the Moscow Helsinki Watch Group* (New York: Morrow, 1988); H. Stuart Hughes, *Sophisticated Rebels: The Political Culture of European Dissent, 1968–1987* (Cambridge, MA: Harvard University Press, 1988); Joshua Rubenstein, *Soviet Dissidents: Their Struggle for Human Rights*, 2nd ed. (Boston: Beacon, 1985). Less attention has been paid to the United States' response to these acts of protest during the 1960s and 1970s. One exception is Barbara Keys, *Reclaiming American Virtue: The Human Rights Revolution of the 1970s* (Cambridge, MA: Harvard University Press, 2014). Existing accounts have largely framed the discussion around Soviet Jewish emigration, and specifically around the Jackson-Vanik Amendment as a struggle between Senator Henry M. Jackson (D-WA) and Kissinger over the wisdom of linking Soviet-American trade to Soviet emigration policy. See, for example, Jeff Bloodworth, "Senator Henry Jackson, the Solzhenitsyn Affair, and American Liberalism," *Pacific Northern Quarterly* (Spring 2006): 75; Robert G. Kaufman, *Henry M. Jackson: A Life in Politics* (Seattle: University of Washington Press, 2000), 4–5, 368; Jeremi Suri, *Henry Kissinger and the American Century* (Cambridge, MA: Harvard University Press, 2007), 244; Mike Bowker and Phil Williams, *Superpower Détente: A Reappraisal* (Newbury Park, CA: Sage, 1988), 163.

2. Although the primary focus of nongovernmental and congressional activism in Eastern Europe was the USSR, human rights abuses in other countries, such as Poland, Romania, Czechoslovakia, the German Democratic Republic, and Yugoslavia, also garnered attention.

3. A conviction for violating Article 70 could result in a seven-year prison sentence followed by two to ten years in internal exile. Violation of Article 190-1 could be punished by three years of imprisonment. Jerry F. Hough, *How the Soviet Union Is Governed* (Cambridge, MA: Harvard University Press, 1979), 279.

4. Yuri Orlov, *Dangerous Thoughts: Memoirs of a Russian Life*, trans. Thomas P. Whitney (New York: Morrow, 1991), 118–22.

5. "Ill Treatment of Prisoners of Conscience in the USSR," Folder 431, AI Indexed Documents, AI IS; "Political Prisoners in the USSR and Their Conditions of Imprisonment," January 30, 1968, ibid.

6. Anatoly Dobrynin, *In Confidence: Moscow's Ambassador to America's Six Cold War Presidents* (New York: Times Books, 1995), 218.

7. See Hope M. Harrison, *Driving the Soviets up the Wall: Soviet–East German Relations, 1953–1961* (Princeton, NJ: Princeton University Press, 2003).

8. Dobrynin, *In Confidence*, 158–59.

9. Alexeyeva, *Soviet Dissent*, 268. I have chosen to use the anglicized version of her name, under which she published in the United States.

10. "Writers in Prison in the USSR," Folder 7, ICM, AI IS. Arthur Goldberg characterized the writers' trial as suppressing their human rights. Press Release, March 6, 1968, Folder 6, Box 52, Part 1, Arthur J. Goldberg Papers, Library of Congress, Washington, DC. Zvi Gitelman argues that the trial of Sinyavsky and Daniel suggested the limits of potential reform to Soviet Jews. Zvi Gitelman, "Soviet Jews: Creating a Cause and a Movement," in *A Second Exodus: The American Movement to Free Soviet Jews*, ed. Murray Friedman and Albert D. Chernin (Hanover, NH: University Press of New England, 1999), 88.

11. Svetlana Savranskaya, "The Battles for the Final Act: The Soviet Government and Dissidents' Efforts to Define the Substance and the Implementation of the Helsinki Final Act" (paper presented at the Conference "European and Transatlantic Strategies in the Late Cold War Period to Overcome the East-West Division of Europe," November 30–December 1, 2007).

12. Richard N. Dean, "Contacts with the West: The Dissidents' View of Western Support for the Human Rights Movement in the Soviet Union," *Universal Human Rights* 2, no. 1 (January–March 1980): 48.

13. Natan Sharansky, *Fear No Evil* (New York: Random House, 1988), 153, 157. Anatoly Shcharansky changed his name to Natan Sharansky upon his immigration to Israel in 1986. Benjamin Nathans argues that longer-term trends in the Soviet Union also played a role. Benjamin Nathans, "The Wild Desire to Leave: On Soviet Jewry," *The Nation*, November 10, 2010. For more on the historical context of Jewish citizenship in and emigration from the Russian empire, see Eric Lohr, *Russian Citizenship: From Empire to Soviet Union* (Cambridge, MA: Harvard University Press, 2012), 113, 178.

14. Alexeyeva, *Soviet Dissent*, 176, 179, 181.

15. For more on the Initiative Group for the Defense of Human Rights in the USSR, see Robert Horvath, "Breaking the Totalitarian Ice: The Initiative Group for the

Defense of Human Rights in the USSR," *Human Rights Quarterly* 36, no. 1 (February 2014): 147–75.

16. Rita Hauser, Address, February 14, 1971, Executive SP 5/IT5, Box 185, Subject Files, WHCF, NPMP.

17. Shestack to Podgorny, September 13, 1973, Folder 18, Box 1164, Organizational Matters Series, ACLU Records.

18. Gilligan, *Defending Human Rights in Russia*, 28–29.

19. Application, October 6, 1973, Folder 75, Feb. 1974 (2), International Executive Committee, AI IS; Gilligan, *Defending Human Rights in Russia*, 40. Their initiative prompted considerable discussion among Amnesty's executive committee. Ennals to Tverdokhlebov, February 27, 1974, Folder 70, International Executive Committee, AI IS; Belck to Colleagues, July 24, 1974, Folder 83, AI IS.

20. For his activism Orlov was barred from working as a scientist. Gilligan, *Defending Human Rights in Russia*, 12; Rumyantzev to Central Committee, September 28, 1973, S.II.2.4.82, Box 46, Andrei Sakharov Papers, Harvard University.

21. Gal Beckerman, *When They Come for Us, We'll Be Gone* (New York: Houghton Mifflin Harcourt, 2010), 114.

22. Ibid., 115.

23. Daniel C. Thomas, "Boomerangs and Superpowers: International Norms, Transnational Networks and U.S. Foreign Policy," *Cambridge Review of International Affairs* 15, no. 1 (2002): 26. See also Sidney Tarrow, *The New Transnational Activism* (Cambridge: Cambridge University Press, 2005), 145; Margaret Keck and Kathryn Sikkink, *Activists Beyond Borders: Advocacy Networks in International Politics* (Ithaca, NY: Cornell University Press: 1998), 12.

24. Dean, "Contacts with the West," 50–51.

25. Historians Mark Bradley and Thomas Borstelmann view *The Gulag Archipelago* as a book that piqued Americans' imagination regarding human rights and transformed external understandings of the Soviet system. In Bradley's telling, Solzhenitsyn's work fueled a focus on individual victims. Mark Philip Bradley, "American Vernaculars: The United States and the Global Human Rights Imagination," *Diplomatic History* 38, no. 1 (January 2014): 16–19; Mark Philip Bradley, *The World Reimagined: Americans and Human Rights in the Twentieth Century* (New York: Cambridge University Press, 2016), 164–70; Thomas Borstelmann, *The 1970s: A New Global History from Civil Rights to Economic Inequality* (Princeton, NJ: Princeton University Press, 2012), 197. In my research, I have not seen evidence that *The Gulag Archipelago* directly influenced Americans' activism. But the Soviet author's 1974 expulsion complicated the Ford administration's response to pressure regarding human rights, particularly as the 1976 election approached. Sarah B. Snyder, "'Jerry, Don't Go': Domestic Opposition to the 1975 Helsinki Final Act," *Journal of American Studies* 44, no. 1 (February 2010): 74–76.

26. Beckerman, *When They Come for Us*, 320.

27. Dean, "Contacts with the West," 51, 53.

28. Ibid., 52. In addition, in September 1973 several Soviet citizens phoned Amnesty's office in London to express their support for the organization's efforts. Press Release, September 15, 1973, Folder 13, ICM, Vienna, September 13–16, 1973, AI IS.

29. Amal'rik was best known in the West for his 1970 essay "Will the Soviet Union Survive until 1984?" See, for example, Press Release, July 19, 1973, Box 260, Accession 3560–005, Henry M. Jackson Papers, University of Washington.

30. Shestack to Podgorny, September 13, 1973, Folder 18, Box 1164, Organizational Matters Series, ACLU Records.

31. Hoopes to Ford, August 30, 1974, CO 158 USSR Executive 10/1/74–10/14/74, Box 50, WHCF, Subject Files: Countries, GRFPL.

32. After the summit Kissinger discussed Moroz's plight with Dobrynin. Clift to Scowcroft, December 14, 1974, USSR (6), Box 17, NSA Presidential Country Files for Europe and Canada, GRFPL.

33. Butman to Ford, September 1, 1974, CO 158 USSR Executive 9/1/74–9/14/74, Box 50, WHCF, Subject Files: Countries, GRFPL.

34. Paula Stern cites the example of Irish-American opposition to the Jay Treaty in 1794. Paula Stern, *Water's Edge: Domestic Politics and the Making of American Foreign Policy* (Westport, CT: Greenwood Press, 1979), xii.

35. Andrew Preston, *Sword of the Spirit, Shield of the Faith: Religion in American War and Diplomacy* (New York: Knopf, 2012), 198, 203–4, 563.

36. Beckerman, *When They Come for Us*, 9.

37. Samuel Moyn, *The Last Utopia: Human Rights in History* (Cambridge, MA: Harvard University Press, 2010), 83; Samantha Power, *A "Problem from Hell": America in the Age of Genocide* (New York: Perennial, 2002), 73. Beckerman asserts, however, that Jews in the United States did not focus on the Holocaust much beyond the attention garnered by the diary of Anne Frank and the subsequent Broadway play and movie. Beckerman, *When They Come for Us*, 43.

38. Although he didn't use the term "cultural genocide," Heschel was explicitly linking the Nazi murder of six million Jews with Soviet efforts to stifle Jewish religious and cultural life in the USSR. Beckerman, *When They Come for Us*, 64–67.

39. Between August 1972 and March 1973 Soviet Jews leaving the Soviet Union paid $7 million in exit fees.

40. The extent of governmental action was often hard to determine. Bernard Gwertzman, "Senate Plan Bars Credits if Soviet Retains Exit Fees," *New York Times*, October 5, 1972, 1; William Korey, "The Jackson-Vanik Amendment in Perspective," *Soviet Jewish Affairs* 18, no. 1 (1988): 31; Elliott to Davis, September 25, 1972, Soviet Jewry 1972 [1 of 4], Box 118, Alpha-Subject Files, Staff Member & Office Files: Leonard Garment, WHCF, NPMP.

41. Beckerman, *When They Come for Us*, 43.

42. Ibid., 58–59.

43. Nathaniel Kurz, "'A Sphere above the Nations?': The Rise and Fall of International Jewish Human Rights Politics" (PhD Diss., Yale University, 2015), 286–87, 292. Michael N. Barnett agrees with Kurz in some respects, arguing that when American Jews did respond to the plight of their coreligionists, this activism was part of what he terms "new tribalism," not a broader commitment to human rights. Michael N. Barnett, *The Star and the Stripes: A History of the Foreign Policies of American Jews* (Princeton, NJ: Princeton University Press, 2016), 156, 175–76.

44. Myrna Shinbaum, "Mobilizing America: The National Conference on Soviet Jewry," in *A Second Exodus*, ed. Murray Friedman and Albert D. Chernin (Hanover, NH: University Press of New England, 1999), 174–75.

45. Beckerman, *When They Come for Us*, 170, 211.

46. News Release, September 6, 1973, Folder 81, International Executive Committee, AI IS.

47. Keys, *Reclaiming American Virtue*, 122. Similarly, the National Conference on Soviet Jewry formed a National Lawyers Committee for Soviet Jews in August 1974.

48. Israel was more involved than it had previously been in supporting efforts both to reach out to Jews in the Soviet Union and to garner support in the United States for Soviet Jewish emigration, which included recruiting secret agents to draw attention to the plight of Soviet Jews by planting sympathetic articles in the press. Noam Kochavi, "Idealpolitik in Disguise: Israel, Jewish Emigration from the Soviet Union, and the Nixon Administration, 1969–1974," *International History Review* 29, no. 3 (September 2007): 559; Beckerman, *When They Come for Us*, 51–52.

49. The group later changed its name to the Student Struggle for Soviet Jewry. Beckerman, *When They Come for Us*, 77–81.

50. Ibid., 203–7, 213–15; Alexeyeva, *Soviet Dissent*, 182.

51. Beckerman, *When They Come for Us*, 216–17, 229.

52. "'Eternal Light Vigil' Highlights Soviet Union's Bias Against Jews," *Jewish Telegraph Agency*, September 20, 1965; Beckerman, *When They Come for Us*, 137.

53. Morris Abram, October 10, 1971, USSR Trip—Sept 1971, Box 1, Series 1, Abram Papers.

54. Activists were concerned with the religious freedom of Christians in the USSR as well. Preston, *Sword of the Spirit*, 564–65.

55. Stern, *Water's Edge*, 195.

56. Beckerman, *When They Come for Us*, 138; Andrew Harrison, *Passover Revisited: Philadelphia's Efforts to Aid Soviet Jews, 1963–1998* (Madison, WI: Farleigh Dickinson University Press, 2001), 29.

57. Marc Schneier, *Shared Dreams: Martin Luther King, Jr., and the Jewish Community* (Woodstock, VT: Jewish Lights, 1999), 119. Beckerman, *When They Come for Us*, 138. I thank James Loeffler for bringing this quotation to my attention.

58. Beckerman, *When They Come for Us*, 138.

59. Drinan also had a large Jewish constituency in Massachusetts.

60. Leo Ribuffo, "Is Poland a Soviet Satellite? Gerald Ford, the Sonnenfeldt Doctrine, and the Election of 1976," *Diplomatic History* 14, no. 3 (1990): 390.

61. According to Stern, Louis Rosenblum of the Union Council for Soviet Jewry first suggested tying Soviet-American trade to freedom of emigration in 1969. Stern, *Water's Edge*, 10–11. William Korey argues that the Jackson-Vanik Amendment was "the first piece of American legislation inspired by the Universal Declaration of Human Rights." Korey, "The Jackson-Vanik Amendment," 29.

62. Macomber to Morgan, May 23, 1967, SOC 14 USSR 1/1/67, Box 3112, CFPF 1967–1969, Social, Record Group 59, NARA; MemCon, April 13, 1967, ibid.

63. Gerald R. Ford, Remarks, December 13, 1971, Rally for Soviet Jewry, New York, NY, December 13, 1971, Box D32, Gerald R. Ford Congressional Papers, GRFPL.

64. H. Con. Res. 324, 93rd Cong., 1st Sess., October 3, 1973.

65. *Hearings Before the House Foreign Affairs Subcommittee on Europe*, 93rd Cong., 2nd Sess., May 8, 15, 22, June 10, 12, 26, July 17, 25, 31, 1974.

66. Jackson to Ford, October 31, 1975, CO 158 Executive 11/1/75–11/30/75, Box 52, WHCF Subject File, GRFPL.

67. Fraser to Kissinger, September 2, 1975, General Correspondence USSR 1975, Box 62, ILHRC.

68. Members of Congress also sought other avenues to influence Soviet leaders directly. For example, Jackson wrote to Brezhnev on behalf of Valentyn Moroz in September 1974 and expressed concern about discrimination against Ukrainians in an October 1975 letter to Brezhnev. Jackson to Brezhnev, September 10, 1974, Folder 13, Box 11, Accession 3560–006, Jackson Papers; Jackson to Brezhnev, October 31, 1975, Folder 145, ibid.

69. Upon his return, Drinan wrote in the *National Catholic Reporter,* "I would like to write that there are signs of hope for religious freedom in the USSR. I cannot. Some 500,000 Christian Baptists have a state-sponsored religious group. But some 100,000 Christian dissidents operate underground, with an estimated 300 of their activists in jail." Raymond A. Schroth, *Bob Drinan: The Controversial Life of the First Catholic Priest Elected to Congress* (New York: Fordham University Press, 2011), 251, 254.

70. Stern, *Water's Edge,* 13.

71. Press Release, March 6, 1968, Folder 6, Box 52, Part 1, Goldberg Papers. According to Drew Middleton of the *New York Times,* Goldberg's speech marked the first time the Johnson administration had publicly criticized the Soviet human rights record. Drew Middleton, "U.S. Scores Trials of Soviet Writers," *New York Times,* March 7, 1968, 1.

72. Press Release, USUN 35, March 8, 1968, Folder 6, Box 52, Part 1, Goldberg Papers.

73. Telegram, U.S. Mission UN to SecState, June 4, 1969, SOC 14–3 ECOSOC 3/1/69, Box 3067, CFPF 1967–1969, Social, Record Group 59, NARA.

74. Despite Kissinger's admonishment, in Safire's view the administration was attentive to the plight of Soviet Jews, and Nixon himself was committed to their cause. William Safire, *Before the Fall: An Inside View of the Pre-Watergate White House* (New York: Da Capo, 1975), 454, 575.

75. Preston, *Sword of the Spirit,* 568. In contrast, Hugh Arnold, based on an analysis of the *Department of State Bulletin* between 1969 and 1976, argues that of the thirty-five times Kissinger addressed the issue of Soviet Jewish emigration, "all but a few of these were defensive or neutral in tone." Hugh M. Arnold, "Henry Kissinger and Human Rights," *Universal Human Rights* 2, no. 4 (October–December 1980): 60.

76. Buchanan to Wexler, August 8, 1968, SOC 14 USSR 5/1/69, Box 3112, CFPF 1967–1969, Social, Record Group 59, NARA.

77. Stern, *Water's Edge,* 13.

78. Beckerman, *When They Come for Us,* 215–16.

79. Edward C. Keefer et al., eds., *Soviet-American Relations: The Détente Years, 1969–1972* (Washington, DC: Government Printing Office, 2007), 587.

80. Stern, *Water's Edge,* 14, 22, 40. Human rights had minimal impact on Soviet-American détente during Nixon's first term. As evidence, a joint Russian and American volume on Soviet-American détente contains only one mention of the term "human rights," which referred to South Asia, not the Soviet record. Keefer, *Soviet-American Relations,* 503.

81. Stern, *Water's Edge,* 44–45.

82. U.S. Policy Toward Soviet Jewry, March 13, 1972, Soviet Jewry 1972 [3 of 4], Box 119, Alpha-Subject Files, Staff Member Office Files: Leonard Garment, WHCF, NPMP.

83. Nixon Tape 866–15b, March 1, 1973, https://nixonlibrary.gov/forresearchers/find/tapes/tape866/866-015b.mp3, accessed April 17, 2016.

84. Andrei Gromyko, *Memoirs* (New York: Doubleday, 1989), 294.

85. Gerald Ford, *A Time to Heal: The Autobiography of Gerald Ford* (New York: Harper & Row, 1979), 139.

86. For an account of how Carter's and Reagan's policies differed from their predecessors', see Sarah B. Snyder, *Human Rights Activism and the End of the Cold War: A Transnational History of the Helsinki Network* (New York: Cambridge University Press, 2011), 81–216.

87. Ford, *A Time to Heal*, 138.

88. Henry Kissinger, *Years of Renewal* (New York: Simon & Schuster, 1999), 114, 128.

89. Henry Kissinger, "Moral Purposes and Policy Choices," *Department of State Bulletin*, October 29, 1973, 529; "Kissinger Cites Risk in Pushing Soviet Too Hard on Emigration," *New York Times*, October 9, 1973, 5. Gromyko's analysis of the question echoed Kissinger's. According to Gromyko, "If we ask ourselves what is the chief human right, the plain answer is, the right to life. This can hardly be refuted: only if you are alive can you enjoy all the other rights—the right to work, to housing, education, medical service, emigration, and so on." Gromyko, *Memoirs*, 293.

90. Theodore Otto Windt Jr., *Presidents and Protesters: Political Rhetoric in the 1960s* (Tuscaloosa: University of Alabama Press, 1990), 182, 188, 186; David Zarefsky, "Presidential Rhetoric and the Power of Definition," *Presidential Studies Quarterly* 34, no. 3 (September 2004): 617. For further discussion of presidential rhetoric, see Jeffrey E. Cohen, "Presidential Rhetoric and the Public Agenda," *American Journal of Political Science* 39, no. 1 (February 1995): 102; Terri Bimes, "Understanding the Rhetorical Presidency," in *The Oxford Handbook of the American Presidency*, ed. George C Edwards III and William G. Howell (New York: Oxford University Press, 2009), 218, 219.

91. At the same conference, Jackson countered with a distinctly different vision of the place of human rights in Soviet-American relations: "Without bringing about an increasing measure of individual liberty in the communist world there can be no genuine détente, there can be no real movement toward a more peaceful world." Press Release, October 11, 1973, Folder 23, Box 244, Accession 3560–005, Jackson Papers.

92. Peter S. Bridges, Oral History Interview, October 24, 2003, ADST. See also Jeremi Suri, *Power and Protest: Global Revolution and the Rise of Détente* (Cambridge, MA: Harvard University Press, 2003), 108.

93. Thompson R. Buchanan, Oral History Interview, March 15, 1996, ADST.

94. Edward Hurwitz, Oral History Interview, August 15, 1996, ADST.

95. Thomas W. Simons Jr., Oral History Interview, July 22, 2004, ADST.

96. Robert G. Kaiser, "Shultz Seen Discussing Trade, Jews," *Washington Post*, March 12, 1973, A16.

97. Dusko Doder, "Soviet Suspend Exit Taxes to Secure U.S. Trade Bill," *Washington Post*, March 22, 1973, A1.

98. Simon's meeting with Brezhnev came several months after he raised the topic of political prisoners with Augusto Pinochet in Chile. Simon's forays outside traditional Treasury Department issues will be discussed further in chapter five. Actions by the Treasury Department, Folder 10, Drawer 23, Series 3b, William E. Simon Papers, Skillman Library, Lafayette College.

99. For a different reading of the amendment, see Anna Su, *Exporting Freedom: Religious Liberty and American Power* (Cambridge, MA: Harvard University Press, 2016), 112, 121.

100. Stern, *Water's Edge*, 42. In William Korey's view, the specter of the Jackson-Vanik Amendment led the Soviets to waive the exit tax. Korey, "The Jackson-Vanik Amendment," 33.

101. Beckerman, *When They Come for Us*, 281. Dobrynin recounts that Vanik told him he was motivated to join forces with Jackson because of Vanik's desire to win support from voters of Eastern European descent in his district. Dobrynin, *In Confidence*, 366.

102. Stern, *Water's Edge*, 35.

103. Nixon Tape 866–15b, March 1, 1973. See also Memorandum of Conversation, May 11, 1973, FRUS, 1969–1976, Vol. XV, 453.

104. Abramovitch et al. to Jackson, April 10, 1974, Folder 15, Box 1, Accession 3560–028, Jackson Papers.

105. Andrei Sakharov, Open Letter to the Congress of the United States, September 14, 1973, Folder 63, Box 10, Accession 3560–006, Jackson Papers.

106. In a sign of how much the Nixon administration wanted to thwart Jackson's initiative, Kissinger sought to trade U.S. supplies in return for Israeli rejection of the amendment. Kochavi, "Idealpolitik in Disguise," 560; Stern, *Water's Edge*, 95.

107. Kissinger, *Years of Renewal*, 270–71, 283. See also memorandum of conversation, March 26, 1974, FRUS, 1969–1976, Vol. XV, 791. Korey, however, argues that the Soviets were less opposed to the amendment than accounts such as Kissinger's memoirs suggest. Korey, "The Jackson-Vanik Amendment," 34–37.

108. Gromyko, *Memoirs*, 293.

109. Kissinger, *Years of Renewal*, 255, 258–60; Perle to Jackson, March 14, 1974, Folder 11, Box 1, Accession 3560–028, Jackson Papers; Ford, *A Time to Heal*, 139.

110. Kissinger to Ford, August 9, 1974, Congressional (1), Box 2, National Security Adviser: Presidential Subject File, GRFPL. See also Kissinger, *Years of Renewal*, 255–60. In a meeting with Kissinger, Brezhnev disputed Jackson's numbers of Soviet Jews who wanted to emigrate, suggesting that Jackson was overstating the case by forty-five thousand. Earlier State Department analysis, however, had shown Brezhnev's numbers to be "in various parts accurate, unintentionally erroneous, and perhaps deliberately misleading." Memcon, October 24, 1974, NSA Kissinger Reports on USSR, China, and Middle East Discussions, Box 1, Staff Assistant Peter Rodman Files, National Security Adviser: Presidential Subject File, GRFPL; Eliot to Kissinger, June 21, 1973, FRUS, 1969–1976, Vol. XV, 522.

111. Jackson to Kissinger, October 18, 1974, Folder 12, Box 1, Accession 3560–028, Jackson Papers; Kissinger to Jackson, October 18, 1974, ibid.; Ford, *A Time to Heal*, 139.

112. Stern, *Water's Edge*, 162–63.

113. Gromyko to Kissinger, October 26, 1974, Folder 17, Box 1, Accession 3560–028, Jackson Papers; Kissinger, *Years of Renewal*, 284.

114. Kissinger, *Years of Renewal*, 308.

115. Peak emigration had been reached in 1973 with thirty-five thousand. Charles McC. Mathias Jr., "Ethnic Groups and Foreign Policy," *Foreign Affairs* 59, no. 5 (Summer 1981): 995.

116. Transcript, *Face the Nation*, 4/4/76—Henry F. Jackson, Box 65, Ron Nessen Files, GRFPL. Analysis by the State Department suggested that in the wake of declining emigration numbers, support for Jackson-Vanik may have been waning by September 1975. "Trade and Emigration: Talking Points," September 1975, 9/18–19/75

USSR—Foreign Minister Gromyko (5), Box 12, NSA Presidential Briefing Material for VIP Visits, GRFPL.

117. See, for example, Joe Renouard, *Human Rights in American Foreign Policy: From the 1960s to the Soviet Collapse* (Philadelphia: University of Pennsylvania Press, 2016), 15. Jackson's lack of charisma and lethargic speaking style were among the factors that thwarted his presidential ambitions. Jeffrey Bloodworth, *Losing the Center: The Decline of American Liberalism, 1968–1992* (Lexington: University Press of Kentucky, 2013), 110, 113.

118. Sarah B. Snyder, "'A Call for U.S. Leadership': Congressional Activism on Human Rights," *Diplomatic History* 37, no. 2 (April 2013): 392. See also Umberto Tulli, "'Whose Rights Are Human Rights?': The Ambiguous Emergence of Human Rights and the Demise of Kissingerism," *Cold War History* 12, no. 4 (November 2012): 586.

119. Stern, *Water's Edge*, 21.

120. Kaufman, *Henry M. Jackson*, 251.

121. Preston, *Sword of the Spirit*, 567.

122. Press Release, February 11, 1977, Folder 7: Human Rights Statement 2–11–77, Box 263, Accession 3560–005, Jackson Papers; Charles Horner, "Human Rights and the Jackson Amendment," in *Staying the Course: Henry M. Jackson and National Security*, ed. Dorothy Fosdick (Seattle: University of Washington Press, 1987), 114; Bloodworth, "Senator Henry Jackson," 71.

123. Horner, "Human Rights," 113, 115–16.

124. Kaufman, *Henry M. Jackson*, 4–5.

125. Ibid., 264.

126. Jackson quoted in Preston, *Sword of the Spirit*, 569.

127. Ibid., 569.

128. In terms of tone, Arnold argues that Kissinger shifted from "perfunctory, obligatory niceties to strong statements of condemnation for violators and calls for adherence to recognized standards." Arnold, "Henry Kissinger and Human Rights," 61–62.

129. According to Kissinger, "When we have been successful, we have not made any public claim for it, because we have thought that the saving of lives was more important than getting credit." Secretary Kissinger, Interviewed by Panel at Portland, OR, *Department of State Bulletin*, August 16, 1976, 242.

130. Davis to Springsteen, May 4, 1976, USSR (37), Box 19, National Security Adviser: Presidential Country Files for Europe and Canada, GRFPL; Clift to Scowcroft, April 22, 1976, ibid.

131. Springsteen to Scowcroft, May 12, 1976, USSR (37), Box 19, National Security Adviser: Presidential Country Files for Europe and Canada, GRFPL.

132. For more discussion of the significance of human rights and ethnic politics in the 1976 election, see Sarah B. Snyder, "Through the Looking Glass: The Helsinki Final Act and the 1976 Election for President," *Diplomacy and Statecraft* 21, no. 1 (March 2010): 87–106.

133. Kuropas to Scowcroft, June 25, 1976, USSR (37), Box 19, National Security Adviser: Presidential Country Files for Europe and Canada, GRFPL.

134. Scowcroft to Kuropas, July 5, 1976, USSR (40), Box 19, National Security Adviser: Presidential Country Files for Europe and Canada, GRFPL; Clift to Scowcroft, June 12, 1976, ibid.

135. Snyder, "Through the Looking Glass," 101.

136. Howe to Rockefeller, November 17, 1976, CO 158 USSR Executive 11/1/76–11/30/76, WHCF, Subject Files, GRFPL.

137. Kissinger was highly skeptical of the process, telling Ford that the human contacts provisions or human rights principle would not "change the Soviet system." Daniel J. Sargent, *A Superpower Transformed: The Remaking of American Foreign Relations in the 1970s* (New York: Oxford University Press, 2015), 216.

138. Beckerman, *When They Come for Us*, 9.

2. A DOUBLE STANDARD ABROAD AND AT HOME?
RHODESIA'S UNILATERAL DECLARATION OF INDEPENDENCE

1. In 1965 only 6 percent of the Rhodesian population (220,000 of four million people) was white.

2. "Universal Declaration of Human Rights," United Nations, http://www.un.org/en/universal-declaration-human-rights/index.html, accessed May 20, 2015.

3. Thomas F. Jackson, *From Civil Rights to Human Rights: Martin Luther King, Jr., and the Struggle for Economic Justice* (Philadelphia: University of Pennsylvania Press, 2007), 223–24, 244.

4. Ibid., 227.

5. Gerald Horne, *From the Barrel of a Gun: The United States and the War Against Zimbabwe, 1965–1980* (Chapel Hill: University of North Carolina Press, 2001), 7; Thomas Borstelmann, *The Cold War and the Color Line: American Race Relations in the Global Arena* (Cambridge, MA: Harvard University Press, 2001), 193.

6. Robert Lagamma, Oral History Interview, August 6, 2008, ADST.

7. "Africa: Southern Rhodesia," *GIST* no. 8 (September 1972).

8. Minutes, Human Rights Advisory Service: Rhodesia Committee, December 23, 1965, File 8, Box 258, MSS Afr.S1681, the Papers of the Africa Bureau, Bodleian Library, Oxford University; Minutes, Human Rights Advisory Service: Rhodesia Committee, December 30, 1965, ibid.; Minutes, Human Rights Advisory Service: Rhodesia Committee, January 18, 1966, ibid. I thank Carl Watts for making me aware of this collection.

9. *Amnesty Action* 1, no. 1 (Fall 1966), General Correspondence: Amnesty International, Box 29, ILRHC.

10. "Sithole Hearing," Folder 90, International Executive Committee, AI IS.

11. Press Release, December 12, 1974, AFR 46 Africa-Rhodesia/Zimbabwe, 1967–1976, Box 1, Series 2: 5, AIUSA Records; Press Release, November 10, 1975, Folder 948, AI IS. As Amnesty International reported in 1976, black Rhodesians facing restrictions on their rights included convicted political prisoners, long-term political detainees, short-term detainees, and restrictees who were confined to certain geographic areas. Amnesty estimated that hundreds of black Rhodesians should be categorized as belonging to each of the first three categories and that hundreds of thousands faced restriction. Amnesty also highlighted reports by short-term detainees indicating that they suffered torture. Amnesty International Briefing Rhodesia/Zimbabwe, March 1976, Rhodesia—Repression, 1976–1973, Box 317, ACOA Addendum.

12. Elizabeth Schmidt, *Foreign Intervention in Africa: From the Cold War to the War on Terror* (New York: Columbia University Press, 2013), 121.

13. See, for example, Andrew DeRoche, *Black, White, and Chrome: The United States and Zimbabwe, 1953–1998* (Trenton, NJ: Africa World Press, 2001), 1, 7–8; David A. Dickson, "U.S. Foreign Policy Toward Southern and Central Africa: The Kennedy and Johnson Years," *Presidential Studies Quarterly* 23, no. 2 (Spring 1993): 308; Robert B. Rakove, *Kennedy, Johnson, and the Nonaligned World* (New York: Cambridge University Press, 2013), 235; Borstelmann, *The Cold War*, 1.

14. For an opposing view, see Barbara Keys, *Reclaiming American Virtue: The Human Rights Revolution of the 1970s* (Cambridge, MA: Harvard University Press, 2014), in which Keys explicitly rules out the United States' stance on Rhodesia as a "general human rights initiative." Instead, she characterizes it as "part of an anticolonial posture" and "an offshoot of antiracial policies at home" (45).

15. See, for example, Press Release, May 5, 1965, Folder 4, Box 193, Adlai E. Stevenson Papers, Public Policy Papers, Seeley G. Mudd Manuscript Library, Princeton University; Anderson Statement, October 8, 1965, A/C.4/SR.1522 (New York: United Nations, 1965); Anderson Statement, November 5, 1965, A/PV.1367 (New York: United Nations, 1965).

16. AmEmbassy Accra to SecState, November 12, 1965, POL 16 RHOD 11/12/65, Box 2606, Political and Defense, CFPF 1964–66, Record Group 59, NARA. Tanzanian President Julius Nyerere also hoped there would be UN action in Southern Rhodesia. AmEmbassy Dar Es Salam to SecState, November 13, 1965, ibid.

17. Indeed, historian Samuel Moyn argues that it was only at the UN that human rights resonated during these years. Samuel Moyn, *The Last Utopia: Human Rights in History* (Cambridge, MA: Harvard University Press, 2010), 3. Roland Burke writes that decolonization had a "revolutionary influence" on the development of human rights. Roland Burke, *Decolonization and the Evolution of International Human Rights* (Philadelphia: University of Pennsylvania Press, 2010), 2.

18. The convention called on states to press "for speedily eliminating racial discrimination in all its forms and manifestations, and to prevent and combat racist doctrines and practices in order to promote understanding between races and to build an international community free from all forms of racial segregation and racial discrimination." Its adherents were bound to "condemn racial segregation and apartheid and undertake to prevent, prohibit and eradicate all practices." UN General Assembly Resolution 2106 (XX), December 21, 1965 (New York: United Nations, 1965).

19. The Security Council made the sanctions more comprehensive in May 1968. Resolution, April 9, 1966, Rhodesia, 1977 (3), Box 151.H.4.2 (F), Donald M. Fraser Papers, Minnesota Historical Society, St. Paul.

20. DeRoche, *Black, White, and Chrome*, 151. Portugal's and South Africa's nonparticipation seriously undermined the sanctions against Southern Rhodesia, and in the CIA's view, the 1966 sanctions "strengthened" the Smith regime rather than undermining it. Intelligence Memorandum: Rhodesia: A Third Round of Sanctions, June 1968, Rhodesia Vol. 1 [2 of 2], Box 743, Country Files: Africa, NSC Files, NPMP. By 1971 UN diplomats expressed frustration that its resolutions "had little or no effect, owing to the arrogant, flagrant and stubborn disregard on the part of South Africa and its racist allies." "Chapter XX: Human Rights Questions," *Yearbook of the United Nations* 25 (1971): 394–446.

21. Telegram, November 13, 1965, POL 16 RHOD, Box 2606, Political and Defense, CFPF 1964–66, Record Group 59, NARA.

22. "Over the Brink," *Washington Post*, November 12, 1965, A16.

23. Randolph and Harrington to Rusk, November 11, 1965, POL 16 Independence Recognition RHOD 12/1/65, Box 2607, Political and Defense, CFPF 1964–66, Record Group 59, NARA.

24. Rhodesia & U.S. Interests, Rhodesia Sanctions Conference, 1974, Box 135, ACOA Addendum; Press Release, October 2, 1973, Rhodesia: Chrome, 1973, Box 311, ACOA Addendum.

25. Gardner to Cleveland, October 31, 1963, Civil Rights, Box 3, Classified Records of Assistant Secretary of State for African Affairs G. Mennen Williams, 1961–1966, Record Group 59, NARA.

26. Comment by Martin Luther King Jr., October 25, 1965, in Martin Luther King Jr., *"In a Single Garment of Destiny": A Global Vision of Justice* (Boston: Beacon Press, 2012).

27. Powell to Johnson, November 15, 1965, POL 16 Independence. Recognition RHOD 12/1/65, Box 2607, Political and Defense, CFPF, 1964–66, Record Group 59, NARA.

28. Wilkins to Johnson, May 4, 1966, GEN CO 250 Rhodesia 11/22/63–1/5/66, CO Box 65, WHCF, LBJPL. Such attention fits into a longer history of anticolonial activism by organizations such as the NAACP. Carol Anderson, *Bourgeois Radicals: The NAACP and the Struggle for Colonial Liberation, 1941–1960* (New York: Cambridge University Press, 2015), 2. At a lower level, a former missionary and a foreign service officer joined together to express their concern about the United States' policy toward Rhodesia. "The United States and Rhodesia," February 16, 1966, Student Nonviolent Coordinating Committee (SNCC) Papers, History Vault, Black Freedom, Part 3, ProQuest; "Why We Are Concerned . . . ," February 17, 1966, ibid.

29. James H. Meriwether, *Proudly We Can Be Africans: Black Americans and Africa, 1935–1961* (Chapel Hill: University of North Carolina Press, 2009), 243–44.

30. Carl Watts, "African Americans and U.S. Foreign Policy: The American Negro Leadership Conference on Africa and the Rhodesian Crisis," in *The U.S. Public and American Foreign Policy*, ed. Andrew Johnstone and Helen Laville (New York: Routledge, 2010), 111.

31. "Southern Africa: The Facts," October 1966, Zimbabwe—ACOA—Fact Sheets—1965–72, Box 152, ACOA Records.

32. A Summary Report of the Washington Office, Washington Office on Africa Reports—1966–1971, Box 45, ACOA Records.

33. Amnesty Action, Rhodesia Political Prisoners, 1979–1973, Box 317, ACOA Addendum.

34. Suggesting a degree of continuity and insularity, ACOA shared many of its prominent supporters—including Eleanor Roosevelt, Roger Baldwin, Charles Diggs, and Reinhold Niebuhr—with other organizations that were concerned with rights in the 1950s and 1960s. Schmidt, *Foreign Intervention in Africa*, 104; David L. Hostetter, *Movement Matters: American Antiapartheid Activism and the Rise of Multicultural Politics* (London: Routledge, 2006), 25, 28–29; Raymond Joseph Parrott, "Struggle for Solidarity: The New Left, Portuguese African Decolonization, and the End of the Cold War Consensus" (PhD Diss., University of Texas–Austin, 2016), 301.

35. American Negro Leadership Conference on Africa Resolutions, September 24–27, 1964, American Negro Leadership Conference on Africa, Box 16, Records of G. Mennen Williams, 1961–66, Record Group 59, NARA.

36. Anthony Lake directed the Carnegie Endowment for International Peace's special project on Rhodesia. Watts, "African Americans," 113.

37. In Watts's analysis, ANLCA also suffered from limited finances, a lack of grassroots support, inefficient lobbying efforts, a weak command of information about Africa, and an anemic organizational structure. Ibid., 108, 110, 111, 116; Hostetter, *Movement Matters*, 30.

38. Lieberg to ACOA and WOA, April 4, 1973, Rhodesian Sanctions, 1973, Box 135, ACOA Addendum.

39. Lieberg to Scotto, May 23, 1974, Rhodesia Sanctions Conference, 1974, Box 135, ACOA Addendum; "Foes of Rhodesia Predict New Mineral Cargoes Here," *New York Times*, July 15, 1972, 5.

40. Other unions such as the United Auto Workers, the AFL-CIO, and the United Steelworkers of America all supported the boycott.

41. Joseph S. Hellwicz, "African Cargo Refused," *Baltimore Sun*, December 13, 1973, C11.

42. Roy Reed, "Rhodesian Goods Protested in U.S.: Blacks in Louisiana Oppose Resumption of Imports," *New York Times*, March 16, 1972, 5; "Two Blacks Arrested as Rhodesian Ore Is Unloaded," *New York Times*, March 21, 1972, 3.

43. "Repeal the Byrd Amendment," Rhodesia Chrome, 1974, Box 311, ACOA Addendum.

44. Some of Britain's steps, such as ending oil shipments to Southern Rhodesia, were more important psychologically and politically than they were likely to be effective. SecState to USUN, December 8, 1965, United Nations Vol. 3, 10/1/65 [4 of 4], Box 67, National Security Files, Agency File, LBJPL. British records show that the government thought the United States could have been more supportive in forcing American companies to abide by sanctions against Rhodesia. Telegram 791, Washington to Foreign Office, March 5, 1966, FO 115/4620, NAUK. CIA analysts did not believe that economic sanctions would be sufficient to cripple Smith's regime. "Repercussions of a Unilateral Declaration of Independence by Southern Rhodesia," October 13, 1965, 72, Rhodesia, Box 8, National Intelligence Estimates, National Security Files, LBJPL.

45. Thomas J. Noer, *Cold War and Black Liberation: The United States and White Rule in Africa, 1948–1968* (Columbia: University of Missouri Press, 1985), 195.

46. Chrome was used in manufacturing stainless steel. Ibid., 105–6.

47. Herman J. Cohen, Oral History Interview, August 15, 1996, ADST.

48. Ryan Irwin, "The Gordian Knot: Apartheid and the Unmaking of the Modern World Order, 1960–1970" (PhD Diss., the Ohio State University, 2010), 119. See also Thomas J. Noer, *Soapy: A Biography of G. Mennen Williams* (Ann Arbor: University of Michigan Press, 2005), 224.

49. British officials tracked fourteen distinct steps taken by the United States between November 1965 and February 1966 to "support" measures taken by the United Kingdom. "Measures Taken by the United States in Support of the United Kingdom Measures Against Southern Rhodesia," March 2, 1966, FCO 115/4620, NAUK.

50. Embargoing oil to Rhodesia required a considerable financial and logistical commitment, as it necessitated implementing an airlift to bring oil to Zambia, which was blocked from access to the sea by Rhodesia. Press Release, April 9, 1966, Rhodesia, 1977 (3), Box 151.H.3.7 (B), Fraser Papers; Noer, *Cold War and Black Liberation*, 197–98, 203–4.

51. "Southern Rhodesia: Background," CO 250 Rhodesia—Nyasaland, Federation of, Box 11 [1 of 2], WHCF, Confidential File, LBJPL.

52. DeRoche, *Black, White, and Chrome*, 159; "Southern Rhodesia," *Administrative History of the Department of State*, Vol. 1, LBJPL. The UN General Assembly's Colonialism Committee and the UN Human Rights Commission both voted to condemn Rhodesian actions; the United States abstained from the Colonialism Committee's statement but supported the Human Rights Commission's resolution. "Two UN Organs Condemn Rhodesia," *Washington Post*, March 8, 1968, A10.

53. Goldberg, who had previously served as secretary of labor and supreme court justice, was appointed ambassador after Stevenson's death in July 1965. Press Release, March 6, 1968, Folder 6, Box 52, Part 1, Arthur J. Goldberg Papers, Library of Congress, Washington, DC.

54. Issraelyan Statement, October 16, 1968, A/C.4/SR.1764, (New York: United Nations, 1968); Finger Statement, October 16, 1968, ibid.

55. Mann to Johnson, December 22, 1965, FRUS, 1964–1968, Vol. XXIV, 876; "Chapter 10: The United Nations," *Administrative History of the Department of State*, Vol. 1, LBJPL.

56. "Chapter XX: Human Rights Questions," *Yearbook of the United Nations* 23 (1969), 496.

57. Katzenbach to Johnson, October 9, 1967, United Nations, Filed by the LBJ Library, Vol. 1 [1 of 2], Box 72, National Security Files, Agency File, LBJPL.

58. Katzenbach to Johnson, May 28, 1968, United Nations, Vol. 10, 4/68–11/68 [3 of 3], Box 70, National Security Files, Agency File, LBJPL.

59. According to Gerald Horne, Rhodesia was a "proxy for U.S. domestic concerns—particularly concerning race and anticommunism." Horne, *From the Barrel*, 71, 161; Noer, *Cold War and Black Liberation*, 221–22; Borstelmann, *The Cold War*, 198–99. The domino theory was used as a rationale for supporting Ian Smith's regime. Vernon McKay, "The Domino Theory of the Rhodesian Lobby," *Africa Report* (June 1967): 55, 58.

60. Noer, *Cold War and Black Liberation*, 209.

61. Acheson's position was likely due to his disregard for anticolonial nationalist movements, his views on race, and his concern about Soviet influence. Douglas Brinkley, *Dean Acheson: The Cold War Years, 1953–1971* (New Haven, CT: Yale University Press, 1992), 303–4; Robert Beisner, *Dean Acheson: A Life in the Cold War* (New York: Oxford University Press, 2006), 525; James Chace, *Acheson: The Secretary of State Who Created the American World* (New York: Simon & Schuster, 1998), 433; *Rhodesia and United States Foreign Policy, Hearings Before the Subcommittee on Africa, Committee on Foreign Affairs*, H. R., 91st Cong., 1st Sess., November 19, 1969.

62. South Africa supplied the United States with needed minerals, port facilities, and supportive votes in the United Nations. Noer, *Cold War and Black Liberation*, 186; DeRoche, *Black, White, and Chrome*, 105–6.

63. Johnson told the attendees at a reception marking the third anniversary of the Organization of African Unity in May 1966, "As a basic part of our national tradition we support self-determination and an orderly transition to majority rule in every quarter of the globe. These principles have guided our American policy from India to the Philippines, from Vietnam to Pakistan. They guide our policy today toward Rhodesia." Lyndon B. Johnson, "Remarks at a Reception Marking the Third Anniversary

of the Organization of African Unity," May 26, 1966, the American Presidency Project, http://www.presidency.ucsb.edu/ws/?pid=27619, accessed April 9, 2017.

64. After Vice President Hubert Humphrey visited Africa, he wrote to Johnson, "The United States must take a clearer and more forthright position on self-determination and majority rule in Africa or lose the confidence and respect of responsible African leaders." Humphrey to Johnson, Vice President Humphrey's African Visit: Report to the President, Box 462, Executive Secretariat Conference Files, Record Group 59, NARA. See also Press Release, April 23, 1968, England (2), Box 145.C.3.2 (F), Fraser Papers.

65. Carl P. Watts, "The United States, Britain, and the Problem of Rhodesian Independence, 1964–1965," *Diplomatic History* 30, no. 3 (June 2006): 443.

66. Ryan M. Irwin, *Gordian Knot: Apartheid and the Unmaking of the Liberal World Order* (New York: Oxford University Press, 2012), 91.

67. Indeed, before Smith's declaration, the United States had devoted far more attention to South Africa and Angola than to Rhodesia. Economically, the total U.S. investment in Rhodesia at the time was only $56 million. Noer, *Cold War and Black Liberation*, 188; Response to National Security Study Memorandum 39: Southern Africa, December 9, 1969, Folder 7, Box H-025, Meeting Files, NSC Institutional Files, Richard Nixon Presidential Library, Yorba Linda, California.

68. Komer to Johnson, October 4, 1965, FRUS, 1964–1968, Vol. XXIV, 814.

69. Komer to Johnson, December 6, 1965, Rhodesia, Box 3, Files of Edward K. Hamilton, National Security Files, LBJPL. The President of Kenya, Jomo Kenyatta, wrote to Johnson to forge a common approach to Southern Rhodesia and noted, "The problem in Southern Rhodesia is a matter of basic human rights." Kenyatta to Johnson, November 10, 1966, CO 250 Rhodesia—Nyasaland, Federation of, Box 11 [1 of 2], WHCF, Confidential File, LBJPL.

70. Rakove, *Kennedy*, 234.

71. Haynes to Fred Panzer, 13 October 1965, CHRONO (Haynes) 3/1/65–6/15/66 [2 of 3], Box 1, Files of Ulric Haynes, National Security Files, LBJPL.

72. Executive Order, January 5, 1967, United Nations, Vol. 6, 12/1/66 [1 of 2], Box 68, National Security Files, Agency File, LBJPL; Summary of Notes of the 567th NSC Meeting, January 25, 1967, Southern Rhodesia, 1/25/67, Box 2, NSC Meetings File, ibid. Surprisingly, Goldberg's biographer David L. Stebenne largely overlooked Goldberg's role in these debates, focusing almost exclusively on Goldberg's involvement on Vietnam during his UN years. David L. Stebenne, *Arthur J. Goldberg: New Deal Liberal* (New York: Oxford University Press, 1996), 352–72.

73. Komer to Johnson, December 6, 1965, Rhodesia, Box 3, Hamilton, National Security Files, LBJPL.

74. Goldberg characterized apartheid as unique from other international human rights problems due to its vast scale, and he urged the United States to reconcile its domestic commitment to racial progress with its policy toward South Africa. Chase to Bundy, September 13, 1965, FRUS, 1964–1968, Vol. XXIV, 1040.

75. When introduced as ambassador, Goldberg declared, "I hope to make real and manifest the assertion of the charter that social justice and better standards of life in larger freedom are indispensable to the achievement of world peace." Press Release, July 20, 1965, United Nations 12/63–8/65 U.S. Representatives at UN, Box 294, National Security Files, Country File, LBJPL.

76. Seymour Maxwell Finger, *Your Man at the UN: People, Politics, and Bureaucracy in Making Foreign Policy* (New York: New York University Press, 1980), 174.

77. Before Smith's declaration of independence, Goldberg had said that the United States would "take the necessary concrete steps" against an independent Rhodesia. Anthony Lake, *The "Tar Baby" Option: American Policy Toward Southern Rhodesia* (New York: Columbia University Press, 1976), 79. Goldberg similarly urged the administration to rethink its approach elsewhere and "embark immediately on a policy of disengagement from South Africa." In Goldberg's view, the United States' stance was inconsistent with American values and the principles of the UN. USUN to RUEHCR/SECSTATE, September 10, 1965, United Nations—Vol. 1, 1965 [2 of 3], Box 66, National Security Files, Agency File, LBJPL.

78. Terrence Lyons, "Keeping Africa off the Agenda," in *Lyndon Johnson Confronts the World: American Foreign Policy, 1963–1968*, ed. Warren I. Cohen and Nancy Bernkopf Tucker (New York: Cambridge University Press, 1994), 291.

79. Lake, *The "Tar Baby" Option*, 97.

80. Lyons, "Keeping Africa off the Agenda," 291.

81. Fraser's comments highlight how the agenda of newly independent countries shaped American policy debates. Lake, *The "Tar Baby" Option*, 119. Representative Benjamin Rosenthal (D-NY) also wrote to Johnson to press him on Sothern Rhodesia, saying, "I urge you to pursue new initiatives to defeat the Rhodesian rebellion, and to protect and stimulate the forces of independence and self-determination in southern Africa." Rosenthal to Johnson, December 16, 1965, GEN CO 250 Rhodesia 11/22/63–1/5/66, CO Box 65, WHCF, LBJPL.

82. Fraser Statement, April 28, 1966, Press Releases, 1965–1966, 149.G.8.9 (B), Fraser Papers.

83. Irwin, "The Gordian Knot," 220–21. Irwin notes that Johnson was motivated, at least in part, by domestic political considerations—the desire to position himself vis-à-vis his political rival Senator Robert F. Kennedy on racial issues.

84. Irwin, *Gordian Knot*, 96.

85. Goldberg to Benjamin Bradlee, December 30, 1966, Folder 1, Box 45, Part 1, Goldberg Papers.

86. Press Release, USUN-27, March 21, 1967, Folder 8, Box 248, Patsy T. Mink Papers, Manuscript Division, Library of Congress, Washington, DC.

87. Speech, April 23, 1966, Folder 8, Box 51, Part 1, Goldberg Papers. See also Speech, June 2, 1966, Folder 9, ibid. At the UN Security Council, Goldberg said, "We are firmly and irrevocably dedicated to the principle of self-determination and independence for the people of Southern Rhodesia, self determination by and for all the people, independence on a basis acceptable to the people of the country as a whole." Press Release, November 12, 1965, Folder 5, Box 15, Part 1, Goldberg Papers.

88. Johnson and Haynes to Johnson, July 13, 1965, FRUS, 1964–1968, Vol. XXIV, 1030.

89. Lake argues that "communication" was a conceptual cover for shifts in policy that benefited Smith's regime. Lake, *The "Tar Baby" Option*, 123, 156. Nixon's policy represented a change from his earlier inclination to link race problems in Africa and the United States. When he returned from a 1957 trip to Ghana as vice president, Nixon reportedly told Eisenhower, "We cannot talk equality to the peoples of Africa and Asia and practice inequality in the United States." Borstelmann, *The Cold War*, 109.

90. Lake, *The "Tar Baby" Option*, 125–26. In May 1970 American officials warned the British that they might have to ease sanctions within six months unless their effectiveness was demonstrated. Papadopoulos to Bevan, May 21, 1970, FCO 36/628, NAUK; Washington to Foreign and Commonwealth Office, June 10, 1970, ibid.

91. Kissinger to Nixon, January 15, 1970, NSDM-38, Box H-213, NSC Institutional Files, NPMP.

92. Horne emphasizes the shift in descriptions of settlers in Rhodesia from "European" to "white," to which Americans, who were often motivated by "white solidarity," could better relate. Horne, *From the Barrel*, 149, 81; Borstelmann, *The Cold War*, 241.

93. Nixon also approved increasing trade promotion with Portuguese territories and South Africa. Kissinger to Nixon, January 15, 1970, NSDM-38, Box H-213, NSC Institutional Files, NPMP.

94. Lake, *The "Tar Baby" Option*, 130.

95. Kissinger to Diggs, October 14, 1970, GEN TA 1/CO Boycotts-Embargos, Box 12, WHCF, NPMP

96. Secretary of State Rogers's Policy Statement on Africa, March 31, 1970, FCO 36/628, NAUK.

97. USIS Text, September 18, 1970, FCO 35/357, NAUK.

98. Lake, *The "Tar Baby" Option*, 139; Background Note, FCO 36/628, NAUK; Note of a Meeting Held in the Oval Room, January 28, 1970, FCO 36/628, NAUK.

99. Press Release, March 6, 1970, Press Release Book 1970 #1, 152.L.9.4 (F), Fraser Papers.

100. National Security Decision Memorandum 47, March 9, 1970, NSDM-47, Box H-214, NSC Institutional Files, NPMP; Kissinger to Nixon, January 15, 1970, NSDM-38, Box H-213, NSC Institutional Files, NPMP; Eliot to Kissinger, March 2, 1970, Rhodesia Vol. 1 [1 of 2], Box 743, Country Files: Africa, NSC Files, NPMP; Rogers to Nixon, March 6, 1970, Rhodesia Vol. 1 [1 of 2], Box 743, Country Files: Africa, NSC Files, NPMP.

101. Lord to Kissinger, December 15, 1969, Folder 2, Box 335, S/P, Record Group 59, NARA.

102. Lord predicted that an increase in "black studies programs" at U.S. universities would increase attention on U.S. policy toward Africa. He also asserted that as Americans turned their attention away from the war in Vietnam, they would become more engaged with Africa. Ibid.

103. Ibid.

104. Ibid.

105. Lord to Kissinger, November 2, 1973, Issues Papers from the Bureaus [1 of 2], Box 382, S/P, Record Group 59, NARA.

106. Lake, *The "Tar Baby" Option*, 198–200.

107. "U.S. Against the Charter," *New York Times*, November 12, 1967, 46.

108. Levine to Haig, May 2, 1972, Congressional Vol. 5, [2 of 2] Box 316, Subject Files, NSC Files, NPMP; Bush to NSC Secretariat, Congressional ibid.

109. Lake, *The "Tar Baby" Option*, 273.

110. Levine and Lehman to Kissinger, May 5, 1972, NSSM-142, Box H-188, NSC Institutional Files, NPMP.

111. Lake, *The "Tar Baby" Option*, 220.

112. Horan and Lehman to Kissinger, July 27, 1973, Congressional Vol. 9, Box 317, Subject Files, NSC Files, NPMP.

113. Lake, *The "Tar Baby" Option*, 216–18; DeRoche, *Black, White, and Chrome*, 197–18.

114. Press Release, July 12, 1972, Press Release 1972, 152.L.9.4 (F), Fraser Papers. Liberal efforts to repeal the Byrd Amendment should also be seen in the context of the 1972 trials of the Wilmington Ten, nine African-American men and one white woman who were charged in connection with arson and a subsequent firefight with emergency workers, which highlighted for many Americans the continuing problems of racial discrimination in the justice system. Later, their plight was framed in human rights terms by Amnesty International. John L. Godwin, *Black Wilmington and the North Carolina Way: Portrait of a Community in the Era of Civil Rights Protest* (Lanham, MD: University Press of America, 2000), 1, 259.

115. Joining him were other members of Congress active on human rights, including Diggs, Peter H. B. Frelinghuysen, Fascell, Findley, Rosenthal, Bingham, Harrington, Ryan, Riegle, Edwards, Drinan, and Rangel among others. Press Releases, 1973, Part 1, 152.L.9.4 (F), Fraser Papers.

116. Donald Fraser, "Rhodesian Sanctions and the Byrd Amendment in the U.S. Congress," June 1974, Fraser Speeches, 1974 Jan–June, 152.L.7.4 (F), Fraser Papers.

117. Methodist leaders also urged members of Congress to repeal the amendment. See, for example, Booth to Biaggi, August 19, 1974, Rhodesia Sanctions Conference, 1974, Box 135, ACOA Addendum; Armstong et al. to Representative, August 15, 1974, ibid.

118. *Congressional Record*, May 23, 1973.

119. "The Case for Restoring Rhodesian Sanctions," Rhodesia Sanctions Conference, 1974, Box 135, ACOA Addendum.

120. Donald Fraser, "Rhodesian Sanctions and the Byrd Amendment in the U.S. Congress," June 1974, Fraser Speeches, 1974 Jan–June, 152.L.7.4 (F) Fraser Papers.

121. Buchanan statement, *Congressional Record*, October 18, 1973. Buchanan had previously supported the amendment but shifted his position after serving as a U.S. representative to the UN. Lake, *The "Tar Baby" Option*, 274.

122. Fact Sheet, September 19, 1975, Folder 3, Box 835, James G. Abourezk Papers, University Libraries, Archives and Special Collections, University of South Dakota.

123. Elliott to Stern, May 18, 1976, CO 1–1 Africa 1/1/76–1/20/76, Box 4, Subject Files, WHCF, GRFPL. Despite his statement, Ford did not work to repeal the amendment. Furthermore, correspondence from his years in the House demonstrates that Ford supported purchasing chrome from Rhodesia. See, for example, Ford to Rickerson, June 12, 1972, Folder 44, Ford Congressional Papers, Box B227, GRFPL. I thank Scott Kaufman for bringing these documents to my attention. For an alternative view, see Carl P. Watts, "'Dropping the F-Bomb': President Ford, the Rhodesian Crisis, and the 1976 Election" (paper presented at the Society for Historians of American Foreign Relations Annual Meeting, June 2014). Watts argues that Ford was committed to finding a solution to Rhodesia, even if it harmed him politically, in part because he felt as though he had already made a political concession by removing Rockefeller from the ticket.

124. Concerns about human rights were not a motivation for Kissinger in these negotiations.

125. Dan Zachary, who worked in the Bureau of African Affairs, remembers that when Kissinger read a draft of his speech for Lusaka, he said, "You Foreign Service officers think you can change the world be [sic] uttering some sentimental crap about democracy and human rights," which suggests some cynicism on Kissinger's part about the initiative. Dan Zachary, Oral History Interview, July 3, 1989, ADST.

126. Henry Kissinger, "United States Policy on Southern Africa," *Department of State Bulletin*, May 31, 1976, 674; DeRoche, *Black, White, and Chrome*, 213. During his April 1976 trip to Africa, Kissinger similarly spoke about human rights, arguing that American opposition to apartheid was "not simply a matter of foreign policy but an imperative of our own moral heritage." Hugh M. Arnold, "Henry Kissinger and Human Rights," *Universal Human Rights* 2, no. 4 (October–December 1980): 66.

127. For more details, see telegram, September 20, 1976, FRUS, 1969–1976, Vol. XXVIII, 574–75. For Kissinger's views, see Memcon, January 19, 1977, ibid., 714–26. For British concerns as the negotiations progressed, see Duff to Crossland, August 23, 1976, FCO 36/1830, NAUK; Record of a Meeting with Dr. Kissinger, September 14, 1976, FCO 36/1833 Anglo/U.S. Joint Planning on Rhodesia, NAUK; Cabinet Memorandum, September 21, 1976, FCO 36/1835, NAUK; Speaking Note, September 22, 1976, FCO 36/1840, NAUK; Record of a Conversation, October 6, 1976, FCO 36/1840, NAUK.

128. DeRoche, *Black, White, and Chrome*, 228.

3. CAUSING US "REAL TROUBLE": THE 1967 COUP IN GREECE

1. George Papandreou served twice as prime minister before being dismissed by the king in 1965. The role of his son, Andreas, in the party was a source of controversy in Greek politics at the time.

2. James Edward Miller, *The United States and the Making of Modern Greece: History and Power, 1950–1974* (Chapel Hill: University of North Carolina Press, 2009), 125. Since the 1947 Truman Doctrine, the United States had been committed to suppressing communism in Greece and had helped to defeat the communists in the Greek Civil War. Svetozar Rajak, "The Cold War in the Balkans, 1945–1956," in *The Cambridge History of the Cold War Volume I: Origins*, ed. Melvyn P. Leffler and Odd Arne Westad (Cambridge: Cambridge University Press, 2010), 205; Evanthis Hatzivassiliou, "Shallow Waves and Deeper Currents: The U.S. Experience in Greece, 1947–1961, Policies, Historicity, and the Cultural Dimension," *Diplomatic History* 38, no. 1 (2014): 89–91; Evanthis Hatzivassiliou, *Greece and the Cold War: Frontline State, 1952–1967* (London: Routledge, 2006), 8.

3. For more on the British reaction, see Effie G. H. Pedaliu, "Human Rights and Foreign Policy: Wilson and the Greek Dictators, 1967–1970," *Diplomacy & Statecraft* 18 (2007): 185–214. On NATO member countries' approaches, see Effie G. H. Pedaliu, "'A Discordant Note': NATO and the Greek Junta, 1967–1974," *Diplomacy & Statecraft* 22, no. 1 (2011): 102–3. For a discussion of the European Economic Community's response, see Eirini Karamouzi, *Greece, the EEC and the Cold War 1974–1979: The Second Enlargement* (London: Palgrave, 2014), 20.

4. Albania withdrew from the Warsaw Pact in 1968.

5. Pauline Mian, "Infringement of Human Rights in Greece and the Response of the United States and the United Nations," Congressional Research Service Annual

Report, 1974; Pedaliu, "Human Rights and Foreign Policy," 195; Pedaliu, "A Discordant Note," 102–3; Adam Garfinkle, "The Nadir of Greek Democracy," in *Friendly Tyrants: An American Dilemma*, ed. Daniel Pipes and Adam Garfinkle (New York: St. Martin's Press, 1991), 73; Konstantina Maragkou, "Favouritism in NATO's Southeastern Flank: The Case of the Greek Colonels, 1967–1974," *Cold War History* 9, no. 3 (August 2009): 354. There were growing concerns within NATO over the regime's human rights violations, with Denmark, the Netherlands, Sweden, and Norway all initiating action before the European Commission on Human Rights against Greece for violating the European Convention on Human Rights in 1967.

6. Keys argues that the outrage in the wake of the 1967 Greek coup underpinned the human rights campaigns that would follow but that it was not one of them because it "did not involve a full-fledged embrace of human rights rhetoric" and because "human rights appeals were part of a broader repertoire of moral and political arguments." Barbara Keys, *Reclaiming American Virtue: The Human Rights Revolution of the 1970s* (Cambridge, MA: Harvard University Press, 2014), 76. Yet, as the record shows, not only did activists concerned with repression in Greece as well as U.S. officials use the language of "human rights" to describe events in Greece, they were also deeply concerned with politically motivated imprisonment, due process, the widespread use of torture, and the conditions of imprisonment in addition to the abrogation of democracy in Greece.

7. Despite playing an important role in antijunta activism, particularly in connection with the European Human Rights Commission, Maria is not a focus of my research, given her Greek citizenship and her concentration on European institutions. James Becket, *Barbarism in Greece* (New York: Walker, 1970), ix.

8. For an example of Becket's writings during those years, see James Becket and Keith D. Griffin, "Revolution in Chile?," *New Republic*, December 29, 1962, 9–11.

9. James Becket, Interview with the Author, December 5, 2016.

10. Ibid.

11. Ibid.

12. Amnesty International, "Situation in Greece," January 27, 1968, Trip to Greece–May 1968, Box 149.G.2 (F), Donald M. Fraser Papers, Minnesota Historical Society, St. Paul; Barbara Keys, "Anti-Torture Politics," in *The Human Rights Revolution: An International History*, ed. Akira Iriye, Petra Goedde, and William I. Hitchcock (Oxford: Oxford University Press, 2012). A second Amnesty International report based on a March 1968 visit to the country alleged that the Greek government had condoned the use of torture. Ann Marie Clark, *Diplomacy of a Conscience: Amnesty International and Changing Human Rights Norms* (Princeton, NJ: Princeton University Press, 2001), 41.

13. AmEmbassy Athens to SecState, March 29, 1968, POL 29 1/1/68, Greece, Box 2154, CFPF 1967–1969, Social, Record Group 59, NARA. A similar interpretation was echoed by journalist C. L. Sulzberger, who was not persuaded that the coup represented a fundamental betrayal of Greek democracy. He pointed out the country's varied forms of government over the years. C. L. Sulzberger, "Greece under the Colonels," *Foreign Affairs* 48 (1969–70): 300.

14. Garfinkle, "The Nadir of Greek Democracy," 71. See, for example, Hans Göran Franck to Johnson, August 4, 1966, AMMO, Box 142, WHCF, Name File, LBJPL; "Human Rights in the Vietnam War," April 21, 1968, U.S. Vietnam Correspondence, 1964–6, Box 36, ILHRC.

15. Fraser et al. to Rusk, November 17, 1967, Greece, 1967, Box 145.C.3.2 (F), Fraser Papers.

16. Macomber to Fraser, May 10, 1967, Greece, 1967, Box 145.C.3.2 (F), Fraser Papers; Rostow to Fraser, May 3, 1967, CO 94 Greece 1/9/66–5/10/67, CO Box 36, WHCF, LBJPL; Fraser to Johnson, 28 April 1967, CO 94 Greece 1/9/66–5/10/67, CO Box 36, WHCF, LBJPL.

17. 5/30/79—Human Rights Conference for the Fed Bar Association, Box 149.C.13.4 (F), Fraser Papers.

18. Memorandum, Trip to Greece—May 1968, Box 149.G.9.2 (F), Fraser Papers.

19. Ibid.

20. Donald Fraser, *Congressional Record*, May 27, 1968, Box 151.H.3.2 (F), Fraser Papers.

21. Press Release, October 2, 1967, Folder 38, Box 73, Series 1: Legislative Files, Donald Edwards Papers, San Jose State University; "A Sad Easter in Greece," Folder 24, Box 74, ibid.

22. Members of Congress to Rusk, November 17, 1967, Folder 35, Box 74, Series 1: Legislative Files, Edwards Papers.

23. Lyons to Colleague, Greek Committee, 1968, Box 151.H.3.3 (B), Fraser Papers.

24. Helen Conispoliatis, "Facing the Colonels: British and American Diplomacy Towards the Colonels' Junta in Greece, 1967–1970" (PhD Thesis, University of Leicester, 2003), 180.

25. Fraser to Reuther, January 6, 1969, Greece: U.S. Committee for Democracy, 1969, Box 151.I.11.6 (F), Fraser Papers.

26. U.S. Committee for Democracy in Greece, "Greece—A Call to Conscience," Trip to Greece—May 1968, Box 149.G.9.2 (F), Fraser Papers; Keys, "Anti-Torture Politics."

27. Minnesotans for Democracy and Freedom, Newsletter No. 5, November 2, 1967, Folder 2, Box 41, Series 1: Legislative Files, Edwards Papers.

28. Greece, 1967–1968, Box 151.H.3.2 (F), Fraser Papers.

29. Groups concerned with democracy in Greece also developed in Chicago, North Carolina, New York, and Washington, DC. "Do You Owe Something to Greece? Help Preserve Her Heritage and Yours," Greece, California Supporters, Carton 2, Frank C. Newman Papers, the Bancroft Library, University of California–Berkeley.

30. Committee to Johnson, August 28, 1967, POL 29 Greece 7/1/67, Box 2154, CFPF 1967–1969, Record Group 59, NARA; Stathis and Mercouris to Friends, November 1967, Folder 2, Box 41, Series 1: Legislative Files, Edwards Papers.

31. Boston Ad Hoc Committee for Freedom in Greece to Johnson, May 2, 1967, CO 94 Greece 11/9/66–5/10/67, Box 36, WHCF, LBJPL; Minutes, August 8, 1967, 1967, Box 1, Series 1: 1, AIUSA Records; Carolyn Lewis, "'Ordinary' People Turn Jail Keys for Idealists," *Washington Post*, October 8, 1967, B4.

32. Pollis to Fraser, June 5, 1968, Folder 4, Box 4, Series 1: Legislative Files, Edwards Papers.

33. Miller, *The United States*, 119.

34. Ibid., 125.

35. Ibid., 138; Margaret Papandreou, *Nightmare in Athens* (Englewood Cliffs, NJ: Prentice-Hall, 1970), 162–63, 170, 191, 298. See also Nick Papandreou, *Father Dancing* (New York: Penguin, 1996), 102–10, for Papandreou's son's perspective on the activity surrounding his father's imprisonment.

36. Academics from Harvard University, Stanford University, Tufts University, the Massachusetts Institute of Technology, Wellesley College, the University of California–Berkeley, the University of Chicago, the University of Pennsylvania, the University of Miami, the University of Michigan, Colorado State University, the University of Minnesota, Purdue University, the University of Washington, the State University of New York–Buffalo, Haverford College, Lincoln University, and the University of California–Santa Barbara wrote to the White House to express their concern for Papandreou. See, for example, Calhoun to Johnson, May 5, 1967, CO 94 Greece 11/9/66–5/10/67, CO Box 35, WHCF, LBJPL; Martin Gansberg, "Johnson to Appeal to Save Jailed Son of Papandreou," *New York Times*, May 8, 1967, 1. Senator Walter Mondale (D-MN) was also among those who wrote to the White House on Papandreou's behalf.

37. Saunders to Rostow, April 26, 1967, Greece Memos & Misc. [1 of 2] 1/66–7/67, Box 126, National Security Files, Country Files, LBJPL.

38. John Kenneth Galbraith, *A Life in Our Times: Memoirs* (Boston: Houghton Mifflin, 1981), 459–60; Martin Gansberg, "Johnson to Appeal to Save Jailed Son of Papandreou," *New York Times*, May 8, 1967, 1. According to Robert Keeley, who served in the U.S. embassy in Athens at the time, the ambassador "was surprised if not dismayed that the most urgent telegraphic traffic he was receiving from Washington, officially and privately, did not carry instructions on the attitude to be taken toward the new regime but consisted mainly of appeals on behalf of Andreas." Robert V. Keeley, *The Colonels' Coup and the American Embassy: A Diplomat's View of the Breakdown of Democracy in Cold War Greece* (University Park: Pennsylvania State University Press, 2010), 133; Conispoliatis, "Facing the Colonels," 146.

39. Galbraith conveyed the economists' pleasure at Johnson's intervention. John Kenneth Galbraith, *Name-Dropping: From FDR On* (New York: Houghton Mifflin, 1999), 150–51; Martin Gansberg, "Johnson to Appeal to Save Jailed Son of Papandreou," *New York Times*, May 8, 1967, 1. Johnson's slur coincided—likely coincidentally—with the State Department's view of Andreas. A State Department memorandum described Andreas Papandreou as "politically naïve, unscrupulous, unstable (with paranoiac tendencies), venal, and above all [with] such an overweening ambition that he would resort to almost any means to achieve his goals." According to Keeley, "anti-Andreas animus" pervaded the American government. Keeley, *The Colonels' Coup*, xxv, 27.

40. Heller to Johnson, April 27, 1967, Foreign Policy Greek Crisis, 04/26–27/67, Box 176, Personal Papers of Joseph Califano, LBJPL.

41. Macomber to Fraser, May 10, 1967, POL 29 Greece 1/1/67, Box 2154, CFPF 1967–69, Record Group 59, NARA. Similar language was used in a letter to Senator William Fulbright (D-AK). Battle to Fulbright, May 11, 1967, ibid.

42. Andreas Papandreou, *Democracy at Gunpoint: The Greek Front* (Garden City, NY: Doubleday, 1970), 27.

43. Papandreou to Johnson, June 21, 1967, CO 94 Greece, CO Box 8 [2 of 2], WHCF, Confidential File, LBJPL; Papandreou, *Nightmare in Athens*, 298.

44. Papandreou, *Democracy at Gunpoint*, 294. Talbot reported to Papandreou after his release that the United States "had not discovered any indication that the regime ever planned to execute him." Nonetheless, Papandreou thanked the embassy for intervening to "save" his life. Telegram, January 9, 1968, FRUS, 1964–1968, Vol. XVI, 721–22. See also Keeley, *The Colonels' Coup*, 165.

45. Saunders to Rostow, April 27, 1967, Greece Memos & Misc. [1 of 2] 1/66–7/67, Box 126, National Security Files, Country Files, LBJPL; Miller, *The United States*, 138.

46. Telegram, April 21, 1967, FRUS, 1964–1968, Vol. XVI, 581.

47. Ibid., 580.

48. Department of State to AmEmbassy Athens, April 22, 1967, POL 29 Greece 1/1/67, Box 2154, CFPF 1967–69, Record Group 59, NARA; Department of State to AmEmbassy Athens, April 27, 1967, ibid.

49. Department of State to AmEmbassy Athens, April 26, 1967, POL 29 Greece 1/1/67, Box 2154, CFPF 1967–69, Record Group 59, NARA.

50. Telegram, April 28, 1967, FRUS, 1964–1968, Vol. XVI, 594–97.

51. Battle to Secretary, April 23, 1967, Greece Memos & Misc. [1 of 2] 1/66–7/67, Box 126, National Security Files, Country Files, LBJPL; Keeley, *The Colonels' Coup*, 95.

52. Memorandum for the Files, April 27, 1967, Greece Memos & Misc. [1 of 2] 1/66–7/67, Box 126, National Security Files, Country Files, LBJPL.

53. "Greek Junta's Plans for Andreas Papandreou," Greece Memos & Misc. [1 of 2] 1/66–7/67, Box 126, National Security Files, Country Files, LBJPL.

54. AmEmbassy Athens to SecState June 1, 1967, POL 29 Greece 1/1/67, Box 2154, CFPF 1967–1969, Social, Record Group 59, NARA; AmEmbassy to SecState, June 6, 1967, ibid.

55. Rousseas to Newman, July 25, 1967, Greece, Andreas G. Papandreou (1 of 3), Carton 2, Newman Papers; Newman to Galbraith, May 17, 1967, ibid.; Newman to Galbraith, May 19, 1967, ibid.; Newman to Pattakos, July 17, 1967, ibid.; Frank C. Newman, Oral History Interview Conducted 1989 and 1991 by Carol Hicke, Regional Oral History Office, University of California–Berkeley, California State Archives State Government Oral History Program.

56. Lyons to Pattakos, August 31, 1967, Folder 1, Box 41, Series 1: Legislative Files, Edwards Papers.

57. In a letter to a citizen who was concerned with Greece, Fraser wrote, "Unfortunately, the attitude of our State Department toward the junta has, in my opinion, remained entirely too friendly." Fraser to Becket, March 26, 1968, Trip to Greece—May 1968, Box 149.G.9.2 (F), Fraser Papers.

58. Becket to Pell, May 22, 1968, Projects—Greece, Box 73, Paul Findley Papers, Illinois State Historical Society, Springfield; Becket, *Barbarism in Greece*, xi; Elise G. Becket, "Athens News March 1973," Folder 3, Box 313, James G. Abourezk Papers, University Libraries, Archives and Special Collections, University of South Dakota; Becket Interview.

59. One notable exception was California state senator Nicholas Petris, who was very active on Greek repression. Petris to Nixon, June 19, 1973, Greece, United States Support, Carton 2, Newman Papers; Petris to Jackson, June 27, 1973, ibid.; Press Release, ibid.

60. Tony Smith, *Foreign Attachments: The Power of Ethnic Groups in the Making of American Foreign Policy* (Cambridge, MA: Harvard University Press, 2000), 63; Clifford P. Hackett, "Congress and Greek American Relations: The Embargo Example," *Journal of the Hellenic Diaspora* 15, nos. 1–2 (Spring–Summer 1988): 8–9.

61. Alexander DeConde, *Ethnicity, Race, and American Foreign Policy: A History* (Boston: Northeastern University Press, 1992), 173; Hackett, "Congress and Greek American Relations," 12.

62. "Philhellenes" were well versed in the classics and Greek culture, which manifested in empathy for Greece. Effie G. H. Pedaliu, "Human Rights and International Security: The International Community and the Greek Dictators," *International History Review* 38, no. 5 (2016).

63. AmEmbassy Athens to SecState, May 13, 1967, Greece Cables, Vol. 2, 1/66–7/67, Box 126, National Security Files, Country Files, LBJPL.

64. Intelligence Memorandum, July 6, 1967, Greece Memos & Misc. [1 of 2] 1/66–7/67, Box 126, National Security Files, Country Files, LBJPL.

65. A White House memorandum in the wake of the coup noted that Dean Rusk had explicitly decided against trying to influence the upcoming Greek election because "the possible political gain is outweighed by the security risks." Rostow reported to Johnson that his aides had decided "that it was becoming less and less appropriate for us to try to influence elections in places like Italy and Greece." Rostow also suggested that the small amount of money under consideration was unlikely to affect the outcome of the election. Rostow to Johnson, May 15, 1967, Greek Coup, 1967, Box 10, National Security Files, Intelligence Files, LBJPL; Memorandum for the Record, March 16, 1967, ibid. Nonetheless, suspicions persist about U.S. involvement. For recent speculation, see Stan Draenos, *Andreas Papandreou: The Making of a Greek Democrat and Political Maverick* (London: I. B. Tauris, 2012), 289–304. See also Philip Deane, *I Should Have Died* (New York: Atheneum, 1977), 123–25.

On the other hand, historian James Miller argues that the United States "neither encouraged or supported" the April 1967 coup. Miller, *The United States*, 135. Louis Klarevas has similarly argued that based on available documentation, although the United States was aware that a coup by the colonels might be possible and did not act to thwart the coup once it broke out, the Johnson administration cannot be seen as responsible for the coup. Louis Klarevas, "Were the Eagle and the Phoenix Birds of a Feather: The United States and the Greek Coup of 1967," *Diplomatic History* 30, no. 3 (June 2006): 475, 494, 506. Evidence suggests that the U.S. ambassador, at least, had no advance knowledge; when Talbot met with the new Greek prime minister immediately thereafter, he expressed frustration at the role of American equipment in the coup. Keeley, *The Colonels' Coup*, 95.

66. Pedaliu, "'A Discordant Note,'" 103. As one scholar has put it, U.S. officials in Athens and Washington were "caught with their pants down" by the coup, which was not predicted. Hatzivassiliou, "Shallow Waves and Deeper Currents," 98.

67. Rostow to Johnson, April 22, 1967, Greece Memos & Misc. [2 of 2], 1/66–7/67, Box 126, National Security Files, Country Files, LBJPL.

68. Rostow to Johnson, April 21, 1967, Greece Memos & Misc. [1 of 2], Box 126, National Security Files, Country Files, LBJPL.

69. Teleconference Between the Department of State and AmEmb Athens, April 24, 1967, Greece, Volume 2, 1/66–7/67, Box 126, National Security Files, Country Files, LBJPL.

70. Rostow to Johnson, April 27, 1967, Greece Memos & Misc. [1 of 2], Box 126, National Security Files, Country Files, LBJPL.

71. Read to Rostow, June 8, 1967, Greece Memos & Misc. [1 of 2], Box 126, National Security Files, Country Files, LBJPL.

72. Barrington King, Oral History Interview, April 18, 1990, ADST.

73. The State Department did monitor human rights abuses in Greece. As of June 9, 1967, it estimated that Greece had five thousand political prisoners incarcerated. Read to Rostow, June 8, 1967, Greece Memos & Misc. [1 of 2] 1/66–7/67, Box 126, National Security Files, Country Files, LBJPL.

74. Rusk to Johnson, July 21, 1967, 1/66–7/67, Box 126, National Security Files, Country Files, LBJPL; Keeley, *The Colonels' Coup*, 97; Reuther to Dirksen, November 13, 1967, Folder 2, Box 41, Series 1: Legislative Files, Edwards Papers.

75. Rostow to Johnson, July 22, 1967, Greece Cables III 8/67–2/68, Box 127, National Security Files, Country Files, LBJPL; Rostow to Johnson, July 21, 1967, Greece, Volume 2, 1/66–7/67, Box 126, ibid.

76. See, for example, Rostow to Johnson, July 22, 1967, Greece, Vol. 3, 1/66–7/67, Box 126, National Security Files, Country Files, LBJPL; Rostow to Manatos, February 21, 1968, Greece, Vol. 3, 8/67–2/68, Box 127, ibid.

77. Rostow to Johnson, July 22, 1967, Greece Cables III 8/67–2/68, Box 127, National Security Files, Country Files, LBJPL. Furthermore, administration officials such as Assistant Secretary of State Lucius Battle argued that the United States should remain engaged with Greece and other authoritarian regimes as a means to shift their practices over time. Battle to Reuther, October 17, 1967, Folder 2, Box 41, Series 1: Legislative Files, Edwards Papers.

78. Rostow to Johnson, July 22, 1967, Greece, Vol. 3, 1/66–7/67, Box 126, National Security Files, Country Files, LBJPL; Rostow to Johnson, September 11, 1967, Greece Cables and Memos, Vol. 4, 3/68–11/68, Box 127, ibid.

79. Edwards to Beck, August 15, 1967, Folder 38, Box 73, Series 1: Legislative Files, Edwards Papers; Macomber to Edwards, August 10, 1867, Folder 1, Box 41, ibid.; Press Release, August 24 1967, Folder 1, Box 41, ibid.; Warnke to Reuther, October 19, 1967, Folder 2, Box 41, ibid. Others in the U.S. government cited the same statistics, which were not uniformly accepted. For example, Elise Becket wrote to the State Department to rebut such figures. Becket to Macomber, March 30, 1968, POL 29 Greece 1/1/68, Box 2154, CFPF 1967–69, Record Group 59, NARA.

80. Katzenbach to Newman, August 24, 1967, POL 29 Greece 7/1/67, Box 2154, CFPF 1967–69, Record Group 59, NARA.

81. Rostow to Newman, September 7, 1967, POL 29 Greece 7/1/67, Box 2154, CFPF 1967–69, Record Group 59, NARA.

82. Report on Trip to Athens, July 22–25, 1967, POL 29 Greece 7/1/67, Box 2154, CFPF 1967–69, Record Group 59, NARA.

83. Amnesty International, "Situation in Greece," January 1, 1968, Folder 431, AI Indexed Documents, AI IS.

84. Ibid.

85. "Situation in Greece: Report by Amnesty International," POL 29, Greece 1/1/68, Box 2154, CFPF 1967–69, Record Group 59, NARA.

86. Document Smuggled out of the Laki Camp, Leros, April 1968, Folder 431, AI Indexed Documents, AI IS.

87. The assistant secretary of state for the Near East and North Africa, Lucius Battle, used divisions between AIUSA and the Amnesty International Secretariat to his advantage, pointing out that the U.S. chapter had "not adopted" the international report. Battle to Pell, April 9, 1968, POL 29 Greece 1/1/68, Box 2154, CFPF 1967–1969,

Social, Record Group 59, NARA. Other observers were skeptical as well. For example, journalist C. L. Sulzberger asserted, "Nor do I believe that torture is official policy." Sulzberger, "Greece under the Colonels," 310. Battle's claims are difficult to reconcile with earlier State Department research from Greece that Amnesty's reporting was "probably substantially true." He may have sought to portray the situation in Greece to an external audience as less serious than it was, or he may have disagreed with the embassy's appraisal. AmEmbassy Athens to SecState, March 29, 1968, POL 29 1/1/68, Greece Box 2154, CFPF 1967–69, Record Group 59, NARA. London *Observer* reporter Philip Deane suggests that journalists such as Sulzberger and American intelligence agents were aware that torture was taking place. Deane, *I Should Have Died*, 133–34.

88. AmEmbassy Athens to SecState, March 29, 1968, POL 29 Greece 1/1/68, Box 2154, CFPF 1967–69, Record Group 59, NARA.

89. Christopher Wren, "Greece: Government by Torture," *Look*, May 27, 1969, 19–21.

90. Rostow to Mantos, June 5, 1968, CO 94 Greece, CO Box 8 [2 of 2], WHCF, Confidential File, LBJPL; Katzenbach to Johnson, June 20, 1968, Greece Cables and Memos Vol. IV 3/68–11/68, Box 127, National Security Files, Country Files, LBJPL.

91. Edwards to Johnson, September 27, 1968, Folder 24, Box 74, Series 1: Legislative Files, Edwards Papers.

92. Press Release, July 22, 1968, Press Releases 1968, 152.L.9.3 (B), Fraser Papers.

93. Donald M. Fraser, "A Few on Greece," *Congressional Record*, May 27, 1968; Press Release, May 27, 1968, Press Releases 1968, Box 152.L.9.3(B), Fraser Papers.

94. Miller, *The United States*, 154.

95. Johnson's response was designed to assuage domestic critics and bolster the prime minister, whom the administration viewed as a moderate force. Rostow to Johnson, January 10, 1968, Greece 10/1/67–1/20/69 [1 of 2], Box 20, National Security Files, Special Head of State Correspondence File, LBJPL.

96. Miller, *The United States*, 157.

97. Rostow to Johnson, October 8, 1968, Greece Vol. VI 3/68–11/68, Box 127, National Security Files, Country Files, LBJPL.

98. Memorandum, Rostow to Johnson, October 8, 1968, FRUS, 1964–1968, Vol. XVI, 767. In Helen Conispoliatis's view, U.S. officials during the Johnson years were only concerned with political prisoners to the extent that their existence complicated lifting the heavy arms embargo against Greece. Conispoliatis, "Facing the Colonels," 208. See, for example, Rostow to Johnson, September 11, 1967, Greece Cables and Memos, Vol. IV 3/68–11/68, Box 127, National Security Files, LBJPL.

99. Mogens Pelt, *Tying Greece to the West: U.S.–West German–Greek Relations 1949–74* (Copenhagen: Museum Tusculanum Press, 2006), 295; Nicholas James Kalogerakos, "Dealing with the Dictators: The United States and the Greek Military Regime, 1967–1974" (DPhil Thesis, Oxford University, 2011), 161. I thank Matthew Jones for sharing this thesis with me.

100. U.S. Policy Toward Greece: Military Assistance, September 24, 1969, Review Group Meeting—Greece 10/2/69, Box H-040, Institutional Files: Meeting Files, NSC, NPMP.

101. AmEmbassy Athens to SecState, October 21, 1968, Greece, Vol. 4, 3/68–11/68, Box 127, National Security Files, Country Files, LBJPL.

102. In addition to maintaining Greece's presence in NATO, U.S. strategic interests in the country included Voice of America sites, a signals intelligence installation on

Crete, a communications facility, and a Greek military base that the U.S. Air Force used. "Greek Options in the Face of Increased Pressure," March 19, 1971, SRG Meeting—Greece (NSSM 116) 3/31/71, Box H-053, NSC Institutional Files, NPMP. According to Kissinger, "When the Nixon administration took office, the Greek military junta was a pariah within NATO." Henry Kissinger, *Years of Renewal* (New York: Simon & Schuster, 1999), 201.

    103. Miller, *The United States*, 158.

    104. Konstantina Maragkou argues that Greece's strategic significance rose with the expulsion of U.S. forces from Wheelus Field in Libya in 1970. Konstantina Maragkou, "The Relevance of Détente to American Foreign Policy: The Case of Greece, 1967–1979," *Diplomacy & Statecraft* 25, no. 4 (2014): 653. In a speech at George Washington University, Greek exile Elias P. Demetracopoulos questioned the underlying rationale for U.S. policy in Greece—that it was supporting military stability in a strategic region. Demetracopoulos argued that the junta had seriously weakened the Greek army and was risking civil war in Greece. He urged the United States, among other measures, to condemn the junta, delay appointing a new ambassador to Athens, end all military aid to the regime, and undertake NATO action to pressure the current leadership to reform. "Greece—A New Viet Nam," April 29, 1969, Folder 11, Box 43, Series 2.2, Frank Church Papers, Special Collections Department, Albertsons Library, Boise State University.

    105. The United States had felt burned by Egyptian leader Gamal Nasser's turn away from the United States in an attempt to defend Egyptian sovereignty. U.S. officials viewed his eventual neutralism as a threat to U.S. interests in the Middle East.

    106. Charles Stuart Kennedy, Oral History Interview, November 17, 1986, ADST.

    107. Miller, *The United States*, 161–62.

    108. SECRET/NODIS, June 26, 1970, VP's Trip to Turkey, Iran, and Greece, 10 and 11/1971, General: Admin and Sub Misc, Vol. V of VI, "Background Books," Box 525, Conference Files, 1949–1972, Record Group 59, NARA.

    109. Kennedy Interview.

    110. King Interview.

    111. Kissinger to Nixon, June 14, 1969, Greece Vol. 1 [2 of 4], Box 593, Country Files: Middle East, NSC Files, NPMP; Miller, *The United States*, 160–61. Not all members of Congress opposed resuming aid to Greece. Representative Edward J. Derwinski, in a letter that indicated a strong focus on Cold War security concerns, urged the new Nixon administration to reevaluate U.S. policy, keeping in mind Greece's "value as a military, naval and diplomatic ally." Derwinski to Kissinger, January 29, 1969, General CO 55 Greece–Beginning–5/31/69, CO Box 33, Subject Files, WHCF, NPMP.

    112. Lord to Kissinger, December 15, 1969, Folder 2, Box 335, S/P, Record Group 59, NARA.

    113. McCarthy to Kissinger, March 31, 1969, General CO 55 Greece Beginning–5/31/69, CO Box 33, Subject Files, WHCF, NPMP; Fraser to Rogers, January 29, 1970, Greece, 147.G.11.1(B), Fraser Papers; Edwards to Sisco, February 3, 1970, Theodorakis, Mikis, Box 84, Series 5: Constituent Subject File, Edwards Papers.

    114. Bayh to Tasca, June 1, 1970, General CO 55 Greece 2/1/69, CO Box 33, Subject Files, WHCF, NPMP. See also Findley to Rogers, October 13, 1969, State, 1969, Box 51, Departmental File, Findley Papers.

    115. Vernon and Mason to Kissinger, June 4, 1973, Executive CO 55 Greece 1/1/73– [1 of 2] CO Box 33, Subject Files, WHCF, NPMP; Woitrin to Kissinger, General CO 55

Greece 1/1/71–, NPMP. Representative Paul Findley also wrote to express his concern about Pesmazoglou, whom he knew personally. Findley to Rogers, June 1, 1973, Legislation—1973, Foreign Relations (General), Box 127, Findley Papers.

116. Although Nixon had decided to resume aid, he had not made his new policy public. Members of Congress to Rogers, July 30, 1969, Folder 35, Box 74, Series 1: Legislative Files, Edwards Papers.

117. Press Release, August 7, 1969, Folder 8, Box 41, Series 1: Legislative Files, Edwards Papers.

118. "Mini-Amnesties and Maxi-Purges in Greece," *Congressional Record*, February 17, 1969.

119. Scheuer to Nixon August 11, 1969, General CO 55 Greece Beginning–5/31/69, CO Box 33, Subject Files, WHCF, NPMP; Statement, September 2, 1969, Folder 34, Box 74, Series 1: Legislative Files, Edwards Papers.

120. Osgood to Kissinger, October 2, 1969, Review Group Meeting—Greece 10/2/69, Box H-040, Institutional Files: Meeting Files, NSC, NPMP. Joseph Sisco, who headed the NSC's Interdepartmental Group for Near East and South Asia, believed that there were more members of Congress who were "hostile to the Greek regime" than those who supported the current government. Sisco to Kissinger, September 26, 1969, VP's Trip to Turkey, Iran, and Greece, 10 and 11/1971, General: Admin and Sub Misc Vol. V of VI "Background Books," Box 525, Conference Files, 1949–1972, Record Group 59, NARA.

121. Talking Points, NSC Review Group, October 2, 1969, Review Group Meeting—Greece 10/2/69, Box H-040, Institutional Files: Meeting Files, NSC, NPMP.

122. Notes, June 17, 1969, Fraser Reports and Speeches, Box 147, G.11.5 (B), Fraser Papers.

123. Davies to MacDermot, March 15, 1971, Greece, United States Support, Carton 2, Newman Papers; IEC/March/70, International Executive Committee, 1970, Folder 413, IEC Minutes, AI IS.

124. Goldblum to Carey, August 21, 1971, Greece, 1970–1971, Box 34, ILHRC.

125. Minutes, June 24, 1971, Folder 9, Box 100, Organizational Matters, ACLU Records.

126. Press Release, October 13, 1972, Greece, 1972–1973, Box 34, ILHRC.

127. Memorandum, October 7, 1969, Review Group Meeting—Greece 10/2/69, Box H-040, Institutional Files: Meeting Files, NSC, NPMP.

128. U.S. Policy toward Greece: Military Assistance, September 24, 1969, Review Group Meeting—Greece 10/2/69, Box H-040, Institutional Files: Meeting Files, NSC, NPMP.

129. Memorandum, October 7, 1969, Box H-040, Institutional Files: Meeting Files, NSC, NPMP.

130. Kissinger to Nixon, December 19, 1969, Greece Vol. 1 [2 of 4], Box 593, Country Files—Middle East, NSC, NPMP. See also Pelt, *Tying Greece to the West*, 296.

131. Miller, *The United States*, 161.

132. In Brown's view, visits to Greece by Secretary of State Rogers and Vice President Agnew demonstrated U.S. support of the junta. Elizabeth Ann Brown, Oral History Interview, May 30, 1995 ADST. The vice president visited Athens in October 1971, which the Greek leadership had long desired. In Agnew's talks with Prime Minister Papadopoulos, the vice president emphasized his desire that Greece take actions that

would mute its critics in the U.S. Congress and elsewhere. AmEmbassy Athens to Sec-State, October 18, 1971, Greece Vol. II [3 of 3], Box 594, Country Files—Middle East, NSC, NPMP. See also Draft Report to the President, VP's Trip to Turkey, Iran, and Greece, 10 and 11/1971, General: Admin and Sub Misc Vol. II of VI, Box 525, Conference Files, 1949–1972, Record Group 59, NARA.

133. Dan Zachary, Oral History Interview, July 3, 1989, ADST.

134. Tasca, "Report on Greece," March 31, 1970, NSSM-116, Box H-181, NSC Institutional Files, NPMP; Sulzberger, "Greece under the Colonels," 302.

135. Tasca, "Report on Greece," March 31, 1970, NSSM-116, Box H-181, NSC Institutional Files, NPMP.

136. Ibid. Resuming military aid to Greece had support among Greek opponents of the junta who were committed to maintaining their country's defenses. AmEmbassy Athens to SecState, August 3, 1970, Greece, Vol. I, January 1969–October 1970, Box 593, Country Files—Middle East, NSC, Richard Nixon Presidential Library, Yorba Linda, CA.

137. Edwards to Chafee, April 22, 1970, Greece, Box 83, Series 1: Legislative Files, Edwards Papers.

138. The White House responded neutrally, saying it "noted your expression of concern." Fraser and Edwards to Nixon, April 10, 1970, Greece, 147.G.11.1(B), Fraser Papers; Timmons to Fraser, April 13, 1970, General CO 55 Greece 12/1/69- CO Box 33, Subject Files, WHCF, NPMP.

139. Press Release, December 19, 1969, Greece, 1968–1974, 149.G.9.5 (B), Fraser Papers.

140. Edwards to Williams, January 27, 1970, Greece, Box 83, Series 1: Legislative Files, Edwards Papers.

141. Press Release, May 22, 1970, Projects—Greece, Box 73, Findley Papers.

142. Sisco to Kissinger, March 8, 1971, VP's Trip to Turkey, Iran, and Greece, 10 and 11/1971, General: Admin and Sub Misc Vol. V of VI "Background Books," Box 525, Conference Files, 1949–1972, Record Group 59, NARA.

143. Telegram to Athens, August 11, 1970, Greece Vol. 1 [1 of 4], Box 593, Country Files—Middle East, NSC, NPMP.

144. "Greece: U.S. Policy," *GIST*, Projects—Greece, Box 73, Findley Papers.

145. Findley to Nixon, October 20, 1970, General CO 55 Greece 12/1/69–, CO Box 33, Subject Files, WHCF, NPMP.

146. Press Release Book 1970 #2, 152.L.9.4 (F), Fraser Papers.

147. Saunders to Kissinger, January 7, 1971, NSSM-116, Box H—1818, NSC Institutional Files, NPMP.

148. Sisco to Kissinger, March 8, 1971, VP's Trip to Turkey, Iran, and Greece, 10 and 11/1971, General: Admin and Sub Misc Vol. V of VI "Background Books," Box 525, Conference Files, 1949–1972, Record Group 59, NARA.

149. Ibid.; Miller, *The United States*, 166.

150. Alexandros Panagoulis Testimony, Greece 1971, 147.G.11.11 (B), Fraser Papers.

151. Peter Thompson, "Human Rights in Greece 1973," Folder 66, International Executive Committee, AI IS.

152. Vitsaxis to Fraser, April 19, 1971, Greece, 1968–1974, 149.G.9.5 (B), Fraser Papers.

153. Don Edwards, "The Greek Junta: No End to the Dictatorship," April 21, 1971, Greece, Box 85, Series 5: Constituent Subject Files, Edwards Papers.

154. Press Release, June 5, 1971, Folder 13, Box 41, Series 1: Legislative Files, Edwards Papers; Members of Congress to Nixon, June 5, 1971, ibid.

155. Testimony, July 12, 1971, Fraser Reports and Speeches, Box 147.G.11.5 (B), Fraser Papers.

156. Press Release, July 13, 1971, Greece, 1968–1974, Box 149.G.9.5 (B), Fraser Papers.

157. In 1969 Senator Pell had sought to cut off all military assistance to Greece, but his effort failed. Senator Rupert Hartke (D-IN) offered a similar initiative in 1970 with the same result.

158. Henry Tanner, "House Group Bids U.S. Stop Aiding Greece, Pakistan," *New York Times*, July 16, 1971.

159. Hays was influenced by a range of factors, including opposition to dictatorships, Greek-Americans in his district, European members of the North Atlantic Assembly, and what he characterized as an affinity for the Greek people. Wayne L. Hays, *Congressional Record*, August 3, 1971, 29113; Hackett, "Congress and Greek American Relations," 8.

160. "A House Committee Rebels," *New York Times*, July 19, 1971. Historian Michael Morgan argues that congressional efforts to suspend aid to Greece in 1971 demonstrated that "democracy and human rights were at least as important to American interests as the containment of communism." Michael Cotey Morgan, "The Seventies and the Rebirth of Human Rights," in *The Shock of the Global: The 1970s in Perspective*, ed. Niall Ferguson et al. (Cambridge, MA: Harvard University Press, 2010), 245.

161. Edwards et al. to Friend, Greece, United States Support, Carton 2, Newman Papers.

162. AmEmbassy Athens to SecState, July 26, 1971, Greece Vol. 2 [2 of 3], Box 594, Country Files—Middle East, NSC, NPMP. See also Pelt, *Tying Greece to the West*, 304.

163. AmEmbassy Athens to SecState, July 11, 1971, FRUS, 1969–1976, Vol. XXIX, 801.

164. Rosenthal and Hamilton to Laird, February 2, 1972, Greece Home Porting Hearings, Box 137, Peter H. B. Frelinghuysen Papers, Public Policy Papers, Department of Rare Books and Special Collections, Princeton University Library; Committee on Foreign Affairs: Report on Hearings on Homeporting in Greece, Frelinghuysen Papers; *Implementation of Homeporting in Greece*, 93rd Cong., 1st Sess., July 16, 19, 30, 1973; Stephen Klaidman, "U.S. to Get Home Port in Greece," *Washington Post*, February 8, 1972, A8; Press Release, February 10, 1972, Greece, 1968–1974, 149.G.9.5(B), Fraser Papers. For more on the reasons for homeporting, see Kalogerakos, "Dealing with the Dictators," 228–33.

165. Presidential Determination 72–11, February 17, 1972, Greece, United States Support, Carton 2, Newman Papers.

166. "McGovern Vows to Halt Aid to Greece if He Is Elected," *New York Times*, July 23, 1972.

167. Kissinger to Nixon, March 7, 1973, Executive CO 55 Greece 1/1/73 [1 of 2], CO Box 33, Subject Files, WHCF, NPMP.

168. Amnesty International reported that the lawyers endured torture during their imprisonment. Kissinger to Nixon, March 7, 1973, Executive CO 55 Greece 1/1/73 [1 of 2], CO Box 33, Subject Files, WHCF, NPMP; Press Release, March 26, 1973, EUR 25 Europe-Greece, 1973, Box 9, Series 5, Record Group 2, AIUSA Records; Telegram, AmEmbassy Athens to SecState, April 21, 1973, Greece Vol. III [2 of 3], Box 594, Country Files—Middle East, NSC, NPMP.

169. Edwards to Colleague, May 30, 1973, Folder 13, Box 41, Series 1: Legislative Files, Edwards Papers.

170. Saunders and Appelbaum to Kissinger, July 5, 1973, Greece Vol. 3 [1 of 3], Box 594, Country Files—Middle East, NSC, NPMP.

171. Exercised by the reimposition of martial law and targeting of student protesters, Edwards asked whether the "Greek government has been using arms supplied to it by the U.S. to control these demonstrations." Edwards to Nixon, November 19, 1973, Greece, 1968–1974, 149.G.9.5 (B), Fraser Papers.

172. Miller, *The United States*, 174–75. In addition, Nicholas Kalogerakos argues that Kissinger was influenced by current talks about the U.S. naval presence on Crete. Kalogerakos, "Dealing with the Dictators," 277.

173. For further discussion, see Miller, *The United States*, 176–200.

174. State Department officials noted that Greeks viewed a "hands-off approach" as support for the junta, which meant that there was no way for the United States to remain truly uninvolved. Lord to Kissinger, February 15, 1974, FRUS, 1969–1976, Vol. XXX, 39–42.

175. Dimitrios Ioannides was the architect of Papadopoulos's ouster. Ibid., 40.

176. Minutes of Secretary's Regional Staff Meeting, March 20, 1974, FRUS, 1969–1976, Vol. XXX, 39.

177. Later in the meeting Kissinger asserted, "Basically we conduct foreign policy here, not domestic policy. We don't muck around with the countries." Ibid., 53, 58.

178. The meeting's transcript suggests that Kissinger put off further discussion until after his upcoming trip to the Soviet Union. Ibid., 53, 58.

179. AI/CAT Publication on Greek Torture Trial, November 1975, Folder 98, International Executive Committee, AI IS.

180. See, for example, Tasca, "Report on Greece," March 31, 1970, NSSM-116, Box H-181, NSC Institutional Files, NPMP.

181. William F. Buckley Jr., "Apology on Greek Torture," *Washington Star*, June 25, 1976, A9.

182. Donald Fraser, "Human Rights and International Relations: Greece, A Case Study," May 14, 1974, Fraser Speeches 1974 Jan–June, 152.L.7.4 (F), Fraser Papers. Fraser's speech was published as "Human Rights and International Relations: A Look Backward at Greece," *Intellect* (October 1974): 28–31.

183. For example, Abram expressed frustration with what he termed the United States' "mute conscience," arguing that U.S. leaders had not "raised a peep against the barbarities of our junta allies in Greece." Morris B. Abram, "America's Mute Conscience," *New York Times*, December 26, 1971, E9.

184. David F. Schmitz, *Thank God They're on Our Side* (Chapel Hill: University of North Carolina Press, 1999), 4.

4. DOES THE UNITED STATES STAND FOR SOMETHING? HUMAN RIGHTS IN SOUTH KOREA

1. In August 1961 Park Chung Hee asked that his name be transliterated as such in all publications and correspondence. I have followed this spelling throughout the

manuscript. Internal State Department records, however, also use Park Chung-hui and Pak Chong-hui.

2. According to the embassy's chargé d'affairs Marshall Green, "Our principles had been too much confined to anti-communism and not enough in affirmative terms of human rights and human responsibilities. The two go closely hand in hand. And in terms of supporting governments that reflect the will of the people." Marshall Green, Oral History Interview, December 13, 1998, ADST.

3. Bong Joong Kim, "Democracy and Human Rights: U.S.–South Korean Relations 1945–1979" (PhD Diss., University of Toledo, 1994), 149. As Daniel A. O'Donohue, who served in the U.S. embassy in Seoul under Ambassador Samuel Berger, said, "Berger had cast his lot with President Park Chung Hee and his military government." Daniel A. O'Donohue, Oral History Interview, May 28, 1996, ADST.

4. Progress Report, August 24, 1961, FRUS, 1961–1963, Vol. XXII, Doc. 242.

5. Ibid.

6. Press Release, November 14, 1961, Korea Subjects Park Visit 11/61–12/61, Box 128, National Security Files, JFKPL.

7. Two days earlier the CIA had warned that the situation in South Korea was "very tense" and at its "most critical" since May 1961. Central Intelligence Agency, "Current Crisis in South Korea and Appraisal as of 14 March 1963," Korea Cables 3/1/63–3/21/63, Box 129, National Security Files, JFKPL.

8. Seoul to Secretary of State, March 15, 1963, Korea Cables 3/1/63–3/21/63, Box 129, National Security Files, JFKPL.

9. Donald Stone Macdonald, U.S.–Korean Relations from Liberation to Self-Reliance: The Twenty-Year Record (Boulder, CO: Westview Press, 1991), 223. See also O'Donohue Interview.

10. Kennedy to Park, March 31, 1963, FRUS, 1961–1963, Vol. XXII.

11. Seoul to Secretary of State, April 2, 1963, Korea Cables 4/63, Box 129, Country Files, National Security Files, JFKPL.

12. Administrative History of the Department of State, Vol. 1, Chap. 7, Special Files, LBJPL.

13. "Silent Sam, the Pressure Man," Time, April 19, 1963.

14. Philip Habib, Oral History Interview, May 24, 1984, ADST; Richard A. Ericson Jr., Oral History Interview, March 27, 1995, ADST. Bong Joong Kim, however, suggests that Park and his team may have created a false crisis "to create the impression that they were flexible enough to listen to American advice." Kim, "Democracy and Human Rights," 181–82.

15. Habib Interview.

16. Gregg Brazinsky, Nation Building in South Korea: Koreans, Americans, and the Making of a Democracy (Chapel Hill: University of North Carolina Press, 2007), 5. Other scholars who have highlighted Korean human rights abuses during the long 1960s include Namhee Lee, "Anticommunism, North Korea, and Human Rights in South Korea: 'Orientalist' Discourse and Construction of South Korean Identity," in Truth Claims: Representation and Human Rights, ed. Mark Bradley and Patrice Petro (New Brunswick, NJ: Rutgers University Press, 2002), 52–53; Kim, "Democracy and Human Rights," 9; Yong-Jick Kim, "The Security, Political, and Human Rights Conundrum, 1974–1979," in The Park Chung Hee Era: The Transformation of South Korea, ed. Byung-Kook Kim and Ezra F. Vogel (Cambridge, MA: Harvard University Press, 2011), 480.

17. Telegram, UN Command to Chairman of the Joint Chiefs of Staff, March 26, 1964, FRUS, 1964–1968, Vol. XXIX, Part 1, 18; Hyun-Dong Kim, *Korea and the United States: The Evolving Transpacific Alliance in the 1960s* (Seoul: Research for Peace and Unification of Korea, 1990), 265, 270; Komer to Bundy, March 26, 1964, FRUS, 1964–1968, Vol. XXIX, Part 1, 19.

18. In Brad Simpson's view, "American nation-building efforts helped define what democracy and stability would mean in South Korea in ways that significantly delayed its emergence and narrowed its meaning." Brad Simpson, "Prudent, Prudent, Tragic: Brazinsky's Arc of Korean Development," *H-Diplo Roundtable Review* 9, no. 17 (2008): 33.

19. Telegram, Seoul to State, June 3, 1964, FRUS, 1964–1968, Vol. XXIX, Part 1, 26; Telegram, Seoul to State, June 6, 1964, ibid., 31. In the words of one observer, to bolster his political power within South Korea, Park "had to ignore the political opposition, manipulate the National Assembly, suppress student dissent, and stifle newspaper criticism." James B. Palais, "'Democracy' in South Korea, 1948–72," in *Without Parallel: The American-Korean Relationship Since 1945*, ed. Frank Baldwin (New York: Pantheon Books, 1974), 338.

20. Telegram, Seoul to State, June 6, 1964, FRUS, 1964–1968, Vol. XXIX, Part 1, 31.

21. Komer to Bundy, June 3, 1964, FRUS, 1964–1968, Vol. XXIX, Part 1, 25.

22. A principal reason that the Johnson administration was reluctant to exert pressure on South Korea was ongoing United States involvement in Vietnam. Johnson's "more flags" program was an effort to demonstrate support for the United States' mission in Vietnam, and South Korea was an important participant, sending fifty thousand troops to fight there. Robert M. Blackburn, *Mercenaries and Lyndon Johnson's "More Flags": The Hiring of Korean, Filipino and Thai Soldiers in the Vietnam War* (Jefferson, MO: McFarland, 1994), 1, 31; Ericson Interview.

23. Background Paper: Political and Economic Situation in Korea, June 22, 1966, Korea, The Secretary's Visit to Seoul, July 8–9, 1966, Box 30, National Security Files, International Meetings and Travel File, LBJPL.

24. CIA Report, June 23, 1967, FRUS, 1964–1968, Vol. XXIX, Part 1, 257; Telegram, Seoul to State, November 25, 1967, ibid., 291.

25. American and South Korean perceptions about the relative egregiousness of these two events complicated relations between the two governments. In the wake of the seizure of the *Pueblo* and the assault on the Blue House, Johnson sought to dissuade South Korean retaliation and did not express his concern over the attack on Park's life, dividing the American and South Korean governments. Mitchell B. Lerner, *The Pueblo Incident: A Spy Ship and the Failure of American Foreign Policy* (Lawrence: University Press of Kansas, 2002), 126–27; Chae-Jin Lee, *A Troubled Peace: U.S. Policy and the Two Koreas* (Baltimore: Johns Hopkins University Press, 2006), 59, 62; O'Donohue Interview; Ericson Interview.

26. Newman to Kim, Arranged Correspondence M–Z, Box 2, Yong-jeung Kim Papers, Rare Book and Manuscript Library, Columbia University.

27. It is not clear that the Korean Affairs Institute's activities went beyond Kim writing to Korean and American leaders to advance his agenda. Kim to Pak, September 13, 1961, Arranged Correspondence A–L, Box 2, Kim Papers.

28. Kim to Rusk, May 13, 1963, Arranged Correspondence M–Z, Box 2, Kim Papers.

29. *The Rights of Man*, May–June 1968, Folder 3, Box 1163, Organizational Matters, ACLU Records.

30. Brazinsky, *Nation Building in South Korea*, 156–57.

31. Robert Boettcher, with Gordon L. Freedman, *Gifts of Deceit: Sun Myong Moon, Tongsun Park, and the Korean Scandal* (New York: Holt, Rinehart & Winston, 1980), 194.

32. Hyug Baeg Im, "The Origins of the *Yushin* Regime: Machiavelli Unveiled," in *The Park Chung Hee Era: The Transformation of South Korea*, ed. Byung-Kook Kim and Ezra F. Vogel (Cambridge, MA: Harvard University Press, 2011), 259.

33. William Stueck, *Rethinking the Korean War: A New Diplomatic and Strategic History* (Princeton, NJ: Princeton University Press, 2002), 202.

34. Ra Jong-oh, "The Korean Security Issue: Congress and Foreign Policy," *Journal of East Asian Affairs* 5, no. 2 (1991): 292.

35. When Agnew arrived in South Korea, he asserted, "Korea's inspiring progress in every area of political, economic, and social life is a source of pride to all men who value freedom." "Much Time Left Free on Agnew's Schedule in Korea," *Courier-Journal*, June 30, 1971, 5. We now know that shortly after Agnew's visit in August 1971, Korean officials recognized that they needed to influence members of Congress to support continuing military assistance, and they undertook a campaign to advance South Korean interests in the legislative branch. Boettcher, *Gifts of Deceit*, 95–96.

36. U.S. records use the spellings Kim Dae Jung, Kim Tae-jung, and Kim Tae-shung. I have used Kim Dae Jung throughout. Telegram from the Embassy in Korea to the Department of State, November 3, 1970, FRUS, 1969–1976, Vol. XIX, Part 1, 190.

37. Report, April 16, 1971, FRUS, 1969–1976, Vol. XIX, Part 1, 234; Kim's fifteen-year-old nephew was arrested in what the State Department viewed as politically motivated case in February 1971. Dorr to Green, February 11, 1971, POL 14 Elections 1971, Box 5, Subject Files of the Office of Korean Affairs, 1966–74, Record Group 59, NARA.

38. Telegram, February 3, 1971, FRUS, 1969–1976, Vol. XIX, Part 1, 226.

39. Park won 6.3 million votes to Kim's nearly 5.4 million votes.

40. Habib became ambassador in 1971. Telegram, Seoul to State, December 13, 1971, FRUS, 1969–1976, Vol. XIX, Part 1, 302.

41. Telegram, Seoul to State, December 23, 1971, FRUS, 1969–1976, Vol. XIX, Part 1, 311.

42. Henneke to Scott, May 6, 1975, CO 78, Box 33, WHCF, Subject Files, GRFPL.

43. Holdridge to Kissinger, October 25, 1972, FRUS, 1969–1976, Vol. XIX, Part 1, 423–24. Brazinsky has condemned American leaders for not acting more forcefully. Brazinsky, *Nation Building in South Korea*, 160.

44. Telegram, Seoul to State, November 18, 1972, FRUS, 1969–1976, Vol. XIX, Part 1, 425–26.

45. Telegram, Seoul to State, November 22, 1972, FRUS, 1969–1976, Vol. XIX, Part 1, 430.

46. Stanley Zuckerman reports that in Seoul, when Nixon stepped off Air Force One and shook Zhou Enlai's hand, there was a "collective gasp" among the South Koreans with whom he watched the event. Stanley Zuckerman, Oral History Interview, July 26, 2004, ADST.

47. C. I. Eugene Kim, "Emergency, Development and Human Rights: South Korea," *Asian Survey* 18, no. 4 (April 1978): 369; Im, "The Origins of the *Yushin* Regime," 233.

48. Kissinger to Nixon, October 17, 1972, FRUS, 1969–1976, Vol. XIX, Part 1, 418–20.

49. Im, "The Origins of the *Yushin* Regime," 252.

50. *Human Rights in South Korea: Implications for U.S. Policy, Hearings Before the Subcommittees on Asian and Pacific Affairs and on International Organizations and Movements of the Committee on Foreign Affairs*, H. R., 93rd Cong., 2nd Sess., July 30, August 5, December 20, 1974.

51. Zuckerman Interview.

52. Ibid.

53. David Blakemore, Oral History Interview, November 7, 1997, ADST.

54. Ibid.

55. As Park's reelection approached, the State Department debated the propriety of Nixon's sending a congratulatory message. At issue was Park's recent authoritarianism, about which U.S. officials "were not consulted" and "not associated." A "cordial but diplomatically correct message" was deemed most appropriate. Eliot to Kissinger, December 22, 1972, FRUS, 1969–1976, Vol. XIX, Part 1, 447.

56. Memcon, January 5, 1973, FRUS, 1969–1976, Vol. E-12. For further discussion, see Don Oberdorfer, "S. Korean Abuses Tolerated," *Washington Post*, May 17, 1976, A1.

57. Boettcher, *Gifts of Deceit*, 3, 8.

58. According to Bruce Cumings, by 1972 the Korean CIA was "a complete rogue institution." Cumings, *Korea's Place in the Sun* (New York: Norton, 2013), 370. U.S. officials had predicted that Kim faced considerable risks earlier in the year. In a memorandum O'Donohue asserted that Kim "must come back to the country, and risk imprisonment, if he wishes to remain an opposition leader." He also noted that Kim's financial secretary had been severely beaten and still had limited abilities to speak. Memorandum for the File, January 4, 1973, POL 5-1 Domestic General 1973, Box 6, Subject Files of the Office of Korean Affairs 1966–1974, Record Group 59, NARA.

59. Boettcher, *Gifts of Deceit*, 226; Donald A. Ranard, "Saving Kim Dae-jung: A Tale of Two Dissident Diplomats," *Boston Globe*, August 24, 2009, A11. See also Jerome Allen Cohen and Edward J. Baker, "U.S. Foreign Policy and Human Rights in South Korea," in *Human Rights in Korea: Historical and Policy Perspectives*, ed. William Shaw (Cambridge, MA: East Asian Legal Studies Program of Harvard Law School, 1991), 178; Brazinsky, *Nation Building in South Korea*, 226–27; O'Donohue Interview; Paul M. Cleveland, Oral History Interview, October 20, 1996, ADST.

60. Donald P. Gregg, Oral History Interview, March 3, 2004, ADST.

61. Donald A. Ranard, "Kim Dae Jung's Close Call: A Tale of Three Dissidents," *Washington Post*, February 23, 2003.

62. Press Release, August 8, 1973, Korea, 1973–1978 (II), 151.H.3.5 (B), Donald M. Fraser Papers, Minnesota Historical Society, St. Paul.

63. William H. Gleysteen Jr., Oral History Interview, June 10, 1997, ADST.

64. Secretary's Staff Meeting Proceedings, January 25, 1974, FRUS, 1969–1976, Vol. E-12.

65. Seoul to Department of State, August 26, 1973, FRUS, 1969–1976, Vol. E-12.

66. Kim Dae Jung, "Nobel Lecture," http://www.nobelprize.org/nobel_prizes /peace/laureates/2000/dae-jung-lecture.html, accessed March 29, 2017.

67. Cleveland Interview.

68. Ibid.

69. Edward Hurwitz, Oral History Interview, August 15, 1996, ADST.

70. George E. Lichtblau, Oral History Interview, December 17, 1991, ADST.

71. J. D. Bindenagel, Oral History Interview, February 3, 1998, ADST.

72. Ericson Interview.

73. According to Habib, growing up among a group of Jewish friends heightened his sensitivity to anti-Semitism. Habib Interview.

74. Lichtblau Interview.

75. Habib, in contrast, "was all over the place and saw everybody. His door was open to anybody and he didn't care about offending the government in any way." Hurwitz Interview.

76. Cleveland Interview. Sneider alienated American missionaries in South Korea when, early in his tenure, he indicated that human rights concerns were only one of many issues with which the embassy was concerned. Ericson Interview.

77. *Human Rights in South Korea: Implications for U.S. Policy, Hearings Before the Subcommittees on Asian and Pacific Affairs and on International Organizations and Movements of the Committee on Foreign Affairs*, H. R., 93rd Cong., 2nd Sess., July 30, August 5, December 20, 1974.

78. Ibid.

79. Ibid.

80. Ericson Interview. As evidence, see, for example, Sourian to Chong-chul Suh, October 19, 1974, Human Rights: Korea—Correspondence September 1, 1974–3/31/1975, Box 1, Entry UD—13D 15, Record Group 59, NARA.

81. Minutes, September 22, 1970, 1974, Box 1, Series 1: 1, AIUSA Records. Based on the content of the minutes and the folder title, it seems more likely that they refer to a meeting in 1974 rather than in 1970, as the document title indicates.

82. Amnesty International, A Report of a Mission to Korea, Folder 4, Box 2, Series 3, George E. Ogle Papers, Archives and Manuscripts Department, Pitts Theology Library, Emory University. Butler based his congressional testimony on his trip report, which highlighted allegations of torture, repression against students, and extended detention without charges. *Human Rights in South Korea: Implications for U.S. Policy, Hearings Before the Subcommittees on Asian and Pacific Affairs and on International Organizations and Movements of the Committee on Foreign Affairs*, H. R., 93rd Cong., 2nd Sess., July 30, August 5, December 20, 1974.

83. Annual Review, 1974–1975, Folder 2812, Box 461, Record Group 3, Rockefeller Brothers Fund, Rockefeller Archive Center, Sleepy Hollow, NY; International League for the Rights of Man, Annual Review, 1976–1977, Folder 2813, ibid.

84. Henderson also publicly noted the abrogation of democracy in South Korea by testifying before Congress and writing to the *New York Times*. Henderson to Editor, *New York Times*, November 8, 1972, 46; Henderson and Thurber to Senator, July 18, 1974, Folder 5, Box 312, James G. Abourezk Papers, University Libraries, Archives and Special Collections, University of South Dakota.

85. WSCF Asia Office to WSCF Movements and Friends, November 1973, Folder 5, Box 312, Abourezk Papers.

86. Reischauer had grown up in Japan in a Presbyterian missionary family.

87. Edwin O. Reischauer, "The Korean Connection: Is It Time to Disengage?," *New York Times*, September 22, 1974, 257.

88. Reischauer to Kissinger, November 29, 1972, General CO 78 Korea 1/1/71–, CO Box 47, Subject Files, WHCF, NPMP.

89. "The U.S. and Repression in Korea," *Los Angeles Times*, July 24, 1974.

90. Memcon, November 16, 1973, FRUS, 1969–1976, Vol. E-12. Ranard argues that "preoccupation with Vietnam clouded top-level Washington thinking" during the early 1970s. Donald L. Ranard, "Korea, Human Rights, and United States Foreign Policy," in *Toward a Humanitarian Diplomacy: A Primer for Policy*, ed. Tom J. Farar (New York: New York University Press, 1980), 197.

91. A number of missionaries remember being motivated to undertake activism in South Korea by unease about racial injustice in the United States or inspiration from figures such as King. Fran Nelson, "We All Know More Bible than We Live By," in *More Than Witnesses: How a Small Group of Missionaries Aided Korea's Democratic Revolution*, ed. Jim Stentzel (Seoul: Korea Democracy Foundation, 2006), 383–84; Jim Sinnott, "Now You Are Free to Speak Out," in ibid., 419; Linda Jones, "From Service to Solidarity," in ibid., 452–53.

92. David A. Hollinger, "The Protestant Boomerang: How the Foreign Missionary Experience Liberalized the Home Culture," Danforth Distinguished Lecture Series, November 18, 2013. I appreciate the John C. Danforth Center on Religion and Politics at Washington University in St. Louis for its efforts to share a transcript of this lecture with me.

93. Randy Rice, "From Isolation to Solidarity," in *More Than Witnesses: How a Small Group of Missionaries Aided Korea's Democratic Revolution*, ed. Jim Stentzel (Seoul: Korea Democracy Foundation, 2006), 108, 109, 114–16, 125; Walter "Butch" Durst, "Missionaries, Cows, and Monday Nights," in ibid., 325; Gene Matthews, "Things They Never Taught Us down on the Farm," in ibid., 218; Sue Rice, "Acting on Our Convictions," in ibid., 353.

94. Durst, "Missionaries, Cows, and Monday Nights," 328.

95. Jones, "From Service to Solidarity," 465.

96. Louise Morris, "What Korea Taught Me about My Country and My Faith," in *More Than Witnesses: How a Small Group of Missionaries Aided Korea's Democratic Revolution*, ed. Jim Stentzel (Seoul: Korea Democracy Foundation, 2006), 148.

97. Faye Moon, "Heartaches No Longer, And Some That Linger," in *More Than Witnesses: How a Small Group of Missionaries Aided Korea's Democratic Revolution*, ed. Jim Stentzel (Seoul: Korea Democracy Foundation, 2006), 176.

98. Making the argument that U.S. involvement could alleviate South Korean repression, Habib asserted that Christian ministers had faced less persecution because of the protection afforded by U.S. interest. Secretary's Staff Meeting Proceedings, January 25, 1974, FRUS, 1969–1976, Vol. E-12.

99. Henry Kissinger, *Years of Renewal* (New York: Simon & Schuster, 1999), 799.

100. In his memoirs Kissinger describes Habib as "no shrinking violet." Kissinger, 530.

101. Habib Interview.

102. Catherine S. Manegold, "Philip C. Habib, a Leading U.S. Diplomat, Dies at 72," *New York Times*, May 27, 1992.

103. Secretary's Staff Meeting Proceedings, January 25, 1974, FRUS, 1969–1976, Vol. E-12. Based on two visits that Kissinger made to South Korea, the deputy chief of mission in Seoul remembers, "Habib was not afraid of Henry and was ready to argue with him when he thought that Kissinger was wrong. I think Kissinger valued this. Phil was quite prepared to shout at Henry when Henry was shouting at him, and shout a little

louder." Francis T. Underhill, Oral History Interview, November 21, 1988, ADST. Given Habib's record, Fraser wrote to the diplomat upon his elevation to assistant secretary with the hope that they could work together on human rights issues in East Asia. Fraser to Habib, September 20, 1974, Human Rights, Box 149.G.13.7 (B), Fraser Papers.

104. Ranard, "Korea," 203.

105. Memcon, May 28, 1974, FRUS, 1969–1976, Vol. E-12.

106. Ranard, "Korea," 203.

107. Don Oberdorfer, "S. Korean Abuses Tolerated," *Washington Post*, May 17, 1976, A1.

108. Ranard, "Korea," 214. According to Marshall Green, Ranard, who had served as head of the embassy's political section at the time of Park's coup, "had a very emotional attachment to the democratic government and democratic process in Korea. He was very much opposed to the military coup. He was not the kind of person that was prepared to forgive and forget." Green Interview.

109. Ranard, "Korea," 214. According to Boettcher, Ranard retired from the foreign service in the fall of 1974 in part due to Kissinger's minimal concern about human rights violations in South Korea. Boettcher, *Gifts of Deceit*, 229.

110. *Human Rights in South Korea: Implications for U.S. Policy, Hearings Before the Subcommittees on Asian and Pacific Affairs and on International Organizations and Movements of the Committee on Foreign Affairs*, H. R., 93rd Cong., 2nd Sess., July 30, August 5, December 20, 1974.

111. George E. Ogle, "Our Hearts Cry with You," in *More Than Witnesses: How a Small Group of Missionaries Aided Korea's Democratic Revolution*, ed. Jim Stentzel (Seoul: Korea Democracy Foundation, 2006), 86–87. South Korea executed the men in April 1975. AmEmbassy Seoul to SecState, June 19, 1975, Access to Archival Databases, Record Group 59, NARA.

112. Ogle was the first missionary expelled from South Korea in ninety years. *Human Rights in South Korea: Implications for U.S. Policy, Hearings Before the Subcommittees on Asian and Pacific Affairs and on International Organizations and Movements of the Committee on Foreign Affairs*, H. R., 93rd Cong., 2nd Sess., July 30, August 5, December 20, 1974; Ogle, "Our Hearts Cry with You," 95, 100; Cumings, *Korea's Place in the Sun*, 371. For more on Ogle's deportation, see "Deportation of a Missionary from the Republic of Korea," Folder 5, Box 2, Series 3, Ogle Papers.

113. See, for example, Don Oberdorfer, "The State v. Woo Hung Sun," *Washington Post*, February 9, 1975, B5. Father James Sinnott was also expelled for his efforts.

114. Kim to Kissinger, September 18, 1974, Arranged Correspondence: U.S. Government (White House & State Department), Box 1, Kim Papers. See also Kim to Nixon, January 26, 1972, General CO 78 Korea 1/1/71–, CO Box 47, Subject Files, WHCF, NPMP.

115. Laise to Kim, October 17, 1974, Arranged Correspondence: U.S. Government (White House & State Department), Box 1, Kim Papers.

116. Patrick Chung, "The 'Pictures in Our Heads': Journalists, Human Rights, and U.S.–South Korean Relations, 1970–1976," *Diplomatic History* 38, no. 5 (2014): 1147–48.

117. Ibid., 1143.

118. Don Oberdorfer, "South Korea: The Smothering of Dissent," July 28, 1974, *Washington Post*, C3.

119. Jim Stentzel, "They Had to Do Something," in *More Than Witnesses: How a Small Group of Missionaries Aided Korea's Democratic Revolution*, ed. Jim Stentzel (Seoul: Korea Democracy Foundation, 2006), 16.

120. Margaret Keck and Kathryn Sikkink, *Activists Beyond Borders: Advocacy Networks in International Politics* (Ithaca, NY: Cornell University Press: 1998), 12; Daniel C. Thomas, "Boomerangs and Superpowers: International Norms, Transnational Networks and U.S. Foreign Policy," *Cambridge Review of International Affairs* 15, no. 1 (2002): 26.

121. Chung, "The 'Pictures in Our Heads,'" 1137.

122. The United States Response to Authoritarianism: East Asia, June 13, 1974, December 1974, Box 347, Entry 5027: S/P, Dirctor's Files (Winston Lord) 1969–77, Record Group 59, NARA.

123. Ibid.

124. Ibid.

125. Ibid.

126. Ibid.

127. *Human Rights in South Korea: Implications for U.S. Policy, Hearings Before the Subcommittees on Asian and Pacific Affairs and on International Organizations and Movements of the Committee on Foreign Affairs*, H. R., 93rd Cong., 2nd Sess., July 30, August 5, December 20, 1974.

128. Ibid.

129. Ingersoll to Morgan, June 27, 1974, Human Rights, 149.G.13.7 (B), Fraser Papers.

130. *Human Rights in South Korea: Implications for U.S. Policy, Hearings Before the Subcommittees on Asian and Pacific Affairs and on International Organizations and Movements of the Committee on Foreign Affairs*, H. R., 93rd Cong., 2nd Sess., July 30, August 5, December 20, 1974.

131. Ibid.

132. Ibid.

133. Ibid.

134. Ibid; Boettcher, *Gifts of Deceit*, 230.

135. *Human Rights in South Korea: Implications for U.S. Policy, Hearings Before the Subcommittees on Asian and Pacific Affairs and on International Organizations and Movements of the Committee on Foreign Affairs*, H. R., 93rd Cong., 2nd Sess., July 30, August 5, December 20, 1974; Boettcher, *Gifts of Deceit*, 139–40, 277.

136. Bingham et al. to Ford, October 24, 1974, South Korea, 1974, 149.G.13.8 (F), Fraser Papers.

137. These efforts ultimately led to a ceiling of $145 million on total military assistance, loans, credits, and other materials. Pub. L. 93-559, December 30, 1974. See also Stephen B. Cohen, "Conditioning U.S. Security Assistance on Human Rights Practices," *American Journal of International Law* 76, no. 2 (April 1982): 255.

138. Gleysteen had spent his childhood in a Presbyterian missionary family in China. Brazinsky, *Nation Building in South Korea*, 226. Two months into the Ford administration, the National Security Council began an evaluation of assistance to South Korea. Despite undertaking such a study, the White House did not shift its public stance on Park's regime. NSSM 211, October 8, 1974, FRUS, 1969–1976, Vol. E-12.

139. Sunoo to Ford, October 8, 1974, CO 78 Korea, Box 33, WHCF, GRFPL.

140. Kim to Ford, November 1, 1974, Arranged Correspondence: U.S. Government (White House & State Department), Box 1, Kim Papers.

141. *Human Rights in South Korea: Implications for U.S. Policy, Hearings Before the Subcommittees on Asian and Pacific Affairs and on International Organizations and Movements of the Committee on Foreign Affairs*, H. R., 93rd Cong., 2nd Sess., July 30, August 5, December 20, 1974.

142. Memcon, November 22, 1974, FRUS, 1969–1976, Vol. E-12.

143. Gerald Ford, *A Time to Heal: The Autobiography of Gerald Ford* (New York: Harper & Row, 1979), 212–13.

144. Press Release, December 12, 1974, Press Release File 1974 Book 2, 152.L.9.5 (B), Fraser Papers; Boettcher, *Gifts of Deceit*, 233–34.

145. Pub. L. 93–559, December 30, 1974.

146. *Human Rights in South Korea: Implications for U.S. Policy, Hearings Before the Subcommittees on Asian and Pacific Affairs and on International Organizations and Movements of the Committee on Foreign Affairs*, H. R., 93rd Cong., 2nd Sess., July 30, August 5, December 20, 1974; Don Oberdorfer, "Hill Seeks Reports on Human Rights in 19 Countries," *Washington Post*, October 4, 1976, A2.

147. As one diplomat has put it, Habib was always careful to frame attention to human rights as achieving "real world objectives." Memcon, June 12, 1975, FRUS, 1969–1976, Vol. E-12; O'Donohue Interview.

148. In O'Donohue's memory, Kissinger was always criticizing his foreign service officers who wanted to do more about South Korean human rights violations, calling them "political scientists," perhaps demonstrating his disdain for his former academic colleagues. Memcon, June 12, 1975, FRUS, 1969–1976, Vol. E-12; O'Donohue Interview.

149. SecState to AmEmbassy Seoul, June 21, 1975, Access to Archival Databases, Record Group 59, NARA.

150. In the face of Sneider's entreaty, Park remained firm in his commitment to keep Emergency Measure 9 in place. AmEmbassy Seoul to SecState, June 23, 1975, Access to Archival Databases, Record Group 59, NARA.

151. Ibid.

152. AmEmbassy Seoul to SecState, June 19, 1975, Access to Archival Databases, Record Group 59, NARA.

153. Telegram, Embassy in Seoul to Department of State, April 18, 1975, FRUS, 1969–1976, Vol. E-12.

154. Ericson Interview.

155. Ibid.

156. *Hearings Before the Subcommittee on International Organizations of the Committee on International Relations*, H. R., 94th Cong., 1st Sess., May 20, 22, June 3, 5, 10, 12, 17, 24, 1975.

157. Ibid.

158. Ibid.

159. Ibid.

160. Both polls were conducted after the fall of Saigon, suggesting that events in Vietnam likely did not affect the shift. Louis Harris, "Oppose Use of Nuclear Weapons to Defend Korea," *Harris Survey*, July 31, 1975.

161. In response to Kissinger's request, Habib did not foresee considerable problems in the short term but suggested that the regime's "survival" in the long term was

unlikely. Habib to Kissinger, July 25, 1975, POL 5–1 Domestic General, October 1975, Box 7, Subject Files of the Office of Korean Affairs, 1966–1974, Record Group 59, NARA.

162. Memcon, August 27, 1975, FRUS 1969–1976, Vol. E-12.

163. "Policy Problems in Korea," FRUS 1969–1976, Vol. E-12.

164. Memorandum of Conversation, September 2, 1975, September 2, 1975—Ford, Schlesinger, Box 15, National Security Adviser—Memoranda of Conversations, GRFPL.

165. Memorandum for the Secretary of Defense, March 16, 1976, FRUS, 1969–1976, Vol. E-12.

166. Ibid.

167. Press Release, March 11, 1976, Korea March '76, Container 95, Call Number 88/214c, Alan Cranston Papers, the Bancroft Library, University of California–Berkeley. Eighteen prominent leaders in South Korea, including Kim Dae Jung, called on Park to resign and for the restoration of democratic government on March 1, 1976. Ranard likened South Korea to Chile in terms of the negative attention it garnered in 1976. Donald L. Ranard, "The U.S. in Korea: What Price Security?," *Worldview* (January/February 1977): 23. The Korean-American Committee for Human Rights in Korea, a DC-based organization, held a rally at the Capitol in March 1976 to press for greater executive and legislative branch pressure on Park. Statement, March 17, 1976, Folder 5, Box 312, Abourezk Papers.

168. Abzug et al. to Ford, April 2, 1976, CO 78–2 1/1/76–1/20/77 Executive, Box 33, WHCF, SF, GRFPL. In an interview with the former *Washington Post* correspondent for South Korea, Ranard revealed that the United States was expressing concern about human rights violations only in public forums and not in private diplomatic sessions. Don Oberdorfer, "S. Korean Abuses Tolerated," *Washington Post*, May 17, 1976, A1.

169. Cranston et al. to Park, September 30, 1976, Folder 5, Box 312, Abourezk Papers.

170. As many as 115 members of Congress may have taken money from an unregistered South Korean lobbyist between 1971 and 1975. Over the same time period, Congress sent $1.5 billion in military assistance to South Korea. Kim, "The Security, Political, and Human Rights Conundrum," 473–74; Maxine Cheshire and Scott Armstrong, "Seoul Gave Millions to U.S. Officials: S. Korea Gave Millions in Cash, Gifts to Congressmen," *Washington Post*, October 24, 1976, 1; Nicholas M. Horrock, "Big Political Scandal Held Possible—Study Still in Early Stage," *New York Times*, October 28, 1976, 89; Ericson Interview.

171. Pub. L. 94–329, June 30, 1976.

172. Dan Morgan, "House Liberals Abandon Effort to Curb Seoul Food Aid," *Washington Post*, May 20, 1976, A2.

173. Ranard, "The U.S. in Korea," 36.

174. Clair Apodaca, *Understanding U.S. Human Rights Policy: A Paradoxical Legacy* (New York: Routledge, 2006), 47–48.

175. Section 502B, 1976 Amendment to the Foreign Assistance Act 1961, Pub. L. 94–329, June 30, 1976.

176. Report on an Amnesty Mission to the Republic of Korea, 27 March–9 April 1975, Folder 4, Box 21, William J. Butler Collection, University of Cincinnati College of Law Archives.

177. George Wald, "The Sins of President Park's Police State: Why Harvard Should Refuse Korean Grants," *Crimson*, February 14, 1977. In another example, Rexford Tucker wrote, pressing Congress not to allow "anti-riot equipment to be sold to Korea

under any conditions." Tucker to Frelinghuysen, September 9, 1974, Legislation-H, Box 82, Peter H. B. Frelinghuysen Papers, Public Policy Papers, Department of Rare Books and Special Collections, Princeton University Library.

178. Henry Kissinger, "America and Asia," *Department of State Bulletin*, August 16, 1976, 217.

179. Ibid., 221.

180. Hugh Arnold, "Henry Kissinger and Human Rights," *Universal Human Rights* 2, no. 4 (October–December 1980): 68.

181. Elliott to Stone, November 24, 1976, CO 78-2 General 9/1/76–1/20/77, Box 34, WHCF, SF, GRFPL.

182. Leslie H. Gelb, "Human-Rights and Morality Issue Runs Through Ford-Carter Debate," *New York Times*, October 8, 1976, 19.

183. There was only a small number of Americans of Korean descent or Korean citizens living in the United States during these years. By 1970 the number of Korean-Americans was only around seventy thousand. Pyong Gap Min, "Korean Americans," in *Asian Americans: Contemporary Trends and Issues*, ed. Pyong Gap Min (London: Pine Forge Press, 2006), 234.

184. Johnson was so concerned with maintaining South Korean participation that he agreed to pay for kimchi for South Korean soldiers serving in Vietnam. Memorandum of Conversation, March 14, 1967, FRUS, 1964–1968, Vol. XXIX, 235–38; Johnson to Pak, March 23, 1967, ibid., 239–41. To meet this need, U.S. AID developed a preserved kimchi that could be sent to Korean soldiers in Vietnam. Ericson Interview.

185. A number of scholars have suggested that Park was immune to greater pressure because the South Korean economy had strengthened such that its dependence on foreign support had greatly diminished. See, for example, Brazinsky, *Nation Building in South Korea*, 255; Kim, "Democracy and Human Rights," 9, 320.

5. TRANSLATING HUMAN RIGHTS INTO THE LANGUAGE OF WASHINGTON: AMERICAN ACTIVISM IN THE WAKE OF THE COUP IN CHILE

1. John Dinges, *The Condor Years: How Pinochet and His Allies Brought Terrorism to Three Continents* (New York: The New Press, 2005), 3.

2. Jan Eckel, "'Under a Magnifying Glass': The International Human Rights Campaign Against Chile in the Seventies," in *Human Rights in the Twentieth Century*, ed. Stefan-Ludwig Hoffmann (New York: Cambridge University Press, 2010), 324. The two hundred thousand Chileans who went into exile under Pinochet resettled in more than 140 countries, creating a dispersed diaspora. Jessica Stites Mor, "Introduction: Situating Transnational Solidarity Within Critical Human Rights Studies of Cold War Latin America," in *Human Rights and Transnational Solidarity in Cold War Latin America*, ed. Jessica Stites Mor (Madison: University of Wisconsin Press, 2013), 8.

3. Seymour M. Hersh, "Kissinger Said to Rebuke U.S. Ambassador to Chile," *New York Times*, September 27, 1974, 18.

4. Solidarity groups developed in Argentina, Canada, Colombia, Costa Rica, Cuba, France, East Germany, Italy, Mexico, Peru, Spain, Sweden, the United Kingdom, the

United States, West Germany, and Venezuela. Alison J. Bruey, "Transnational Concepts, Local Contexts: Solidarity at the Grassroots in Pinochet's Chile," in *Human Rights and Transnational Solidarity in Cold War Latin America*, ed. Jessica Stites Mor (Madison: University of Wisconsin Press, 2013), 126.

5. AmEmbassy Santiago to RUEHC, September 12, 1973, Coup Cables, Country Files: Latin America, NSC Records, NPMP.

6. Press Release, September 12, 1973, Folder 7, Box 5, Freedom House Records, Public Policy Papers, Seeley G. Mudd Manuscript Library, Princeton University.

7. Subject: Chile—Initial Operational and Policy Questions, September 17, 1973, WSAG Meeting Chile 9/20/73, Box H-094, NSC Institutional Files, NPMP. The embassy, however, doubted that there had been mass executions. Telegram, September 24, 1973, Department of State, FRUS, 1969–1976, Vol. E-11, Part 2, 385.

8. Van Gosse, "Unpacking the Vietnam Syndrome: The Coup in Chile and the Rise of Popular Anti-Interventionism," in *The World the '60s Made: Politics and Culture in Recent America*, ed. Van Gosse and Richard Moser (Philadelphia: Temple University Press, 2003), 103.

9. Historian Vanessa Walker argues that the 1969 Rockefeller Report's characterization of military governments as stabilizing forces provided the "intellectual underpinnings" of Nixon's policy toward Latin America. Vanessa Walker, "Ambivalent Allies: Advocates, Diplomats, and the Struggles for an 'American' Human Rights Policy" (PhD Diss., University of Wisconsin–Madison, 2011), 37.

10. Subject: Chile—Initial Operational and Policy Questions, September 17, 1973, WSAG Meeting Chile 9/20/73, Box H-094, NSC Institutional Files, NPMP.

11. Brazil was a possible alternative source for Chile's short-term military needs.

12. Peter Kornbluh, *The Pinochet File: A Declassified Dossier on Atrocity and Accountability* (New York: The New Press, 2003), 203.

13. Subject: Chile—Initial Operational and Policy Questions, September 17, 1973, WSAG Meeting Chile 9/20/73, Box H-094, NSC Institutional Files, NPMP.

14. Kennedy and Jorden to Kissinger, September 19, 1973, WSAG Meeting Chile 9/20/73, Box H-094, NSC Institutional Files, NPMP.

15. Ibid.

16. SecState to AmEmbassy Santiago, September 24, 1973, Chile 1 Jan 73–31 Mar 1974, (Agusto Pinochet Files Removed from NSC Boxes 777–8), Country Files: Latin America, NSC, NPMP. It is difficult to assess the State Department's appraisal of the situation in Santiago—was there a lack of knowledge in Washington about the junta's human rights violations? Or was there only a degree of denial in a statement that the United States "is impressed with early indications of GOC [government of Chile] respect for human rights"? As a testament to Chilean sensitivity, embassy officials in Washington closely followed congressional speeches regarding Chile as well as its portrayal in the American press; indeed, the Chilean government believed it was being persecuted by the *Washington Post* and *New York Times* due to these outlets' emphasis on individual rights. According to the ambassador, U.S. news sources inevitably oppose a "government that is accused of suppressing freedom of the press, union rights, having dismissed Congress, of having suspended the activities of certain political parties and outlawed other parties as well as violated human rights." EmbaChile to MinRel, November 30, 1973, Fondo: Paises EEUU: Vol. 172, Año 1973, MREC; No. 01482/526, November 5, 1973, ibid.; No. 047, June 22, 1975, Fondo: Paises EEUU, Año

1976, EMBCH EE-UU R (1–65), MREC; No. 578, June 24, 1976, Fondo: Paises EEUU, Vol. E. EE. UU OF. ORD. R. 320–580, Año 1976, MREC. In June 1975 the Chilean government withdrew *Washington Post* reporter Joanne Omang's press credentials over her dissemination of "false information" about the Chilean government. "Chile Bans Post Reporter," *Washington Post*, June 20, 1975, A21.

17. Eckel, "'Under a Magnifying Glass,'" 323; Yves Dezalay and Bryant Garth, *The Internationalization of Palace Wars: Lawyers, Economists, and the Contest to Transform Latin American States* (Chicago: University of Chicago Press, 2002), 146; Verónica Validivia Ortiz de Zárate, "Terrorism and Political Violence During the Pinochet Years: Chile, 1973–1989," *Radical History Review* 85 (Winter 2003): 182; Louis Bickford, "The Archival Imperative: Human Rights and Historical Memory in Latin America's Southern Cone," *Human Rights Quarterly* 21, no. 4 (November 1999): 1103–4. Increased human rights activism in Latin America should also be seen in the context of the 1968 Medellin Conference, which addressed the rights and needs of indigenous people and the poor in Latin America. Manzar Foroohar, "Liberation Theology: The Response of Latin American Catholics to Socioeconomic Problems," *Latin American Perspectives* 13, no. 3 (1986): 37–58; Cecilio De Lora, "From the Vatican II to Medellin," *Horizonte* 9, no. 24 (2011): 1233–45.

18. Dezalay and Garth, *The Internationalization of Palace Wars*, 52–53.

19. Tanya Harmer, "The View from Havana: Chilean Exiles in Cuba and Early Resistance to Chile's Dictatorship, 1973–1977," *Hispanic American Historical Review* 6, no. 1 (2016): 114, 136. David Featherstone defines solidarity as "a relation forged through political struggle which seeks to challenge forms of oppression." David Featherstone, *Solidarity: Hidden Histories and Geographies of Internationalism* (New York: Zed Books, 2012), 5.

20. Harmer, "The View from Havana," 137.

21. Baez to Kissinger, September 19, 1973, General CO 33 Chile 1/1/73–, Box 17, Subject Files, WHCF, NPMP. AIUSA members in California wrote to Kissinger as well. Duncan and Sagan to Kissinger, September 19, 1973, ibid.

22. Prominent Americans, including Baez; writers Truman Capote, Norman Mailer, and Susan Sontag; and former attorney general Ramsey Clark, similarly spoke out against conditions in Chile. "Friends of Chile," May 9, 1974, Folder 3, Box 35, CPUSA.

23. Rose Styron, "Terror in Chile II: The Amnesty Report," *New York Review of Books*, May 30, 1974. Patrick Kelly, however, raises questions about the accuracy of Styron's reporting. Patrick William Kelly, *Sovereign Emergencies: Latin America and the Making of Global Human Rights Politics* (New York: Cambridge University Press, 2018).

24. Anthony Lewis, "The Meaning of Torture," *New York Times*, May 30, 1974, 37.

25. Activism related to Chilean human rights abuses was undoubtedly shaped by earlier efforts to oppose the military dictatorship in Brazil. James N. Green, "Clerics, Exiles, and Academics: Opposition to the Brazilian Military Dictatorship in the United States, 1969–1974," *Latin American Politics and Society* 45, no. 1 (Spring 2003): 88, 111.

26. Eric Pace, "Conditions in Chile Protested by Writers and Publisher Here," *New York Times*, September 28, 1973, 2.

27. Non-Intervention in Chile, "Campaign for Disappeared Political Prisoners in Chile," Flyers, Leaflets, Press Releases and Brochures, 1973–1976, Undated 1 of 2, Box 56, WOLA Records; Benedetta Calandra, "The 'Good Americans': U.S. Solidarity

Networks for Chilean and Argentinean Refugees, 1973–1983," *Historia Actual Online* (2010): 23. Historian Van Gosse has described the network as being "committed to a more militant style of protest." Gosse, "Unpacking the Vietnam Syndrome," 107.

28. The sponsors of the Chile Committee for Human Rights included members of Congress Abourezk, Drinan, Fraser, and Harrington as well as private citizens such as Julian Bond, Ramsey Clark, John Kenneth Galbraith, and Rose Styron. Chile Committee for Human Rights, Flyers, Leaflets, Press Releases and Brochures, 1973–1976, Undated 1 of 2, Box 56, WOLA Records; "Dear Friends," September 1977, Chile: Human Rights Violations, Box 66, Victor G. Reuther Collection, Walter P. Reuther Library, Wayne State University; Newsletter, CIA, Chile-Human Rights, Box 2, Michael Harrington Papers, Salem State College Library; Gosse, "Unpacking the Vietnam Syndrome," 104–5; National Legislative Conference on Chile, Articles and Papers 1969–1974, Undated 1 of 2, Box 54, WOLA Records; Jack Anderson and Les Whitten, "Repression Continuing in Chile: The Washington Merry-Go-Round," *Washington Post*, October 25, 1975, B26.

29. Grant 74–189, Reel 2792, Ford Foundation Records, Rockefeller Archive Center, Sleepy Hollow, NY; Grant 07400364, Reel 1188, ibid.; Inderjeet Parmar, *Foundations of the American Century: The Ford, Carnegie, and Rockefeller Foundations in the Rise of American Power* (New York: Columbia University Press, 2012), 212; William Korey, *Taking On the World's Repressive Regimes: The Ford Foundation's International Human Rights Policies and Practices* (New York: Palgrave Macmillan, 2007), 26; Lewis H. Diuguid, "Chilean Ex-Leaders May Be Freed," *Washington Post*, August 16, 1974, A20.

30. Other groups such as the U.S. Committee for Justice to Latin American Political Prisoners, the Chile Committee for Human Rights, Non-Intervention in Chile, the Chile Human Rights Research Project, and the Washington Office for Human Rights in Chile were also involved in U.S.-based activism related to Chilean human rights abuses. In addition, there was a range of local committees devoted to Chile in states across the country such as California, Colorado, Illinois, Massachusetts, Michigan, Minnesota, Missouri, New York, Oregon, Pennsylvania, Washington, and Wisconsin.

31. It is interesting that those so affiliated with the Allende government would turn to the embassy that was closely associated with its downfall.

32. AmEmbassy Santiago to SecState, May 24, 1974, Chile 1 April 1974-, (Agusto Pinochet Files Removed from NSC Boxes 777–8), Country Files: Latin America, NSC, NPMP.

33. Agenda Item 9b (i), May 1974, Folder 79, International Executive Committee, AI IS. After his return, Porter briefed State Department officials on his observations in Chile. Telegram, May 14, 1974, FRUS, 1969–1976, Vol. E-11, Part 2, 450.

34. The National Council of Churches, the United Methodist Church, the U.S. Catholic Conference, and the Quixote Center were instrumental in WOLA's establishment. Joseph Eldridge, Remarks, November 3, 1976, Early History, Box 27, WOLA Records; Virginia Bouvier, "The Washington Office on Latin America: Charting a New Path in U.S.–Latin American Relations," Box 28, WOLA Records; Edward L. Cleary, *The Struggle for Human Rights in Latin America* (Westport, CT: Praeger, 1997), 142–44; Darren G. Hawkins, *International Human Rights and Authoritarian Rule in Chile* (Lincoln: University of Nebraska Press, 2002), 57. The Washington Office on Latin America and the Washington Office on Africa both worked out of the United Methodist Building in Washington, DC. For more on the organizations' ties, see Raymond

Joseph Parrott, "Struggle for Solidarity: The New Left, Portuguese African Decolonization, and the End of the Cold War Consensus" (PhD Diss., University of Texas at Austin, 2016), 475–76.

35. Eldridge does not think it was a coincidence that he and George Ogle both became involved in human rights issues, observing his Methodist missionary orientation program's significance in shaping his worldview and Ogle's participation in the same process. Joseph Eldridge, Interview with the Author, April 13, 2016. David Hollinger notes that the explosion of membership in human rights organizations happened at the same time that liberal Protestant missions dramatically decreased in number. David A. Hollinger, "The Protestant Boomerang: How the Foreign Missionary Experience Liberalized the Home Culture," Danforth Distinguished Lecture Series, November 18, 2013.

36. Eldridge Interview.

37. Ibid.

38. "Dear Friend of Chile," June 1974, Early History, Box 27, WOLA Records; La Voy to Latin America Strategy Committee, June 26, 1974, ibid. Several years after WOLA was founded, Representative Ed Koch (D-NY) wrote to one of its early staff members to recount the "tremendous impact" that WOLA had had as well as its responsibility for "untold headaches to the State Department." Koch to LaVoy, September 29, 1976, ibid.

39. According to Fraser, "We knew that their information was reliable. We knew their commitment to human rights was complete." Donald M. Fraser, "A Turning Point in Congress," *Cross Currents* (November 2004): 5.

40. "Campaign to End Torture in Chile," Folder 1, Box 35, CPUSA.

41. Proposal for a National Petition Campaign," Folder 1, Box 35, CPUSA. Antijunta activists described their overlap with the antiwar movement in demographic terms— that each was supported by a "fundamentally white, middle class constituency." "To All Peace Activists," July 31, 1974, Folder 3, ibid.

42. NCCSC to Velasquez, July 25, 1974, Folder 22, Box 39, CPUSA.

43. See, for example, H. Con. Res. 309, September 20, 1973; H. Con. Res. 308, September 20, 1973; H. Con. Res. 319, October 1, 1973; Lars Schoultz, *Human Rights and United States Policy Toward Latin America* (Princeton, NJ: Princeton University Press, 1981), 74; Ralph G. Carter and James M. Scott, *Choosing to Lead: Understanding Congressional Foreign Policy Entrepreneurs* (Durham, NC: Duke University Press, 2009), 142–43.

44. SecState to AmEmbassy Santiago, September 27, 1973, Chile, 1 Jan. 73–31 Mar. 1974, (Agusto Pinochet Files Removed from NSC Boxes 777–8), Country Files: Latin America, NSC, NPMP.

45. Barbara Keys, *Reclaiming American Virtue: The Human Rights Revolution of the 1970s* (Cambridge, MA: Harvard University Press, 2014), 149.

46. Schneider attributed his own interest in human rights and Latin America to his time in the Peace Corps. His decision to become a volunteer was shaped by the context of the civil rights movement and his undergraduate years during the 1960s at UC Berekely, where he remembers protesting against the House Un-American Activities Committee. Mark Schneider, Oral History Interview, February 2, 2009, Edward M. Kennedy Oral History Project, Miller Center, University of Virginia; Mark Schneider, Interview with the Author, August 14, 2017.

47. Schneider Interview, February 2, 2009; Edward M. Kennedy, *True Compass: A Memoir* (New York: Twelve, 2011), 127, 177; Edward M. Kennedy, Oral History Interview, March 23, 2005, Edward M. Kennedy Oral History Project. Interest in human rights often spread in Congress, and particularly in the House, through a "socializing effect," whereby it moved from one subcommittee to another. David P. Forsythe, *Human Rights and U.S. Foreign Policy: Congress Reconsidered* (Gainesville: University of Florida Press, 1988), 143. In a different interpretation, Joe Renouard characterizes some of Kennedy's attention to human rights as political opportunism. Joe Renouard, *Human Rights in American Foreign Policy: From the 1960s to the Soviet Collapse* (Philadelphia: University of Pennsylvania Press, 2016), 63.

48. *Refugee and Humanitarian Problems in Chile, Senate Subcommittee to Investigate Problems Connected with Refugees and Escapees Hearing*, 93rd Cong., 1st Sess., September 28, 1973.

49. Ibid.; "Human Rights in Chile," *Washington Post*, October 5, 1973, A28. The Chilean foreign minister met with Kennedy in an attempt to influence his amendment. EmbaChile to Relaciones Internacionales, October 12, 1973, Fondo: Paises EEUU: Vol. 175, Año 1973, MREC. Chilean officials again met with Kennedy in June 1974 and sharply resisted his "suggestions" about internal Chilean judicial practices. Telex 677, June 14, 1974, Fondo: Paises EEUU, Vol. 188, Año 1974, MREC. Kennedy opposed giving Chile $24 million to buy U.S. wheat because of the human rights violations there. The credit, however, was extended by the U.S. government. "Kennedy Against Chile Sale," *New York Times*, October 7, 1973, 37; Terri Shaw, "Chile Gets U.S. Loan for Wheat," *Washington Post*, October 6, 1973, A11.

50. *Refugee and Humanitarian Problems in Chile: Part II, Hearing Before the Subcommittee to Investigate Problems Connected with Refugees and Escapees of the Committee on the Judiciary*, Senate, 93rd Cong., 2nd Sess., July 28, 1974.

51. AmEmbassy Santiago to SecState, September 27, 1973, Chile 1 Jan 73–31 Mar 1974, (Agusto Pinochet Files Removed from NSC Boxes 777–8), Country Files: Latin America, NSC, NPMP. Samuel F. Hart, who was economic counselor in the embassy at the time of the coup, remembers saying to members of the junta, "I want you to know that time is running out, and the goodwill of the United States is running out, because of your behavior—the murders, the detentions, the disappearances, those kind of things." Samuel F. Hart, Oral History Interview, June 12, 1992, ADST.

52. AmEmbassy Santiago to SecState, September 27, 1973, Chile 1 Jan 73–31 Mar 1974, (Agusto Pinochet Files Removed from NSC Boxes 777–8), Country Files: Latin America, NSC, NPMP.

53. "U.S. Envoy Expresses Concern to Chile Junta," *Washington Post*, October 3, 1973, A12; Kornbluh, *The Pinochet File*, 155.

54. AmEmbassy Santiago to SecState, October 12, 1973, Reprinted in Kornbluh, *The Pinochet File*, 184.

55. MemCon, October 11, 1973, FRUS, 1969–1976, Vol. E-11, Part 2, 396–97.

56. AmEmbassy Santiago to SecState, September 21, 1973, Coup Cables, Country Files: Latin America, NSC, NPMP.

57. SecState to AmEmbassy Santiago, September 25, 1973, Chile 1 Jan 73–31 March 1974, (Agusto Pinochet Files Removed from NSC Boxes 777–8), Country Files: Latin America, NSC, NPMP. Concern about summary executions in Chile should also be

seen in the context of the Supreme Court decision in *Furman v. Georgia* (1972), which declared capital punishment unconstitutional.

58. *Refugee and Humanitarian Problems in Chile, Senate Subcommittee to Investigate Problems Connected with Refugees and Escapees Hearing,* 93rd Cong., 1st Sess., September 28, 1973.

59. Horman to Fulbright, October 25, 1973, Chile, 1973, Box 149.G.12.5 (B), Donald M. Fraser Papers, Minnesota Historical Society, St. Paul. Joyce Horman, Charles's widow, also wrote to Fulbright to express her frustration at American inaction on the news that Charles had been detained. Horman to Fulbright, November 12, 1973, ibid. Charles Horman's parents each wrote to Fraser in advance of planned hearings on U.S. policy toward Chile in order to assist the representative in preparing questions to ask State Department officials. Horman to Fraser, June 6, 1974, Human Rights, Box 149.G.13.7 (B), Fraser Papers; Horman to Fraser, June 8, 1974, Human Rights, 149.G.13.7 (B), Fraser Papers.

60. No. 455, November 15, 1973, Fondo: Paises EEUU: Vol. 176, Año 1973, MREC. As of January 22, 1974, the Ministry of Foreign Affairs had not replied, prompting the U.S. embassy to inquire again. No. 030, Fondo: Paises EEUU, Vol. 187, Año 1974, MREC. Although the embassy in Washington asked for further information, the Chilean government did not answer the embassy's questions. Telex 95, January 25, 1974, Fondo: Paises EEUU, Vol. 189, Año 1974, MREC; Translation of Chilean Foreign Ministry Note No. 2364, February 6, 1974, Horman Case FOIA, Jan.–Feb. 1974, Box 1, Heraldo Muñoz Papers, David M. Rubenstein Library, Duke University. See also Telex 158, February 7, 1974, Fondo: Paises EEUU, Vol. 188, Año 1974, MREC.

61. SecState to AmEmbassy Santiago, November 27, 1973, Chile 1 Jan 73–31 Mar 1974, (Agusto Pinochet Files Removed from NSC Boxes 777–8), Country Files: Latin America, NSC, NPMP.

62. No. 14, January 14, 1974, Fondo: Paises EEUU, Vol. 187, Año 1974, MREC.

63. Like Newman, Becket also transferred his energies from Greece to Chile, working for the United Nations high commissioner on refugees regarding refugees from Chile among other issues. James Becket, Interview with the Author, December 5, 2016.

64. "Report to Amnesty International on our Mission to Santiago Chile (November 1973)," Feb. 1974 (3), Folder 76, International Executive Committee, AI IS. See also Frank C. Newman, Oral History Interview by Carol Hicke, 1989 and 1991, Regional Oral History Office, University of California–Berkeley, California State Archives State Government Oral History Program. According to Patrick Kelly, the Amnesty International report "was the first formal international attempt to alert the world to human rights abuses taking place in Chile." Patrick William Kelly, "The 1973 Chilean Coup and the Origins of Transnational Human Rights Activism," *Journal of Global History* 8, no. 1 (March 2013): 176.

65. Press Release, January 20, 1974, Folder 948, AI IS. Newman also testified before Congress in the wake of his mission. The Chilean embassy in Washington closely followed congressional hearings and reported back to Santiago on the testimony of Newman and others. Telex 1093, December 7, 1973, Fondo: Paises EUU: Vol. 175, Año 1973, MREC; No. 01752/613, December 13, 1973, Fondo: Paises EEUU: Vol. 172, Año 1973, MREC. Ennals had written directly to Pinochet the previous month to indicate his concern about torture, executions, and denial to counsel in Chile. *Human Rights in Chile, Hearings Before the House Foreign Affairs Subcommittees on Inter-American*

Affairs and on International Organizations and Movements, 93rd Cong., 2nd Sess., December 7, 1973, May 7, 23, June 11, 12, 18, 1974.

66. See, for example, "To All National Sections and Chile Action Groups," January 21, 1974, Folder 76, International Executive Committee, AI IS; Kelly, "The 1973 Chilean Coup," 172.

67. "Torture in Post-Coup Chile," June 1974, Folder 28, International Executive Committee, AI IS.

68. Walker, "Ambivalent Allies," 64.

69. WILPF Intervention, February 26, 1974, Folder 40, Box 41, CPUSA.

70. Report of the Chicago Commission of Inquiry into the Status of Human Rights in Chile, February 16–23, 1974, Folder 38, Box 35, CPUSA.

71. International Commission of Jurists, Final Report of Mission to Chile, April 1974, Folder 3, Box 46, Series 2.2, Frank Church Papers, Special Collections Department, Albertsons Library, Boise State University. For more on the ICJ, see Howard B. Tolley Jr., *International Commission of Jurists: Global Advocates for Human Rights* (Philadelphia: University of Pennsylvania Press, 1994). For further discussion of torture methods in Chile, see Darius Rejali, *Torture and Democracy* (Princeton, NJ: Princeton University Press, 2007), 206.

72. International Commission of Jurists, Final Report of Mission to Chile, April 1974, Folder 3, Box 46, Series 2.2, Church Papers. When American papers such as the *New York Times* reported on the ICJ's findings, Chilean embassy officials worried that such reports could have a "very negative effect" on public opinion, Congress, and the U.S. government. Telex 589, May 17, 1974, Fondo: Paises EEUU, Vol. 188, Año 1974, MREC.

73. International Commission of Jurists, Final Report of Mission to Chile, April 1974, Folder 3, Box 46, Series 2.2, Church Papers.

74. *Human Rights in Chile, Hearing Before the Subcommittees on International Organizations and Movements and on the Inter-American Affairs of the Committee on Foreign Affairs*, H. R., 93rd Cong., 2nd Sess., November 19, 1974.

75. In order to combat the ICJ's reports and testimony, the Chilean embassy took out an advertisement in the *Washington Post* entitled "The Truth about the 'International Commission of Jurists' and Its Attack on Chile." The Chilean government suggested that its critics did nothing more than parrot the propaganda of Radio Moscow, which routinely broadcast content from two Chilean journalists based in the Soviet Union. Their programming included music and news from Chile and enabled transnational connections among Chileans who had been dispersed by the coup. Ibid.

76. "Report on the Status of Human Rights in Chile," October 25, 1974, OEA/Ser.L/V/II.34, Inter-American Commission on Human Rights, http://www.cidh.org/countryrep/Chile74eng/TOC.htm, accessed March 30, 2017; David Binder, "Chile Accused of Torture by OAS Investigators," *New York Times*, December 10, 1974, 8; Lewis H. Diuguid, "OAS Study Hits Torture in Chile," *Washington Post*, December 9, 1974, A1.

77. Wright to Fraser, November 6, 1973, Chile, 1973, 149.G.12.5 (B), Fraser Papers.

78. Kubisch to Secretary, November 16, 1973, Digital National Security Archive.

79. SecState to AmEmbassy Santiago, March 30, 1974, Chile 1 Jan 73–31 Mar 1974, (Agusto Pinochet Files Removed from NSC Boxes 777–8), Country Files: Latin America, NSC, NPMP. In addition, Popper wrote to express concern that without some

guidance on tactics at the UN, Chile could become a "pariah state." AmEmbassy Santiago to SecState, February 22, 1974, ibid. In a January 1974 discussion of arms sales to Chile, however, Kissinger asserted, "We should not engage in a massive lecturing to them of what is best for their country." Secretary's Staff Meeting, January 31, 1974, Transcripts of Secretary of State Henry Kissinger's Staff Meetings, 1973–1977, Office of the Secretary of State, Lot Files, Record Group 59, NARA.

80. Popper had served as deputy assistant secretary for international organizations from 1965 to 1969. In that capacity, he was involved in planning U.S. involvement in the United Nations International Year for Human Rights, but no evidence suggests that his previous experience shaped his actions in Santiago. AmEmbassy Santiago to SecState, April 3, 1974, Chile 1 April 1974–, (Agusto Pinochet Files Removed from NSC Boxes 777–8), Country Files: Latin America, NSC, NPMP.

81. Ibid.

82. Popper raised similar issues with another member of the junta several days later. AmEmbassy Santiago to SecState, April 4, 1974; AmEmbassy Santiago to SecState, April 8, 1974, Chile 1 April 1974–, (Agusto Pinochet Files Removed from NSC Boxes 777–8), Country Files: Latin America, NSC, NPMP.

83. AmEmbassy Santiago to SecState, April 9, 1974, Chile 1 April 1974–, (Agusto Pinochet Files Removed from NSC Boxes 777–8), Country Files: Latin America, NSC, NPMP.

84. "U.S. Expresses Concern," *Washington Post*, April 16, 1974, A14.

85. *Human Rights in Chile, Hearings Before the House Foreign Affairs Subcommittees on Inter-American Affairs and on International Organizations and Movements*, 93rd Cong., 2nd Sess., December 7, 1973, May 7, 23, June 11, 12, 18, 1974.

86. Ibid.

87. Secretary's Staff Meetings, June 10, 1974, Transcripts of Secretary of State Henry Kissinger's Staff Meetings, 1973–1977, Office of the Secretary of State, Lot Files, Record Group 59, NARA.

88. *Human Rights in Chile, Hearings Before the House Foreign Affairs Subcommittees on Inter-American Affairs and on International Organizations and Movements*, 93rd Cong., 2nd Sess., December 7, 1973, May 7, 23, June 11, 12, 18, 1974. Working for the Justice Department in the American South in 1962 and 1963 shaped Clark's commitment to the rights, political, civil, social, and economic, of African Americans. Katherine A. Scott, *Reining In the State: Civil Society and Congress in the Vietnam and Watergate Eras* (Lawrence: University Press of Kansas, 2013), 35–44, 49.

89. *Human Rights in Chile, Hearings Before the House Foreign Affairs Subcommittees on Inter-American Affairs and on International Organizations and Movements*, 93rd Cong., 2nd Sess., December 7, 1973, May 7, 23, June 11, 12, 18, 1974.

90. Ibid.

91. Fraser's questioning of Shlaudeman revealed a litany of rights still being abused by the Chilean government. Ibid.

92. Fraser to Vidal, January 8, 1975, Chile 1975, 149.G.9.7 (B), Fraser Papers. The Chilean embassy closely followed Fraser's efforts to link Chilean human rights violations and military assistance to that country. Oficio DRI No. 1751/416, June 11, 1974, Fondo: Paises EEUU, Vol. 185, Año 1974, MREC.

93. Holton to Fraser, November 5, 1974, *Human Rights in Chile, Hearing Before the Subcommittees on International Organizations and Movements and on the*

Inter-American Affairs of the Committee on Foreign Affairs, H. R., 93rd Cong., 2nd Sess., November 19, 1974.

94. Pub. L. 93–559, December 30, 1974; Forsythe, *Human Rights*, 102; Stephen B. Cohen, "Conditioning U.S. Security Assistance on Human Rights Practices," *American Journal of International Law* 76, no. 2 (April 1982): 255; Rogers, Vest, and McCloskey to Kissinger, March 4, 1975, FRUS, 1969–1976, Vol. E-11, Part 2, 494–500. In addition, Kennedy expressed frustration that the two countries that were getting the most food aid through Public Law 480 were South Korea and Chile, "two very dictatorial regimes." *Refugee and Humanitarian Problems in Chile: Part III, Hearing Before the Senate Judiciary Subcommittee to Investigate Problems Connected with Refugees and Escapees*, 94th Cong., 1st Sess., October 2, 1975. Within the NSC in June 1975, U.S. officials debated both the legality and the political advisability of resuming military sales to Chile. Low to Kissinger, June 6, 1975, Chile (2), Box 3, Presidential Country Files for Latin America, National Security Adviser, GRFPL. Forsythe, *Human Rights*, 102. In Apodaca's view, Congress implemented country-specific legislation when it felt that its will was being ignored by the White House. Clair Apodaca, *Understanding U.S. Human Rights Policy: A Paradoxical Legacy* (New York: Routledge, 2006), 43–44.

95. Eldridge Interview. See Foreign Assistance Act of 1974, Pub. L. 93–559, December 30, 1974, for final language.

96. Kissinger hoped that if he met with Kennedy, the secretary of state could "swing him around." Transcript of the Secretary of State's Regional Staff Meeting, December 3, 1974, FRUS, 1969–1976, Vol. E-11, Part 2, 473.

97. SecState to USDel, June 22, 1976, June 20–28, 1976—Paris, Munich, London, San Juan, Puerto Rico TOSEC (2), Box 39, NSA Trip Briefing Books and Cables for Henry Kissinger, National Security Adviser, GRFPL.

98. Transcript of the Secretary of State's Staff Meeting, January 31, 1974, FRUS, 1969–1976, Vol. E-11, Part 2, 422.

99. Pub. L. 94–329, June 30, 1976; Kennedy Remarks, *Congressional Record*, February 18, 1976, 3598–9; Richard D. Lyons, "Senate Votes Overhaul of Military Aid," *New York Times*, February 19, 1976, 73. In October 1975 the United States decided not to request foreign military sales credit or military assistance program training for Chile during fiscal year 1976 due to internal opposition to such funding. Press Guidance, October 6, 1975, Digital National Security Archive. For more discussion on congressional limits on arms sales to Chile, see John R. Bawden, "Cutting Off the Dictator: The United States Arms Embargo of the Pinochet Regime, 1974–1988," *Journal of Latin American Studies* 45 (2013): 513–43. Bawden, however, focuses on the impact of congressional amendments on Pinochet's continued presence in power rather than Congress's objective, which was to end U.S. complicity in the junta's repression.

100. In a meeting with Chilean officials in July 1976, Scowcroft argued that through the pipeline of approval, the United States had been able to send more military assistance to Chile than was expected given congressional opposition. MemCon, July 12, 1976, Chile—Political, Military (3), Box 1, NSC Latin American Affairs Staff Files: Country File, National Security Adviser, GRFPL; Richard D. Lyons, "Senate Votes Overhaul of Military Aid," *New York Times*, February 19, 1976, 73; Schoultz, *Human Rights*, 255–56. Furthermore, Congress imposed a limit of $90 million on economic aid to Chile for the 1976 fiscal year.

101. Pub. L. 93–189, December 17, 1973; Pub. L. 93–559, December 30, 1974. Chilean officials in Washington wanted to signal to Kissinger how much they appreciated that he had enabled "the flow of supplies to continue" at a time of emergency for Chile. Earlier reporting from the Chilean embassy had noted the intense lobbying of members of Congress by State Department officials in an effort to preserve assistance to Chile. EmbaChile to MinRel, February 6, 1975, Fondo: Paises EEUU, Vol. 195, Año 1975, MREC; EmbaChile to Direlame, August 1, 1974, Fondo: Paises EEUU, Vol. 190, Año 1974, MREC.

102. Spencer Rich, "Chile Arms Pledge Called 'Shoddy Deal,'" *Washington Post*, June 25, 1976, A17.

103. "Chapter XXIV: Human Rights Questions," *Yearbook of the United Nations* 28 (1974): 617–91; Laurie S. Wiseberg and Harry M. Scoble, "The International League for Human Rights: The Strategy of a Human Rights NGO," *Georgia Journal of International & Comparative Law* 7 (1977): 303; Kathleen Teltsch, "UN Votes to Urge Chile to Release Political Prisoners," *New York Times*, November 7, 1974, 6.

104. "Chapter XXV: Human Rights Questions," *Yearbook of the United Nations* 29 (1975): 587–643. Pinochet had sought to minimize American frustration at the cancellation of the working group's visit, asking the U.S. ambassador to meet with him at home shortly thereafter. There the two debated the wisdom of the cancellation, with Popper arguing that the Chilean decision complicated U.S. support. SecState to USDEL, July 11, 1975, July 9–12, 1975—Europe TOSEC (5), Box 16, NSA Trip Briefing Books and Cables for Henry Kissinger, National Security Adviser, GRFPL; David Binder, "U.S. Aide Rebukes Chile for Barring UN Inquiry," *New York Times*, July 12, 1975, 7.

105. A/10285, October 7, 1975 (New York: United Nations, 1975).

106. UN General Assembly Resolution 3448 (XXX), December 9, 1975.

107. Daniel P. Moynihan, "Amnesty for Political Prisoners," *Wall Street Journal*, November 14, 1975, 14; Press Release, November 12, 1975, Folder 8, Box 248, Patsy T. Mink Papers Manuscript Division, Library of Congress, Washington, DC. For more on Moynihan's aggressive stance at the United Nations, see Daniel Patrick Moynihan, with Suzanne Weaver, *A Dangerous Place* (Boston: Little, Brown, 1978), 205–8; Godfrey Hodgson, *The Gentleman from New York: Daniel Patrick Moynihan* (New York: Houghton Mifflin, 2000), 234–43; Daniel J. Sargent, *A Superpower Transformed: The Remaking of American Foreign Relations in the 1970s* (New York: Oxford University Press, 2015), 198.

108. Paul Hoffman, "U.S., in UN, Asks All Lands to End Political Jailing," *New York Times*, November 13, 1975, 1.

109. See, for example Adolfo Jankelevich, "Telling the United States about Chile," *New York Times*, September 27, 1975, 29; Juan de Onis, "Evidence Growing on Torture in Chile," *New York Times*, October 19, 1975, 3. Foreign governments sought to telegraph their condemnation of the Chilean junta not only through the UN but also through the Organization of American States.

110. Colman McCarthy, "The Chilean Junta's Advertising Campaign," *Washington Post*, December 10, 1974, A20; Schoultz, *Human Rights*, 52. The CIA supported propaganda about the junta for domestic and international consumption. Kornbluh, *The Pinochet File*, 207.

111. Telex 978, August 16, 1974, Fondo: Paises EEUU, Vol. 190, Año 1974, MREC. See also Hawkins, *International Human Rights*, 57; Harmer, "The View from Havana," 138.

112. Low to Scowcroft, February 10, 1976, CO 33 Chile, 10/1/75–1/20/77 Executive, Box 12, Subject Files, WHCF, GRFPL. Anderson was keenly interested in the role of the U.S. government and U.S. corporations in destabilizing Allende. In Anderson's view, U.S. actions in Chile fit into a broader pattern of efforts to "pauperize left-wing governments and replace them with military dictatorships." See, for example, Jack Anderson, "ITT and the Allende Government," *Washington Post*, September 26, 1974, G13; Jack Anderson, "The Economic War Against Allende," *Washington Post*, November 3, 1974, C7.

113. See, for example, Jack Anderson and Les Whitten, "U.S. Aid to Chile Growing Larger," *Washington Post*, October 11, 1975, A24; Jack Anderson, "Respecting the Torturers in Chile," *Washington Post*, January 11, 1976, F7.

114. Cleary, *The Struggle for Human Rights*, 147; Hawkins, *International Human Rights*, 57.

115. Department of State Briefing Paper, Latin American and Human Rights, August 1974, President Ford: Briefings, August–September 1974, Box 11, NSC Latin American Affairs Staff: Files, National Security Adviser, GRFPL.

116. Ibid.

117. Ibid.

118. Thomas D. Boyatt, Oral History Interview, March 8, 1990, ADST.

119. Anthony Lewis, "For Which We Stand: II," *New York Times*, October 2, 1975, 38.

120. Eldridge Interview.

121. Seymour M. Hersh, "Kissinger Said to Rebuke U.S. Ambassador to Chile," *New York Times*, September 27, 1974, 18. Popper later recalled, "We were in basic sympathy with the point of view of the human rights proponents in the United States. This was a pretty rough regime." David Popper, "Reminiscences of David Popper" (1980), p. 122, Columbia Center for Oral History Archives, Rare Book and Manuscript Library, Columbia University.

122. Seymour M. Hersh, "Kissinger is Challenged on Chile Policy," *New York Times*, September 28, 1974, 9. Fraser sought to meet with Kissinger to discuss Hersh's story, but the Secretary of State did not wish to engage with Fraser on the issue. *Human Rights in Chile, Hearing Before the Subcommittees on International Organizations and Movements and on the Inter-American Affairs of the Committee on Foreign Affairs*, H. R., 93rd Cong., 2nd Sess., November 19, 1974.

123. Fraser to Kissinger, October 9, 1974, Chile, 1974, 149.G.13.8 (F), Fraser Papers.

124. Seymour M. Hersh, "Kissinger Said to Rebuke U.S. Ambassador to Chile," *New York Times*, September 27, 1974, 18.

125. Ibid, 18.

126. The Chilean embassy in Washington followed Anderson's columns and cabled to Santiago regarding one that revealed Amy Conger's treatment. Telex 770, Fondo: Paises EEUU, Vol. 188, Año 1974, MREC; Jack Anderson, "Respecting the Torturers in Chile," *Washington Post*, January 11, 1976, F7; Jack Anderson, "U.S. Woman Details Chile Torture," *Washington Post*, November 27, 1974, B13.

127. Jack Anderson, "U.S. Woman Details Chile Torture," *Washington Post*, November 27, 1974, B13. State Department records indicate that Conger's account of the abuse she endured was less severe when she shared it with embassy officials in Santiago. Karkashian to Bowdler, December 5, 1974, State Department FOIA Reading Room.

128. Therefore the United States asked the Ministry of Foreign Relations to investigate Conger's treatment while detained. No. 523, Fondo: Paises EEUU, Vol. 187, Año 1974, MREC.

129. Conger to Findley, November 20, 1974, Legislation—1974 Foreign Relations A–M, Box 133, Legislative File, Paul Findley Papers, Illinois State Historical Society, Springfield.

130. Findley to Bowen, December 9, 1974, Legislation—1974 Foreign Relations A–M, Box 133, Legislative File, Findley Papers.

131. Rogers's answer was unlikely the one Kissinger had expected. Or perhaps it was; Kissinger accused Rogers's bureau of "egging" Kennedy on. Findley to Bowen, December 9, 1974. Interestingly, Rogers had led the Johnson administration's task force on Rhodesia. In addition, he previously worked on the Alliance for Progress from 1962 to 1965. Outside of his State Department work, Rogers had been involved in civil rights and in his current role, he was pushing his bureau to pay attention to human rights concerns, including through the designation of a human rights officer and the compilation of reports on recipient countries' human rights records. William D. Rogers, Oral History Interview, July 8, 1992, ADST.

132. Kornbluh, *The Pinochet File*, 226.

133. Transcript of Secretary of State's Staff Meeting, October 6, 1975, FRUS, 1969–1976, Vol. E-11, Part 2, 556–57. In Kennedy aide Mark Schneider's memory, Rogers was an ally to members of Congress active on human rights, and Schneider assumed Rogers would "push" Kissinger "as much as he could." Schneider Interview, August 14, 2017.

134. Secretary's Regional Staff Meeting, December 5, 1974, National Security Archive, nsarchive.gwu.edu/NSAEBB/NSAEBB212/index.htm, accessed April 29, 2015.

135. The Secretary's Principals' and Regionals' Staff Meeting, December 20, 1974, Digital National Security Archive.

136. The Secretary's Regionals' and Principals' Staff Meeting, December 23, 1974, Digital National Security Archive.

137. See, for example, MemCon, July 28, 1975, FRUS, 1969–1976, Vol. E-11, Part 2, 531.

138. Transcript of Secretary of State's Staff Meeting, October 6, 1975, FRUS, 1969–1976, Vol. E-11, Part 2, 554–55.

139. Telex 813, December 24, 1974, Fondo: Paises EEUU, Vol. 188, Año 1974, MREC.

140. SecState to AmEmbassy Santiago, December 27, 1974, Chile-State Department Telegrams: From SECSTATE-NODIS, Box 3, Presidential Country Files for Latin America, National Security Adviser, GRFPL.

141. Ibid.; Walters to Kissinger, January 7, 1975, FRUS, 1969–1976, Vol. E-11, Part 2, 488.

142. AmEmbassy Lima to SecState, March 13, 1975, Peru—State Department Telegrams to SECSTATE-NODIS, Box 6, Presidential Country Files for Latin America, National Security Adviser, GRFPL.

143. Low to Davis, April 2, 1975, President Ford—Speech Draft—April 1975, Foreign Policy Address to Congress, Box 12, NSC Latin American Affairs Staff Files, National

Security Adviser, GRFPL; AmEmbassy Santiago to SecState, April 7, 1975, Chile—State Department Telegrams: To SECSTATE-EXDIS, Box 3, ibid.

144. In another case, when in August 1975 Pinochet expressed interest in meeting with Ford when he traveled to New York for the UN General Assembly, the White House sought to discourage the idea, suggesting that Popper tell Pinochet that the president was already overcommitted during that time. Low to Scowcroft, August 8, 1975, Chile (2), Box 3, Presidential Country Files for Latin American, National Security Adviser, GRFPL.

145. Bilateral Talks During OASGA, April 1975, Organization of American States— Bilateral Briefing Book (1), Box 1, National Security Adviser: Presidential Country Files for Latin America, GRFPL.

146. Ibid.

147. AmEmbassy Santiago to Department of State, May 18, 1975, State Department FOIA Reading Room; Walker, "Ambivalent Allies," 144.

148. Low to Scowcroft, July 1, 1975, Chile—Political, Military (1), Box 1, NSC Latin American Affairs Staff Files, National Security Adviser, GRFPL.

149. Bloomfield to Rogers and Ryan, July 11, 1975, National Security Archive Electronic Briefing Book 212, http://nsarchive.gwu.edu/NSAEBB/NSAEBB212/, accessed April 14, 2016.

150. Chile, Wilson Accretion, 9/75–12/75, Box 6, James M. Wilson Papers, GRFPL.

151. Low to Kissinger, September 23, 1975, Chile—Political, Military (1), Box 1, NSC Latin American Affairs Staff Files: Country Files, National Security Adviser, GRFPL.

152. Telcon, June 3, 1976, Digital National Security Archive. Rogers was promoted to under secretary of state for economic affairs and was replaced by his deputy, Harry Shlaudeman, in June 1976.

153. "Terror Under the Junta," *Time*, June 16, 1975.

154. Press Release, July 8, 1975, Press Release File 1975 Book 1, 152.L.9.5 (B), Fraser Papers.

155. MemCon, July 18, 1975, FRUS, 1969–1976, Vol. E-11, Part 2, 528.

156. *Human Rights in Chile, Hearing Before the Subcommittee on International Organizations of the Committee on International Relations*, H. R., 94th Cong., 1st Sess., December 9, 1975.

157. Ibid.; Jack Anderson and Les Whitten, "Chile's Junta Invades the Schools," *Washington Post*, April 24, 1975, G13; Jack Anderson and Les Whitten, "Chile Resorts to Book Burning," *Washington Post*, August 30, 1975, E21.

158. *Human Rights in Chile, Hearing Before the Subcommittee on International Organizations of the Committee on International Relations*, H. R., 94th Cong., 1st Sess., December 9, 1975.

159. Seymour M. Hersh, "CIA Chief Tells House of $8-Million Campaign Against Allende in '70-'73," *New York Times*, September 8, 1974, 1. Colby also admitted to the Church Committee in July 1975 that the CIA had sought to precipitate a coup, and his admission quickly leaked. Kornbluh, *The Pinochet File*, 217.

160. "Mrs. Allende Hits U.S. Role in Chile Coup," *Washington Post*, November 8, 1974, A15; Allende to Editor, *New York Times*, September 22, 1974, 38.

161. David Binder, "A Suit to Curb CIA Activities Announced by Rep. Harrington," *New York Times*, December 28, 1974, 8.

162. Lord had expressed concern about "meddling" in Chile via "clandestine action" in 1971. He wrote to Kissinger that he was "depressed, and, at the risk of sounding naïve, shocked" at the idea. Lord to Kissinger, March 23, 1971, Feb '71, Box 339, S/P, Record Group 59, NARA; Keys, *Reclaiming American Virtue*, 173.

163. Kornbluh, *The Pinochet File*, 225.

164. Wilson to Robinson, June 10, 1976, Wilson Accretion, 1/76–8/76, Box 6, James M. Wilson Papers, GRFPL.

165. Report to the Congress on the Human Rights Situation in Countries Receiving U.S. Security Assistance, November 14, 1975, Folder 6, Box 3, James G. Abourezk Papers, University Libraries, Archives and Special Collections, University of South Dakota. See also Keys, *Reclaiming American Virtue*, 174; Apodaca, *Understanding U.S. Human Rights Policy*, 47–48.

166. Keys, *Reclaiming American Virtue*, 175.

167. MemCon, May 9, 1975, FRUS, 1969–1976, Vol. E-11, Part 2, 507.

168. MemCon, September 29, 1975, National Security Archive, nsarchive.gwu.edu/ NSAEBB/NSAEBB212/index.htm, accessed April 29, 2015.

169. Kathryn Sikkink, *Mixed Signals: U.S. Human Rights Policy and Latin America* (Ithaca, NY: Cornell University Press, 2004), 107.

170. DINA was established in June 1974, and CIA cooperation began shortly thereafter. Kornbluh, *The Pinochet File*, 157–60.

171. Muñoz gives the date of Contreras's visit as August 1975, but I could not confirm evidence of an earlier visit. Heraldo Muñoz, *The Dictator's Shadow: Life under Augusto Pinochet* (New York: Basic Books, 2008), 96.

172. Dinges, *The Condor Years*, 102.

173. Jack Anderson and Les Whitten, "2 Chilean Aides Get U.S. Red Carpet," *Washington Post*, October 16, 1975, B22; Kornbluh, *The Pinochet File*, 215. Marxists, via Radio Moscow and other avenues, worked to highlight the regime's abuses. Benedetta Calandra, "Exile and Diaspora in an Atypical Context: Chileans and Argentineans in the United States (1973–2005)," *Bulletin of Latin American Research* 32, no. 3 (2013): 316.

174. NCCSC Program of Work for 1975, January 1975, Folder 4, Box 35, CPUSA.

175. NCCSC Letter, May 3, 1975, Folder 33, Box 118, CPUSA; Proposal, November 1, 1975, Folder 4, Box 35, CPUSA; "For Immediate Action," December 13, 1975, Folder 4, Box 35, CPUSA; "For Immediate Action," October 13, 1975, Folder 4, Box 35, CPUSA.

176. National Legislative Conference on Chile, Folder 5, Box 35, CPUSA.

177. "Stop the Chilean Death Ship," Harrington—CIA/Chile—Correspondence, Box 4, Harrington Papers. In 1974 thousands of people protested the ship's visit. National Chile Center to Key Contacts, June 4, 1976, Folder 5, Box 35, CPUSA. In 1976 protests greeted the *Esmeralda* in Rhode Island, New Jersey, New York, and Maryland. Minutes, Executive Committee Meeting, June 21, 1976, Folder 31, Box 118, CPUSA.

178. *U.S. Relations with Latin America, Senate Subcommittee on Western Hemisphere Affairs*, 94th Cong., 1st Sess., February 27, 1975.

179. Simon had previously traded bonds for Salomon Brothers. In Daniel Sargent's view, Simon was a "defender of capitalism" and a "fierce partisan of the market." Sargent, *A Superpower Transformed*, 179.

180. Press Release, May 7, 1976, Chile, Brazil, and Mexico Visit: 1976, Series 4, William E. Simon Papers, Skillman Library, Lafayette College; Muñoz, *The Dictator's Shadow*, 90.

181. Keys, *Reclaiming American Virtue*, 206.

182. Adopted Prisoners from Chile, Folders 13–14, Drawer 18, Series 3b, Simon Papers. When sending the treasury secretary more names of prisoners of concern, Styron wrote, "Your enthusiasm is contagious." Styron to Simon, April 10, 1976, ibid. She later sent him information about prisoners who had been adopted in the Soviet Union and Yugoslavia. See, for example, Styron to Simon, ibid.

183. Allem to Simon, Folders 13–14, Drawer 18, Series 3b, Simon Papers. Schneider remembers that Kennedy had a personal relationship with Simon, thought he was "decent," and wanted to support Simon's efforts. Schneider Interview, August 14, 2017.

184. Simon's visit was characterized in internal documents as part of a "major initiative in early 1976 to press for greater observance of fundamental human rights." Arrival Statement, May 7, 1976, Folder 52, Drawer 18, Series 3b, Simon Papers; Actions by the Treasury Department, Folder 10, Drawer 23, ibid.

185. AmEmbassy Santiago to SecState, May 8, 1976, Simon, William, Box 90, William L. Seidman Files, GRFPL.

186. Simon to Ford, May 24, 1976, Simon, William, Box 90, William L. Seidman Files, GRFPL.

187. José Zalaquett, "Human Rights in Chile," *New York Times*, May 26, 1976, 27.

188. Trucco to Editor, *New York Times*, May 12, 1976, Fondo: Paises EEUU, Vol. E. EE.UU OF. ORD. R. 320–580, Año 1976, MREC.

189. MemCon, June 1, 1976, FRUS, 1969–1976, Vol. E-3, Doc. 259.

190. SecState to USDEL, June 25, 1976, June 6–13, 1976, Latin American TOSEC (1), Box 36, NSA Trip Briefing Books and Cables for HAK, National Security Adviser, GRFPL.

191. Kornbluh, *The Pinochet File*, 231.

192. Scowcroft to Ford, June 9, 1976, June 6–13, 1976, Latin America: HAK Messages for the President, Box 36, NSA Trip Briefing Books and Cables for Henry Kissinger, National Security Adviser, GRFPL; MemCon, June 8, 1976, Chile (3), Box 3, Presidential Country Files for Latin America, National Security Adviser, GRFPL; Henry Kissinger, *Years of Renewal* (New York: Simon & Schuster, 1999), 758.

193. MemCon, June 8, 1976, Chile (3), Box 3, Presidential Country Files for Latin America, National Security Adviser, GRFPL.

194. Ibid.

195. Harmer, "The View from Havana," 110.

196. Statement by Secretary Kissinger, June 8, 1976, *Department of State Bulletin*, July 5, 1976, 1–5.

197. Kissinger, *Years of Renewal*, 749.

198. Ibid., 755.

199. MemCon, June 14, 1975, FRUS, 1969–1976, Vol. E-11, Part 2, 625.

200. Jones to Kaufman, June 11, 1976, Amnesty International: Correspondence, Box 4, Subseries 1.6, Ivan I. Morris Papers, Rare Book and Manuscript Library, Columbia University. Schoultz argues that Kissinger's OAS speech should be taken to have

conveyed to American diplomats that "the value of human rights in United States policy toward Latin America had increased considerably." Schoultz, *Human Rights*, 111–12.

201. "Human Rights in Latin America," *Wall Street Journal*, June 24, 1976, 16.

202. Only ten days earlier Letelier had spoken at a concert in New York that was headlined by Joan Baez. Karen DeYoung and Milton Coleman, "Victim Denounced Policies of Junta," *Washington Post*, September 22, 1976, A1.

203. Orlando Letelier, "A Testament," *New York Times*, September 27, 1976, 31.

204. Efforts to seek justice by the Letelier and Moffit families, members of Congress, and eventually officials in other branches of the government would go on for years.

205. Brownell and Mozeleski to Janka, September 21, 1976, Chile—Political, Military (3), Box 1, NAC Latin American Affairs Staff Files: Country Files, National Security Adviser, GRFPL.

206. For more on how the murders of Letelier and Moffitt complicated U.S.-Chilean relations during the Carter and Reagan years, see Todd Landam, "Pinochet's Chile: The United States, Human Rights, and International Terrorism," *Human Rights & Human Welfare* 4 (2004): 95; Kornbluh, *The Pinochet File*, 354. John Dinges asserts that "U.S. officials knew enough to have stopped" the Letelier assassination and that they only "launched a flawed and foreshortened effort to do so." Dinges, *The Condor Years*, 248.

207. See, for example, *Congressional Record—Senate*, September 21, 1976, 31463, 31466. As Mark Schneider put it, "The assassination had an impact on everyone who had been following Chile." Schneider Interview, August 14, 2017.

208. Philip A. McCombs, "Murder of Diplomat Deplored; Probe Is Urged by Senator," *Washington Post*, September 22, 1976, A9.

209. The Ford administration had already decided not to seek military assistance for Chile in 1977. The limit of $27.5 million on economic assistance, which was put in place by Congress for the 1977 fiscal year, was due to concerns about Chilean human rights violations.

210. Trucco to Carter, October 27, 1976, Fondo: Paises EEUU, Año 1976, EMBCH EE-UU R (1–65), MREC.

211. See, for example, Jack Anderson and Les Whitten, "Chile Envoy Sent Carter Nasty Letter," *Washington Post*, November 30, 1976, C15; Embajador to MinRel, November 15, 1976, Fondo: Paises EEUU, Año 1976, EMBCH EE-UU R (1–65), MREC.

212. Muñoz, *The Dictator's Shadow*, 108. Shortly after Carter's election, Chile announced that it was releasing nearly three hundred prisoners. John Dinges, "Chile Says It Will Free Prisoners," November 16, *Washington Post*, A1; AmEmbassy Santiago to SecState, November 17, 1976, Folder 10, Drawer 23, Series 3b, Simon Papers; Vanessa Walker, "At the End of Influence: The Letelier Assassination, Human Rights, and Rethinking Intervention in U.S.–Latin American Relations," *Journal of Contemporary History* 46, no. 1 (January 2011): 119. This announcement was the culmination of releases that had been ongoing since September 1974, through which more than seven hundred Chileans had been released. It is not known if this timing was only coincidental, or if there was something more to it. John Dinges, "Chile Says It Will Free Prisoners," *Washington Post*, November 17, 1976, A1; Muñoz, *The Dictator's Shadow*, 109.

213. In the words of Thomas Quigley of the U.S. Catholic Conference, the coup was "the event that catalyzed everything else." Quoted in Kelly, "The 1973 Chilean Coup," 166.

214. Tanya Harmer, *Allende's Chile and the Inter-American Cold War* (Chapel Hill: University of North Carolina Press, 2011), 261. See also Boyatt Interview.

215. Popper, "The Reminiscences of David Popper" (1980), p. 95.

216. Patrick William Kelly, "The Latin American Roots of the Ford Foundation's Human Rights Philanthropy" (paper presented at the Society for Historians of American Foreign Relations Annual Meeting, June 2015).

217. Lubna Z. Qureshi, *Nixon, Kissinger, and Allende: U.S. Involvement in the 1973 Coup in Chile* (Lanham, MD: Lexington Books, 2009), 86.

218. Seymour M. Hersh, *The Price of Power: Kissinger in the Nixon White House* (New York: Summit, 1983), 263.

219. AmEmbassy Santiago to Department of State, May 18, 1975, State Department FOIA Reading Room.

220. Schoultz, *Human Rights*, 370–71; Calandra, "The 'Good Americans,'" 26. See also The Secretary's Regionals' and Principals' Staff Meeting, December 23, 1974, Digital National Security Archive. As one congressional staffer put it, the "credibility gap" of the White House was of "cosmic proportions." Keys, *Reclaiming American Virtue*, 168.

221. Terri Shaw, "American Groups Hit Chile," *Washington Post*, March 11, 1974, A18.

222. Church to Day, October 29, 1973, Folder 2, Box 46, Series 2.2, Church Papers. Even before the coup in Chile, Church opposed U.S. support for "dictators" as it was "an affront to our democratic traditions," and he argued that the United States needed a "general reorientation" of its foreign policy. He argued, "When we supply the tanks later used to batter down the gates of the Presidential Palace during a military coup d-etat in Lima; when we furnish the tear gas and mace, along with the training, for putting down protest in the streets of Rio de Janeiro; then we have, by our own choice, identified the United States with that element in Latin America which epitomizes static, authoritarian rule." Church to Moore, November 19, 1969, Folder 12, Box 44, Series 2.2, Church Papers; Speech at the Center for Inter-American Relations Inc., October 10, 1969, Folder 15, Box 17, Series 8.1, Church Papers. Mark Schneider remembers that the members of Congress most involved on human rights in Greece, Brazil, and Chile were those who had also been active opposing the war in Vietnam. Schneider Interview, August 14, 2017.

223. Carlos Chipoco and Lars Schoultz, Program Evaluation, 1981 Ford Evaluation, Box 28, WOLA Records.

224. Schneider attributes specifically his experience living under military rule as El Salvador sought to transition toward democracy to shaping his later activism. Schneider Interview, February 2, 2009; Schneider Interview, August 14, 2017

225. Fagen to Fulbright, October 8, 1973, Articles and Papers 1970, 1973–1974, Undated, Box 54, WOLA Records. Latin American Studies, as a discipline in the United States, dated from the twentieth century, with considerable growth between the 1930s and 1970s. Parmar, *Foundations of the American Century*, 186.

226. Margaret Power and Julie A. Charlip, "On Solidarity," *Latin American Perspectives* 36, no. 6 (November 2009): 8; Hawkins, *International Human Rights*, 81. Many Chileans were opposed to or hesitant to migrate to the United States, given its opposition to Allende's government and its close relationship with Pinochet's junta, and the United States was slow to welcome Chilean refugees. Calandra, "Exile and Diaspora," 319; Calandra, "The 'Good Americans,'" 27. As of 1970, there were only 15,393

Chilean-born residents of the United States. This number had grown to 35,127 by 1980. Region and Country or Area of Birth of the Foreign-Born Population: 1960 to 1990, U.S. Bureau of the Census.

227. Virginia Bouvier, "The Washington Office on Latin America: Charting a New Path in U.S.–Latin American Relations," Box 28, WOLA Records.

228. Jack Anderson and Les Whitten, "Visit to Torture Central," *Washington Post*, June 5, 1976, C15. Orlando Letelier's presence in Washington was important for WOLA, and it relied on his contacts to facilitate Eldridge's visit to Chile with Harkin and other members of Congress. Eldridge Interview.

229. Press Release, March 17, 1976, Folder 54, Box 21, Legislative Working Files, Thomas R. Harkin Collection, Drake University Archives and Special Collections. The Senate Judiciary Subcommittee to Investigate Problems Connected with Refugees and Escapees also sent a delegation to Chile. Members of the April 1974 study mission reported, "A continuing and systematic disregard for human rights exists in Chile." *Refugee and Humanitarian Problems in Chile: Part II, Hearing Before the Subcommittee to Investigate Problems Connected with Refugees and Escapees of the Committee on the Judiciary*, Senate, 93rd Cong., 2nd Sess., July 28, 1974.

230. Keys, *Reclaiming American Virtue*, 9.

231. There were identifiable political prisoners in Chile, including former members of Allende's cabinet, who were imprisoned on Dawson Island, and most notably Communist Party head Luis Corvalán, who was released through a prisoner exchange with the Soviet Union in 1976. Olga Ulianova, "Corvalán for Bukovsky: A Real Exchange of Prisoners During an Imaginary War: The Chilean Dictatorship, the Soviet Union, and U.S. Mediation, 1973–1976," *Cold War History* 14, no. 3 (2014): 315–36.

232. The impact of these steps on Pinochet, however, is less discernible, as his regime remained in power until 1990.

6. "A CALL FOR U.S. LEADERSHIP": CONGRESSIONAL ACTIVISM ON HUMAN RIGHTS

This chapter builds upon an article previously published as Sarah B. Snyder, "'A Call for U.S. Leadership': Congressional Activism on Human Rights," *Diplomatic History* 37, no. 2 (April 2013): 372–97.

1. The hearings' significance has been acknowledged by several scholars, including Kathryn Sikkink, Clair Apodaca, William Michael Schmidli, and Barbara Keys. Kathryn Sikkink, *Mixed Signals: U.S. Human Rights Policy and Latin America* (Ithaca, NY: Cornell University Press, 2004), 49; Clair Apodaca, *Understanding U.S. Human Rights Policy: A Paradoxical Legacy* (New York: Routledge, 2006), 34; William Michael Schmidli, "Institutionalizing Human Rights in U.S. Foreign Policy: U.S.-Argentine Relations, 1976–1980," *Diplomatic History* 35, no. 2 (April 2011): 365; William Michael Schmidli, *The Fate of Freedom Elsewhere: Human Rights and U.S. Cold War Policy Toward Argentina* (Ithaca, NY: Cornell University Press, 2013), 63–65; Barbara Keys, "Congress, Kissinger, and the Origins of Human Rights Diplomacy," *Diplomatic History* 34, no. 5 (November 2010): 823–51; Barbara Keys, *Reclaiming American Virtue: The Human Rights Revolution of the 1970s* (Cambridge, MA: Harvard University Press, 2014), 76–77. See also David Weissbrodt, "Human Rights Legislation and U.S. Foreign

Policy," *Georgia Journal of International and Comparative Law* 7 (1977): 238; Umberto Tulli, "'Whose Rights Are Human Rights?': The Ambiguous Emergence of Human Rights and the Demise of Kissingerism," *Cold War History* 12, no. 4 (November 2012): 577.

2. Robert David Johnson, *Congress and the Cold War* (New York: Cambridge University Press, 2006), xiv, xix. Richard Falk terms the same group "pragmatic idealists" for believing that "American national interests are best served by conducting foreign policy mainly within a moral framework." Richard Falk, "The Human Rights Country Reports," *World Issues* (October/November 1978): 19. Daniel Sargent suggests that two worldviews, with considerable middle ground, informed those committed to increasing attention to human rights in U.S. foreign policy in the early 1970s. First, those he terms "globalists" believed "human rights were both an expression of new kinds of social interdependence and a necessary legal-ethical foundation for the new global order." Others, whom he refers to as "idealists," are said to be drawn to human rights as "a means to reaffirm America's leadership among nations after Vietnam." Daniel Sargent, "From Internationalism to Globalism: The United States and the Transformation of International Politics in the 1970s" (PhD Diss., Harvard University, 2008), 415–18. See also John F. Manley, "The Rise of Congress in Foreign Policy-Making," *Annals of the American Academy of Political and Social Science* 397 (September 1971): 60–70. Church used the term "confirmed internationalist" to describe members of Congress who supported the UN, Peace Corps, and "sensible foreign-aid programs." Frank Church, "How Many Dominican Republics and Vietnams Can We Take On?," *New York Times Magazine*, November 28, 1965.

3. Congressional activism on human rights was often implemented through what has been termed "subcommittee government." David P. Forsythe, *Human Rights and U.S. Foreign Policy: Congress Reconsidered* (Gainesville: University of Florida Press, 1988), 102.

4. Donald M. Fraser, "Freedom and Foreign Policy," *Foreign Policy* 26 (Spring 1977): 143.

5. House staff member Robert B. Boettcher argues that travel to the Soviet Union in 1972 and the violations that Fraser witnessed there also influenced his decision to hold hearings on human rights. Robert B. Boettcher, "The Role of Congress in Deciding United States Human Rights Policies," in *Dynamics of Human Rights in U.S. Foreign Policy*, ed. Natalie Kaufman Hevener (New Brunswick, NJ: Transaction Books, 1981), 281.

6. 5/30/79—Human Rights Conference for the Fed Bar Association, Box 149.C.13.4 (F), Donald M. Fraser Papers, Minnesota Historical Society, St. Paul.

7. Arthur M. Schlesinger Jr., *The Imperial Presidency* (Boston: Houghton Mifflin, 1973). By the early 1970s, Frank Church identified Congress's approach as being more "self-assertive, more mindful of its constitutional rights and prerogatives, more independent of the Executive Branch." Frank Church, "American Foreign Policy in Transition: Who Will Shape It? The Role of Congress," February 3, 1971, Folder 3, Box 11, Series 7.9, Frank Church Papers, Special Collections Department, Albertsons Library, Boise State University.

8. Jonathan Bingham to *Washington Post*, May 14, 1971, Foreign Affairs (General and Miscellaneous), 1971, Box 8, Action Files, Jonathan Bingham Papers, Bronx Historical Society, New York.

9. Andrew Bennett, "Who Rules the Roost? Congressional-Executive Relations on Foreign Policy after the Cold War," in *Eagle Rules? Foreign Policy and American Primacy in the Twenty-First Century*, ed. Robert J. Lieber (Upper Saddle River, NJ: Prentice Hall, 2002), 9; Thomas Cronin, "A Resurgent Congress and the Imperial Presidency," *Political Science Quarterly* 95, no. 2 (Summer 1980): 219. For further discussion of the Mansfield Amendment, see Daniel J. Sargent, *A Superpower Transformed: The Remaking of American Foreign Relations in the 1970s* (New York: Oxford University Press, 2015), 58. Political scientists Ralph G. Carter and James M. Scott have outlined four different means by which members of Congress can exert influence: direct legislative; indirect legislative, which refers to activities such as holding hearings or drafting reports; direct nonlegislative, such as one-on-one meetings with political leaders; and indirect nonlegislative, such as using the media to draw attention to an issue. Members of Congress concerned with human rights sought to use all four methods. Ralph G. Carter and James M. Scott, *Choosing to Lead: Understanding Congressional Foreign Policy Entrepreneurs* (Durham, NC: Duke University Press, 2009), 146. Fraser's hearings also fit into a pattern of rising use of public congressional hearings, dating from the McCarthy hearings and including Fulbright's hearings on the war in Vietnam and the Church committee hearings. Patrick Chung, "The 'Pictures in Our Heads': Journalists, Human Rights, and U.S.–South Korean Relations, 1970–1976," *Diplomatic History* 38, no. 5 (2014): 14.

10. Fraser's occupation of the subcommittee chair was due in part to the Legislative Reorganization Act of 1970, which limited to one the number of subcommittees a member could chair at a time. New rules enabled greater authority for congressional subcommittees, and Fraser took advantage of these changes. Congressional staffs also expanded, enabling members of Congress to focus on more issues and in greater depth. Donald Fraser, Correspondence with the Author, January 27, 2009; Vanessa Walker, "Ambivalent Allies: Advocates, Diplomats, and the Struggles for an 'American' Human Rights Policy" (PhD Diss., University of Wisconsin–Madison, 2011), 127; Daniel A. O'Donohue, Oral History Interview, May 28, 1996, ADST.

11. Salzberg characterized Fraser as "a very liberal congressperson, and idealistic . . . in many respects" who "had been concerned with the lack of attention to human rights, [the] lack of priority in the Kissinger/Nixon foreign policy." Salzberg had previously served as the International Court of Justice representative to the UN and had completed graduate work in international human rights. John P. Salzberg Interview, "The Life and Legacy of George Lister: Reconsidering Human Rights, Democracy, and U.S. Foreign Policy," Bernard and Audre Rapoport Center for Human Rights and Justice, University of Texas School of Law. According to Lars Schoultz, "Salzberg maintained contact with virtually everyone who had an interest in the human rights component of United States foreign policy." Lars Schoultz, *Human Rights and United States Policy Toward Latin America* (Princeton, NJ: Princeton University Press, 1981), 160. Eldridge has claimed that John Salzberg was the "architect" of Fraser's hearings, but Schoultz has aptly argued that such interpretations minimize the contributions of members of Congress such as Fraser and Kennedy and suggest that members "are so malleable as to be pushed into such controversial, extremely time-consuming positions simply because they are lobbied by their aides." Walker, *Ambivalent Allies*, 132; Schoultz, *Human Rights*, 160.

12. "Human Rights in the World Community: A Call for U.S. Leadership," December 10, 1973, Speeches 1973, 152.L.7.3 (B), Fraser Papers.

13. Fraser Correspondence, January 27, 2009.

14. *International Protection of Human Rights: The Work of International Organizations and the Role of U.S. Foreign Policy*, 93rd Cong., 1st Sess., August–December 1973.

15. Notes, October 15, 1975, Binder, Box 149.C.12.4 (F), Fraser Papers.

16. According to Fraser, "only a few members of the subcommittee took an active interest." Fraser Correspondence, January 27, 2009. Political scientist Edward Cleary described the human rights hearings as the work of "obscure congressmen." Edward L. Cleary, *The Struggle for Human Rights in Latin America* (Westport, CT: Praeger, 1997), 146.

17. Salzberg Interview, "The Life and Legacy of George Lister."

18. H. R. Gross's part in the hearings indicated his lack of support for Fraser's agenda, and he disclaimed the subcommittee's resulting report. Similarly, two others withheld their endorsement of the report. Dan Morgan, "House Unit Stresses Humanity," *Washington Post*, March 27, 1974, A2. According to Fraser, Gross may have seen the hearings as "attacks on countries that he felt were friends of the U.S." Fraser Correspondence, January 27, 2009.

19. "Biographical Note," Dante B. Fascell Congressional Papers, 1955–1993, University of Miami Special Collections, http://proust.library.miami.edu/findingaids/?p=collections/findingaid&id=750, accessed August 25, 2017.

20. Schoultz characterizes Fascell's record on human rights legislation in the 1970s as "fairly erratic," noting that he voted against the Harkin Amendment and a number of other human rights initiatives, although he did support a prohibition on military sales to Chile. Schoultz, *Human Rights*, 146.

21. Findley to Beaty, December 9, 1974, Civil Rights, 1974, Box 132, Legislative File, Paul Findley Papers, Illinois Historical Society, Springfield.

22. Press Release, November 18, 1963, Mr. Findley's Civil Rights Statement, Box 228, Findley Papers. He argued that it was "a matter of simple justice. We don't discriminate against Negroes in collecting taxes, so I don't think we can fairly discriminate against them in making available the facilities which are financed by these taxes." Findley to Friends, November 1, 1963, Civil Rights—1963, Box 96, Legislative File, Findley Papers.

23. See, for example, Findley to Ran, October 18, 1973, Foreign Relations (General), 1973, Box 127, Legislative File, Findley Papers; Findley to Knapp, November 29, 1973, ibid.; Findley to Hering, February 23, 1973, ibid.; Findley to Gardner, May 24, 1971, Vietnam—Calley Letters (1), Box 121, ibid.

24. The subcommittee also intended to examine potential bureaucratic reorganization at the UN, as Fraser believed it was not adequately organized to protect human rights effectively. Fraser to Rogers, July 26, 1973, Foreign Affairs Committee, [1973], 149.G.12.5 (B), Fraser Papers. Fraser aide Robert Boettcher argues that Fraser initially hoped his hearings would inspire more American support for UN human rights efforts. Instead, he shifted his focus to U.S. support for repressive regimes. Robert Boettcher, with Gordon L. Freedman, *Gifts of Deceit: Sun Myong Moon, Tongsun Park, and the Korean Scandal* (New York: Holt, Rinehart & Winston, 1980), 231–32.

25. Press Release, September 11, 1973, Foreign Affairs—1973—Meeting Notices, Box 63, Findley Papers; Salzberg to Fraser, July 5, 1973, Foreign Affairs: International Human Rights Hearings, 149.G.12.5 (B), Fraser Papers.

26. Press Release, September 11, 1973, Foreign Affairs—1973—Meeting Notices, Box 63, Findley Papers.

27. *International Protection of Human Rights: The Work of International Organizations and the Role of U.S. Foreign Policy*, 93rd Cong., 1st Sess., August–December 1973.

28. Ibid.

29. Ibid.

30. Ibid. For further discussion of Shestack's argument that concern for international human rights is in the United States' interest, see Jerome Shestack, "Human Rights, the National Interest, and U.S. Foreign Policy," *Annals of the American Academy of Political and Social Science* 506 (November 1989): 19–21.

31. *International Protection of Human Rights: The Work of International Organizations and the Role of U.S. Foreign Policy*, 93rd Cong., 1st Sess., August–December 1973.

32. Committee on Foreign Affairs, House of Representatives, *Human Rights in the World Community: A Call for U.S. Leadership, Report of the Subcommittee on International Organizations and Movements of the Committee on Foreign Affairs* (Washington, DC: Government Printing Office, 1974).

33. Ibid.

34. Fraser Correspondence, January 27, 2009.

35. Salzberg Interview, "The Life and Legacy of George Lister."

36. Fraser Correspondence, January 27, 2009.

37. Notes, October 15, 1975, Binder, Box 149.C.12.4 (F), Fraser Papers.

38. Richard Schifter Interview, "The Life and Legacy of George Lister."

39. David Binder, "U.S. Urged to Act on Human Rights," *New York Times*, March 28, 1974, 17. Based on State Department records, Runyon appears to have been an early proponent of a robust "human rights policy," as an August 1974 memo termed it. "Human Rights Policy," August 12, 1974, Human Rights: S/P Study—Policy Planning Vol. 2, Box 2, entry UD 13D 15, Record Group 59, NARA. Barbara Keys's story of these changes is one of limited, begrudging steps taken by Henry Kissinger's State Department under Gerald Ford to stave off potentially more-far-reaching concessions to an activist Congress. Keys, "Congress, Kissinger," 831.

40. Henry Kissinger, "Moral Purposes and Policy Choices," *Department of State Bulletin*, October 29, 1973, 528–29; "Kissinger Cites Risk in Pushing Soviet Too Hard on Emigration," *New York Times*, October 9, 1973, 5.

41. Richard Nixon, Commencement Address at the United States Naval Academy, June 5, 1974, American Presidency Project, www.presidency.ucsb.edu/ws/?pid=4236, accessed April 3, 2010.

42. When an aide indicated that the attendees had not been finalized, Kissinger fumed, "Are you telling me you have set up a meeting with an unknown group that is dedicated to a set of propositions which you know they are going to get me into trouble?" Transcript, Secretary's Staff Meeting, October 22, 1974, FRUS, 1969–1976, Vol. E-3, Doc. 244.

43. Noting that Fraser had opposed his nomination for Secretary of State, Kissinger asked, "What is the chance of getting Don Fraser on my side?" Ibid.

44. Ibid. Throughout Kissinger's meetings with his staff, he and his aides deploy sports metaphors to discuss their competition with members of Congress over human rights issues, using football, baseball, and wrestling imagery to convey that they are competing against Fraser, Kennedy, and others. Secretary's Regional Staff Meeting, December 5, 1974, National Security Archive, nsarchive.gwu.edu/NSAEBB/ NSAEBB212/index.htm, accessed April 29, 2015.

45. Furthermore, Ingersoll's regular communication with Fraser seemed to have positively influenced the representative's appraisal of State Department efforts. Ranard to Sneider, July 17, 1974, FRUS, 1969–1976, Vol. E-3, Doc. 239.

46. SecState to USLO Peking, November 27, 1974, People's Republic of China–State Department Telegrams: from SECSTATE-NODIS (3), Box 14, NSA Presidential Country Files for East Asia and the Pacific, National Security Adviser, GRFPL. For a revealing portrait of Kissinger's personality, see Barbara Keys, "Henry Kissinger: The Emotional Statesman," Diplomatic History 35, no. 4 (September 2011): 587–609.

47. Memorandum of Conversation, December 17, 1974, FRUS, 1969–1976, Vol. E-3, Doc. 245.

48. Ibid.

49. Ibid.

50. Fraser to Mondale et al., January 29, 1975, Human Rights, 1974–1978 (3), Box 151.H.4.2 (F), Fraser Papers; Congressional Meeting with Secretary Kissinger, July 22, 1975, Cranston Human Rights Amendment, Container 264, Alan Cranston Papers, the Bancroft Library, University of California–Berkeley.

51. Buffum proposed tasking one person within each regional bureau to follow human rights issues as a temporary measure to improve the department's image on the problem while the broader studies were undertaken. Transcript, the Acting Secretary's Principals' and Functionals' Staff Meeting, June 12, 1974, FRUS, 1969–1976, Vol. E-3, Doc. 236.

52. Ibid.

53. Ibid.

54. Brown to Kissinger, August 8, 1974, FRUS, 1969–1976, Vol. E-3, Doc. 241.

55. Levenson to Brown, May 14, 1974, Human Rights D/HA, Box 7, Records of the Deputy Secretary of State Charles W. Robinson, 1976–1977, Record Group 59, NARA.

56. The secretary's office occupied the seventh floor of the main State Department building in Foggy Bottom. Ibid.

57. Fraser to Kissinger, June 27, 1974, Folder 21, Box 7, George Lister Papers, Benson Latin American Collection, University of Texas Libraries, the University of Texas at Austin.

58. Fraser to Ingersoll, July 10, 1974, Human Rights, Box 149.G.13.7 (B), Fraser Papers.

59. Ingersoll became deputy secretary of state in 1974. Ingersoll to Fraser, April 18, 1975, State Department, 1975, Box 149.G.9.7 (B), Fraser Papers. For further discussion of Wilson's tenure, see Keys, "Congress, Kissinger"; Edwin S. Maynard, "The Bureaucracy and Implementation of U.S. Human Rights Policy," Human Rights Quarterly 11, no. 2 (May 1989): 178–79.

60. Ingersoll to Eastland, April 18, 1975, FRUS, 1969–1976, Vol. E-3, Doc. 250. When describing Wilson's experience to Jacob Javits, Robert Ingersoll emphasized bureaucratic talents, not specialized knowledge. Ingersoll to Javits, May 10, 1975, Human

Rights and Humanitarian Affairs—Office Organization and Personnel Matters, Box 1, James M. Wilson Papers, GRFPL.

61. Ronald D. Palmer, Oral History Interview, May 15, 1992, ADST.

62. Ibid.

63. "U.S. Policies on Human Rights and Authoritarian Regimes," 1974, General Records of the Department of State, S/P, Director's Files, Box 348, Record Group 59, NARA. I appreciate Daniel Sargent's willingness to share this document with me. For a summary of the policy planning staff's study and detail on authorship, see Summary: U.S. Policies on Human Rights and Authoritarian Regimes, FRUS, 1969–1976, Vol. E-3, Doc. 243; Briefing Paper on Human Rights, FRUS, 1969–1976, Vol. E-3, Doc. 264.

64. The legal adviser determined that "the principle of non-interference is not in itself a legal bar to official U.S. cognizance of human rights problems in a foreign country," arguing, "there is now ample legal justification for diplomatic representations to a state concerning its treatment of its own nationals where such treatment violates minimum standards of international law." Yet the report's author noted that such a legal determination did not mean that countries would not nonetheless regard such expressions of concern as interference. Summary: U.S. Policies on Human Rights and Authoritarian Regimes, FRUS, 1969–1976, Vol. E-3, Doc. 243.

65. "U.S. Policies on Human Rights and Authoritarian Regimes," 1974, General Records of the Department of State, S/P, Director's Files, Box 348, Record Group 59, NARA.

66. Fraser to All Signatories, September 18, 1974, "Dear Colleague—Kissinger," 1974, Box 151.H.3.3 (B), Fraser Papers; Press Release, September 22, 1974, Box 151.H.3.3 (B), Fraser Papers.

67. Holton to Fraser, October 23, 1974, Captive Nations, 1973–1974, Fraser Papers.

68. Abourezk to Cranston, August 29, 1973, Amendments to Foreign Aid Bill for FY 1974, Container 264, Cranston Papers.

69. James G. Abourezk, *Advise and Dissent: Memoirs of South Dakota and the U.S. Senate* (Chicago: Lawrence Hill Books, 1989), 131; James Abourezk, Interview with the Author, October 6, 2016; A. J. Langguth, "U.S. Has a 45-Year History of Torture," *Los Angeles Times*, May 3, 2009. Barbara Keys also highlights Abourezk's concern for political prisoners in South Vietnam. Keys, *Reclaiming American Virtue*, 135.

70. Foreign Assistance Act 1973, 93rd Cong., 1st Sess. In April 1974 the State Department asked for widespread reporting on the treatment of political prisoners from its embassies.

71. Ingersoll to Morgan, June 27, 1974, Folder 5, Box 312, James G. Abourezk Papers, University Libraries, Archives and Special Collections, University of South Dakota. For further discussion of Abourezk and his amendments, see Keys, *Reclaiming American Virtue*, 133–40.

72. Ingersoll to Morgan, July 28, 1974, FRUS, 1969–1976, Vol. E-3, 240; Fiscal Year 1975 Foreign Assistance Request, 93rd Cong., 2nd Sess., June 4, 5, 11, 12, 13, 18, 19, 20, 26, July 1, 2, 10, 11, 1974. See also Apodaca, *Understanding U.S. Human Rights Policy*, 35.

73. Foreign Assistance Act of 1974, 93rd Cong., 2nd Sess. Clair Apodaca sees the language of "gross violations" as presenting a problem in definition, in that it was connected with the degree of violation as well as the number of people affected and for a significant duration of time. Apodaca, *Understanding U.S. Human Rights Policy*, 38.

74. Keys writes that Kissinger "was willing to engage in quite blatant evasion" of 502B. Keys, "Congress, Kissinger," 840.

75. Clair Apodaca, "U.S. Human Rights Policy and Foreign Assistance: A Short History," *Ritsumekian International Affairs* 3 (2005): 66; Stephen B. Cohen, "Conditioning U.S. Security Assistance on Human Rights Practices," *American Journal of International Law* 76, no. 2 (April 1982): 268.

76. McCloskey to Koch, PGOV: Congressional, Box 1, Bureau of Human Rights and Humanitarian Affairs: Subject Files, 1976–77, Record Group 59, NARA.

77. Cohen, "Conditioning U.S. Security Assistance," 252.

78. Ibid., 277. David Forsythe argues that general human rights legislation is not useful because "the votes are not there to force the executive to follow the letter—or indeed some times even the spirit—of the laws adopted." David P. Forsythe, "Congress and Human Rights in U.S. Foreign Policy: The Fate of General Legislation," *Human Rights Quarterly* 9, no. 3 (August 1987): 382.

79. Donald M. Fraser, "Human Rights and U.S. Foreign Policy: Some Basic Questions Regarding Principles and Practice," *International Studies Quarterly* 23, no. 2 (June 1979): 179.

80. Keys, "Congress, Kissinger," 824, 850.

81. Benedetta Calandra, "The 'Good Americans,': U.S. Solidarity Networks for Chilean and Argentinean Refugees, 1973–1983," *Historia Actual Online* (2010): 26.

82. Harris/CCFR Survey of American Public Opinion and U.S. Foreign Policy December 1974. In the survey 36 percent "agreed strongly," and 32 percent "agreed somewhat." Mario Del Pero argues that Americans were only temporarily willing to have a realist foreign policy and that by Nixon's second term, there was greater concern with morality. Mario Del Pero, *The Eccentric Realist: Henry Kissinger and the Shaping of American Foreign Policy* (Ithaca, NY: Cornell University Press, 2010), 6, 8, 129–30.

83. SecState to AmEmbassy Nicosia, February 20, 1975, FRUS, 1969–1976, Vol. E-3, Doc. 247.

84. SecState to All Diplomatic and Consular Posts, August 2, 1975, FRUS, 1969–1976, Vol. E-3, Doc. 253.

85. James M. Wilson Jr., Oral History Interview, March 31, 1999, ADST. Foreign service officer Donald C. Johnson worried that new legislation could lead to U.S. intervention in the internal affairs of other countries and turn U.S. embassies into "detective bureaus." Donald C. Johnson, "Congress, the Executive, and Human Rights Legislation," *Foreign Service Journal* (December 1976): 19.

86. Keys, *Reclaiming American Virtue*, 173.

87. Wilson remembers Kissinger insisted that Ronald Palmer write a general report, which sent members of Congress "through the roof." Wilson Interview; Bernard Gwertzman, "U.S. Blocks Rights Data on Nations Getting Arms," *New York Times*, November 19, 1975, 89.

88. Report to the Congress on the Human Rights Situation in Countries Receiving U.S. Security Assistance, November 14, 1975, Folder 6, Box 3, Abourezk Papers.

89. Ibid.

90. Statements on Previous Debate Concerning Human Rights, Folder 4, Box 3, Abourezk Papers.

91. Bernard Gwertzman, "U.S. Blocks Data On Nations Getting Arms," *New York Times*, November 19, 1975, 89.

92. Press Release, December 9, 1975, Folder 1, Box 3, Abourezk Papers.

93. Alan Cranston Testimony, Folder 5, Box 3, Abourezk Papers.

94. Ford to Senate, 1976/05/07 S2662 International Security Assistance and Arms Export Control Act (Vetoed) (3), Box 44, White House Records Office: Legislative Case Files, GRFPL; Cannon to Ford, June 30, 1976, 6/30/76 HR12203, Foreign Assistance and Related Programs Appropriation Act of 1976 (1), Box 48, ibid.; Cohen, "Conditioning U.S. Security Assistance," 252–53.

95. Pub. L. 94–329, June 30, 1976.

96. Lord to Deputy Secretary, November 10, 1976, Human Rights D/HA, Box 7, Records of the Deputy Secretary of State Charles W. Robinson, 1976–1977, Record Group 59, NARA; *Conference Report on International Security Assistance and Arms Export Control Act of 1976*, 94th Cong., 2nd Sess., April 6, 1976.

97. Wilson to McManaway, November 10, 1976, AMGT: Establishment Office, Box 1, Bureau of Human Rights and Humanitarian Affairs: Subject Files, 1976–1977, Record Group 59, NARA.

98. The Harkin Amendment was drafted by Joe Eldridge of WOLA and Edward Snyder of the Friends Committee on National Legislation. It surprisingly passed in the House when it was supported by Representative Wayne Hays and other conservatives who were opposed to foreign assistance. In 1975 the Harkin Amendment was extended to cover Food for Peace funds. The Ford administration, seeing the "needy people" clause as a loophole, basically ignored the Harkin Amendment. Schoultz, *Human Rights*, 196–97, 208.

99. Apodaca, *Understanding U.S. Human Rights Policy*, 41–42.

100. DeSibour to Davis, FR 14–1 Executive 9/10/76–10/14/76, WHCF, GRFPL.

101. Although the report on Chile acknowledged problems with the Chilean legal system, its language was often formulated passively: "Reports exist of torture or cruel, inhuman or degrading treatment and punishment of political detainees." The report on South Korea described a range of political and civil rights that were "limited by law or Presidential decree." Borg to Scowcroft, November 9, 1976, FO 3–2 Executive 11/20/76 (1), WHCF, GRFPL.

102. Fraser to Jenkins, October 12, 1976, HU Executive 1/1/76–1/20/77, Box 1, WHCF, GRFPL.

103. Kenneth Hill, Oral History Interview, March 28, 2014, ADST.

104. Fraser Correspondence, January 27, 2009. See also Falk, "The Human Rights Country Reports," 21.

105. See, for example, Wilson to Deputy Secretary, November 8, 1976, FRUS, 1969–1976, Vol. E-3, 262. He had already been working to ensure that human rights officers were consulted on congressional correspondence and commercial export licenses, slowly integrating the issue into U.S. foreign policy formulation. Wilson to Assistant Secretaries of Geographic Bureaus, December 1, 1976, PGOV: Congressional, Box 1, Bureau of Human Rights and Humanitarian Affairs: Subject Files, 1976–1977, Record Group 59, NARA; Wilson to Atherton, November 10, 1976, PGOV: Congressional, Box 1, Bureau of Human Rights and Humanitarian Affairs: Subject Files, 1976–1977, Record Group 59, NARA.

106. Salzberg to Lake, December 3, 1976, International Relations Committee: Subcommittee on International Organizations—1977 (V), Box 151.H.3.6 (F), Fraser Papers.

107. Aldrich was concerned with convincing observers abroad and in Congress that the new administration cared about human rights. George H. Aldrich, "A Sensible Human Rights Policy," Human Rights 1975–1977, Box 1, Wilson Papers, GRFPL.

108. Wilson to the Deputy Secretary Designate, January 21, 197, Human Rights General 1975–1977, Box 1, Wilson Papers, GRFPL.

109. Keys argues that the Bureau of Human Rights and Humanitarian affairs had "virtually no influence on policy" in the Kissinger years. Instead, during Kissinger's tenure the bureau "performed an important educative function, inculcating a new mindset, establishing new diplomatic precedents and procedures, and setting in motion the process through which human rights developed in a normal part of foreign-policy considerations." Keys, "Congress, Kissinger," 833–34. Keys uses the terminology "bureau" to describe Wilson's office, although it was not formally designated as such until October 27, 1977. In Apodaca's view, early human rights officers in the State Department did not have sufficient authority. Apodaca, *Understanding U.S. Human Rights Policy*, 49.

110. Sandra L. Vogelgesang, "Human Rights and U.S. Foreign Policy: Executive-Congressional Interaction," June 1977, Folder 3, Box 220, Council on Foreign Relations Studies Department Files, Public Policy Papers, Department of Rare Books and Special Collections, Princeton University Library.

111. Fraser Correspondence, January 27, 2009.

112. Schifter Interview, "The Life and Legacy of George Lister."

113. Ibid.

114. David D. Newsom, Oral History Interview, June 17, 1991, ADST.

115. Donald Fraser, *Congressional Record*, September 30, 1976, 151, Part 2.

116. Steven Pinker, *The Better Angels of Our Natures: Why Violence Has Declined* (New York: Penguin, 2011), 168.

CONCLUSION

1. The figures central to *From Selma to Moscow* are almost entirely male, perhaps because of the limited opportunities in these years for women in law and the foreign service, two of the key professions from which human rights activists emerged. Women made up less than 10 percent of law students until the 1972–1973 school year, only rising above 20 percent in the 1974–1975 school year. First Year and Total JD Enrollment by Gender, 1947–2011, https://www.americanbar.org/content/dam/aba/administrative/legal_education_and_admissions_to_the_bar/statistics/jd_enroll ment_1yr_total_gender.authcheckdam.pdf, accessed March 30, 2017. Furthermore, in the 1960s women in the legal profession experienced considerable discrimination. Cynthia Grant Bowman, "Women in the Legal Profession from the 1920s to the 1970s: What Can We Learn from Their Experience about Law and Social Change?," *Maine Law Review* 61, no. 1 (2009): 10. Similarly, the number of women entering the foreign service each year did not rise above 20 percent until 1974, and only 8.9 percent of the foreign service officers appointed in the years 1961–1970 were women. Between 1966 and 1974, the percentage of women appointed was more than 10 percent in only three years: 1968, 1972, and 1973. Women never made up more than 10 percent of the overall foreign

service between 1960 and 1970. Holmer Calkin, *Women in the Department of State: Their Role in American Foreign Affairs* (Washington, DC: Department of State, 1978). Among missionaries, who often traveled abroad as couples, activism was more balanced in terms of gender. As the 1970s progressed, women became increasingly active. Jean H. Quataert, "Women, Development, and Injustice: The Circuitous Origins of the New Gender Perspectives in Human Rights Visions and Practices in the 1970s" (paper presented at "A New Global Morality? The Politics of Human Rights and Humanitarianism in the 1970s," Freiburg Institute for Advanced Studies, Freiburg, Germany, June 2010); Karen Brown Thompson, "Women's Rights Are Human Rights," in *Restructuring World Politics: Transnational Social Movements, Networks, and Norms*, ed. Sanjeev Khagram, James V. Riker, and Kathryn Sikkink (Minneapolis: University of Minnesota Press, 2002), 105. An important moment was the 1975 United Nations International Women's Year, which advanced the cause of women's rights by enabling women to confront "discrimination and injustices in multiple settings in societies around the world." Quataert, "Women, Development, and Injustice." See also Georgina Ashworth, "The United Nations 'Women's Conference' and International Linkages in the Women's Movement," in *Pressure Groups in the Global System*, ed. Peter Willetts (New York: St. Martin's Press, 1982), 125–47; Jocelyn Olcott, "Globalizing Sisterhood: International Women's Year and the Politics of Representation," in *The Shock of the Global: The 1970s in Perspective*, ed. Niall Ferguson et al. (Cambridge, MA: Harvard University Press, 2010), 281–93.

2. "Toward an Expanded Program," 1968, Folder 3, Box 1163, Organizational Matters, ACLU Records.

3. Policy Goals and Structure of the International League for the Rights of Man, July 20, 1967, International Year for Human Rights (1968)—Correspondence, 1964–67, Box 43, ILRHC.

4. Moody to RBF, Files, January 8, 1975, Folder 2812, Box 461, Record Group 3, Rockefeller Brothers Fund, Rockefeller Archives Center, Sleepy Hollow, NY.

5. Barbara Keys, *Reclaiming American Virtue: The Human Rights Revolution of the 1970s* (Cambridge, MA: Harvard University Press, 2014), 184. See also Steven Hopgood, *The Endtimes of Human Rights* (Ithaca, NY: Cornell University Press, 2013), xi.

6. See, for example, Ludmilla Alexeyeva, *Soviet Dissent: Contemporary Movements for National, Religious, and Human Rights* (Middletown, CT: Wesleyan University Press, 1985), 291–92; Ludmilla Alexeyeva and Paul Goldberg, *The Thaw Generation: Coming of Age in the Post-Stalin Era* (Pittsburgh: University of Pittsburgh Press, 1990), 254, 284; Roland Burke, "'How Time Flies': Celebrating the Universal Declaration of Human Rights in the 1960s," *International History Review* 38, no. 3 (2016): 413. To give just one measure of those attitudes, an October 1968 poll conducted among Minnesotans showed that only 15.3 percent of respondents were "well satisfied" with the job the UN was doing. Minnesota Poll No. 281, October 3–6, 1968, the Roper Center for Public Opinion Research.

7. Joseph Eldridge, Interview with the Author, April 13, 2016.

8. Ronald D. Palmer, Oral History Interview, May 15, 1992, ADST; James M. Wilson, "Diplomatic Theology—An Early Chronicle of Human Rights at State," Human Rights and Humanitarian Affairs—Wilson Memoir, Box 1, James M. Wilson Papers, GRFL.

9. Chicago Council on Foreign Relations Survey, 1974.

10. Of those, 48.9 percent "strongly" agreed. Chicago Council on Foreign Relations Survey, 1974.

11. Miles S. Pendleton Jr., Oral History Interview, June 22, 1998, ADST.

12. Thomas Borstelmann, *The 1970s: A New Global History from Civil Rights to Economic Inequality* (Princeton, NJ: Princeton University Press, 2012), 184; Barbara Keys, "Congress, Kissinger, and the Origins of Human Rights Diplomacy," *Diplomatic History* 34, no. 5 (November 2010): 823–51; William Michael Schmidli, "Institutionalizing Human Rights in U.S. Foreign Policy: U.S.-Argentine Relations, 1976–1980," *Diplomatic History* 35, no. 2 (April 2011): 351–78; Richard Falk, "The Human Rights Country Reports," *World Issues* (October/November 1978): 19. See also Thomas E. Quigley, "The Role of the Churches in Human Rights Promotion," Churches Early Years, Box 28, WOLA Records.

13. Roberta Cohen, Oral History Interview, September 26, 2008, ADST.

14. Aryeh Neier, *The International Human Rights Movement: A History* (Princeton, NJ: Princeton University Press, 2012), 1–4.

BIBLIOGRAPHY

GOVERNMENT DOCUMENTS

Unpublished

Archivo General Histórico, Ministerio de Relaciones Exteriores de Chile, Santiago, Chile

General Records of the Department of State, Record Group 59, National Archives and Records Administration, College Park, MD

Gerald R. Ford Presidential Library, Ann Arbor, MI

John F. Kennedy Presidential Library, Boston

Lyndon Baines Johnson Presidential Library, Austin, TX

National Archives, Kew, United Kingdom

Records of the United States Information Agency, Record Group 306, National Archives and Records Administration, College Park, MD

Richard Nixon Presidential Library, Yorba Linda, CA

Richard Nixon Presidential Materials Project, College Park, MD

United Nations Archives, Geneva

Published

"Africa: Southern Rhodesia." *GIST* no. 8 (September 1972).

"Chapter XX: Human Rights Questions." *Yearbook of the United Nations* 25 (1971): 394–446.

"Chapter XX: Human Rights Questions." *Yearbook of the United Nations* 23 (1969): 483–556.

"Chapter XXIV: Human Rights Questions." *Yearbook of the United Nations* 28 (1974): 617–91.

"Chapter XXV: Human Rights Questions." *Yearbook of the United Nations* 29 (1975): 587–643.

Department of State. *Foreign Relations of the United States, 1961–1963: Volume XIV, Berlin Crisis, 1961–1962.* Washington, DC: Government Printing Office, 1993.

Department of State. *Foreign Relations of the United States, 1961–1963: Volume XXII, Northeast Asia.* Washington, DC: Government Printing Office, 1996.

Department of State. *Foreign Relations of the United States, 1961–1963: Volume XXV, Organization of Foreign Policy; Information Policy; United Nations; Scientific Matters.* Washington, DC: Government Printing Office, 2001.

Department of State. *Foreign Relations of the United States, 1964–1968: Volume XIV, Soviet Union.* Washington, DC: Government Printing Office, 2001.

Department of State. *Foreign Relations of the United States, 1964–1968: Volume XVI, Cyprus; Greece; Turkey.* Washington, DC: Government Printing Office, 2000.

Department of State. *Foreign Relations of the United States, 1964–1968: Volume XXIV, Africa.* Washington, DC: Government Printing Office, 1995.

Department of State. *Foreign Relations of the United States, 1964–1968: Volume XXXIV, Energy Diplomacy and Global Issues.* Washington, DC: Government Printing Office, 1999.

Department of State. *Foreign Relations of the United States, 1969–1976: Volume E-3, Documents on Global Issues, 1973–1976.* Washington, DC: Government Printing Office, 2009.

Department of State. *Foreign Relations of the United States, 1969–1976: Volume E-5, Part 1, Documents on Sub-Saharan Africa, 1969–1972.* Washington, DC: Government Printing Office, 2005.

Department of State. *Foreign Relations of the United States, 1969–1976: Volume E-11, Part 2, Documents on South America, 1973–1976.* Washington, DC: Government Printing Office, 2015.

Department of State. *Foreign Relations of the United States, 1969–1976: Volume E-12, Documents on East and Southeast Asia, 1973–1976.* Washington, DC: Government Printing Office, 2011.

Department of State. *Foreign Relations of the United States, 1969–1976: Volume XV, Soviet Union, June 1972–August 1974.* Washington, DC: Government Printing Office, 2011.

Department of State. *Foreign Relations of the United States, 1969–1976: Volume XIX, Part 1, Korea, 1969–1972.* Washington, DC, Government Printing Office, 2015.

Department of State. *Foreign Relations of the United States, 1969–1976: Volume XXVIII, Southern Africa.* Washington, DC: Government Printing Office, 2011.

Department of State. *Foreign Relations of the United States, 1969–1976: Volume XXX, Greece; Cyprus; Turkey, 1973–1976.* Washington, DC: Government Printing Office, 2007.

Keefer, Edward C., David C. Geyer, and Douglas E. Selvage, eds. *Soviet-American Relations: The Détente Years, 1969–1972.* Washington, DC: Government Printing Office, 2007.

Public Papers of the Presidents of the United States: Lyndon B. Johnson, 1965: Volume II. Washington, DC: Government Printing Office, 1966.

MANUSCRIPT COLLECTIONS

Abourezk, James G., Papers. University Libraries, Archives and Special Collections, University of South Dakota.

Abram, Morris B., Papers. Manuscript, Archives, and Rare Book Library, Emory University.

Ad Hoc Committee on the Human Rights and Genocide Treaties Records. Tamiment Library, New York University.

American Civil Liberties Union Records. Public Policy Papers, Department of Rare Books and Special Collections, Princeton University Library.

American Committee on Africa Records. Amistad Research Center, New Orleans.

American Committee on Africa Records Addendum. Amistad Research Center, New Orleans.

Amnesty International International Secretariat Archives. International Institute for Social History, Amsterdam.

Amnesty International USA Archives. Center for Human Rights Documentation and Research, Rare Book and Manuscript Library, Columbia University Library.

Baldwin, Roger N., Papers. Public Policy Papers, Seeley G. Mudd Manuscript Library, Princeton University.

Ball, George, Papers. Public Policy Papers, Seeley G. Mudd Manuscript Library, Princeton University.

Berger, Samuel D., Papers. Jacob Rader Marcus Center of the American Jewish Archives, Cincinnati.

Bingham, Jonathan, Papers. Bronx Historical Society, New York.

Bitker, Bruno, Papers. University of Wisconsin–Milwaukee.

Butler, William J., Collection. College of Law Archives, University of Cincinnati.

Church, Frank, Papers. Special Collections Department, Albertsons Library, Boise State University.

Cleveland, Harlan, Papers. Public Policy Papers, Seeley G. Mudd Manuscript Library, Princeton University.

Communist Party of the United States of America Papers. Tamiment Library/Robert F. Wagner Labor Archives, New York University.

Council on Foreign Relations Studies Department Files. Public Policy Papers, Seeley G. Mudd Manuscript Library, Princeton University Library.

Cranston, Alan, Papers. The Bancroft Library, University of California–Berkeley.

Dodd, Thomas J., Papers. Thomas J. Dodd Research Center, Storrs, CT.

Edwards, Donald, Papers. San Jose State University.

Fascell, Dante, Papers. University of Miami.

Field, George, Collection. Public Policy Papers, Seeley G. Mudd Manuscript Library, Princeton University.

Findley, Paul, Papers. Illinois State Historical Society, Springfield.

Ford Foundation Records. Rockefeller Archive Center, Sleepy Hollow, NY.

Fraser, Donald M., Papers. Minnesota Historical Society, St. Paul.

Freedom House Records. Public Policy Papers, Seeley G. Mudd Manuscript Library, Princeton University.

Frelinghuysen, Peter H. B., Papers. Public Policy Papers, Seeley G. Mudd Manuscript Library, Princeton University.

Goldberg, Arthur J., Papers. Library of Congress, Washington, DC.

Harkin, Thomas R., Collection. Drake University Archives and Special Collections.

Harrington, Michael, Papers. Salem State College Library.

Humphrey, Hubert, Papers. Minnesota Historical Society, St. Paul.

International League for Human Rights Collection. New York Public Library.

Jackson, Henry M., Papers. University of Washington.

Kim, Yong-jeung, Papers. Rare Book and Manuscript Library, Columbia University.

Lister, George, Papers. Benson Latin American Collection, University of Texas Libraries.

Mink, Patsy T., Papers. Manuscript Division, Library of Congress, Washington, DC.

Morris, Ivan I., Papers. Rare Book and Manuscript Library, Columbia University.

Muñoz, Heraldo, Papers. David M. Rubenstein Library, Duke University.

Newman, Frank C., Papers. The Bancroft Library, University of California–Berkeley.

Ogle, George E., Papers. Archives and Manuscripts Department, Pitts Theology Library, Emory University.

Papers of the Africa Bureau. Bodleian Library, Oxford University.

Peace Collection. Swarthmore College.

Proxmire, William, Collection. Wisconsin Historical Society, Madison.

Reuther, Victor G., Collection. Walter P. Reuther Library, Wayne State University.

Rockefeller Brothers Fund. Rockefeller Archive Center, Sleepy Hollow, NY.

Rosenthal, Benjamin, Congressional Papers. Rosenthal Library, Queens College, City University of New York.

Sakharov, Andrei, Archives. Houghton Library, Harvard University.

Schlesinger, James R., Papers. Manuscript Division, Library of Congress, Washington, DC.

Simon, William E., Papers. Skillman Library, Lafayette College.

Social Action Vertical File. Wisconsin Historical Society, Madison.

Stevenson, Adlai E., Papers. Public Policy Papers, Seeley G. Mudd Manuscript Library, Princeton University.

Student Nonviolent Coordinating Committee (SNCC) Papers. ProQuest History Vault, Black Freedom, Part 3.

Washington Office on Latin America Records. David M. Rubenstein Library, Duke University.

Wilkins, Roy, Papers. Manuscript Division, Library of Congress, Washington, DC.

Yost, Charles, Papers. Public Policy Papers, Seeley G. Mudd Manuscript Library, Princeton University.

INTERVIEWS

Abourezk, James. Interview with the Author, October 6, 2016.

Becket, James. Interview with the Author, December 5, 2016.

Eldridge, Joseph. Interview with the Author, April 13, 2016.

Foreign Affairs Oral History Collection, Association for Diplomatic Studies and Training, Library of Congress, Washington, DC.

Fraser, Donald. Interview with the Author, January 27, 2009.

Grant, Martha. Interview with Donald Fraser, April 6, 2008.

Kennedy, Edward M. Oral History Project, Miller Center, University of Virginia.

Newman, Frank C. Oral History Interview Conducted 1989 and 1991 by Carol Hicke. Regional Oral History Office, University of California–Berkeley, California State Archives State Government Oral History Program.

Salzberg, John. Interview with the Author, September 23, 2016.

Salzberg, John P. Interview. "The Life and Legacy of George Lister: Reconsidering Human Rights, Democracy, and US Foreign Policy." Bernard and Audre Rapoport Center for Human Rights and Justice, University of Texas School of Law.

Schifter, Richard. Interview. "The Life and Legacy of George Lister: Reconsidering Human Rights, Democracy, and U.S. Foreign Policy." Bernard and Audre Rapoport Center for Human Rights and Justice, University of Texas School of Law.

Schneider, Mark. Interview with the Author, August 14, 2017.

Simpson, Brad. Interview with Donald Fraser, May 2008.

UNPUBLISHED MANUSCRIPTS

Amos, Jennifer Ann. "Soviet Diplomacy and Politics on Human Rights, 1945–1977." PhD Diss., University of Chicago, 2012.

Bohlen, Casey. "Cold War Faith, International Encounters, and the Origins of Student Civil Rights Activism." Paper Presented at the Organization of American Historians Annual Meeting, April 2016.

Conispoliatis, Helen. "Facing the Colonels: British and American Diplomacy Towards the Colonels' Junta in Greece, 1967–1970." PhD Thesis, University of Leicester, 2003.

Farer, Tom J. "How Can U.S. Policy Provide Effective Support for Human Rights in the Soviet Union?" On File in Donald Fraser Papers.

Focer, Ada J. "Frontier Internship in Mission, 1961–1974: Young Christians Abroad in a Post-Colonial and Cold War World." PhD Diss., Boston University, 2016.

Hager, Michael. "Powerful Influence: The United States in Chile." MA Thesis, California State University–Dominguez Hills, 2001.

Harrison, Hope. "Ulbricht and the Concrete 'Rose': New Archival Evidence on the Dynamics of Soviet–East German Relations and the Berlin Crisis, 1958–1961." Working Paper No. 5, Cold War International History Project, Woodrow Wilson International Center for Scholars, Washington, DC.

Higgin, Hannah Nicole. "Disseminating American Ideals in Africa, 1949–1969." DPhil Thesis, University of Cambridge, 2014.

Hodgman, Edward Bailey. "Détente and the Dissidents: Human Rights in U.S.-Soviet Relations, 1968–1980." PhD Diss., University of Rochester, 2003.

Hollinger, David A., "The Protestant Boomerang: How the Foreign Missionary Experience Liberalized the Home Culture." Danforth Distinguished Lecture Series, November 18, 2013.

Irwin, Ryan. "The Gordian Knot: Apartheid and the Unmaking of the Modern World Order: 1960–1970." PhD Diss., Ohio State University, 2010.

Jensen, Steven. "The Breakthrough Decade? International Human Rights Diplomacy and Law in the 1960s." Paper Presented at the Society for Historians of American Foreign Relations Annual Meeting, June 2013.

Kalogerakos, Nicholas James. "Dealing with the Dictators: The United States and the Greek Military Regime, 1967–1974." DPhil Thesis, Oxford University, 2011.

Kelly, Patrick William. "The Latin American Roots of the Ford Foundation's Human Rights Philanthropy." Paper Presented at the Society for Historians of American Foreign Relations Annual Meeting, June 2015.

Kim, Bong Joong. "Democracy and Human Rights: U.S.–South Korean Relations 1945–1979." PhD Diss., University of Toledo, 1994.

Kurz, Nathaniel A. "'A Sphere above the Nations?': The Rise and Fall of International Jewish Human Rights Politics." PhD Diss., Yale University, 2015.

Liem, Wol-san. "Telling the 'Truth' to Koreans: U.S. Cultural Policy in South Korea During the Early Cold War, 1947–1967." PhD Diss., New York University, 2010.

Michael, Daniel L. "Nixon, Chile and Shadows of the Cold War: U.S.-Chilean Relations During the Government of Salvador Allende, 1970–1973." PhD Diss., George Washington University, 2005.

Morris, Stephen J. "The Soviet-Chinese-Vietnamese Triangle in the 1970s: The View from Moscow." Working Paper No. 25, Cold War International History Project, Woodrow Wilson International Center for Scholars, Washington, DC.

Parrott, Raymond Joseph. "Struggle for Solidarity: The New Left, Portuguese African Decolonization, and the End of the Cold War Consensus." PhD Diss., University of Texas at Austin, 2016.

Popper, David. "The Reminiscences of David Popper," (1980). Rare Book and Manuscript Library, Columbia University.

Quataert, Jean H. "Women, Development, and Injustice: The Circuitous Origins of the New Gender Perspectives in Human Rights Visions and Practices in the 1970s." Paper Presented at "A New Global Morality? The Politics of Human Rights and Humanitarianism in the 1970s," Freiburg Institute for Advanced Studies, June 2010.

Sargent, Daniel. "From Internationalism to Globalism: The United States and the Transformation of International Politics in the 1970s." PhD Diss., Harvard University, 2008.

Savranskaya, Svetlana. "The Battles for the Final Act: The Soviet Government and Dissidents' Efforts to Define the Substance and the Implementation of the Helsinki Final Act." Paper Presented at European and Transatlantic Strategies in the Late Cold War Period to Overcome the East-West Division of Europe Conference, November 30–December 1, 2007.

Vik, Hanne Hagtvedt. "The United States, the American Legal Community and the Vision of International Human Rights Protection, 1941–1953." PhD Diss., University of Oslo, 2009.

Walker, Vanessa. "Ambivalent Allies: Advocates, Diplomats, and the Struggles for an 'American' Human Rights Policy." PhD Diss., University of Wisconsin–Madison, 2011.

Watts, Carl P. "'Dropping the F-Bomb': President Ford, the Rhodesian Crisis, and the 1976 Election." Paper Presented at the Society for Historians of American Foreign Relations Annual Meeting, June 2014.

——. "Ripe for Settlement? Kissinger's Attempted Mediation of the Rhodesian Conflict." Paper Presented at the Society for Historians of American Foreign Relations Annual Meeting, June 2013.

BIBLIOGRAPHY

ARTICLES

Abram, Morris B. "The UN and Human Rights." *Foreign Affairs* 47, no. 4 (January 1969): 363–74.

Allen, Tim, and David Sityan. "A Right to Interfere? Bernard Kouchner and the New Humanitarianism." *Journal of International Development* 12 (2000): 825–42.

Alston, Philip. "Book Review: Does the Past Matter? On the Origins of Human Rights." *Harvard Law Review* 126 (2013): 2043–81.

Apodaca, Clair. "U.S. Human Rights Policy and Foreign Assistance: A Short History." *Ritsumekian International Affairs* 3 (2005): 63–80.

Apodaca, Clair, and Michael Stohl. "United States Human Rights Policy and Foreign Assistance." *International Studies Quarterly* 43, no. 1 (March 1999): 185–98.

Arnold, Hugh M. "Henry Kissinger and Human Rights." *Universal Human Rights* 2, no. 4 (October–December 1980): 57–71.

Barrett, Andrew W. "Gone Public: The Impact of Going Public on Presidential Legislative Success." *American Politics Research* 32, no. 3 (May 2004): 338–70.

Bawden, John R. "Cutting Off the Dictator: The United States Arms Embargo of the Pinochet Regime, 1974–1988." *Journal of Latin American Studies* 45 (2013): 513–43.

Bell, Peter D. "The Ford Foundation as a Transnational Actor." *International Organization* 25, no. 3 (Summer 1971): 465–78.

Bickford, Louis. "The Archival Imperative: Human Rights and Historical Memory in Latin America's Southern Cone." *Human Rights Quarterly* 21, no. 4 (November 1999): 1097–122.

Birnbaum, Karl E. "Human Rights and East-West Relations." *Foreign Affairs* 55 (July 1977): 783–99.

Bloodworth, Jeff. "Senator Henry Jackson, the Solzhenitsyn Affair, and American Liberalism." *Pacific Northern Quarterly* (Spring 2006): 69–77.

Borstelmann, Thomas. "'Hedging Our Bets and Buying Time': John Kennedy and Racial Revolution in the American South and Southern Africa." *Diplomatic History* 24, no. 3 (Summer 2000): 435–63.

Bowman, Cynthia Grant. "Women in the Legal Profession from the 1920s to the 1970s: What Can We Learn from Their Experience about Law and Social Change?" *Maine Law Review* 61, no. 1 (2009): 1–25.

Bradley, Mark Philip. "American Vernaculars: The United States and the Global Human Rights Imagination." *Diplomatic History* 38, no. 1 (January 2014): 1–21.

Brier, Robert. "Beyond the Quest for a 'Breakthrough': Reflections on the Recent Historiography of Human Rights." *European History Yearbook* 16 (2015): 155–73.

Buchanan, Tom. "Amnesty International in Crisis, 1966–67." *Twentieth Century British History* 15, no. 3 (2004): 267–89.

——. "'The Truth Will Set You Free': The Making of Amnesty International." *Journal of Contemporary History* 37, no. 4 (2002): 575–97.

Buckley, William F., Jr. "Human Rights and Foreign Policy: A Proposal." *Foreign Affairs* 58, no. 4 (Spring 1980): 775–96.

Bundy, William P. "Dictatorships and American Foreign Policy." *Foreign Affairs* 54, no. 1 (October 1975): 51–60.

Burke, Roland. "Flat Affect? Revisiting Emotion in the Historiography of Human Rights." *Journal of Human Rights* 16, no. 2 (2015): 123–41.

——. "'How Time Flies': Celebrating the Universal Declaration of Human Rights in the 1960s." *International History Review* 38, no. 3 (2016): 394–420.

Byrnes, Robert F. "United States Policy Towards Eastern Europe: Before and After Helsinki." *Review of Politics* 37 (October 1975): 435–63.

Calandra, Benedetta. "Exile and Diaspora in an Atypical Context: Chileans and Argentineans in the United States (1973–2005)." *Bulletin of Latin American Research* 32, no. 3 (2013): 311–24.

——. "The 'Good Americans': U.S. Solidarity Networks for Chilean and Argentinean Refugees, 1973–1983." *Historia Actual Online* (2010): 21–35.

Cargas, Sarita. "Questioning Samuel Moyn's Revisionist History of Human Rights." *Human Rights Quarterly* 38, no. 2 (May 2016): 41–25.

Chung, Patrick. "The 'Pictures in Our Heads': Journalists, Human Rights, and U.S.-South Korean Relations, 1970–1976." *Diplomatic History* 38, no. 5 (2014): 1136–55.

Clavin, Patricia. "Defining Transnationalism." *Contemporary European History* 14, no. 4 (2005): 421–39.

Clymer, Kenton. "Jimmy Carter, Human Rights, and Cambodia." *Diplomatic History* 27, no. 2 (April 2003): 245–77.

Cmiel, Kenneth. "The Emergence of Human Rights Politics in the United States." *Journal of American History* 86, no. 3 (December 1999): 1231–50.

——. "The Recent History of Human Rights." *American Historical Review* 109, no. 1 (2004): 117–35.

Cohen, Jeffrey E. "Presidential Rhetoric and the Public Agenda." *American Journal of Political Science* 39, no. 1 (February 1995): 87–107.

Cohen, Stephen B. "Conditioning U.S. Security Assistance on Human Rights Practices." *American Journal of International Law* 76, no. 2 (April 1982): 246–79.

Colby, Jason M. "'A Chasm of Values and Outlook': The Carter Administration's Human Rights Policy in Guatemala." *Peace & Change* 35, no. 4 (October 2010): 561–93.

Cronin, Thomas. "A Resurgent Congress and the Imperial Presidency." *Political Science Quarterly* 95, no. 2 (Summer 1980): 209–37.

Dean, Richard N. "Contacts with the West: The Dissidents' View of Western Support for the Human Rights Movement in the Soviet Union." *Universal Human Rights* 2, no. 1 (January–March 1980): 47–65.

De Lora, Cecilio. "From the Vatican II to Medellin." *Horizonte* 9, no. 24 (2011): 1233–45.

Dezalay, Yves, and Bryant Garth. "From the Cold War to Kosovo: The Rise and Renewal of the Field of International Human Rights." *Annual Review of Law and Social Science* (2006): 231–55.

Dickson, David A. "U.S. Foreign Policy Toward Southern and Central Africa: The Kennedy and Johnson Years." *Presidential Studies Quarterly* 23, no. 2 (Spring 1993): 301–15.

Donnelly, Jack. "Human Rights at the United Nations, 1955–85: The Question of Bias." *International Studies Quarterly* 32, no. 2 (September 1988): 275–303.

Drezner, Daniel W. "Ideas, Bureaucratic Politics, and the Crafting of Foreign Policy." *American Journal of Political Science* 44, no. 4 (October 2000): 733–49.

Eckel, Jan. "The International League for the Rights of Man, Amnesty International, and the Changing Fate of Human Rights Activism from the 1940s Through the 1970s." *Humanity* 4, no. 2 (Summer 2013): 183–214.

Elbaum, Max. "What Legacy from the Radical Internationalism of 1968?" *Radical History Review* 82 (Winter 2002): 37–64.

Evans, Tony. "Hegemony, Domestic Politics and the Project of Universal Human Rights." *Diplomacy & Statecraft* 6, no. 3 (November 1995): 616–44.

Fair, John D. "The Intellectual JFK: Lessons in Statesmanship from British History." *Diplomatic History* 30, no. 1 (January 2006): 119–42.

Falk, Richard. "The Human Rights Country Reports." *World Issues* (October/November 1978): 19–21.

Fenderson, Jonathan, James Stewart, and Kabria Baumgartner. "Expanding the History of the Black Studies Movement: Some Prefatory Notes." *Journal of African American Studies* 16 (2012): 1–20.

Flynn, Gregory A. "The Content of European Détente." *Orbis* 20 (Summer 1976): 401–16.

Foroohar, Manzar. "Liberation Theology: The Response of Latin American Catholics to Socioeconomic Problems." *Latin American Perspectives* 13, no. 3 (1986): 37–58.

Forsythe, David P. "Congress and Human Rights in U.S. Foreign Policy: The Fate of General Legislation." *Human Rights Quarterly* 9, no. 3 (August 1987): 382–404.

——. "Human Rights and the International Committee of the Red Cross." *Human Rights Quarterly* 12 (1990): 265–89.

——. "Human Rights in U.S. Foreign Policy: Retrospect and Prospect." *Political Science Quarterly* 105, no. 3 (Autumn 1990): 435–54.

——. "The United Nations and Human Rights, 1945–1985." *Political Science Quarterly* 100, no. 2 (Summer 1985): 249–69.

Frankfurt, Harry. "The Importance of What We Care About." *Syntheses* 53, no. 2 (November 1982): 257–72.

Fraser, Cary. "Crossing the Color Line in Little Rock." *Diplomatic History* 24, no. 2 (Spring 2000): 233–64.

Fraser, Donald M. "Freedom and Foreign Policy." *Foreign Policy* 26 (Spring 1977): 140–56.

——. "Human Rights and International Relations: A Look Backward at Greece." *Intellect* (October 1974): 28–31.

——. "Human Rights and U.S. Foreign Policy: Some Basic Questions Regarding Principles and Practice." *International Studies Quarterly* 23, no. 2 (June 1979): 174–85.

——. "New Directions in Foreign Aid." *World Affairs* 129, no. 4 (January, February, March 1967): 244–50.

——. "Title IX: The Dynamics of Growth in Developing Nations." *Foreign Service Journal* (March 1970): 12–14.

——. "A Turning Point in Congress." *Cross Currents* (November 2004): 5.

Fraser, Donald M., and John P. Salzberg. "Foreign Policy and Effective Strategies for Human Rights." *Universal Human Rights* 1, no. 1 (January–March 1979): 11–18.

Green, James N. "Clerics, Exiles, and Academics: Opposition to the Brazilian Military Dictatorship in the United States, 1969–1974." *Latin American Politics and Society* 45, no. 1 (Spring 2003): 87–117.

Green, William C. "Human Rights and Détente." *Ukrainian Quarterly* 36, no. 2 (1980): 138–49.

Gross, Franz B. "The U.S. National Interest and the UN." *Orbis* (April 1963): 367–85.

Grubbs, Larry. "'Workshop of a Continent': American Representations of Whiteness and Modernity in 1960s South Africa." *Diplomatic History* 32, no. 3 (June 2008): 405–39.

Hackett, Clifford P. "Congress and Greek American Relations: The Embargo Example." *Journal of the Hellenic Diaspora* 15, nos. 1–2 (Spring–Summer 1988): 5–32.

Hall, Jacquelyn Dowd. "The Long Civil Rights Movement and the Political Uses of the Past." *Journal of American History* 91, no. 4 (March 2005): 1233–63.

Hall, Simon. "Protest Movements in the 1970s: The Long 1960s." *Journal of Contemporary History* 43, no. 4 (2008): 655–72.

Harmer, Tanya. "Fractious Allies: Chile, the United States, and the Cold War, 1973–76." *Diplomatic History* 37, no. 1 (2013): 109–43.

———. "The View from Havana: Chilean Exiles in Cuba and Early Resistance to Chile's Dictatorship, 1973–1977." *Hispanic American Historical Review* 6, no. 1 (2016): 109–46.

Hartley, Anthony. "John Kennedy's Foreign Policy." *Foreign Policy* 4 (Autumn 1971): 77–87.

Hartmann, Hauke. "U.S. Human Rights Policy under Carter and Reagan, 1977–1981." *Human Rights Quarterly* 23 (2001): 402–30.

Hatzivassiliou, Evanthis. "Shallow Waves and Deeper Currents: The U.S. Experience in Greece, 1947–1961, Policies, Historicity, and the Cultural Dimension." *Diplomatic History* 38, no. 1 (2014): 83–110.

Hitchcock, William I. "The Rise and Fall of Human Rights? Searching for a Narrative from the Cold War to the 9/11 Era." *Human Rights Quarterly* 37, no. 1 (February 2015): 80–106.

Hoffmann, Stefan-Ludwig. "Human Rights and History." *Past and Present* 232 (August 2016): 279–310.

Horvath, Robert. "Breaking the Totalitarian Ice: The Initiative Group for the Defense of Human Rights in the USSR." *Human Rights Quarterly* 36, no. 1 (February 2014): 147–75.

Hunt, Lynn. "The Long and the Short of the History of Human Rights." *Past and Present* 233 (November 2016): 323–31.

Jacobs, Meg, and Julian E. Zelizer. "Swinging Too Far to the Left." *Journal of Contemporary History* 43, no. 4 (October 2008): 689–93.

Johnson, Donald C. "Congress, the Executive, and Human Rights Legislation." *Foreign Service Journal* (December 1976): 18–20, 28.

Jong-oh, Ra. "The Korean Security Issue: Congress and Foreign Policy." *Journal of East Asian Affairs* 5, no. 2 (1991): 287–312.

Kaufman, Natalie Hevener, and David Whiteman. "Opposition to Human Rights Treaties in the United States Senate: The Legacy of the Bricker Amendment." *Human Rights Quarterly* 10 (1988): 309–37.

Kelly, Patrick William. "The 1973 Chilean Coup and the Origins of Transnational Human Rights Activism." *Journal of Global History* 8, no. 1 (March 2013): 165–86.

Kelly, Tobias. "What We Talk about When We Talk about Torture." *Humanity* 2, no. 2 (Summer 2011): 327–43.

Kendrick, Frank J. "The United States and the International Protection of Human Rights." *North Dakota Quarterly* (Spring 1968): 29–45.

Kerber, Linda K. "We Are All Historians of Human Rights." *Perspectives on History* (October 2006).

Keys, Barbara. "Congress, Kissinger, and the Origins of Human Rights Diplomacy." *Diplomatic History* 34, no. 5 (November 2010): 823–51.

——. "Henry Kissinger: The Emotional Statesman." *Diplomatic History* 35, no. 4 (September 2011): 587–609.

Keys, Barbara, Jack Davies, and Elliot Bannan. "The Post-Traumatic Decade: New Histories of the 1970s." *Australasian Journal of American Studies* 33, no. 1 (July 2014): 1–17.

Kim, C. I. Eugene. "Emergency, Development and Human Rights: South Korea." *Asian Survey* 18, no. 4 (April 1978): 363–78.

Kim, Seung-Young. "American Elites' Strategic Thinking Toward Korea: From Kennan to Brzezinski." *Diplomacy & Statecraft* 12, no. 1 (March 2001): 185–212.

Klarevas, Louis. "Were the Eagle and the Phoenix Birds of a Feather: The United States and the Greek Coup of 1967." *Diplomatic History* 30, no. 3 (June 2006): 471–508.

Kochavi, Noam. "Idealpolitik in Disguise: Israel, Jewish Emigration from the Soviet Union, and the Nixon Administration, 1969–1974." *International History Review* 29, no. 3 (September 2007): 550–72.

Korey, William. "Human Rights Treaties: Why Is the U.S. Stalling?" *Foreign Affairs* 45, no. 3 (April 1967): 414–24.

——. "The Jackson-Vanik Amendment in Perspective." *Soviet Jewish Affairs* 18, no. 1 (1988): 29–47.

Landam, Todd. "Pinochet's Chile: The United States, Human Rights, and International Terrorism." *Human Rights & Human Welfare* 4 (2004): 91–99.

Loescher, G. D. "U.S. Human Rights Policy and International Financial Institutions." *The World Today* 33, no. 12 (December 1977): 453–63.

Macdonald, Donald S. "American Imperialism: Myth or Reality?" *Korea and World Affairs* 10, no. 3 (Fall 1986): 575–98.

Manley, John F. "The Rise of Congress in Foreign Policy-Making." *Annals of the American Academy of Political and Social Science* 397 (September 1971): 60–70.

Maragkou, Konstantina. "Favouritism in NATO's Southeastern Flank: The Case of the Greek Colonels, 1967–1974." *Cold War History* 9, no. 3 (August 2009): 347–66.

——. "The Relevance of Détente to American Foreign Policy: The Case of Greece, 1967–1979." *Diplomacy & Statecraft* 25, no. 4 (2014): 646–68.

Mathias, Charles McC., Jr. "Ethnic Groups and Foreign Policy." *Foreign Affairs* 59, no. 5 (Summer 1981): 975–98.

Maynard, Edwin S. "The Bureaucracy and Implementation of U.S. Human Rights Policy." *Human Rights Quarterly* 11, no. 2 (May 1989): 175–248.

Mazower, Mark. "The Strange Triumph of Human Rights, 1933–1950." *Historical Journal* 47, no. 2 (2004): 379–98.

McCrudden, Christopher. "Human Rights Histories." *Oxford Journal of Legal Studies* 35, no. 1 (Spring 2015): 179–212.

McKay, Vernon. "The Domino Theory of the Rhodesian Lobby." *Africa Report* (June 1967): 55–58.

Montias, John Michael. "Communist Rule in Eastern Europe." *Foreign Affairs* 43, no. 2 (January 1965): 331–48.

Nathans, Benjamin. "The Dictatorship of Reason: Aleksandr Vol'Pin and the Idea of Rights under 'Developed Socialism.'" *Slavic Review* 66, no. 4 (Winter 2007): 630–63.

——. "Talking Fish: On Soviet Dissident Memoirs." *Journal of Modern History* 87, no. 3 (September 2015): 579–614.

Nolan, Cathal J. "The Last Hurrah of Conservative Isolationism: Eisenhower, Congress, and the Bricker Amendment." *Presidential Studies Quarterly* 22, no. 2 (1992): 337–49.

Onslow, Sue. "A Question of Timing: South Africa and Rhodesia's Unilateral Declaration of Independence, 1964–65." *Cold War History* 5, no. 2 (2005): 129–59.

Ortiz de Zárate, Verónica Validivia. "Terrorism and Political Violence During the Pinochet Years: Chile, 1973–1989." *Radical History Review* 85 (Winter 2003): 182–90.

Pedaliu, Effie G. H. "'A Discordant Note': NATO and the Greek Junta, 1967–1974." *Diplomacy & Statecraft* 22, no. 1 (2011): 101–20.

——. "Human Rights and Foreign Policy: Wilson and the Greek Dictators, 1967–1970." *Diplomacy & Statecraft* 18 (2007): 185–214.

——. "Human Rights and International Security: The International Community and the Greek Dictators." *International History Review* 38, no. 5 (2016): 1014–39.

Pérez, Louis A. "Fear and Loathing of Fidel Castro: Sources of U.S. Policy Toward Cuba." *Journal of Latin American Studies* 34, no. 2 (May 2002): 227–54.

Phillips, Jared Michael. "Toward a Better World: LBJ, Niebuhr, and American Human Rights, 1964–1966." *Ozark Historical Review* 38 (Spring 2009): 31–50.

Power, Margaret. "The U.S. Movement in Solidarity with Chile in the 1970s." *Latin American Perspectives* 36, no. 6 (November 2009): 46–66.

Power, Margaret, and Julie A. Charlip. "On Solidarity." *Latin American Perspectives* 36, no. 6 (November 2009): 3–9.

Rabe, Stephen. "After the Missiles of October: John F. Kennedy and Cuba, November 1962 to November 1963." *Presidential Studies Quarterly* 30, no. 4 (December 2000): 714–26.

——. "The Caribbean Triangle: Betancourt, Castro, and Trujillo and U.S. Foreign Policy, 1958–1963." *Diplomatic History* 20, no. 1 (Winter 1996): 55–78.

——. "John F. Kennedy and Constitutionalism, Democracy, and Human Rights in Latin America: Promise and Performance." *New England Journal of History* 52 (Fall 1995): 38–57.

Ranard, Donald L. "The U.S. in Korea: What Price Security?" *Worldview* (January–February 1977): 23–26, 35–37.

——. "What We Should Do about Korea." *Worldview* (June 1976): 23–26, 35.

Ribuffo, Leo. "Is Poland a Soviet Satellite? Gerald Ford, the Sonnenfeldt Doctrine, and the Election of 1976." *Diplomatic History* 14, no. 3 (1990): 385–404.

Rodrigues, Luís Nuno. "'Today's Terrorist is Tomorrow's Statesman': The United States and Angolan Nationalism in the Early 1960s." *Portuguese Journal of Social Science* 3, no. 2 (2004): 115–40.

Romano, Renee. "No Diplomatic Immunity: African Diplomats, the State Department, and Civil Rights, 1961–1964." *Journal of American History* (September 2000): 546–79.

Rubinstein, Joshua. "The Enduring Voice of the Soviet Dissidents." *Columbia Journalism Review* (September/October 1978): 32–39.

Sandholtz, Wayne. "United States Military Assistance and Human Rights." *Human Rights Quarterly* 38, no. 4 (November 2016): 1070–1101.

Schmidli, William Michael. "Institutionalizing Human Rights in U.S. Foreign Policy: U.S.-Argentine Relations, 1976–1980." *Diplomatic History* 35, no. 2 (April 2011): 351–78.

Schmitz, David F., and Natalie Fousekis. "Frank Church, the Senate, and the Emergence of Dissent on the Vietnam War." *Pacific Historical Review* 63, no. 4 (November 1994): 561–81.

Schmitz, David F., and Vanessa Walker. "Jimmy Carter and the Foreign Policy of Human Rights: The Development of a Post–Cold War Foreign Policy." *Diplomatic History* 28 (January 2004): 113–43.

Schulman, Bruce J. "The Empire Strikes Back—Conservative Responses to Progressive Social Movements in the 1970s." *Journal of Contemporary History* 43, no. 4 (2008): 695–700.

Schwartz, Thomas Alan. "'Henry . . . Winning an Election Is Terribly Important': Partisan Politics in the History of U.S. Foreign Relations." *Diplomatic History* 33, no. 2 (April 2009): 173–90.

Scoble, Harry M., and Laurie S. Wiseberg. "Human Rights and Amnesty International." *Annals of the American Academy of Political and Social Science* 413 (May 1974): 11–26.

Shannon, Matthew K. "American-Iranian Alliances: International Education, Modernization, and Human Rights During the Pahlavi Era." *Diplomatic History* 39, no. 4 (2015): 661–88.

——. "'Contacts with the Opposition': American Foreign Relations, the Iranian Student Movement, and the Global Sixties." *Sixties: A Journal of History, Politics, and Culture* 4, no. 1 (June 2011): 1–29.

Shestack, Jerome. "Human Rights, the National Interest, and U.S. Foreign Policy." *Annals of the American Academy of Political and Social Science* 506 (November 1989): 17–29.

Shestack, Jerome J., and Roberta Cohen. "International Human Rights: A Role for the United States." *Virginia Journal of International Law* 14, no. 4 (1974): 673–701.

Simpson, Bradley R. "Denying the 'First Right': The United States, Indonesia, and the Ranking of Human Rights by the Carter Administration, 1976–1980." *International History Review* 31, no. 4 (December 2009): 798–826.

——. "Ideal Illusions: How the U.S. Government Co-Opted Human Rights." *Critical Asian Studies* 44, no. 2 (2012): 329–38.

——. "The Many Meanings of National Self-Determination." *Current History* (November 2014): 312–17.

——. "Prudent, Prudent, Tragic: Brazinsky's Arc of Korean Development." *H-Diplo Roundtable Review* 9, no. 17 (2008): 27–33.

Smith, Jason Scott. "The Strange History of the Decade: Modernity, Nostalgia, and the Perils of Periodization." *Journal of Social History* 32, no. 2 (Winter 1998): 263–85.

Snyder, Sarah B. "'A Call for U.S. Leadership': Congressional Activism on Human Rights." *Diplomatic History* 37, no. 2 (April 2013): 372–97.

——. "Exporting Amnesty International to the United States: Transatlantic Human Rights Activism in the 1960s." *Human Rights Quarterly* 34, no. 3 (August 2012): 779–99.

——. "'Jerry, Don't Go': Domestic Opposition to the 1975 Helsinki Final Act." *Journal of American Studies* 44, no. 1 (February 2010): 67–81.

——. "Through the Looking Glass: The Helsinki Final Act and the 1976 Election for President." *Diplomacy & Statecraft* 21, no. 1 (March 2010): 87–106.

Sorensen, Theodore C. "JFK's Strategy of Peace." *World Policy Journal* 20, no. 3 (Fall 2003): 2–6.

Stevens, Daniel. "Public Opinion and Public Policy: The Case of Kennedy and Civil Rights." *Presidential Studies Quarterly* 32, no. 1 (March 2002): 111–36.

Stevens, Simon. "'From the Viewpoint of a Southern Governor': The Carter Administration and Apartheid, 1977–81." *Diplomatic History* 36 (November 2012): 843–80.

Sulzberger, C. L. "Greece under the Colonels." *Foreign Affairs* 48 (1969–1970): 300–311.

Tama, Jordan. "From Private Consultation to Public Crusade: Assessing Eisenhower's Legislative Strategies on Foreign Policy." *Congress & the Presidency* 40, no. 1 (2013): 41–60.

Tananbaum, Duane A. "The Bricker Amendment Controversy: Its Origins and Eisenhower's Role." *Diplomatic History* 9, no. 1 (1985): 73–93.

Thomas, Daniel C. "Boomerangs and Superpowers: International Norms, Transnational Networks and U.S. Foreign Policy." *Cambridge Review of International Affairs* 15, no. 1 (2002): 25–44.

Trenta, Luca. "The Champion of Human Rights Meets the King of Kings: Jimmy Carter, the Shah, and Iranian Illusions and Rage." *Diplomacy & Statecraft* 24, no. 3 (2013): 476–98.

Tsutsui, Kikyoteru, and Christine Min Wotipka. "Global Civil Society and the International Human Rights Movement: Citizen Participation in Human Rights International Nongovernmental Organizations." *Social Forces* 83, no. 2 (December 2004): 587–620.

Tuck, Stephen. "Reconsidering the 1970s—The 1960s to a Disco Beat?" *Journal of Contemporary History* 43, no. 4 (2008): 617–20.

Tucker, Nancy Bernkopf. "Taiwan Expendable? Nixon and Kissinger Go to China." *Journal of American History* (June 2005): 109–35.

Tulis, Jeffrey K. "*The Rhetorical Presidency* in Retrospect." *Critical Review* 19, nos. 2–3 (2007): 481–500.

Tulli, Umberto. "'Whose Rights are Human Rights?': The Ambiguous Emergence of Human Rights and the Demise of Kissingerism." *Cold War History* 12, no. 4 (November 2012): 573–93.

Ulianova, Olga. "Corvalán for Bukovsky: A Real Exchange of Prisoners During an Imaginary War: The Chilean Dictatorship, the Soviet Union, and U.S. Mediation, 1973–1976," *Cold War History* 14, no. 3 (2014): 315–36.

Vance, Cyrus R. "The Human Rights Imperative." *Foreign Policy* 63 (Summer 1986): 3–19.

Walker, Vanessa. "At the End of Influence: The Letelier Assassination, Human Rights, and Rethinking Intervention in U.S.–Latin American Relations." *Journal of Contemporary History* 46, no. 1 (January 2011): 109–35.

Watts, Carl P. "G. Mennen Williams and Rhodesian Independence: A Case Study in Bureaucratic Politics." *Michigan Academician* 36 (2004): 225–46.

——. "The United States, Britain, and the Problem of Rhodesian Independence, 1964–1965." *Diplomatic History* 30, no. 3 (June 2006): 439–70.

Weissbrodt, David. "Human Rights Legislation and U.S. Foreign Policy." *Georgia Journal of International and Comparative Law* 7 (1977): 231–87.

Whang, Roy, "An Opposition Leader's Mysterious Death." *Far Eastern Economic Review* (September 12, 1975): 18.

Wiseberg, Laurie S., and Harry M. Scoble. "The International League for Human Rights: The Strategy of a Human Rights NGO." *Georgia Journal of International & Comparative Law* 7 (1977): 289–313.

Xydis, Stephen G. "Coups and Countercoups in Greece, 1967–1973." *Political Science Quarterly* 89, no. 3 (Autumn 1974): 507–38.

Yergin, Daniel. "Politics and Soviet-American Trade: Three Questions." *Foreign Affairs* (January 1, 1977): 517–38.

Zarefsky, David. "Presidential Rhetoric and the Power of Definition." *Presidential Studies Quarterly* 34, no. 3 (September 2004): 607–19.

Zelikow, Philip. "American Policy and Cuba, 1961–1963." *Diplomatic History* 24, no. 2 (Spring 2000): 317–34.

BOOKS

Memoirs

Abourezk, James G. *Advise & Dissent: Memoirs of South Dakota and the U.S. Senate.* Chicago: Lawrence Hill Books, 1989.

Abram, Morris B. *The Day Is Short: An Autobiography.* New York: Harcourt Brace Jovanovich, 1982.

Amal'rik, Andrei. *Notes of a Revolutionary.* Trans. Guy Daniels. New York: Knopf, 1982.

Ball, George W. *The Past Has Another Pattern: Memoirs.* New York: Norton, 1982.

Brown, Winthrop G. *Postmark Asia: Letters of American Diplomat to His Family Written from India, Laos and Korea, 1957–1966.* Published by the author, n.d.

Deane, Philip. *I Should Have Died.* New York: Atheneum, 1977.

Dobrynin, Anatoly. *In Confidence: Moscow's Ambassador to America's Six Cold War Presidents.* New York: Times Books, 1995.

Ford, Gerald. *A Time to Heal: The Autobiography of Gerald Ford.* New York: Harper & Row, 1979.

Galbraith, John Kenneth. *A Life in Our Times: Memoirs.* Boston: Houghton Mifflin, 1981.

——. *Name-Dropping: From FDR On.* New York: Houghton Mifflin, 1999.

Gromyko, Andrei. *Memoirs.* New York: Doubleday, 1989.

Johnson, Lyndon B. *The Vantage Point: Perspectives on the Presidency, 1963–1969.* New York: Holt, Rinehart & Winston, 1971.

Keeley, Robert V. *The Colonels' Coup and the American Embassy: A Diplomat's View of the Breakdown of Democracy in Cold War Greece.* University Park: Pennsylvania State University Press, 2010.

Kennedy, Edward M. *True Compass: A Memoir.* New York: Twelve, 2011.

Kissinger, Henry. *The White House Years.* Boston: Little, Brown, 1979.

——. *Years of Renewal.* New York: Simon & Schuster, 1999.

——. *Years of Upheaval.* New York: Little, Brown, 1982.

Moynihan, Daniel Patrick, with Suzanne Weaver. *A Dangerous Place.* Boston: Little, Brown, 1978.

Muñoz, Heraldo. *The Dictator's Shadow: Life under Augusto Pinochet*. New York: Basic Books, 2008.

Nixon, Richard. *Memoirs*. New York: Grosset & Dunlap, 1978.

Orlov, Yuri. *Dangerous Thoughts: Memoirs of a Russian Life*. Trans. Thomas P. Whitney. New York: William Morrow, 1991.

Papandreou, Andreas. *Democracy at Gunpoint: The Greek Front*. Garden City, NY: Doubleday, 1970.

Papandreou, Margaret. *Nightmare in Athens*. Englewood Cliffs, NJ: Prentice-Hall, 1970.

Papandreou, Nick. *Father Dancing*. New York: Penguin, 1996.

Rusk, Dean. *As I Saw It*. New York: Norton, 1990.

Safire, William. *Before the Fall: An Inside View of the Pre-Watergate White House*. New York: Da Capo, 1975.

Schlesinger, Arthur M., Jr. *A Thousand Days: John F. Kennedy in the White House*. Boston: Houghton Mifflin, 1965.

Schwarz, Karen. *What You Can Do for Your Country: An Oral History of the Peace Corps*. New York: William Morrow, 1991.

Sharansky, Natan. *Fear No Evil*. New York: Random House, 1988.

Stevenson, Adlai E. *Looking Outward: Years of Crisis at the United Nations*. Ed. Robert T. Schiffer and Selma Schiffer. New York: Harper & Row, 1961.

Wilkins, Roy, with Tom Mathews. *Standing Fast: The Autobiography of Roy Wilkins*. New York: Da Capo, 1994.

Secondary Sources

Agnew, Jean-Christophe, and Roy Rosenzweig, eds. *A Companion to Post-1945 America*. Malden, MA: Blackwell, 2002.

Alexeyeva, Lyudmila. *Soviet Dissent: Contemporary Movements for National, Religious, and Human Rights*. Middletown, CT: Wesleyan University Press, 1985.

Alexeyeva, Lyudmila, and Paul Goldberg. *The Thaw Generation: Coming of Age in the Post-Stalin Era*. Pittsburgh: University of Pittsburgh Press, 1990.

Anderson, Carol. *Bourgeois Radicals: The NAACP and the Struggle for Colonial Liberation, 1941–1960*. New York: Cambridge University Press, 2015.

Apodaca, Clair. *Understanding U.S. Human Rights Policy: A Paradoxical Legacy*. New York: Routledge, 2006.

Ashabranner, Brent. *A Moment in History: The First Ten Years of the Peace Corps*. Garden City, NY: Doubleday, 1971.

Ashworth, Georgina. "The United Nations 'Women's Conference' and International Linkages in the Women's Movement." In *Pressure Groups in the Global System*, ed. Peter Willetts, 125–47. New York: St. Martin's Press, 1982.

Baldwin, Frank, ed. *Without Parallel: The American-Korean Relationship since 1945*. New York: Pantheon, 1974.

Balogh, Brian. *The Associational State: American Governance in the Twentieth Century*. Philadelphia: University of Pennsylvania Press, 2015.

Barnett, Michael N. *The Star and the Stripes: A History of the Foreign Policies of American Jews*. Princeton, NJ: Princeton University Press, 2016.

Beckerman, Gal. *When They Come for Us, We'll Be Gone.* New York: Houghton Mifflin Harcourt, 2010.

Becket, James. *Barbarism in Greece.* New York: Walker, 1970.

Beisner, Robert. *Dean Acheson: A Life in the Cold War.* New York: Oxford University Press, 2006.

Bennett, Andrew. "Who Rules the Roost? Congressional-Executive Relations on Foreign Policy after the Cold War." In *Eagle Rules? Foreign Policy and American Primacy in the Twenty-First Century,* ed. Robert J. Lieber, 47–68. Upper Saddle River, NJ: Prentice Hall, 2002.

Bimes, Terri. "Understanding the Rhetorical Presidency." In *The Oxford Handbook of the American Presidency,* ed. George C Edwards III and William G. Howell, 208–31. New York: Oxford University Press, 2009.

Blackburn, Robert M. *Mercenaries and Lyndon Johnson's "More Flags": The Hiring of Korean, Filipino and Thai Soldiers in the Vietnam War.* Jefferson, NC: McFarland, 1994.

Bloodworth, Jeffrey. *Losing the Center: The Decline of American Liberalism, 1968–1992.* Lexington: University Press of Kentucky, 2013.

Boettcher, Robert B. "The Role of Congress in Deciding United States Human Rights Policies." In *Dynamics of Human Rights in U.S. Foreign Policy,* ed. Natalie Kaufman Hevener, 279–90. New Brunswick, NJ: Transaction Books, 1981.

Boettcher, Robert, with Gordon L. Freedman. *Gifts of Deceit: Sun Myong Moon, Tongsun Park, and the Korean Scandal.* New York: Holt, Rinehart & Winston, 1980.

Borgwardt, Elizabeth. *A New Deal for the World: America's Vision for Human Rights.* Cambridge, MA: Belknap, 2005.

Borstelmann, Thomas. *The Cold War and the Color Line: American Race Relations in the Global Arena.* Cambridge, MA: Harvard University Press, 2001.

——. *The 1970s: A New Global History from Civil Rights to Economic Inequality.* Princeton, NJ: Princeton University Press, 2012.

Bowker, Mike, and Phil Williams. *Superpower Détente: A Reappraisal.* Newbury Park, CA: Sage, 1988.

Boykin, John. *Cursed Is the Peacemaker: The American Diplomat Versus the Israeli General, Beirut 1982.* Belmont, CA: Applegate, 2002.

Bradley, Mark Philip. *The World Reimagined: Americans and Human Rights in the Twentieth Century.* New York: Cambridge University Press, 2016.

Bradley, Mark, and Patrice Petro, eds. *Truth Claims: Representation and Human Rights.* New Brunswick, NJ: Rutgers University Press, 2002.

Branch, Taylor. *Parting the Waters: America in the King Years, 1954–63.* New York: Simon & Schuster, 1988.

Brands, H. W., ed. *Beyond Vietnam: The Foreign Policies of Lyndon Johnson.* College Station: Texas A&M University Press, 1999.

——. *The Wages of Globalism: Lyndon Johnson and the Limits of American Power.* New York: Oxford University Press, 1995.

Brazinsky, Gregg. *Nation Building in South Korea: Koreans, Americans, and the Making of a Democracy.* Chapel Hill: University of North Carolina Press, 2007.

Brinkley, Douglas. *Dean Acheson: The Cold War Years, 1953–1971.* New Haven, CT: Yale University Press, 1992.

Brodine, Virginia, and Mark Selden, eds. *Open Secret: The Kissinger-Nixon Doctrine in Asia*. New York: Harper & Row, 1972.

Brownell, Josiah. *The Collapse of Rhodesia: Population Demographics and the Politics of Race*. New York: I. B. Tauris, 2011.

Bruey, Alison J. "Transnational Concepts, Local Contexts: Solidarity at the Grassroots in Pinochet's Chile." In *Human Rights and Transnational Solidarity in Cold War Latin America*, ed. Jessica Stites Mor, 120–42. Madison: University of Wisconsin Press, 2013.

Brysk, Alison, ed. *Globalization and Human Rights*. Berkeley: University of California Press, 2002.

Burke, Roland. *Decolonization and the Evolution of International Human Rights*. Philadelphia: University of Pennsylvania Press, 2010.

Calkin, Holmer. *Women in the Department of State: Their Role in American Foreign Affairs*. Washington, DC: Department of State, 1978.

Carroll, Peter. *It Seemed Like Nothing Happened: The Tragedy and Promise of America in the 1970s*. New York: Holt, Rinehwart & Winston, 1982.

Carter, Ralph G., and James M. Scott. *Choosing to Lead: Understanding Congressional Foreign Policy Entrepreneurs*. Durham, NC: Duke University Press, 2009.

Chace, James. *Acheson: The Secretary of State Who Created the American World*. New York: Simon & Schuster, 1998.

Clark, Ann Marie. *Diplomacy of a Conscience: Amnesty International and Changing Human Rights Norms*. Princeton, NJ: Princeton University Press, 2001.

Cleary, Edward L. *The Struggle for Human Rights in Latin America*. Westport, CT: Praeger, 1997.

Clogg, Richard, ed. *Greece in the 1980s*. New York: St. Martin's Press, 1983.

Cohen, Jerome Allen, and Edward J. Baker. "U.S. Foreign Policy and Human Rights in South Korea." In *Human Rights in Korea: Historical and Policy Perspectives*, ed. William Shaw, 171–220. Cambridge, MA: East Asian Legal Studies Program of Harvard law School, 1991.

Cohen, Warren I., and Nancy Bernkopf Tucker, eds. *Lyndon Johnson Confronts the World: American Foreign Policy, 1963–1968*. New York: Cambridge University Press, 1994.

Colman, Jonathan. *The Foreign Policy of Lyndon B. Johnson*. Edinburgh: Edinburgh University Press, 2010.

Cranston, Maurice. *What Are Human Rights?* New York: Taplinger, 1973.

Cumings, Bruce. *Korea's Place in the Sun*. New York: Norton, 2013.

Curry, Jane Leftwich, ed. *Dissent in Eastern Europe*. New York: Praeger, 1983.

Dallek, Robert. *Flawed Giant: Lyndon Johnson and His Times, 1961–1973*. New York: Oxford University Press, 1998.

——. *John F. Kennedy: An Unfinished Life, 1917–1963*. New York: Penguin, 2003.

Daum, Andreas W. *Kennedy in Berlin*. Trans. Dona Geyer. New York: Cambridge University Press, 2008.

Davies, Gareth. *From Opportunity to Entitlement: The Transformation and Decline of Great Society Liberalism*. Lawrence: University Press of Kansas, 1996.

Davy, Richard, ed. *European Détente: A Reappraisal*. London: Sage for the Royal Institute of International Affairs, 1992.

DeConde, Alexander. *Ethnicity, Race, and American Foreign Policy: A History*. Boston: Northeastern University Press, 1992.

Del Pero, Mario. *The Eccentric Realist: Henry Kissinger and the Shaping of American Foreign Policy*. Ithaca, NY: Cornell University Press, 2010.

DeRoche, Andrew. *Black, White, and Chrome: The United States and Zimbabwe, 1953–1998*. Trenton, NJ: Africa World Press, 2001.

Dezalay, Yves, and Bryant G. Garth. *The Internationalization of Palace Wars: Lawyers, Economists, and the Contest to Transform Latin American States*. Chicago: University of Chicago Press, 2002.

Dinges, John. *The Condor Years: How Pinochet and His Allies Brought Terrorism to Three Continents*. New York: New Press, 2005.

Domber, Gregory F. *Empowering Revolution: America, Poland and the End of the Cold War*. Chapel Hill: University of North Carolina Press, 2014.

Draenos, Stan. *Andreas Papandreou: The Making of a Greek Democrat and Political Maverick*. London: I. B. Tauris, 2012.

Dudziak, Mary. *Cold War Civil Rights: Race and the Image of American Democracy*. Princeton, NJ: Princeton University Press, 2000.

Dumbrell, John. *American Foreign Policy: Carter to Clinton*. New York: St. Martin's Press, 1997.

——. *The Carter Presidency: A Re-Evaluation*. New York: St. Martin's Press, 1993.

Durst, Walter "Butch." "Missionaries, Cows, and Monday Nights," in *More Than Witnesses: How a Small Group of Missionaries Aided Korea's Democratic Revolution*, ed. Jim Stentzel, 279–307. Seoul: Korea Democracy Foundation, 2006.

Eckel, Jan. "'Under a Magnifying Glass': The International Human Rights Campaign Against Chile in the Seventies." In *Human Rights in the Twentieth Century*, ed. Stefan-Ludwig Hoffmann, 321–42. New York: Cambridge University Press, 2010.

Eckel, Jan, and Samuel Moyn, eds. *The Breakthrough: Human Rights in the 1970s*. Philadelphia: University of Pennsylvania Press, 2014.

Edwards, George C., III. *On Deaf Ears: The Limits of the Bully Pulpit*. New Haven, CT: Yale University Press, 2003.

Edwards, George C., III, and William G. Howell, eds. *The Oxford Handbook of the American Presidency*. New York: Oxford University Press, 2009.

Falk, Barbara J. *The Dilemmas of Dissidence in East-Central Europe: Citizen Intellectuals and Philosopher Kings*. New York: Central European University Press, 2003.

Farar, Tom J., ed. *Toward a Humanitarian Diplomacy: A Primer for Policy*. New York: New York University Press, 1980.

Featherstone, David. *Solidarity: Hidden Histories and Geographies of Internationalism*. New York: Zed Books, 2012.

Ferguson, Niall, Charles S. Maier, Erez Manela, and Daniel J. Sargent, eds. *The Shock of the Global: The 1970s in Perspective*. Cambridge, MA: Harvard University Press, 2010.

Field, Thomas C. *From Development to Dictatorship: Bolivia and the Alliance for Progress in the Kennedy Era*. Ithaca, NY: Cornell University Press, 2014.

Finger, Seymour Maxwell. *Your Man at the UN: People, Politics, and Bureaucracy in Making Foreign Policy*. New York: New York University Press, 1980.

Firestone, Bernard J., and Alexej Ugrinsky, eds. *Gerald R. Ford and the Politics of Post-Watergate America*. New York: Greenwood Press, 1992.

Foot, Rosemary. "The Cold War and Human Rights." In *The Cambridge History of the Cold War Volume III: Endings*, ed. Melvyn P. Leffler and Odd Arne Westad, 445–65. Cambridge: Cambridge University Press, 2010.

——. *Rights Beyond Borders: The Global Community and the Struggle over Human Rights in China*. New York: Oxford University Press, 2000.

Forsythe, David P., ed. *Human Rights and U.S. Foreign Policy: Congress Reconsidered*. Gainesville: University of Florida Press, 1988.

——, ed. *The United States and Human Rights: Looking Inward and Outward*. Lincoln: University of Nebraska Press, 2000.

Fosdick, Dorothy, ed. *Staying the Course: Henry M. Jackson and National Security*. Seattle: University of Washington Press, 1987.

Frankfurt, Harry G. *The Importance of What We Care About: Philosophical Essays*. New York: Cambridge University Press, 1988.

Friedman, Murray, and Albert D. Chernin, eds. *A Second Exodus: The American Movement to Free Soviet Jews*. Hanover, NH: University Press of New England, 1999.

Gaddis, John Lewis. *George F. Kennan: An American Life*. New York: Penguin, 2011.

Garfinkle, Adam. "The Nadir of Greek Democracy." In *Friendly Tyrants: An American Dilemma*, ed. Daniel Pipes and Adam Garfinkle, 63–90. New York: St. Martin's Press, 1991.

Gavin, Francis J., and Mark Atwood Lawrence, eds. *Beyond the Cold War: Lyndon Johnson and the New Global Challenges of the 1960s*. New York: Oxford University Press, 2014.

Geary, Daniel. *Beyond Civil Rights: The Moynihan Report and Its Legacy*. Philadelphia: University of Pennsylvania Press, 2015.

Giglio, James N. *The Presidency of John F. Kennedy*. 2nd ed., revised. Lawrence: University Press of Kansas, 2006.

Gilligan, Emma. *Defending Human Rights in Russia: Sergei Kovalyov, Dissident and Human Rights Commissioner, 1969–2003*. New York: Routledge, 2004.

Gitelman, Zvi. "Soviet Jews: Creating a Cause and a Movement," in *A Second Exodus: The American Movement to Free Soviet Jews*, ed. Murray Friedman and Albert D. Chernin, 84–96. Hanover, NH: University Press of New England, 1999.

Glendon, Mary Ann. *Rights Talk: The Impoverishment of Political Discourse*. New York: Free Press, 1991.

Godwin, John L. *Black Wilmington and the North Carolina Way: Portrait of a Community in the Era of Civil Rights Protest*. Lanham, MD: University Press of America, 2000.

Goedde, Petra, "Challenging Cultural Norms," in *Global Interdependence: The World after 1945*, ed. Akira Iriye, 589–649. Cambridge, MA: Belknap Press of Harvard University Press, 2014.

Goldberg, Paul. *The Final Act: The Dramatic, Revealing Story of the Moscow Helsinki Watch Group*. New York: Morrow, 1988.

Goluboff, Risa L. *The Lost Promise of Civil Rights*. Cambridge, MA: Harvard University Press, 2007.

——. *Vagrant Nation: Police Power, Constitutional Change, and the Making of the 1960s*. New York: Oxford University Press, 2016.

Gordon, Linda. *Heroes of Their Own Lives: The Politics and History of Family Violence, Boston 1880–1960*. New York: Viking, 1988.

Gosse, Van. "Unpacking the Vietnam Syndrome: The Coup in Chile and the Rise of Popular Anti-Interventionism." In *The World the '60s Made: Politics and Culture in Recent America*, ed. Van Gosse and Richard Moser, 100–113. Philadelphia: Temple University Press, 2003.

Gosse, Van, and Richard Moser, ed. *The World the '60s Made: Politics and Culture in Recent America*. Philadelphia: Temple University Press, 2003.

Grandin, Greg. *The Last Colonial Massacre: Latin America in the Cold War*. Chicago: The University of Chicago Press, 2004.

Gready, Paul, ed. *Fighting for Human Rights*. New York: Routledge, 2004.

Green, James N. *We Cannot Remain Silent: Opposition to the Brazilian Military Dictatorship in the United States*. Durham, NC: Duke University Press, 2010.

Hall, Michael R. *Sugar and Power in the Dominican Republic: Eisenhower, Kennedy, and the Trujillos*. Westport, CT: Greenwood Press, 2000.

Hall, Simon. *Peace and Freedom: The Civil Rights and Antiwar Movements in the 1960s*. Philadelphia: University of Pennsylvania Press, 2005.

——. *Rethinking the American Anti-War Movement*. New York: Routledge, 2012.

Hanhimäki, Jussi. *The Flawed Architect: Henry Kissinger and American Foreign Policy*. New York: Oxford University Press, 2004.

Harmer, Tanya. *Allende's Chile and the Inter-American Cold War*. Chapel Hill: University of North Carolina Press, 2011.

Harrison, Andrew. *Passover Revisited: Philadelphia's Efforts to Aid Soviet Jews, 1963–1998*. Madison, WI: Farleigh Dickinson University Press, 2001.

Harrison, Hope M. *Driving the Soviets up the Wall: Soviet–East German Relations, 1953–1961*. Princeton, NJ: Princeton University Press, 2003.

Haslam, Jonathan. *The Nixon Administration and the Death of Allende's Chile: A Case of Assisted Suicide*. New York: Verso, 2005.

Hatzivassiliou, Evanthis. *Greece and the Cold War: Frontline State, 1952–1967*. London: Routledge, 2006.

Hawkins, Darren G. *International Human Rights and Authoritarian Rule in Chile*. Lincoln: University of Nebraska Press, 2002.

Heiss, Mary Ann, and S. Victor Papcosma, eds. *NATO and the Warsaw Pact: Intrabloc Conflicts*. Kent, OH: Kent State University Press, 2008.

Hersh, Seymour M. *The Price of Power: Kissinger in the Nixon White House*. New York: Summit, 1983.

Hevener, Natalie Kaufman, ed. *Dynamics of Human Rights in U.S. Foreign Policy*. New Brunswick: Transaction, 1981.

Hinton, Elizabeth. *From the War on Poverty to the War on Crime: The Making of Mass Incarceration in America*. Cambridge, MA: Harvard University Press, 2016.

Hodgson, Godfrey. *The Gentleman from New York: Daniel Patrick Moynihan*. New York: Houghton Mifflin, 2000.

Hoffman, Elizabeth Cobbs. *All You Need is Love: The Peace Corps and the Spirit of the 1960s*. Cambridge, MA: Harvard University Press, 1998.

Hoffmann, Stefan-Ludwig, ed. *Human Rights in the Twentieth Century*. New York: Cambridge University Press, 2010.

Hollinger, David A. *After Cloven Tongues of Fire: Protestant Liberalism in Modern American History*. Princeton, NJ: Princeton University Press, 2013.

Hopgood, Stephen. *The Endtimes of Human Rights*. Ithaca, NY: Cornell University Press, 2013.

Horn, Gerd-Rainer, and Padraic Kenney, eds. *Transnational Moments of Change: Europe 1945, 1968, 1989*. New York: Rowman & Littlefield. 2004.

Horne, Gerald. *From the Barrel of a Gun: The United States and the War Against Zimbabwe, 1965–1980*. Chapel Hill: University of North Carolina Press, 2001.

Horner, Charles. "Human Rights and the Jackson Amendment." In *Staying the Course: Henry M. Jackson and National Security*, ed. Dorothy Fosdick, 109–28. Seattle: University of Washington Press, 1987.

Horvath, Robert. *The Legacy of Soviet Dissent: Dissidents, Democratization and Radical Nationalism in Russia*. New York: Routledge Curzon, 2005.

Hostetter, David L. *Movement Matters: American Antiapartheid Activism and the Rise of Multicultural Politics*. London: Routledge, 2006.

Hough, Jerry F. *How the Soviet Union Is Governed*. Cambridge, MA: Harvard University Press, 1979.

Howland, Douglas, and Luise White, eds. *The State of Sovereignty: Territories, Laws, Populations*. Bloomington: Indiana University Press, 2009.

Hughes, H. Stuart. *Sophisticated Rebels: The Political Culture of European Dissent, 1968–1987*. Cambridge, MA: Harvard University Press, 1988.

Ignatieff, Michael, ed. *American Exceptionalism and Human Rights*. Princeton, NJ: Princeton University Press, 2005.

——. *The Rights Revolution*. Toronto: Anasi, 2000.

Im, Hyug Baeg. "The Origins of the *Yushin* Regime: Machiavelli Unveiled." In *The Park Chung Hee Era: The Transformation of South Korea*, ed. Byung-Kook Kim and Ezra F. Vogel, 233–61. Cambridge, MA: Harvard University Press, 2011.

Iriye, Akira. *Global Community: The Role of International Organizations in the Making of the Contemporary World*. Berkeley: University of California Press, 2002.

——, ed. *Global Interdependence: The World after 1945*. Cambridge, MA: Belknap Press of Harvard University Press, 2014.

——. Introduction to *Global Interdependence: The World after 1945*, ed. Akira Iriye, 3–8. Cambridge, MA: Belknap Press of Harvard University Press, 2014.

——. "The Transnationalization of Humanity." In *Global Interdependence: The World after 1945*, ed. Akira Iriye, 727–70. Cambridge, MA: Belknap Press of Harvard University Press, 2014.

Iriye, Akira, Petra Goedde, and William I. Hitchcock, eds. *The Human Rights Revolution: An International History*. Oxford: Oxford University Press, 2012.

Iriye, Akira, and Rana Mitter. Foreword to *1968 in Europe: A History of Protest and Activism, 1956–1977*, ed. Martin Klimke and Joachim Scharloth, vii–viii. New York: Palgrave Macmillan, 2008.

Irwin, Ryan M. *Gordian Knot: Apartheid and the Unmaking of the Liberal World Order*. New York: Oxford University Press, 2012.

Isaacson, Walter. *Kissinger: A Biography*. New York: Simon & Schuster, 1992.

Isserman, Maurice, and Michael Kazin. *America Divided: The Civil War of the 1960s*. New York: Oxford University Press, 2000.

Jackson, Thomas F. *From Civil Rights to Human Rights: Martin Luther King, Jr., and the Struggle for Economic Justice*. Philadelphia: University of Pennsylvania Press, 2007.

Jensen, Steven L. B. *The Making of International Human Rights, 1945–1993: The 1960s, Decolonization, and the Reconstruction of Global Values*. New York: Cambridge University Press, 2016.

Johns, Andrew L. *Vietnam's Second Front: Domestic Politics, the Republican Party, and the War*. Lexington: University Press of Kentucky, 2010.

Johnson, Robert David. *Congress and the Cold War*. New York: Cambridge University Press, 2006.

Johnstone, Andrew, and Helen Laville, eds. *The U.S. Public and American Foreign Policy*. New York: Routledge, 2010.

Jones, Linda. "From Service to Solidarity." In *More Than Witnesses: How a Small Group of Missionaries Aided Korea's Democratic Revolution*, ed. Jim Stentzel, 411–40. Seoul: Korea Democracy Foundation, 2006.

Karamouzi, Eirini. *Greece, the EEC and the Cold War 1974–1979: The Second Enlargement*. London: Palgrave, 2014.

Katzmann, Robert A., ed. *Daniel Patrick Moynihan: The Intellectual in Public Life*. Baltimore: Johns Hopkins University Press, 1998.

Kaufman, Natalie Hevener. *Human Rights Treaties and the Senate: A History of Opposition*. Chapel Hill: University of North Carolina Press, 1990.

Kaufman, Robert G. *Henry M. Jackson: A Life in Politics*. Seattle: University of Washington Press, 2000.

Katsiaficas, George. *Asia's Unknown Uprisings: Volume I: South Korean Social Movements in the 20th Century*. Oakland, CA: PM Press, 2012.

Kazin, Michael. *American Dreamers: How the Left Changed a Nation*. New York: Knopf, 2011.

Keck, Margaret, and Kathryn Sikkink. *Activists Beyond Borders: Advocacy Networks in International Politics*. Ithaca, NY: Cornell University Press: 1998.

Kelly, Patrick William. *Sovereign Emergencies: Latin America and the Making of Global Human Rights Politics*. New York: Cambridge University Press, 2018.

Kelly, Tobias. *This Side of Silence: Human Rights, Torture, and the Recognition of Cruelty*. Philadelphia: University of Pennsylvania Press, 2012.

Keys, Barbara J. "Anti-Torture Politics." In *The Human Rights Revolution: An International History*, ed. Akira Iriye, Petra Goedde, and William I. Hitchcock, 201–22. Oxford: Oxford University Press, 2012.

——. *Reclaiming American Virtue: The Human Rights Revolution of the 1970s*. Cambridge, MA: Harvard University Press, 2014.

King, Martin Luther, Jr. *"In a Single Garment of Destiny": A Global Vision of Justice*. Boston: Beacon, 2012.

Kim, Byung-Kook, and Ezra F. Vogel, eds. *The Park Chung Hee Era: The Transformation of South Korea*. Cambridge, MA: Harvard University Press, 2011.

Kim, Hyun-Dong. *Korea and the United States: The Evolving Transpacific Alliance in the 1960s*. Seoul: Research for Peace and Unification of Korea, 1990.

Kim, Yong-Jick. "The Security, Political, and Human Rights Conundrum, 1974–1979." In *The Park Chung Hee Era: The Transformation of South Korea*, ed. Byung-Kook Kim and Ezra F. Vogel, 457–82. Cambridge, MA: Harvard University Press, 2011.

Kirk, Donald, and Choe Sang Hun, eds. *Korea Witness: 135 Years of War, Crisis and News in the Land of the Morning Calm*. Seoul: EunHaeng NaMu, 2006.

Klimke, Martin. *The Other Alliance: Student Protest in West Germany & the United States in the Global Sixties*. Princeton, NJ: Princeton University Press, 2010.

Klimke, Martin, and Joachim Scharloth, eds. *1968 in Europe: A History of Protest and Activism, 1956–1977*. New York: Palgrave Macmillan, 2008.

——. "1968 in Europe: An Introduction." In *1968 in Europe: A History of Protest and Activism, 1956–1977*, ed. Martin Klimke and Joachim Scharloth, 1–9. New York: Palgrave Macmillan, 2008.

Korey, William. *Taking on the World's Repressive Regimes: The Ford Foundation's International Human Rights Policies and Practices*. New York: Palgrave Macmillan, 2007.

Kornbluh, Felicia. *The Battle for Welfare Rights: Politics and Poverty in Modern America*. Philadelphia: University of Pennsylvania Press, 2007.

Kornbluh, Peter. *The Pinochet File: A Declassified Dossier on Atrocity and Accountability*. New York: New Press, 2003.

Krenn, Michael L. *Black Diplomacy: African Americans and the State Department, 1945–1969*. London: Sharpe, 1999.

Lake, Anthony. *The "Tar Baby" Option: American Policy Toward Southern Rhodesia*. New York: Columbia University Press, 1976.

Lassen, Eva Maria, and Erik Andre Andersen, eds. *Europe and the Americas: Transatlantic Approaches to Human Rights*. Leiden: Brill Nijhoff, 2015.

Lauren, Paul Gordon. *Evolution of International Human Rights*. Philadelphia: University of Pennsylvania Press, 2003.

Lee, Chae-Jin. *A Troubled Peace: U.S. Policy and the Two Koreas*. Baltimore: Johns Hopkins University Press, 2006.

Lee, Namhee. "Anticommunism, North Korea, and Human Rights in South Korea: 'Orientalist' Discourse and Construction of South Korean Identity." In *Truth Claims: Representation and Human Rights*, ed. Mark Bradley and Patrice Petro, 43–72. New Brunswick, NJ: Rutgers University Press, 2002.

——. *The Making of Minjung: Democracy and the Politics of Representation in South Korea*. Ithaca, NY: Cornell University Press, 2007.

Lee, Sang-Dawn. *Big Brother, Little Brother: The American Influence on Korean Culture in the Lyndon B. Johnson Years*. New York: Lexington Books, 2002.

Leffler, Melvyn P., and Odd Arne Westad, eds. *The Cambridge History of the Cold War, Volume I: Origins*. Cambridge: Cambridge University Press, 2010.

——. *The Cambridge History of the Cold War, Volume III: Endings*. Cambridge: Cambridge University Press, 2010.

Lerner, Mitchell B. *Looking Back at LBJ: White House Politics in a New Light*. Lawrence: University Press of Kansas, 2005.

——. *The Pueblo Incident: A Spy Ship and the Failure of American Foreign Policy*. Lawrence: University Press of Kansas, 2002.

Lieber, Robert J., ed. *Eagle Rules? Foreign Policy and American Primacy in the Twenty-First Century*. Upper Saddle River, NJ: Prentice Hall, 2002.

Lohr, Eric. *Russian Citizenship: From Empire to Soviet Union*. Cambridge, MA: Harvard University Press, 2012.

Lyons, Terrence. "Keeping Africa off the Agenda." In *Lyndon Johnson Confronts the World: American Foreign Policy, 1963–1968*, ed. Warren I. Cohen, and Nancy Bernkopf Tucker, 245–78. New York: Cambridge University Press, 1994.

Macdonald, Donald Stone. *U.S.-Korean Relations from Liberation to Self-Reliance: The Twenty-Year Record*. Boulder, CO: Westview Press, 1991.

Malkki, Liisa H. *The Need to Help: The Domestic Arts of International Humanitarianism*. Durham, NC: Duke University Press, 2015.

Mariager, Rasmus, Karl Molin, and Kjersti Brathagen, eds. *Human Rights During the Cold War*. London: Routledge, 2014.

Marshall, Charles Burton. *Crisis over Rhodesia: A Skeptical View*. Baltimore: Johns Hopkins University Press, 1967.

Marwick, Andrew. "'1968' and the Cultural Revolution of the Long Sixties (c. 1958–c. 1974)." In *Transnational Moments of Change: Europe 1945, 1968, 1989*, ed. Gerd-Rainer Horn and Padraic Kenney, 81–94. New York: Rowman & Littlefield, 2004.

Matthews, Gene. "Things They Never Taught Us down on the Farm." In *More Than Witnesses: How a Small Group of Missionaries Aided Korea's Democratic Revolution*, ed. Jim Stentzel, 196–242. Seoul: Korea Democracy Foundation, 2006.

Mazower, Mark. *Governing the World: The History of an Idea*. New York: Penguin, 2012.

McAdam, Doug, Sidney Tarrow, and Charles Tilly. *Dynamics of Contention*. New York: Cambridge University Press, 2001.

Meriwether, James H. *Proudly We Can Be Africans: Black Americans and Africa, 1935–1961*. Chapel Hill: University of North Carolina Press, 2002.

Miller, James Edward. *The United States and the Making of Modern Greece: History and Power, 1950–1974*. Chapel Hill: University of North Carolina Press, 2009.

Min, Pyong Gap, ed. *Asian Americans: Contemporary Trends and Issues*. London: Pine Forge Press, 2006.

——. "Korean Americans." In *Asian Americans: Contemporary Trends and Issues*, ed. Pyong Gap Min, 230–59. London: Pine Forge Press, 2006.

Moon, Faye. "Heartaches No Longer, and Some that Linger." In *More Than Witnesses: How a Small Group of Missionaries Aided Korea's Democratic Revolution*, ed. Jim Stentzel, 148–80. Seoul: Korea Democracy Foundation, 2006.

Mor, Jessica Stites, ed. *Human Rights and Transnational Solidarity in Cold War Latin America*. Madison: University of Wisconsin Press, 2013.

——. "Introduction: Situating Transnational Solidarity Within Critical Human Rights Studies of Cold War Latin America." In *Human Rights and Transnational Solidarity in Cold War Latin America*, ed. Jessica Stites Mor, 3–18. Madison: University of Wisconsin Press, 2013.

Morgan, Michael Cotey. "The Seventies and the Rebirth of Human Rights." In *The Shock of the Global: The 1970s in Perspective*, ed. Niall Ferguson et al., 237–50. Cambridge, MA: Harvard University Press, 2010.

Morris, Louise. "What Korea Taught Me about My Country and My Faith." In *More Than Witnesses: How a Small Group of Missionaries Aided Korea's Democratic Revolution*, ed. Jim Stentzel, 113–47. Seoul: Korea Democracy Foundation, 2006.

Moskowitz, Moses. *International Concern with Human Rights*. Dobbs Ferry, NY: Oceana Publications, 1976.

Mower, A. Glenn. *The United States, the United Nations, and Human Rights: The Eleanor Roosevelt and Jimmy Carter Eras.* Westport, CT: Greenwood Press, 1979.

Moyn, Samuel. *Human Rights and the Uses of History.* New York: Verso, 2014.

——. *The Last Utopia: Human Rights in History.* Cambridge, MA: Harvard University Press, 2010.

Muehlenbeck, Philip E. *Betting on the Africans: John F. Kennedy's Courting of African Nationalist Leaders.* New York: Oxford University Press, 2012.

Muskie, Edmund S., Kenneth Rush, and Kenneth W. Thompson, eds. *The President, the Congress, and Foreign Policy.* Lanham, MD: University Press of America, 1986.

Neary, Ian. *Human Rights in Japan, South Korea and Taiwan.* New York: Routledge, 2002.

Neier, Aryeh. *The International Human Rights Movement: A History.* Princeton, NJ: Princeton University Press, 2012.

Nelson, Fran. "We All Know More Bible than We Live By." In *More Than Witnesses: How a Small Group of Missionaries Aided Korea's Democratic Revolution,* ed. Jim Stentzel, 348–56. Seoul: Korea Democracy Foundation, 2006.

Nelson, Michael. *Resilient America: Electing Nixon in 1968, Channeling Dissent, and Dividing Government.* Lawrence: University Press of Kansas, 2014.

Nesbitt, Francis Njubi. *Race for Sanctions: African Americans Against Apartheid, 1946–1994.* Bloomington: Indiana University Press, 2004.

Newsom, David D. *The Diplomacy of Human Rights.* Lanham, MD: University Press of the American for Institute for the Study of Diplomacy, Georgetown University, 1986.

Nichols, Christopher McKnight. *Promise and Peril: America at the Dawn of a Global Age.* Cambridge, MA: Harvard University Press, 2011.

Noer, Thomas J. *Cold War and Black Liberation: The United States and White Rule in Africa, 1948–1968.* Columbia: University of Missouri Press, 1985.

——. *Soapy: A Biography of G. Mennen Williams.* Ann Arbor: University of Michigan Press, 2005.

Ogle, George E. "Our Hearts Cry with You." In *More Than Witnesses: How a Small Group of Missionaries Aided Korea's Democratic Revolution,* ed. Jim Stentzel, 67–99. Seoul: Korea Democracy Foundation, 2006.

——. *South Korea: Dissent Within the Economic Miracle.* London: Zen Books, 1990.

Olcott, Jocelyn. "Globalizing Sisterhood: International Women's Year and the Politics of Representation." In *The Shock of the Global: The 1970s in Perspective,* ed. Niall Ferguson et al. 281–93. Cambridge, MA: Harvard University Press, 2010.

Palais, James B. "'Democracy' in South Korea, 1948–72." In *Without Parallel: The American-Korean Relationship since 1945,* ed. Frank Baldwin, 318–57. New York: Pantheon, 1974.

Parmar, Inderjeet. *Foundations of the American Century: The Ford, Carnegie, and Rockefeller Foundations in the Rise of American Power.* New York: Columbia University Press, 2012.

Paterson, Thomas G., ed. *Kennedy's Quest for Victory: American Foreign Policy, 1961–1963.* New York: Oxford University Press, 1989.

Pelt, Mogens. *Tying Greece to the West: U.S.–West German-Greek Relations 1949–74.* Copenhagen: Museum Tusculanum Press, 2006.

Pérez, Louis A., Jr. *Cuba and the United States: Ties of Singular Intimacy.* 3rd ed. London: University of Georgia Press, 2003.

Peterson, Christian Philip. *Globalizing Human Rights: Private Citizens, the Soviet Union, and the West.* New York: Routledge, 2012.

Pinker, Steven. *The Better Angels of Our Natures: Why Violence Has Declined.* New York: Penguin, 2011.

Pipes, Daniel, and Adam Garfinkle, eds. *Friendly Tyrants: An American Dilemma.* New York: St. Martin's Press, 1991.

Power, Samantha. *"A Problem from Hell": America and the Age of Genocide.* New York: Perennial, 2002.

Preston, Andrew. *Sword of the Spirit, Shield of the Faith: Religion in American War and Diplomacy.* New York: Knopf, 2012.

Quataert, Jean H. *Advocating Dignity: Human Rights Mobilizations in Global Politics.* Philadelphia: University of Pennsylvania Press, 2009.

Qureshi, Lubna Z. *Nixon, Kissinger, and Allende: U.S. Involvement in the 1973 Coup in Chile.* New York: Lexington Books, 2009.

Rajak, Svetozar. "The Cold War in the Balkans, 1945–1956." In *The Cambridge History of the Cold War, Volume I: Origins,* ed. Melvyn P. Leffler and Odd Arne Westad, 198–220. Cambridge: Cambridge University Press, 2010.

Rakove, Robert B. *Kennedy, Johnson, and the Nonaligned World.* New York: Cambridge University Press, 2013.

Ranard, Donald L. "Korea, Human Rights, and United States Foreign Policy." In *Toward a Humanitarian Diplomacy: A Primer for Policy,* ed. Tom J. Farar, 177–226. New York: New York University Press, 1980.

Rejali, Darius. *Torture and Democracy.* Princeton, NJ: Princeton University Press, 2007.

Renouard, Joe. *Human Rights in American Foreign Policy: From the 1960s to the Soviet Collapse.* Philadelphia: University of Pennsylvania Press, 2016.

Rice, Randy. "From Isolation to Solidarity." In *More Than Witnesses: How a Small Group of Missionaries Aided Korea's Democratic Revolution,* ed. Jim Stentzel, 100–12. Seoul: Korea Democracy Foundation, 2006.

Rice, Sue. "Acting on Our Convictions." In *More Than Witnesses: How a Small Group of Missionaries Aided Korea's Democratic Revolution,* ed. Jim Stentzel, 308–25. Seoul: Korea Democracy Foundation, 2006.

Robertson, Geoffrey. *Crimes Against Humanity: The Struggle for Global Justice.* 3rd ed. New York: The New Press, 2006.

Rodgers, Daniel T. *Age of Fracture.* Cambridge, MA: Belknap, 2011.

Rosati, Jerel A. *The Carter Administration's Quest for Global Community: Beliefs and Their Impact on Behavior.* Columbia: University of South Carolina Press, 1987.

Rossinow, Doug. *Visions of Progress: The Left-Liberal Tradition in America.* Philadelphia: University of Pennsylvania Press, 2008.

Roubatis, Yiannis P. *Tangled Webs: The U.S. in Greece, 1947–1967.* New York: Pella Publishing, 1987.

Rubenstein, Joshua. *Soviet Dissidents: Their Struggle for Human Rights.* 2nd ed. Boston: Beacon Press, 1985.

Rubin, Barry M., and Elizabeth P. Spiro, eds. *Human Rights and U.S. Foreign Policy.* Boulder, CO: Westview Press, 1979.

Ryan, Yvonne. *Roy Wilkins: The Quiet Revolutionary and the NAACP.* Lexington: University Press of Kentucky, 2014.

Ryu, Youngju. *Writers of the Winter Republic: Literature and Resistance in Park Chung Hee's Korea.* Honolulu: University of Hawai'i Press, 2016.

Said, Abdul Aziz, ed. *Ethnicity and U.S. Foreign Policy.* New York: Praeger, 1977.

Sargent, Daniel J. *A Superpower Transformed: The Remaking of American Foreign Relations in the 1970s.* New York: Oxford University Press, 2015.

Schlesinger, Arthur M., Jr. *The Imperial Presidency.* Boston: Houghton Mifflin, 1973.

Schmidli, William Michael. *The Fate of Freedom Elsewhere: Human Rights and U.S. Cold War Policy Toward Argentina.* Ithaca, NY: Cornell University Press, 2013.

Schmidt, Elizabeth. *Foreign Intervention in Africa: From the Cold War to the War on Terror.* New York: Columbia University Press, 2013.

Schmitz, David F. "Senator Frank Church and Opposition to the Vietnam War and the Imperial Presidency." In *Vietnam and the American Political Tradition*, ed. Randall B. Woods, 121–48. New York: Cambridge University Press, 2003.

——. *Thank God They're on Our Side.* Chapel Hill: University of North Carolina Press, 1999.

——. *The United States and Right-Wing Dictatorships.* New York: Cambridge University Press, 2006.

Schneier, Marc. *Shared Dreams: Martin Luther King, Jr., and the Jewish Community.* Woodstock, VT: Jewish Lights, 1999.

Schoultz, Lars. *Human Rights and United States Policy Toward Latin America.* Princeton, NJ: Princeton University Press, 1981.

Schroth, Raymond A. *Bob Drinan: The Controversial Life of the First Catholic Priest Elected to Congress.* New York: Fordham University Press, 2011.

Schulzinger, Robert D. "Richard Nixon, Congress, and the War in Vietnam, 1969–1974." In *Vietnam and the American Political Tradition: The Politics of Dissent*, ed. Randall B. Woods, 282–300. New York: Cambridge University Press, 2003.

Schwartz, Thomas Alan. *Lyndon Johnson and Europe: In the Shadow of Vietnam.* Cambridge, MA: Harvard University Press, 2003.

Scott, Katherine A. *Reining in the State: Civil Society and Congress in the Vietnam and Watergate Eras.* Lawrence: University Press of Kansas, 2013.

Sellars, Kristen. *The Rise and Rise of Human Rights.* London: Sutton, 2002.

Sewell, Bevan, and Scott Lucas, eds. *Challenging U.S. Foreign Policy: America and the World in the Long Twentieth Century.* New York: Palgrave, 2011.

Shaw, William, ed. *Human Rights in Korea: Historical and Policy Perspectives.* Cambridge, MA: Harvard University Press, 1991.

Shinbaum, Myrna. "Mobilizing America: The National Conference on Soviet Jewry." In *A Second Exodus*, ed. Murray Friedman and Albert D. Chernin, 173–80. Hanover, NH: University Press of New England, 1999.

Sikkink, Kathryn. *Mixed Signals: U.S. Human Rights Policy and Latin America.* Ithaca, NY: Cornell University Press, 2004.

Sinnott, Jim. "Now You Are Free to Speak Out." In *More Than Witnesses: How a Small Group of Missionaries Aided Korea's Democratic Revolution*, ed. Jim Stentzel, 375–410. Seoul: Korea Democracy Foundation, 2006.

Simpson, Bradley R. *Economists with Guns: Authoritarian Development and U.S.-Indonesian Relations, 1960–1968.* Stanford, CA: Stanford University Press, 2008.

Skilling, H. Gordon. *Samizdat and an Independent Society in Central and Eastern Europe*. London: Macmillan Press, 1989.

Smith, Tony. *Foreign Attachments: The Power of Ethnic Groups in the Making of American Foreign Policy*. Cambridge, MA: Harvard University Press, 2000.

Snyder, Sarah B. *Human Rights Activism and the End of the Cold War: A Transnational History of the Helsinki Network*. New York: Cambridge University Press, 2011.

Sorensen, Ted. *Kennedy: The Classic Biography*. Rev. ed. New York: Harper Perennial, 2009.

Sorley, Lewis. *Arms Transfers under Nixon: A Policy Analysis*. Lexington: University Press of Kentucky, 1983.

Stammers, Neil. *Human Rights and Social Movements*. New York: Pluto Press, 2009.

Stebenne, David L. *Arthur J. Goldberg: New Deal Liberal*. New York: Oxford University Press, 1996.

Stentzel, Jim, ed. *More Than Witnesses: How a Small Group of Missionaries Aided Korea's Democratic Revolution*. Seoul: Korea Democracy Foundation, 2006.

——. "They Had to Do Something." In *More Than Witnesses: How a Small Group of Missionaries Aided Korea's Democratic Revolution*, ed. Jim Stentzel, 19–40. Seoul: Korea Democracy Foundation, 2006.

Stern, Paula. *Water's Edge: Domestic Politics and the Making of American Foreign Policy*. Westport, CT: Greenwood Press, 1979.

Stern, Steve J. *Battling for Hearts and Minds: Memory Struggles in Pinochet's Chile, 1973–1988*. Durham, NC: Duke University Press, 2006.

Stroup, Sarah S. *Borders Among Activists: International NGOs in the United States, Britain, and France*. Ithaca, NY: Cornell University Press, 2012.

Stueck, William. *Rethinking the Korean War: A New Diplomatic and Strategic History*. Princeton, NJ: Princeton University Press, 2002.

Su, Anna. *Exporting Freedom: Religious Liberty and American Power*. Cambridge, MA: Harvard University Press, 2016.

Suri, Jeremi. *Henry Kissinger and the American Century*. Cambridge, MA: Harvard University Press, 2007.

——. *Power and Protest: Global Revolution and the Rise of Détente*. Cambridge, MA: Harvard University Press, 2003.

Tananbaum, Duane. *The Bricker Amendment Controversy: A Test of Eisenhower's Political Leadership*. Ithaca, NY: Cornell University Press, 1988.

Tarrow, Sidney. *The New Transnational Activism*. Cambridge: Cambridge University Press, 2005.

Thompson, Karen Brown. "Women's Rights Are Human Rights." In *Restructuring World Politics: Transnational Social Movements, Networks, and Norms*, ed. Sanjeev Khagram et al., 96–122. Minneapolis: University of Minnesota Press, 2002.

Thompson, Kenneth W., ed. *The Kennedy Presidency: Seventeen Intimate Perspectives of John F. Kennedy*. Lanham, MD: University Press of America, 1985.

Tilly, Charles. *Social Movements, 1768–2004*. Boulder, CO: Paradigm Publishers, 2004.

Tilly, Charles, and Sidney Tarrow. *Contentious Politics*. Boulder, CO: Paradigm Publishers, 2007.

Tofel, Richard J. *Sounding the Trumpet: The Making of John F. Kennedy's Inaugural Address*. Chicago: Ivan R. Dee, 2005.

Tolley, Howard B., Jr. *International Commission of Jurists: Global Advocates for Human Rights*. Philadelphia: University of Pennsylvania Press, 1994.

Tucker, Nancy Bernkopf. *Strait Talk: United States–Taiwan Relations and the Crisis with China*. Cambridge, MA: Harvard University Press, 2009.

——. *Taiwan, Hong Kong, and the United States, 1945–1992: Uncertain Friendships*. New York: Twayne, 1994.

Tullis, Jeffrey K. *The Rhetorical Presidency*. Princeton, NJ: Princeton University Press, 1987.

Tyrell, Ian. *Transnational Nation: United States History in Global Perspective since 1789*. New York: Palgrave Macmillan, 2007.

Van Oudenaren, John. *Détente in Europe: The Soviet Union and the West since 1953*. Durham, NC: Duke University Press, 1991.

Villaume, Poul, Rasmus Mariager, and Helle Porsdam, eds. *The "Long 1970s": Human Rights, East-West Détente, and Transnational Relations*. London: Routledge, 2016.

Watts, Carl Peter. "African Americans and U.S. Foreign Policy: The American Negro Leadership Conference on Africa and the Rhodesian Crisis." In *The U.S. Public and American Foreign Policy*, ed. Andrew Johnstone and Helen Laville, 107–22. New York: Routledge, 2010.

——. *Rhodesia's Unilateral Declaration of Independence: An International History*. New York: Palgrave Macmillan, 2012.

White, Luise, and Douglas Howland, eds. *The State of Sovereignty: Territories, Laws, Populations*. Bloomington: Indiana University Press, 2009.

Windt, Theodore Otto, Jr. *Presidents and Protesters: Political Rhetoric in the 1960s*. Tuscaloosa: University of Alabama Press, 1990.

Windt, Theodore, with Beth Ingold, eds. *Essays in Presidential Rhetoric*. Dubuque, IA: Kendall/Hunt Publishing, 1983.

Woods, Randall B. *LBJ: Architect of American Ambition*. Cambridge, MA: Harvard University Press, 2006.

——, ed. *Vietnam and the American Political Tradition: The Politics of Dissent*. New York: Cambridge University Press, 2003.

Zeiler, Thomas W. *Dean Rusk: Defending the American Mission Abroad*. Wilmington, NC: Scholarly Resources, 2000.

Zelizer, Julian E. *On Capitol Hill: The Struggle to Reform Congress and Its Consequences, 1948–2000*. New York: Cambridge University Press, 2004.

INDEX

Reagan, Ronald, 39, 113, 166, 189n86, 240n206

realpolitik, 56, 132, 155

Red Cross. *See* International Committee of the Red Cross

refuseniks, 20, 21, 22, 29. *See also* Soviet Union: Jewish emigration from

Reischauer, Edwin O., 99, 218n86

Republic of Korea (ROK). *See* South Korea

Reuther, Victor, 65

rhetoric, 33, 37, 46, 55, 57, 113, 123, 168, 171, 202n6

Rhodesia News Summary, 176n19

Rhodesia. *See* Southern Rhodesia

Ribicoff, Abraham, 28

Rice, Randy, 100

Riegle, Donald W., Jr., 83

Rockefeller, Nelson, 40, 200n123, 225n9

Roe, Robert, 156

Rogers, William D., 134, 135, 137, 139, 140, 142, 170, 236n131, 236n133, 237n132

Rogers, William P., 54, 93, 210n132

Romania, 184n2

Roosevelt, Eleanor, 194n34

Rosenblum, Louis, 187n61

Rosenthal, Benjamin, 64, 151, 167, 198n81, 200n115

Rostow, Walt, 71, 73, 75, 76, 206n65

Rousseas, Stephen, 66, 69

Rubin, Vitaly, 35

Rumsfeld, Donald, 111

Runyon, Charles, III, 155, 158, 246n39

Rusk, Dean, 9, 11, 45, 52, 72, 73, 92, 206n65

Russia, 5, 25, 29, 37. *See also* Soviet Union

Ryan, Leo, 106

Safire, William, 30, 188n74

Sagan, Ginetta, 5

Sakharov, Andrei, 21, 26, 29, 35

Salzberg, John, 150, 151, 154, 166, 170, 244n11

samizdat, 20, 22

Sargent, Daniel, 13, 182n85, 238n179, 243n2

Saunders, Harold, 82

Schifter, Richard, 166

Schlesinger, James, 111

Schmitz, David, 12, 86

Schneider, Mark, 236n133, 239n183, 240n207, 241n222; as aide to Ted Kennedy, 122, 140; time in El Salvador, 145, 228n46, 241n224; work in the Carter administration, 171. *See also* Kennedy, Edward "Ted"

Schwartz, James, 69

Scowcroft, Brent, 39, 233n100

Second Vatican Council. *See* Catholic Church

Section 32 of the Foreign Assistance Act of 1973. *See* Foreign Assistance Act of 1973

Section 116 of the Foreign Assistance Act of 1961. *See* Foreign Assistance Act of 1961

Section 301 of the International Security Assistance and Arms Control Export Act of 1976. *See* International Security Assistance and Arms Control Export Act of 1976

Section 502B of the Foreign Assistance Act of 1974. *See* Foreign Assistance Act of 1974

Senate Judiciary Senate Subcommittee to Investigate Problems Connected with Refugees and Escapees, 122, 123, 242n229. *See also* Congress, U.S.

Senate Subcommittee on Foreign Assistance, 165. *See also* Congress, U.S.

Sharansky, Natan. *See* Shcharansky, Anatoly

Shcharansky, Anatoly, 21, 29, 35, 184n13

Shestack, Jerome, 25, 152, 246n30

Shlaudeman, Harry W., 128, 232n91, 237n152

Shultz, George P., 34

Sikkink, Kathryn, 139

Silva, Raúl, 142, 146

Simon, William, 34, 140–41, 189n98, 238n179, 239n183, 239n184

Siniavsky, Andrei, 20

Sisco, Joe, 81, 82, 85, 210n120